RENEWALS 458-4574

Date Due

Biotechnology

Between Commerce and Civil Society

Biotechnology

Nico Stehr

editor

Transaction Publishers
New Brunswick (U.S.A.) and London (U.K.)

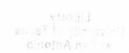

Library of Congress Catalog Number: 2004041240
ISBN: 0-7658-0224-4
Printed in Canada

Library of Congress Cataloging-in-Publication Data

Biotechnology : between commerce and civil society / Nico Stehr, editor.
    p. cm.
    Includes bibliographical references and index.
    ISBN 0-7658-0224-4 (cloth : alk. paper)
    1. Biotechnology—Social aspects. 2. Biotechnology industries. I. Stehr, Nico.

TP248.23.B5625 2004
303.48'3—dc22

2004041240

Contents

Part III
Major Societal Institutions and Biotechnology:
The Law, the State, and the Economy

Part IV
Biotechnology and Civil Society: Case Studies

Preface and Acknowledgements

Nico Stehr

That new scientific knowledge is no longer merely the key to unlocking the secrets of nature and society but represents the "becoming" of a world, of the ways in which we conduct our affairs and of how we reflexively comprehend the changes underway as the result of novel technical artefects and scientific knowledge has become even more evident to most ever since the practical fruits of biotechnology have both grasped our imagination and generated worldwide debate and concern.

In many countries, and since the mid-nineties more and more intensely, biotechnology, and particularly the techniques of genetic modification, are the centre of disputes and conflicts not only in the scientific community but among the public at large, the media, national parliaments, a growing number of commissions charged with assessing the implications of biotechnology, transnational organization such as the OECD, non-governmental organizations and last but not least the heads of state, for example, the G8 Heads of Government who in 1999 at their meeting in Cologne, Germany asked for a "study of the implications of biotechnology and other aspects of food safety".

The debates on biotechnology shift between images of utopia and dystopia advocating a brilliant future for humankind (see Hellstein 2002) or in despairing terms, a collapse of human civilization and the nature of human nature (Reed 2002).

Given the evident social, cultural and economic importance of biotechnology for modern societies, the issues raised and implied by development in biotechnology surely underscore the observation that these issues, and in this instance in particular, are much too important to be left to the natural science community, the politicians, the ethicists or business. The social sciences have gained a voice in the contested debates and in the sober examination of the economic, social and cultural implications of biotechnology. Among the social sciences, the economic point of view has been heard most stridently proclaiming for example, as the eminent economist Lester Thorow did, [1] the advent of a new economic order based on biotechnology and predicting that the importance of biotechnology as the technology of the future will far exceed that of the information technologies, in particular the Internet. This volume is designed to illustrate the contributions anthropology, law, political science and sociology are making to the ongoing discussions about the role of biotechnology in modern societies.

With a single exception all the papers included in this anthology were first presented at an international conference in the *Kulturwissenschaftliche Institut* (Center for Advanced Cultural Studies) in Essen, Germany, September 5–7, 2002. It is a pleasure to thank the people who helped me to create this anthology: I am very grateful to the Director of the Center, Professor Jörn Rüsen as well as the Heinrich-Böll Stiftung, Berlin for supporting the conference on "Biotechnology: Between Commerce and Civil Society". My sincere thanks also go to Dr. Norbert Jegelka, the managing director of the Center, his persistant enthusiasm and usual facility to smooth administrative hurdles. All participants and guests of the conference benefited immensely from Doris Alemara's organizational skills. Mrs. Almenara and the staff of the Center made it easy for all who took part in the conference to feel at home in the *Kulturwissenschaftliche Institut.*

Note

1. Quoted in "Biotech fuelling latest revolution, economist says," *Globe and Mail* Wednesday, November 24, 1999. A few years earlier, though in necessarily ambivalent terms, bioindustry analysts made equally far-ranging predictions about the economic impact of biotechnology: by the year 2025 between seventy and forty percent of the global economy will have, at its base, some form of biotechnology (cited in Hindmarsh, Lawrence and Norton 1998:3).

References

Hellstein, Iina (2002), "Selling the life sciences: promises of a better future in biotechnology advertisements," *Science as Culture* 11:459–479.
Hindmarsh, Richard, Geoffrey Lawrence and Janet Norton (1998), "Bio-utopia: the way forward," in: Richard Hindmarsh, Geoffrey Lawrence and Janet Norton (eds.), *Altered Genes. Reconstructing Nature: The Debate.* London: Allen & Unwin. 3–23.
Reed, Matthew (2002), "Rebels from the crown down: the organic movement's revolt against agricultural biotechnology," *Science as Culture* 11:481–504.

Introduction
Biotechnology: Between Commerce and Civil Society

Nico Stehr

An examination of the new frontiers of science and society has to be embedded in an understanding of at least the rough contours of modern societies' development toward what has been called *knowledge societies* (Stehr 1994), the emergence of *knowledge-based economies* (with biotechnology industries often seen as a core strategy for economic development) and the transformation of the knowledge-guiding interests in *social research* devoted to an understanding of the social role of knowledge itself.

Knowledge is no longer the key, if it ever was, to unlocking the secrets of the world; rather, it is the becoming of a world. The recognition of this role of knowledge in society is gradually leading to significant changes in the knowledge-guiding interests in those fields of study that concern themselves with the different roles of knowledge in society. Yet the traditional form of the sociology of knowledge (for example, in its most prominent contemporary form of science studies) is to this day primarily interested in the social foundations or dependence of knowledge. The connection—or as Max Scheler, one of the pioneers of the traditional sociology of knowledge, put it—the "intimate linkage" (Scheler [1924] 1960:193) between class and ideology, labor and knowledge, society and truth, or interests and knowledge-guiding interests constitutes and in many ways still represents the primary research focus of inquiries into knowledge. The interest in the social foundations of knowledge as the research focus of the sociology of knowledge originally emerges out of epistemology. But in the tradition of epistemological themes, the question of the genesis of knowledge, its conditions and its consequences, continues to form the core concern of the sociology of knowledge (Mannheim [1929] 1965:164–167).

The sociology of knowledge has of course—aside from self-exemplifying questions about the foundations of its own consciousness—problematized the

1

societal role of knowledge (for example in the sense of *Herrschaft kraft Wissen* [authority based on knowledge] Weber [1922] 1964: 339), and the sociology of knowledge also displays an interest in the social role of the carriers of knowledge (for example intellectuals, bureaucrats, experts, and cultural elites) and the civilizational transformation of forms of knowledge (for instance in the work of Norbert Elias 1983).

Nonetheless, and using economic concepts to describe the core foci of the sociology of knowledge as still widely practiced, interest centers on the supply, and not the demand or the consumption, of knowledge. At the same time, the traditional research guiding interest always saw knowledge as something akin to a dependent variable.

The emphasis of the production of knowledge, which is of course an important issue, forms the almost singular interest of science studies as we know them. The multi-faceted laboratory studies are a part of this focus (e.g. Latour and Woolgar 1986), as well as the controversial finalization debate of some two decades ago (Böhme et al. 1973); and more recently, the thesis of new forms of the production of knowledge—labeled, for example, "post-normal science" (Funtowicz and Ravetz 1993), "mode 2" (Gibbons et al. 1994; Nowotny et al 2001) or "postacademic science" (Ziman 1994). In the context of these observations about science, knowledge of course is not viewed as a closed, autonomous canon; rather, it is the *societal orientation of science*, as Gernot Böhme (Böhme 1993:19) puts it, that assures us what kind of knowledge we ultimately have in science, and what social processes are responsible for the inner structure of knowledge and its conceptual apparatus.

The transformation of the standard sociology of knowledge approach in the postwar era away from questions concerned with the production and supply of knowledge to issues more concerned with the demand for knowledge can perhaps best be traced to various theories of modern society, for example to Helmut Schelsky's (1961) notion of the emergence of a scientific-technical civilization; or to the pessimistic vision of the dawn of the technical state, as argued by Herbert Marcuse ([1964] 1989); or later, the much more upbeat idea of the emergence of post-industrial society (Bell, 1964; 1973) and its socialist equivalent, the scientific-technological revolution (Richta, 1971; see also Stehr 1994:99–174). The notable commonalties of the different theories of modern societies just enumerated extend—despite their manifest political and economic differences—to the observation that the primacy of the relations between human and machines in production is replaced by the rise in the economic significance of knowledge.

Initially, however, there were few if any explicit connections between these theories of modern society and the sociology of science and knowledge, especially when it comes to the images of the social production and utilization of scientific and technical knowledge in theories of modern society.

Daniel Bell and other authors who discovered knowledge as the new axial principle of modern society spend little time reflecting on the nature of knowledge, how it was produced, or why, for that matter, there appeared to be a growing demand for knowledge in society. To use what has become a cliché, theoretical knowledge was treated as a black box.

Yet the various theories of society that stressed the new social role of knowledge primarily within and for the economic system touch upon and reflect societal transformations forcing us to shift to knowledge-guiding interests much concerned with the use or the impact of knowledge on the life world and the kind of society we will live in. What is required, then, is a shift from a mainly supply-side driven perspective to a demand-side view of knowledge in modern societies. Nonetheless, the intellectual origins of such a theoretical interest may be found in the classical sociology of knowledge.

The Field of Biotechnology

Although the term "biotechnology," apparently first coined in 1917 by a Hungarian farmer (Bud 1991:422), is not an essentially contested term, definitions do vary considerably within and across countries as well as in different periods in history (see e.g. Office of Technology Assessment, 1984; National Science Board 1984). Depending on one's definition, we are dealing, for example, with a field of research and practical operations that gradually evolved over more than a century, out of industrial application in brewing and baking. More recently, biotechnology is seen as a scientific and practical activity resulting from the use of *recombinant techniques*. Thus, biotechnology now commonly refers to a diversity of "new genetic technologies" in different scientific disciplines, applied in a wide range of sectors of society such as health care, agriculture, chemicals, and environmental control (also Frederick Buttel's introduction to the second section of the anthology).[1] Other terms tend to emphasize the social utility (Griffiths and Wald 1999) rather than the disciplinary roots of biotechnology (Markle and Robin 1985:70–71; Bud 1991).

Whether one chooses to stress biotechnology as the possible key to future prosperity, to focus on its intellectual and practical origins, or to put forward some other conception, the definition has powerful ramifications. The meaning assigned to the term affects the kind of social, economic and political support biotechnology encounters. The specific concept affects judgments about the present state of research in biotechnology, compared to what has been accomplished and what may be attained in the future. And prevailing definitions reflect and change with emerging technical and scientific developments as well as public attitudes (Davison, Barns and Schibeci 1997) and economic interests.

The most common reference, as indicated, in the still emerging development of biotechnology from the late 1970s is its use of and dependence on molecular biology in general, and recombinant DNA techniques in particular. Such a conception gives expression to convictions among scientists, business people, politicians, various strands of public discourse, the media and other groups that the boundaries between science and technology may be penetrated more readily than in the past; and that an integration of technology with biological processes will be a major frontier not only in science but also in the commercial exploitation of their combined developments. The same conception testifies to the conviction that we are only beginning systematically to explore the frontiers of biotechnology as well as the diverse impacts of biotechnology on individuals and society. Thus, one scientist compares the *present* state of knowledge in biotechnology to that of the punch-card era in computing science and its application in the 1950s.[2] But even if intellectual and practical developments in biotechnology are only beginning to evolve, discussions about the likely social effects and costs are already in full swing and are likely to intensify in the next years, opening a diverse field of new issues for social science research. The present collection of essays signifies the intensity with which social research is ready to take up the challenge of investigating a wide range of contentious issues in the contentious context of biotechnology between commerce and civil society.

Biotechnology and Civil Society

Anxieties and concerns about the social consequences of new scientific knowledge and novel technologies are not of recent origin. Nor are elusive promises of the plain blessings of science for humankind and the mitigation of human suffering that scientific advances entail. But a persuasive case can be made that we have reached a new, modern stage. The first controlled genetic experiment did not occur until 1972. The first human being conceived outside a woman's body was born in 1978. The controversial discussions of recombinant DNA, embryonic stem cells, genetically modified foods, the prospects of lethal and "nonlethal" biotechnology weapons, genetic engineering of the human germline, the neurosciences, the reconstruction of the genome of the ancestor of the human being, neurogenetics, and reproductive cloning exemplify some of the novel issues we are confronting in vigorously contested debates.

Concerns about the societal consequences of an unfettered expansion of (natural) scientific knowledge in general, and biotechnology in particular, are now being raised more urgently, and are moving to the center of public disputes in society, in the scientific community, in the media (see the contribution by Susanna Priest and Toby Ten Eyck in this volume), and in the legal system (see the contribution by Alexander Somek in this anthology), and to the top of the political agenda. Governments will have to engage in new political activity and will be held accountable to new standards (see, for example, the essay by Herbert Gottweis in this collection). Public conflicts, frictions, and disputes over the implementation of knowledge, seen by at least some as attacks against science, will no longer mainly take place *a posteriori*.

The Societal Regulation of Biotechnology

Given the general willingness to review the once taken-for-granted assessment of the social role of *new* scientific knowledge, it is no longer uncommon that the discussion in many societies about the role of biotechnology leads to demands that such knowledge and its impact be managed in some way, regulated, or even suppressed altogether. The question has now become, for example, how can we protect and defend a shared and even sacred human essence that may be devoured by a marvelously powerful science? It would be too easy to dismiss calls for such intervention by the state, the law or other institutions in society as an irrational or antimodern response. The objections raised to biotechnology, the concerned questions asked and the resistance mobilized refer back, of course, to the image that we have of our ourselves, according to which we are arranging our life—an image and a world reality that appear to be under threat.

But what knowledge needs to be regulated, and whose responsibility is it? And what knowledge do we require in the context of regulative knowledge politics? Do we need to regulate new scientific knowledge as closely as, or even more strictly than, one regulates traffic, for instance? If not, on what grounds? If so, for what reasons, and protecting what interests? If strict restrictions apply, could absolute prohibitions (for example, outlawing human germline gene therapy) be enforced? Is knowledge about to become a private good (again)? What will be the identity of some of the major actors involved, and how will knowledge politics be organized? These are some of the questions that need to be raised and examined not only by ethicists, politicians, philosophers, theologians and journalists but also by social scientists. This anthology is one effort toward such a new agenda of research and reflection in the social sciences.

In the following paragraphs, I will try to deal with some of the issues that pertain specifically to the origins of the growing chorus of voices demanding that new knowledge, particularly, the broad range of "new genetic knowledge," be regulated rather than promoted, as was the case just a decade ago in most developed societies.

Knowledge Politics and Civil Society

Why is knowledge politics emerging? Why are there growing efforts to exert power over knowledge? Why are we, perhaps in growing numbers, not prepared simply to accept the apparently "natural" progression; to take for granted the relentless, exponential development of scientific knowledge, of technical artifacts and their application, as a key to unlocking the mysteries of the world, as a release from pain and freedom from suffering, as the basis for a better and more just society, or as a means to greater prosperity; or to believe that more knowledge represents an emancipation from all kinds of troubling ills and harsh constraints? The straightforward, or at least traditional, assumption that specialized knowledge ought to command respect in general, and that any increase in knowledge automatically brings with it an increase in benefits to humankind in particular, is becoming porous and vulnerable. [3] The idea that the *uselessness* of science is a virtue, and that the uses that humans "have drawn from science have contributed to their misery" (Chargaff 1975:21) is still only a marginal voice, rarely heard. The optimistic faith, uttered without any qualms and nurtured in a period of unprecedented economic growth in the 1950s and early 1960s, that science, whatever its specific function, gives satisfaction, and that a constant expansion of "knowledge" might even prompt a displacement of politics and ideology (Brooks 1965; Lane 1966; Bell 1960, 1973), has been thoroughly demystified (e.g. Wilensky 1967; King and Melanson 1972).[4]

If one no longer regards the fabrication and use of additional scientific knowledge as a humanitarian project, as in harmony with the aspirations of different publics and "as an unquestioned ultimate good, one is willing to consider its disciplined direction" (Sinsheimer 1978:23). The fear that we know too much, and the threat that we are about to assume the role of God (or are about to commence a "self-transformation of the species" [Habermas 2001:42]; also Janich and Weingarten 2002),[5] increasingly replaces the concern that *we do not know enough* and that we are to a large degree poorly informed. Francis Fukuyama (2002:7), to name but one other prominent recent voice, therefore suggests in his new book, *Our Posthuman Future: Consequences of the Biotechnology Revolution*, that "the most significant threat posed by biotechnology is the possibility that it will alter human nature and thereby move us into a 'posthuman' stage of history." The social costs of biotechnological developments, once implemented, are enormous. The break that Fukuyama, at least, sees between forms of society is fundamental; as is the threat to basic human aspirations—to such core rights as equality and justice, which form the foundation of what we now define as civil society. It is difficult, if not impossible, to anticipate exactly what these new forms of biotechnical knowledge will be and what their social consequences might be. However, our visionary record of foretelling social transformations, technical developments and the exact enlargement of scientific knowledge is not exactly impressive and unerring.

Nonetheless, resistance, objections, apprehension and alarm replace the rhetoric of hope and the conviction, which until recently dominated societal discourse about new developments in science and technology in modern societies, that *new* knowledge enlarges our sense of human dignity and autonomy (Mulkay 1993:735–739). Objections to science and apprehension about the alleged benefits of science are not new, of course; nor are the many concerns about the consequences of biotechnologies that I have mentioned without their missionary detractors. The human ability to "manipulate" the nature of our nature, as the result of new capacities of action originating from biogenetics, is certainly not universally viewed with apprehension; it is also understood and promoted, as one would expect, by such interested actors as biotechnology firms, as well as by others, presumably more "neutral" observers, as a form of emancipation and an enlargement of both our dignity and our autonomy (Markl 2003; Zizek 2003). However, the extent of the public support from such sources for a mostly unregulated application of biogenetics and an attitude of laissez-faire individualism in this new field of political activity is small, and pales in comparison to the welcome in society that scientific and technological breakthroughs once enjoyed.

Moreover, the social relations between the scientific communities, scientists as experts, society and the public have changed. Scientists no longer almost automatically inspire trust (cf. Miller 1983: 90–93; Cozzens and Woodhouse 1995:540–548). On the contrary, we believe less and less in experts, although we employ them more and more. Yet without some element of trust exhibited by ordinary members of society towards experts, expertise would vanish. Nonetheless, experts today are constantly involved in a remarkable number of controversies. The growing policy field of setting limits to the presence of certain ingredients in foodstuffs, of safety regulations, risk management and hazard control, has often had the unanticipated effect of ruining the reputation of experts and the notion of certainty once closely allied with knowledge. As long as an issue remains a contested matter, especially a publicly contentious matter, the power and influence of experts and counter-experts are limited (see Mazur 1973; Nelkin 1975); once a decision has been made and a question settled, the authority of experts becomes almost uncontested as well. The work required to transform a contested matter into an uncontested issue is linked to the ability of experts to mobilize social and cultural resources in *relevant* contexts (see Limoges, 1993). The boundaries of science are less definite and the channels of influence on science, or as some might see it, the economic and political levers of intervention in scientific affairs, have become both more evident and even more legitimate (cf. Rip 1997).

All of this, in retrospect, more firmly than ever signals the end of the golden age of science and technology, in which science served as a symbol of secular progress and civilizational advance and enjoyed enormous freedom and autonomy of inquiry. The golden age of science and technology ended in the early part of the last century. But its demise has become more visible only since the end of the Second World War.

The emergence of knowledge politics occurs with some delay in response to the exceptional growth and speed with which knowledge and technical capacities are added in modern societies. Appropriating Adolph Lowe's (1971:563) astute insights, it is a change from social realities in which "things" simply "happened" (at least from the point of view of most people) to a social world in which more and more things are "made" to happen. An increasingly malleable world or more advanced society may be described as a *knowledge society* because of the penetration of all its spheres by scientific and technical knowledge. What Adolph Lowe some three decades ago was unable to anticipate is the possibility that human agency not only extends to massively reorganizing its social as well as its natural environment, but that human agency may also take control of and rearrange its own genetic structure and molecular basis, resulting of course in what is then seen as a *posthuman* subject and posthuman future (see Hayles 1999; Simon 2003 and the essay by Steve Best and Douglas Kellner in this volume).

In knowledge societies, the individual's capability of doing and being whatever she/he desires is considerably enhanced at multiple levels of activity. The *societal* changes I have in mind can also be described in the following way: in the case of large and influential social institutions, but also in the case of individuals and small social groups, the weight in the relationship between autonomy and conditionality is shifting. The sum total of conditionality and autonomy is not constant. Both autonomy and conditionality of social action are capable of growing; they may also decline. In knowledge societies, the degree of apprehended autonomy of individuals and small social groups increases, while the extent of conditionality shrinks. In the case of large collectivities such as the state, large corporations, science, the church, etc., the extent to which their conduct is conditioned may decline as well, but their autonomy or ability to impose their will does not increase in proportion. While the limits of what can be done are re-written, the responsibility for the changes that are underway must be shared by larger segments of society.[6] The societal changes will be affected by and affect the kinds of changes that biotechnology will have for individuals, as well as for future generations and nature as we now know it.

What is evident is that the social and natural boundaries of what at one time appeared to be solidly beyond the ability of all of us to change, alter or manage are rapidly moved and penetrated. The transcendence of these limits applies, for example, to the possibility that we may come to review the validity of the now discarded Lamarckian idea that deliberately induced genetic transformations in one individual may in fact be passed to one's offspring in the future. The result, of course, is that new knowledge and new technical abilities as capacities to act are also perceived as a peril posed to every woman, man, and child; not merely as a threat and a burden to privacy, the status quo, the course of life and the understanding of what life is, but also as a danger to the very nature of creation. For as the biologist Robert Sinsheimer (1976:599) put it, shortly after the discovery of the possibility of genetic engineering by recombinant DNA techniques:

> With the advent of synthetic biology we leave the security of that web of natural evolution that, blindly and strangely, bore us and all of our fellow creatures. With each step we will be increasingly on our own. The invention and introduction of new self-reproducing, living forms may well be irreversible. How do we prevent grievous missteps, inherently unretractable? Can we in truth foresee the consequences, near- and long-term, of our interventions? By our wits mankind has become the master of the extant living world. Will short-sighted ingenuity now spawn new competitors to bedevil us?

The concern that we know too much is no longer – as was the case in the seventies of the last century, for example – that we are amassing a large store of trivial and practically irrelevant knowledge at a high price that promises no useful gains (Lübbe 1977:14). The fear of an information, or even knowledge, overload [7] has been replaced by concerns about the accumulation of novel knowledge that appears to have questionable social consequences. In that sense, at least, current concerns about science represent a return to conflicts that science has experienced in the past. But in contrast to past disputes, when discussions about the societal consequences of science were driven by complaints about its lack of social and economic utility in tackling major social problems of the day, today concern is focused on a surplus of effects – especially with respect to traditional world views, the established life-worlds and the limits to what can be manipulated in nature and society.

It would be mistaken to conclude, however, given the prominence assigned to developments in molecular biology in this essay, following of course its dominance in recent public debates about the social impact of science and technology, that the issue of knowledge politics either is confined to these fields of science or is a wholly civilian matter. As Joseph S. Nye, the former Chairman of the U.S. National Intelligence Council, and William A. Owens, a former Vice Chairman of the U.S. Joint Chiefs of Staff (in the Clinton administration), make plain, knowledge politics extends to military uses. [8] But knowledge politics in its military version also extends to fields other than biotechnology and information warfare; it could include, for example, the field of meteorology (see Stehr 2003:126–129). In addition, other fields of science and technology will likely generate new knowledge that will be subject to regulation and control; for example, in the fields of medical science, pharmacology, demography or criminology.

The Social Orientation of Biotechnology

> *In a democracy, the public must be the ultimate arbiter of decisions which affect it, but it is unrealistic and impractical to appeal every issue – especially complex, technically oriented issues to a public process.*
>
> —Harvey Brooks (1984)

In all modern societies, we now find elaborate drug regulations and corresponding agencies that register, test, control or permit pharmaceutical substances to enter the market as legalized drugs. Until a few decades ago, decisions about the production and marketing of chemicals as drugs were typically made by corporations, by individual pharmacists, or by physicians (cf. Bodewitz et al. 1987). As new scientific knowledge is "applied," it becomes embedded in social contexts external to science. As a part of such embeddedness, knowledge is subject to the kinds of (latent) control mechanisms and social constraints found in and constitutive for these contexts. It simply cannot escape the selectivity that issues from such external contexts, even if only in efforts designed to generate trust in a certain artifact or solution offered by novel knowledge.

In as much as knowledge becomes the constitutive principle of modern society, the production, distribution and especially the application of knowledge can avoid political struggles and conflicts less than ever. The distribution and implementation (and with it the fabrication) of knowledge increasingly become domains of extensive deliberation by expert committees (e.g. International Council for Science 2003) and citizen groups, objects of explicit legislation and targets of political and economic decisions.

The dissemination and application of knowledge do not occur in the imaginary world of perfect, unimpeded competition and equality of opportunities. As a result, a *politics of knowledge* must confront the consequences of the social distribution of knowledge, especially the stratified access to and utilization of knowledge. It remains an open question, for example, to what extent dispossession of knowledge generates social conflicts, and in what specific ways such struggles manifest themselves.

But predictions about the intellectual, social and economic gaps nourished and sustained by new knowledge overestimate the extent to which knowledge and its use can in fact be controlled by the institutions of civil society. It will be increasingly difficult to regulate knowledge, in spite of the many efforts that will undoubtedly be made. Efforts to control knowledge encounter contradictions. Sustaining economic growth, for example, requires an expansion of knowledge. And knowledge that expands rapidly is difficult to control. The expansion of knowledge enlarges the segment of knowledge-based occupations. Knowledge expansion and knowledge dissemination rely on conditions that are themselves inimical to control. However, one thing is evident: future conflicts, tensions and opportunities generated by knowledge and by artifacts emerging from biotechnology will be enourmous. And the public involvement and emerging tools for public involvement (see Wynne, 2001) in responding proactiviely and *a posteriori* to biotechnological developments will became a central arena of political, commercial, legal and ideological deliberation and struggle in decades ahead. But what is equally evident is that the future social and commercial orientation of biotechnology—in an almost self-exemplifying manner—is uncertain and open to many trajectories.

Notes

1. Namatie Traore and Antoine Rose (2003) have examined the uptake of biotechnology by Canadian industry. Their findings indicate that the health sector in Canada leads the way in biotechnology utilization, followed by agriculture, food processing and the environment sector. As far as specific techniques are concerned, biochemistry and immunology based biotechnologies are the most used, followed by bioprocessing based biotechnology and DNA based biotechnologies.
2. Hans Schöler in *Frankfurter Allgemeine Sonntagszeitung*, May 5, 2003, p. 55.
3. Now that the idea that progress in science must invariably equal progress in human affairs is no longer widely taken for granted, it is worth briefly mentioning that the equation that has fallen into disrepute did not find strong support until the age of Francis Bacon, who of course did much to expedite its acceptance and promotion himself. Bacon was very cognizant that the identification of advances in science and society could not be taken for granted, but had to be established, especially among the ruling classes. In much of antiquity the idea of progress was completely absent, and in the Middle Ages human progress was not expected to arrive with or derive from the secular sciences (cf. Böhme 1992). If one wants to date, or point to historical events that represent, the beginnings of knowledge politics, one has to refer to what is called the nuclear age, the atom bomb of 1945 in particular; but also to the development of (and resistance to) nuclear power and the initial public nuclear protests in the 1950s (Weart 1988). The political discussion of the "moral" status of nuclear science prompts John Dewey ([1927] 1954:231), in his afterword written in July 1946 to *The Public and Its Problems*, to point out that though "aspects of the *moral* problem of the status of physical science have been with us for a long time...the consequences of the physical sciences...failed to obtain the kind of observation that would bring the conduct and state of science into a specifically *political* field. The use of these sciences to increase the destructiveness of war was brought to such a sensationally obvious focus with the splitting of the atom that the political issue is now with us..."
4. In knowledge societies, the social role of "ideology" will actually be invigorated, in as much as the demystification of the nature of knowledge and the experience

of contending expert advice will encourage, even legitimate, actors' reliance on their normative perspectives, rather than fostering the "knowledge" that was supposed to displace ideology (cf. King and Melanson 1972:100).

5. Habermas ([1998] 2001:164) opposes human cloning and does so by analogy with slavery, on the grounds that no "person may so dispose over another person, may so control his possibilities for acting, in such a way that the dependent person is deprived of an essential part of his freedom. This condition is violated if one person decides the genetic makeup of another." The essential difference between the outcomes of (deliberate) cloning and "standard" (spontaneous?) human reproduction is, however, difficult to detect or sustain with respect to the moral prohibition Habermas wants us to adhere to.

6. I have examined these changes of and consequences for modern societies in greater detail in *The Fragility of Modern Societies* (Stehr 2001).

7. There are useful reminders that the idea of "information overload" is not unique to our era but stretches back centuries: for example, during the early modern period between 1550–1750, Europe *experienced* a kind of information explosion, for during this period "the production, circulation, and dissemination of scientific and scholarly texts accelerated tremendously" (see Rosenberg 2003:1).

8. As Nye and Owens (1996: 20) underline in their recent article, "knowledge, more than ever before, is power...The information advantage [of the U.S.] can strengthen the intellectual link between U.S. foreign policy and military power and offer new ways of maintaining leadership in alliances and ad hoc coalitions."

References

Bell, Daniel (1973) *The Coming of Post-Industrial Society*. New York: Basic Books.

Bell, Daniel (1964) "The post-industrial society," In: Eli Ginzberg ed., *Technology and Social Change*. New York: Columbia University Press, S. 44–59.

Bell, Daniel (1960) *The End of Ideology*. Glencoe, Ill.: Free Press.

Bodewitz, Henk J.H.W., Henk Buurma and Gerard H. de Vries (1987) "Regulatory science and the social management of trust in medicine," in: Wiebe E. Bijker, Thomas P. Hughes and Trevor Pinch (eds.), *The Social Construction of Technological Systems: New Directions in the Sociology and History of Technology*. Cambridge, Massachusetts: MIT Press, pp. 243–259.

Böhme, Gernot (1992) *Coping with Science*. Boulder, Colorado: Westview Press.

Böhme, Gernot, van den Daele, Wolfgang und Wolfgang Krohn (1973) "Die Finalisierung der Wissenschaft," *Zeitschrift für Soziologie* 2:128–144.

Brooks, Harvey (1984) "The resolution of technically intensive public policy disputes," *Science, Technology, & Human Values* 9: 39–50.

Brooks, Harvey (1965) "Scientific concepts and cultural change," *Daedalus* 94: 66–83.

Bud, Robert (1991) "Biotechnology in the twentieth century," *Social Studies of Science* 21:415–457.

Chargaff, Erwin (1975) "Profitable wonders: A few thoughts on nucleid acid research," *The Sciences* 17: 21–26.

Cozzens, Susan E. and Edward J. Woodhouse (1995) "Science, government, and the politics of knowledge," in: Sheila Jasanoff, Gerald E. Markle, James C. Peterson and Trevor Pinch (eds.), *Handbook of Science and Technology Studies*. Revised Edition. Thousand Oaks, California: Sage, pp. 533–553.

Davison, Aidan, Ian Barns and Renato Schibeci (1997) "Problematic publics: a critical review of surveys of public attitudes toward biotechnology," *Science, Technology, & Human Values* 22:317–348.

Dewey, John ([1927] 1954) *The Public and its Problems*. Athens, Ohio: Ohio University Press.

Elias, Norbert (1983) *Engagement and Distanzierung. Arbeiten zur Wissenssoziologie I*. Frankfurt am Main: Suhrkamp.

Fukuyama, Francis (2002) *Our Posthuman Future: Consequences of the Biotechnology Revolution*. New York: Farrar, Straus, and Giroux.

Funtowicz, Silvio O. und Jeffrey R. Ravetz (1993) "The emergence of post-normal science, in: René von Schomberg ed., *Science, Politics and Morality. Scientific Uncertainty and Decision Making*. Dordrecht: Kluwer.

Gibbons, Michael et al. (1994) *The New Production of Knowledge. The Dynamics of Science and Research in Contemporary Societies*. London: Sage.

Griffiths, Michael and Salomon Wald (1999) "Biotechnology for industrial sustainability," *STI Review* No. 25:65–97.

Habermas, Jürgen (2001) *Die Zukunft der menschlichen Natur: Auf dem Weg zu einer liberalen Eugenik?* Frankfurt am Main: Suhrkamp.

Habermas, Jürgen ([1998] 2001) "An argument against human cloning. Three replies," in: Jürgen Habermas, *The Postnational Constellation. Political Essays*. Oxford: Polity Press.

Hayles, N. Katherine (1999) *How We Became Posthuman: Virtual Bodies in Cybernetics, Literature, and Informatics*. Chicago: University of Chicago Press.

International Council for Science (2003) *New Genetics, Food and Agriculture: Science Discoveries –Societal Dilemmas*. Paris. ICFS.

Janich, Peter and Michael Weingarten (2002) "Verantwortung ohen Verständnis? Wie die Ethikdebatte zur Gentechnik von deren Wissenschaftstheorie abhängt," *Journal for General Philosophy of Science* 33:85–120.

King, Lauriston R. and Philip H. Melanson (1972) "Knowledge and politics: some experiences from the 1960's," *Public Policy* 20: 83–101.

Lane, Robert E. (1966) "The decline of politics and ideology in a knowledgeable society," *American Sociological Review* 31:649–662.

Latour, Bruno and Steve Woolgar (1986) *Laboratory Life. The Construction of Scientific Facts*. With a new postcript. Princeton, New Jersey: Princeton University Press.

Limoges, Camille (1993) "Expert knowledge and decision-making in controversy contexts," *Public Understanding of Science* 2:417–426.

Lowe, Adolph (1971) "Is present-day higher learning 'relevant'?," *Social Research* 38: 563–580.

Lübbe, Hermann (1977) *Wissenschaftspolitik. Planung-Politik—Relevanz*. Zürich: Interfrom.

Mannheim, Karl ([1929] 1965) *Ideologie und Utopie*. Frankfurt am Main: G. Schulte-Bulmke.

Marcuse, Herbert ([1964] 1989) *Der eindimensionale Mensch. Studien zur Ideologie der fortgeschrittenen Industriegesellschaft*. Schriften 7. Frankfurt am Main: Suhrkamp.

Markl, Hubert (2003), "Ist der Mensch biotechnisch optimierbar?," *Wirtschaft & Wissenschaft* 11:32–45.

Markle, Gerald E. and Stanley S. Robin (1985) "Biotechnology and the social reconstruction of molecular biology," *Science, Technology, & Human Values* 10:70–79.

Mazur, Allan (1973) "Disputes between experts," *Minerva* 11: 243–262.

Miller, Jon D. (1983) *The American People and Science Policy*. New York: Pergamon.

Mulkay, Michael (1993) "Rhetorics of hope and fear in the great embryo debate," *Social Studies of Science* 23:721–742.

National Science Board (1984) *Research Related to Biotechnology*. Volumes 1 and 2. Washington, DC: National Science Foudation.

Nelkin, Dorothy (1975) "The political impact of technical expertise," *Social Studies of Science* 5:35–54.

Nowotny, Helga, Peter Scott and Michael Gibbons (2001) *Re-Thinking Science. Knowledge and the Public in an Age of Uncertainty*. Oxford: Polity Press.

Nye, Joseph S. and William A. Owens (1996) "America's information edge," *Foreign Affairs* 75: 20–34.

Office of Technology Assessment (1984) *Commercial Biotechnology: An International Analysis*. Washington, DC: U.S. Government Printing Office.

Richta, Radovan (1971) *Politische Ökonomie des 20. Jahrhunderts*.Berlin: Makol.

Rip, Arie (1997) "A cognitive approach to relevance of science," *Social Science Information* 36: 615–640.

Rosenberg, Daniel (2003) "Early modern information overlaod," *Journal of the History of Ideas* 64:1–9.

Scheler, Max ([1924] 1960) *Die Wissensformen und die Gesellschaft*. Bern und München: Francke.

Schelsky, Helmut (1961) *Der Mensch in der wissenschaftlichen Zivilisation*. Köln/Opladen: Westdeutscher Verlag.

Simon, Bart (2003) "Toward a critique of posthuman futures," *Cultural Critique* (Winter): 1–9.

Sinsheimer, Robert L. (1978) "The presumptions of science," *Daedalus* 107:23–35.

Sinsheimer, Robert L. (1976) "Recombinant DNA – on our own," *BioScience* 26:599.

Stehr, Nico (2003) *Wissenspolitik. Die Überwachung des Wissens*. Frankfurt am Main: Suhrkamp.

Stehr, Nico (2001), *The Fragility of Modern Societies. Knowledge, Information and Risk*. London: Sage.

Stehr, Nico (1994) *Knowledge Societies*. London: Sage.

Traore, Mamatic and Antoine Rose (2003) "Determinants of biotechnology utilization by Canadian industry," *Research Policy (in press)*.

Weart, Spencer R. (1988) *Nuclear Fear. A History of Images*. Cambridge, Massachusetts: Harvard University Press.

Weber, Max ([1922] 1964) *The Theory of Social and Economic Organization*. Edited with an Introduction by Talcott Parsons. New York: Free Press.

Wilensky, Harold L. (1967) *Organizational Intelligence – Knowledge and Government and Industry*. New York: Basic Books.

Wynne, Brian (2001) "Creating public alienation: Expert cultures of risk and ethics on GMO's," *Science as Culture* 10:445–481.

Ziman, John (1994) *Prometheus Bound: Science in a Dynamic "Steady State."* Cambridge: Cambridge University Press

Zizek, Slavoj (2003) "Bring me my Philips Mental Jacket," *London Review of Books* 25 (No.10), May 22.

Part I

Biotechnology and Civil Society: Historical and Theoretical Perspectives

Introduction
Historical Perspectives on Re-Shaping
Knowledge, Re-Shaping Society

Eugene A. Rosa

The goal of this section is to situate biotechnology in both distant and proximate historical contexts and to evaluate the three chapters that follow within those contexts.

The Biotechnology Revolution

Biotechnology, a voracious rubric comprising a wide range of biological possibilities, holds unprecedented potential for translating basic knowledge of fundamental biological processes into numerous applications. So Herculean in magnitude is biotechnology's potential that its realization, everyone agrees, will be revolutionary—revolutionary in our fundamental knowledge of the building blocks of life, revolutionary in how we view humans and other species, revolutionary in our moral judgments and ethical norms, and revolutionary in how we socially and politically organize ourselves. The 21st century, then, portends to be the century of the biotechnology revolution. For many scientists, citizens, and institutional actors the revolution is the highway to a bio-utopian future. For others it foretells of catastrophic disasters including the creation of monstrosities. Sociological insight warns of many bumps in the road, whatever the route of the highway.

Now poised on the verge of this revolution, what sociological wisdom can we offer for assessing the potential for a bio-utopian future: for anticipating the difficult issues that will confront society, for understanding the fault lines of the inevitable changes, and for informing the polity and other key institutions challenged with the management of the changes? One painfully obvious approach to developing this wisdom might be to look to the history of past science-society revolutions.

Scientific Revolutions and Social Change:
Distant Historical Context

Each of the previous two centuries has witnessed scientific breakthroughs that have resulted in revolutionary change for science and for society. With the discovery of the 2nd Law of Thermodynamics in the 19th century by French engineer, Sadi Carnot, the science of energetics was not only born but that knowledge unleashed a unprecedented spate of technological innovations that catapulted the incipient and struggling industrial revolution rapidly toward fruition. With the harnessing of the atom in the middle of the 20th century the field of sub-atomic physics was not only born but it also unleashed a keen quest to develop applications, military and peaceful, for this awesome conversion of matter to energy.

Broad lessons are contained in these two science-society revolutions, the most obvious and relevant being the pervasive and far-reaching changes to society resulting from paradigmatic changes in the scientific knowledge and worldview. Equally clear is that each resulted in a wide variety of benefits for society while simultaneously introducing a wide variety of risks—often risks unknown to history—and numerous unintended consequences. But these ostensible changes were revealed to us only in hindsight, begging the question of whether they could have been anticipated at the times of their unfolding?

While re-affirming the undeniable—and the banally obvious—connection between science, technology, and social change the revolutions of the 19th and 20th century are limited in their purchase of the likely direction to be taken by the biotechnology revolution. The 2nd Law of the 19th century was the scientific codification of practical solutions—mainly prototypical versions of the steam engine—in an attempt to improve on practical applications and on efficiency. The harnessing of the atom was intimately bound up with the exigencies of geopolitics—a desire by the United States to beat Germany in the believed race to develop an atomic bomb and the desire to end World War II.

Neither revolution had the historical nor the sociological hindsight available to the biotechnology revolution, neither had the long lead-time in which the biotechnology revolution is unfolding, and neither had the social and political sensibilities of the postmodern age. As pointed out by Stehr in the "Introduction" of this volume, societies are no longer content to engage in *a posteriori* cleanups of the realized risks and consequences stemming from the application of scientific knowledge. Instead, science is faced with unprecedented pressures of public scrutiny and legitimacy. Thus, gaining sociological purchase on the biotechnology revolution poses not just the unique challenges of any "first-of-a-kind" endeavor, but also, awkwardly put, poses uniquely unique challenges because of the nature of its knowledge (about the structure of living things) and the clearly significant re-structuring the application of that knowledge will generate.

Biotechnology as Postmodern Hydra

While considerable debate swirls around the fortunes of biotechnology, there is universal agreement about its polysemous character. It is a many-headed Hydra that provides grist for literally every societal mill: science, technology, theory (scientific and socio-political), commodification, politics, ethics, morals, and all others. Its most challenging features, and the most disturbing for many observers, is not the immense scientific puzzle solving that lies ahead, but the fundamental ethical, moral, and political challenges that do. For it is these challenges that will force us to probe deeply into such primal issues as: What defines a human being now and in the future? What defines an animal? What defines a species? What defines hybrid gene pools?

Francis Fukuyama, having recently revived the history he previously ended to proclaim the potential for a "posthuman" future (2002), distills the biotechnology revolution into four pathways to the future:

(i) a cognitive revolution in our understanding of genetic causes; (ii) neuropharmacology; (iii) life extension, and (iv) genetic engineering. The first of these (i), represented by such major endeavors as Genome projects, can be summed up for our purposes here with the legal phrase, *res ipsa loquitor*, the thing speaks for itself. Two of the others, and by extension a third, are empirically and analytically unpacked in two of the chapters that follow—the one by Nikolas Rose on neuropharmacology (with implications for life extension) and the other by Steven Best and Douglas Kellner on genetic engineering, especially cloning.

(ii) The Neurochemical Self and (iii) Life Extension. Rose presents a compelling suite of empirical evidence to make his case that many of us are becoming, perhaps like the hatched "people" taking soma in Aldous Huxley's *Brave New World,* "neurochemical selves," selves whose personalities are viewed as plastic raw material to be adjusted to suit desirable moods or medically prescribed behaviors. Mental illness and other coping challenges have become defined as brain disorders, symptom-treatable like any other chronic disease (e.g. diabetes) with medication—indeed, with a parade of medications over the past half-century, from Thorazine and tranquilizers to the contemporary family of "smart drugs" such as Prozac, Zoloft, Paxil, and Xanax. Indeed, Rose argues that one of the most profound consequences of this re-definition of repertoire of psychological maladies is the "transformation of personhood" where the sentient individual shaped by social, economic and biographical contingencies is replaced by the "somatic individual" swallowing customized chemical cocktails from a growing pharmacopoeia.

But Rose, not content to just describe the neurochemical self, nor the proximate factors causing it, explicates a set of reinforcing structural forces that gave rise to, perpetuates, and threatens to increase the number of somatic individuals. Converging toward a structural ossification of the psychiatric drug market are the insatiable profit appetites of the pharmaceutical companies, the creativity of public relations firms and the marketing of illnesses, the neurochemical paradigm driving the big business of psychiatry (supplanting Freudian approaches to treatment), the deinstitutionalization and other cost-containment incentives of the state and its health care systems, and, for many, the demand for drive-in solutions to problems now defined in terms of health and illness.

Left unaddressed in Rose's chapter, though specifically recognized, is the question about trends in the use of commercial pharmaceuticals more generally. For paralleling the broad trends documented by Rose is another, broader trend that doubtless reinforces—perhaps causally drives—the convergences in the psychiatric drug market. And it is this trend that connects Fukuyama's neuropharmacology pathway with the life extension one. An unchallenged value driving the medical profession is the desire to extend human life, and the 20th century has witnessed a dramatic increase in life expectancies nearly everywhere. In many respects life extension has been achieved through the successful treatment of catastrophic illnesses, with the consequence that by living longer people become afflicted with chronic illnesses—asthma, diabetes, cardiovascular and kidney diseases, various cancers, Alzheimer's, Arthritis, and others (Tenner, 1996).

But a recent compilation by Johns Hopkins University adds "mental illness" to this list, suggesting that drug use for physical and mental symptoms is traceable to a common cause—the rebound effects from the general growth of chronic illnesses. Furthermore, as hinted at by Rose there remains the question over the age distribution of neurochemical users, since the rise in use may be driven by the need to treat a variety of dementias afflicting an aging population.

(iv) Clone This. Were a postmodern Rip Van Winkle to arise from a twenty-year slumber to read the chapter by Best and Kellner he would doubtless suspect that he was reading the product of a fertile science fiction mind. Test tube babies, humans with xenotransplants, cyborgs, cryogenically suspended individuals, germ line engineered offspring, cloned humans, clones of cloned animals—these fantastic possibilities would all but confirm his suspician. But, such is not the case. All these things are already a reality or just over the horizon. For many observers they represent the most controversial pathway of the biotechnology revolution comprising, as they do, not only science, but also "religion, politics, economics, democracy, ethics and the meaning and nature of human beings and all life forms."

Best and Kellner tease out the complex issues shrouding the controversy over genetic engineering through a careful analysis of its upper bound case—cloning, possibly the most direct route to a posthuman future. Cloning, the exact replication of cells to produce new cells, tissues, organs, whole animals or even humans, holds untold promise for therapeutic applications, but spurs an unbounded imagination of pain to animals and to humans, of the creation of monstrosities, and of the control of science by the narrowly shaped motives of corporate interests. Cloning also draws into sharp relief the most disquieting biotechnology issues: What constitutes a human being, now and in the future? What are the long-term social and ecological consequences of the teleological tinkering with evolution? Best and Kellner provide a well-crafted survey of the cloning-related genetic engineering applications, tying them to the moral, ethical, and political issues they engender.

Their analyses distinguish between therapeutic (currently using embryonic stem cells, the body's master cells) and human reproductive cloning. They categorically reject the latter but conclude that the benefits of stem cell cloning in curing many deliberating diseases far outweigh the disposal of few-day old embryos. Their conclusion speaks volumes to the deep moral and ethical issues raised, for it is based upon a pragmatic, consequentialist stance where benefits are judged to trump risk. But, avoiding a principled, deontological stance, leaves the way open for pro-cloners, such as Antinori and Zavos, to adopt precisely the same argument to reach a conclusion repugnant to Best and Kellner.

Contested Solutions

The important point here is not the resolution of this knotty philosophical problem, but that one of the most acute problems for biotechnology, as it is for other risky technologies, is how to reach decisions under conditions of intractable uncertainty? This is where the big gun issues of biotechnology lie: in the selection of the social, political, and moral intelligence most fitting to direct and regulate its development, to shape the agendas of science and of society, and to retain our sense of the homo sapiens as essentially a human being. One approach favored by Best and Kellner, consistent with Habermas and part of a rapidly growing movement in technology assessment, is to democratize the procedures of decision making by extending the scientific, medical, and ethical discourse to the lay public. The appropriate products of this dialogical process would be laws, regulations, and regulatory agencies that would be shaped by and remain open to public input and scrutiny.

Fukuyama (2002), fearful of a runaway biotechnology that leads to a "posthuman future," a future like that portrayed in *Brave New World* where everyone is healthy and happy but have ceased to be human beings, offers a narrowly neo-liberal solution to the threat. Resigned to a relentless march of the biotechnology revolution, his solution to this fear is to restrain the free-market processes by establishing an infrastructure of international and national government regulations and controls.

Hired Guns

Fuller's chapter weighs in with both guns aimed at the limitations of Fukuyama's view of the future with the recapture of a theoretical history that first takes us back 200 years to the beginnings of a socialist temperament and later to the emergence of the discipline of sociology. It then takes us forward to demonstrate that the ideologies dominating the biotechnology revolution—the coalition of paternalistic social conservatism with the ecological left in opposition to market liberals—is little more than new wine in centuries-old bottles. This divide not only repeats, respectively, the divide between 19th century liberal Whigs and conservative Tories, but also reveals the unre-solved tension in both positions over the balance between the egalitarianism of individual liberty and the responsibility to the collective well-being. For Fuller, the synthesis of this tension was both the "genius of socialism," and the fundament for the emergent discipline of sociology.

In contrast, the neoliberal ideology dominating contemporary biotechnol-ogy has declared society dead—a fictitious reification. Furthermore, it has morphed its traditional actor *Homo Economicus* with a new actor, *Homo Geneticus*, the first focused upon its financial investments and the second on its genetic investments. Missing is the dialectic honing that comes from a dialogical process that engages a socialist sensibility with its collective conceptualization of our species and the collective focus of our concern for the welfare of this species. After all, each individual is the statistical and contingent outcome of actions in a dynamic gene pool that contains common genetic information millions of years old.

Fuller's worry beads are wrapped around this decline in the socialist sensibility and in the abrogation by sociology of its role in not only explicat-ing social conditions, but also in developing theoretically informed strategic and policy recommendations. Sociology's intellectual shortfall can be traced to amnesia about John Stuart Mill's distributional ideals[1]. Fuller argues force-fully for a neo-Millian sociology and for a conceptualization of society as not simply *persona ficta,* but as viable entity for understanding *la condition humaine.* He sees in the genetic science underlying the biotechnology revolu-tion, owing to its inherently statistical status, a remarkably attractive opportu-nity for the revival of both socialism and social science.

Fuller takes aim at the ecological left, in part because of its zoocentric principles, and at the Risk Society thesis of Beck (1992) and Giddens (1990), because of its abandonment of traditional welfare concerns—with its refocus of concern from the distribution of goods to the distribution of bads. But, by situating these perspectives in a traditional Left-Right continuum, he misdirects attention away from the potential eco-disasters of biotechnology and from the larger axiomatic connection between an ecologically viable base and the perpetuation of societies, whether conceived as gene pools or as a *res publica*. After all, a concern for the re-distribution of society's spoils is ineluctably dependent upon the existence of a society in the first place, a hoary presupposition whose contemporary status is very much in question. Furthermore, a focus on the egalitarianism of risks by deflecting attention away from the re-distribution issue, sheds light on social welfare that affects all citizens, rich and poor.

Genomes and Geopolitics: Recent Historical Context

This volume was prepared in 2003, a year of several landmark "semicentennials" or 50th anniversaries. The first of these—and the one that launched the topic of this volume—was the breaking of the genetic code in 1953 with the discovery of the helical structure of the basic building block of life, deoxyribonucleic acid, DNA. As basic science it represented knowledge of the genetic information that translates DNA into the structures and functions of species. To recur to questions organizing this discussion, how does one assess the awesome potential, for good or ill, of this essential knowledge? One approach to such an assessment comes from examining the revolution immediately preceding it, knowledge of the structure of the atom.

In 1953 a second significant event occurred, the now famous speech by President Dwight D. Eisenhower before the United Nations arguing for thoughtful and peaceful uses of the atom. The development and dropping of atomic bombs by the United States to end World War II had not only unleashed a destructive force more powerful than history had ever known but also revealed a deeper understanding of the structure of the atom than science had ever known. Knowledge for making bombs was simultaneously knowledge of causation (how to convert mass to energy) and knowledge of technology (how to initiate and control the conversion). Since knowledge increases available options and "capacities to act," the natural question to follow was how the vast potential of such fundamental scientific and technical knowledge could be transformed into benefits for the human race.

The Eisenhower speech was the clarion declaration of the coming energy-utopia where the uncontrolled fission of atomic bombs could be controlled in order to create vast quantities of energy from puny amounts of fuel. Envisioned then, as now, was the use of nuclear energy to generate electricity, with the expectation that nuclear would eventually replace coal, gas, and oil as the fuel for generators. But the vision of the time was far grander than this, for it projected the development of nuclear military craft (since realized), a nuclear powered airplane (attracting a failed $1 billion U.S. investment), nuclear ocean freighters and passenger ships, and nuclear reactors to power space ships. Even more astounding was the expectation that nuclear explosives could be used for peaceful applications, such as in building canals and harbors, or in redirecting large water sources (such as the Amazon River) to areas most in need of the water, or underground explosions to enable oil and gas supplies to flow more smoothly.

It is uncompromisingly clear in hindsight that the grand vision of nuclear's future was a dream never to be realized. Nearly all the projected uses for the technology have been abandoned. And the one remaining civilian use, nuclear electricity the most viable application, has failed to date to attain even a fraction of its expected generating possibilities, has been rejected by many countries, and is stalemated in many of the countries that have adopted it. What happened to energy-utopia? The short answer is that a number of historical, economic, political and forces converged to conspire against the technology. Looming large among these forces is a persistent public rejection of nuclear energy (Rosa and Dunlap, 1994), due to the operating and disposal risks of the technology and to a persistent mistrust of the institutions developing and managing the technology.

At an even deeper level of consciousness the technology attracts an essential tension—an obdurate binary, an unshakeable ambivalence. Against its utopian promise it conjures horrific images of dread and easily imagined chimera, due—it is theorized—to the lengthy Western ambivalence over knowledge and manipulation of life-forces[2] (Weart,1988). Counterbalancing images of utopian atom-powered cities on earth and other planets and images of unlimited energy are the doomsday images of radioactive monsters, exploding planets, weird ray devices, and the specter of nuclear holocaust. Typically the psyche trumps the utopian with the dystopian.

Long before the atom was harnessed it was known that radiation (i.e. radiating energy), due to the transmutation from one element into another, had powerful effects on living creatures. That knowledge, a precursor to images of the atom, initiated the deep ambivalence—was radiation an elixir or poison?—that continues to this day. The continuing public ambivalence over nuclear energy offers at least one key lesson to the incipient biotechnology revolution, for it embeds many of the features that will determine the fate of that revolution: extraordinary potential for benefits accompanied by high risk and great uncertainty, high susceptibility to negative imagery, and the uncertainty over institutional trust[3]. Thus, whether biotechnology reaches the utopian heights envisioned by its promoters, or whether it becomes stalemated will inexorably depend upon how publics everywhere weigh the risks, reflect on bio-imagery, and invest in institutional trust.[4]

Advanced Modernity and Risk

The principal milestones in advancing the biological sciences and in advancing the technologies for converting basic knowledge into useful procedures and products occurred during the contemporary period of advanced modernity. It was during this same period that societies acquired a heightened sensibility about the risks associated with products of science. Indeed, risk, uncertainty, and decision-making are at the core of the three chapters that follow (Jaeger, Renn, Rosa, and Webler, 2001.

Genetics, a key feature of the biotechnology revolution, shares with risk the ontological status as a statistical phenomenon, ineluctably embedding probabilities and uncertainties in their predictions of future outcomes. In this context, the challenge of weighing the potential benefits of biotechnology against the potential risks and the unintended consequences is part of a larger issue (Rosa, 1998); does high modernity generate risks (Beck, 1992; Giddens, 1990) accompanied by vulnerabilities and "fragilities" (Stehr, 2001) at a pace faster than societies can develop effective oversight and institutional structures for managing those risks? Furthermore, the question draws into sharp relief the theme of this volume, namely the question of whether it is possible to create oversight structures that preserve the fundaments of civil society and democratic processes.

Coda

A final 1953 semicentennial can shed light on whether society shall proceed with the biotechnological revolution and how the revolution, by restructuring both basic and applied knowledge, may restructure society. On May 29, 1953 New Zealander Edmund Hilary and Sherpa Tenzing Norgay summated Mount Everest, the first humans documented to do so. The universal answer to the ineluctable question of "why should they climb Everest" is, as everyone knows, "because it was there." Though banal in its surface meaning, the answer embeds a collection of deeper meanings encompassing complex processes and social forces.

It embeds, among other things, the pre-supposition—endemic to all technical solutions—that the mountain can be conquered, that it entails serious risks, but that the rewards of reaching the summit are worth those risks. Though orders of magnitude greater, these, too, are the forces that will determine the future of biotechnology—and the re-shaping of society. There is every likelihood that biotechnology will march forward, not only "because the knowledge is there," but also because "what science values is there," "what people value is there," "what corporations value is there," and especially "because what other powerful interests value is there." The challenge, then, is to ensure that biotechnology marches to the tune of civil society—to a respect for law, for due process, for public preferences and welfare, and for political legitimacy—not to narrow institutional, corporate, or state interests. Should the biotechnology revolution overcome this challenge it will enjoy an accomplishment unknown to previous science-society revolutions.

Notes

1. Works of John Stuart Mill have been embraced by sociology and the social sciences more generally, but not in the way favoured by Fuller. Causal reasoning in the social sciences can be traced to the deep influence of Mill's *System of Logic* where, in an ambitious attempt to account for both logic, the methods of science, and their applicability to social as well as purely natural phenomena, he specified his methods for inductive inference: the Method of Agreement, the Method of Difference, the Joint Method of Agreement and Difference, the Method of Residues, and the Method of Concomitant Variation. Lost in the legacy to the social sciences—due to G.E. Moore's "naturalistic fallacy" which was absorbed as a guiding pre-supposition of logical positivism—was Mill's normative component, his concern for social welfare. The net effect, in support of Fuller's point, is that the social sciences are, via method, inadvertent partners in the neo-liberal temperament.

2. The persistent belief shared by Chinese Middle Eastern and European alchemists of an inseparable connection between the essence of matter and life itself. Indeed, they were guided to their furnaces by the belief that by manipulating the life-force they could master the growth processes of matter, including human matter—flesh and bones.

3. Arguably the analogy between nuclear and biology is not overdrawn. For example, fission, the term used to describe the splitting of an atom, was adopted from cell division in biology; proliferation is another nuclear borrowing from biology; and a biological imagery, mushroom shaped, was chosen from a variety of possible images to describe the cloud of a nuclear explosion.

4. Fukuyama (2002) mistakenly argues that biotechnology is unique because it mixes obvious benefits with subtle harms and this distinguishes it from nuclear weapons and nuclear energy that were recognized to be dangerous from their beginnings. Nuclear weapons then, as now, and nuclear power, even more so, were believed to offer a number of obvious benefits while containing a number of subtle (low level doses of radiation for example) and not-so-subtle (the possibility of a nuclear catastrophe) harms.

References

Beck, Ulrich, ([1986] 1992) *Risk Society: Toward a New Modernity,* trans by Mark Ritter. London: Sage.

Fukuyama, Francis (2002) *Our Posthuman Future: Consequences of the Biotechnology Revolution.* New York: Farrar, Straus and Giroux.

Giddens, Anthony. (1990) *The Consequences of Modernity.* Stanford, CA: Stanford University Press.

Jaeger, Carlo, Ortwin Renn, Eugene A. Rosa, and Thomas Webler (2001) *Risk, Uncertainty, and Rational Action.* London: Earthscan Press.

Rosa, Eugene A. and Riley E. Dunlap (1994) "Nuclear Power: Three Decades of Public Opinion," Public *Opinion Quarterly* 58(3): 295–325.

Rosa, Eugene A. (1998) "Metatheoretical foundations for post-normal risk," with commentary by Jerry Ravetz and Silvio Funtowicz, *Journal of Risk Research* 1(1): 15–48.

Stehr, Nico 2001) *The Fragility of Modern Societies: Knowledge and Risk in the Information Age.* London: Sage.

Tenner, Edward (1996) *Why Things Bite Back: Technology and the Revenge of Unintended Consequences.* New York: Knopf.

Weart, Spencer R. 1988. *Nuclear Fear: A History of Images.* Cambridge, MA: Harvard University Press.

1

Back to the Future with Bioliberalism: Or, the Need to Reinvent Socialism and Social Science in the 21st Century

Steve Fuller

Introduction: The Disappearance of Society in the Bioliberal Era

S igns of the times appear in the most unlikely places. In the 3 October 1987 issue of *Women's Own*, a supermarket magazine targeting UK housewives, Prime Minister Margaret Thatcher made the most notorious and profound assertion of her career:

> I think we've been through a period where too many people have been given to understand that if they have a problem, it's the government's job to cope with it. 'I have a problem, I'll get a grant.' 'I'm homeless, the government must house me.' They're casting their problem on society. And, you know, *there is no such thing as society*. There are individual men and women, and there are families. And no government can do anything except through people, and people must look to themselves first. It's our duty to look after ourselves and then, also to look after our neighbour. People have got the entitlements too much in mind, without the obligations. There's no such thing as entitlement, unless someone has first met an obligation.

This assertion unleashed a torrent of social scientific, social theoretic, and socialistic critique, perhaps most notably the earnest Fabian Society pamphlet (no. 536), 'Does society exist?' Authored by Brian Barry, an analytic philosopher who was then Professor of Political Theory at the London School of Economics, the pamphlet dutifully weighed the arguments on both sides of the issue before concluding that, contrary to Mrs Thatcher's assertion, society does indeed exist. While Barry may have succeeded in assuaging the fears of

Labour Party operatives, little had he realized that Thatcher was anticipating what is nowadays, generally speaking, a rather respectable and self-styled 'progressive' view across the arts and sciences. I call this emergent sensibility *bioliberalism*. However, in world-historic terms it marks a great leap backward to the moment when the market first asserted itself against traditional forms of social life—the 'great transformation' in European history described in Karl Polanyi (1944). For Polanyi, this moment created the original need for socialism. Whether something similar will happen this time remains an open question.

My argument is informed by a prediction that I hope will be self-defeating. I believe that, unless steps are taken to the contrary, we are in the process of systematically forgetting the intuitions that were common to the founders of socialism as a distinct political movement and social science as an autonomous body of knowledge. The most fundamental common intuition was that *humanity is a project in the making*, one achieved by organizing a certain kind of animal in a certain range of ways. This is the primary normative meaning of 'society' in the modern sense, and the nation-state has been its main legal executor. From this standpoint, while humanity is very much within the potential of *homo sapiens,* the species need not develop in that direction. Indeed, history has thrown up many ways of retarding and even pre-empting what is fairly called the 'socialist' project, once all members of *homo sapiens* are not treated as full participants in its construction.

The socialist project has been traditionally inhibited or destroyed from two directions. One involves specifying a clear hierarchy within *homo sapiens* that makes it unlikely that all of its members can ever be equal participants in the project of humanity. The other involves the reverse motion of flattening the distinction between *homo sapiens* and other animals, such that the concept of humanity loses its metaphysical grounding altogether, and socialism is thus seen as too restrictive. In the early 19th century, humanistically inclined conservatives occupied the former position, and naturalistically inclined liberals the latter. Feudalism and Darwinism defined this polar opposition, both conceptually and historically.

In the early 21st century, the allegiances may be scrambled, but their collective consequence no less crowds out the prospects for the realization of the socialist project. In this respect, the new biotechnology marks not a radical break with the past, but an excuse to turn back the clock—specifically 200 years. That such a thing could happen is a by-product of these postmodern times, in which the very idea of progress (and hence regress) in the moral and political spheres is considered such a non-starter that there is never anything to 'gain' or 'lose', objectively speaking, by calling into question the project of humanity. The collective mind simply becomes distracted by other matters. At the same time, for those not so driven to distraction, the new biotechnology *does* provide opportunities for a reinvention of both socialism and social science.

Recalling the Past Link between Socialism and Social Science

To be sure, during the Cold War, and especially in the United States, the link between 'socialism' and 'social science' was treated as little more than an accident of spelling. (At least, so I was told as an undergraduate sociology major at Columbia in 1977.) At that time, under the historiographical influence of Raymond Aron and Robert Nisbet, sociology was said to have emerged as a reaction to the French Revolution of 1789, which in the name of Reason had tried to replace, in one fell swoop, centuries of traditional order with a planned society. Sociology, at its best, realized that this Enlightenment utopia was really a totalitarian nightmare in disguise, which would always fail to contain the paradoxical yet resilient character of human nature, as expressed in so-called 'organic' institutions like the family and the church. (From a strictly legal standpoint, one to which the original German sociologists were especially sensitive, these two institutions had radically different bases—the family being involuntary and the church voluntary. Nevertheless, that fact did not trouble the Cold Warriors, who focused on the anti-statism common to the two institutions.) In this genealogy, the arch French diplomatic observer of American affairs, Alexis de Tocqueville, figured as a founding father of the discipline, whereas one of his most avid readers and Auguste Comte's British publicist, John Stuart Mill, did not. The difference, of course, was that de Tocqueville anticipated the Cold Warrior's sense that democracy forces a trade-off between liberty and equality, whereas Mill held to the more 'socialist' idea that the two virtues could be jointly maximized with the rational redistribution of excess wealth.

Notwithstanding this Cold War attempt to manipulate sociology's past, it is difficult to deny that the fortunes of socialism and social science have risen and fallen together. In what follows, I assume a common post-Cold War view about the background against which sociology was originally defined, namely, the Industrial Revolution in late 18th and early 19th century Britain. Instead of the planned society, the implicit foe of the nascent sociological discipline was the emergent capitalist form of life that threatened to level the hard-won difference between civilized society and brute animal existence. Depending on the Enlightenment philosopher one chooses, this difference had been won in classical Athens or republican Rome but, in any case, had regressed in the Middle Ages when a Plato-inspired hereditary hierarchy was used to protect Christianity from the threat of Islam, which claimed its spiritual mantle by promising a genuine brotherhood of humanity equal under the eyes of Allah. However, for the Enlightenment wits, this threat was rebuffed by what (only since 1945) is called the 'Scientific Revolution', which was in the process of liberating ('secularising') Christianity of its feudal residue.

At this point, it is worth remarking that the twinned fate of socialism and social science is not so very different from the relationship between the ecology movement and environmental science, despite the efforts of the latter's practitioners to distance themselves from the former's advocates. (What differentiates the eco-twins from the socio-twins, of course, is that political-scientific support for the eco-twins is ascendant.) In the case of both social science and environmental science, it is important to stress that the issue here is the *autonomy* of this body of knowledge from more established forms of humanistic and natural scientific knowledge. After all, Thatcher never denied the existence of human beings or even of such self-organizing social units as families. Similarly, she did not deny that we have animal natures and live in a physical environment. However, it is clear that she would have the normative and policy concerns that have distinguished the social (and environmental) sciences subsumed under more traditional socio-epistemic formations. And with the help of unwittingly obliging intellectuals, that is indeed happening.

The US lawyer-activist Jeremy Rifkin has seen half the story. In what he calls the 'age of biology', Rifkin (2001) rightly observes an ideological realignment, with social conservatives and the ecological left combined in opposition to the utilitarian view of life associated with biotechnology that is shared by the free market liberals and what remains of the Marxists. However, Rifkin regards this realignment as new, when in fact it marks a return to the ideological state of play during the Industrial Revolution before the rise of socialism. The early 19th century debate was even couched as an anti—vs. pro-growth argument, as it is today—only with the factory, not the laboratory, functioning as the lightning rod for people's hopes and fears. Back then protectors of the land and developers of industry occupied clear ideological positions that were mutually exclusive and jointly exhaustive. They were called Tories (Conservatives) and Whigs (Liberals), and their corresponding forms of knowledge were later immortalized by Matthew Arnold as the 'cultured' (humanists) and the 'philistine' (natural scientists) at a time when Britain was still innocent of a 'third culture' of social science (Lepenies 1988). At that time, the Tories were the paternalistic protectors of the inveterate poor, while the Whigs regarded poverty as a retarded state of enterprise from which the poor had to be released.

Nowadays the two groups are defined as Ecologists and Neo-Liberals, respectively, and their spheres of concern have somewhat expanded. Ecologists extend their paternalism across species, while Neo-Liberals believe that the state inhibits everyone's—not merely the poor's—enterprising spirit. The ideological space marked by this pre- and post-socialist world is captured in Table 1.1.

Table 1.1
The Political Landscape before and after Socialism

	PROTECTIONIST	EMANCIPATIONIST
ANTHROPOCENTRIC	19th c. Conservatism	21st c. Neo-Liberalism
SPECIES EGALITARIAN	21st c. Ecologism	19th c. Liberalism

One key difference between the 19th and the 21st century expressions of this matrix is the exact nature of the thing that the opposing ideologues wish either to protect or to free. In the 19th century, that thing was *labour power.* Conservatives wanted to restrict labour both physically (i.e. the ability of individuals to move house to find work) and conceptually (i.e. family and guild prerogatives on the intergenerational transmission of property, trade, and craft). In contrast, Liberals promised freedom along both dimensions: On the one hand, Liberals wanted to sever people's hereditary ties to the land that legally inhibited the construction of factories and people living near these places of work; on the other, they wanted to dissociate labour from a specific human embodiment, which effectively reduced labour to a form of what Marx called 'variable capital' that was ultimately replaceable by the 'fixed capital' of technology. In the 21st century, the object of ecological protection and neo-liberal emancipation is *genetic potential* (Fuller 2002a: chaps. 2–3). Thus, ecologists campaign for a global intellectual property regime that prohibits 'bioprospectors' from appropriating the genetic potential of indigenous peoples and the patenting of animal and plant species. Meanwhile, neo-liberals envisage the aim of intellectual property legislation as simply the removal of barriers from people freely trading—and being held responsible for—their genetic potential as they would anything else in their possession. Moreover, the neo-liberals follow the practice of past liberals of foreseeing the replacement of the natural with the artificial, as the traded organic material is eventually superseded by synthetic biochemical versions that produce the same effects at less cost and risk.

What had yet to exist in the early 19th century—and what is disappearing in the early 21st century—are the various shades of red that used to cut such a dashing figure across the political landscape of Europe as socialist and social democratic parties, as well as their distinctive forms of knowledge. To be sure, these parties continue to exist, if only by virtue of organizational inertia—an ironic twist to the fate of the social democrats recounted in Roberto Michels' 1911 classic, *Political Parties.* Yet, as has become especially clear in the UK and Northern Europe, the old socialist parties are subject to strong countervailing forces from the ecologists and the neo-liberals. A more muted version of this tension can be even found within the US Democratic Party (e.g. the strength of the recent presidential candidacies of the ecologically minded Ralph Nader and the neo-liberal Ross Perot).

Socialism as the Dialectical Synthesis
of Conservatism and Liberalism

We tend to forget that one of socialism's achievements was to wed a broadly utilitarian, pro-science and pro-industry policy perspective to an overarching sense of responsibility for all of humanity, especially its most vulnerable members. It essentially completed the secularisation of Christianity promised by the Enlightenment (MacIntyre 1994). This movement started with the 'religion of humanity' of the Marquis de Condorcet and Auguste Comte, extended through the various socialist movements of the last 200 years, and was most successfully realized in the heyday of the welfare state in the third quarter of the 20th century. As Hegel and Marx might have it, the genius of socialism was to generate an egalitarian political ethic from a dialectical synthesis of the two countervailing forms of inegalitarianism that came to be consolidated by the end of the 18th century: conservative paternalism and liberal voluntarism. For the first time, a form of politics took seriously the idea—at least as a regulative ideal of collective action—that all people belonged equally to *homo sapiens.*

Socialism's inegalitarian roots remain latent in the Marxist motto: 'From each according to their ability (the liberal credo) to each according to their need' (the conservative credo). Marxists imagined that a spontaneously mutually beneficial division of labour would eventuate in a classless society. But what if we do not yet live in 'society degree zero' (the revolutionary moment) and classes are already in existence? In the 19th century, conservatives could see in the Marxist slogan the need to reproduce dependency relations, whereas liberals could read it as a call for the free exchange goods and services. Both conservatives and liberals imagined that a legally sanctioned system of stratification would result in either case, be it based on ascription or achievement. Moreover, each not only justified their own position but also demonised that of their opponents, as in Charles Dickens' fictional portrait of the heartless liberal, Thomas Gradgrind, in *Hard Times* and Bram Stoker's satirization of the parasitic Austro-Hungarian aristocrat, Count Dracula. The difference between these two forms of inegalitarianism are illustrated in Table 1.2.

The conservative strategy was to reproduce the current social order, no matter the opportunity costs, whereas the liberals wanted to invest current wealth most efficiently, no matter the social dislocation that resulted. For British liberals, the Poor Laws, which devoted 80% of local taxes to providing the poor with a modicum of food and shelter, could be better spent on roads and other capital investments to attract industry, thereby creating jobs that would enable the poor to provide for themselves by contributing to the nation's overall wealth. In contrast, the conservatives believed that the cost of maintaining a secure life was a stable hierarchy, which implied the perpetual reproduction of feudal dependency relations between the rich and the poor. To destabilize this hierarchy would be to incur untold damage, including unnecessary death. But for the liberals the far greater cost of stability was that the poor were never given the opportunity to rise to their appropriate level of merit (or die, if they prove incapable of adapting to the needs of the market), which impeded the overall productivity of society. Liberal political economists regarded the amount of unused inherited land as the ultimate symbol of this squandered potential.

Thus, the liberals began to query how class divisions were drawn: why sheer property ownership rather than earned income or merit? What is touted as the 'individualism' of liberal political philosophy is simply the realization that class divisions are conventional, if only because everyone is endowed with the same innate capacities but differ in their opportunities to employ those capacities. Liberals aspired to a world in which people could dispose of their capacities just as landowners could of their property: Ideally, you would be judged by what you did with your 'possessions' in this extended sense, in a free environment. As we shall see, this perspective has come to be reinvented as we acquire greater knowledge of specifically biological capacities. In any case, liberals agreed with conservatives on the need for some sort of principle of cumulative advantage but disagreed on its basis. In particular, what was an appropriate principle of *inheritance*? Legal theories of succession presupposed rather ancient biological views about the passage of competence across generations of family members that created grounds for a son's entitlement to manage his father's estate or assume his trade (e.g. primogeniture). It was this common concern with the transmission of accumulated advantage—what Richard Dawkins (1982) has renovated as the 'extended phenotype'—that would come to distinguish both liberals and conservatives from socialists most clearly.

The Rise and Fall of the Welfare Concept: From Sociology to Socialism on the Cheap

The question of inheritance—the inter-generational transmission of property—was central to the establishment of sociology in Germany, France, and the United States. The concept of welfare was meant to capture a collective inheritance to which each member of society contributed and from which each benefited, though—as Marx stressed—*not* according to some default biologically based principle. In the final quarter of the 19th century, all three nation-states transformed the legal basis for incorporating individuals into the

Table 1.2
The Two Inegalitarian Sources of Modern Socialism

	CONSERVATIVE PATERNALISM	LIBERAL VOLUNTARISM
LEGACY TO SOCIALISM	State ensures that the able provide for the needy	State ensures that the needy become able
VISION OF ARISTOCRATS	Hereditary Protectors of Tradition	Wasters of Unearned Advantage
VISION OF BOURGEOISIE	Mercenary Destroyers of Tradition	Investors in Earned Advantage
VISION OF POOR	Vulnerable Wards	Financial Burden
LEGAL PRECEDENT	Poor Laws	Enclosure Laws
ECONOMIC POLICY	Minimum Wage	Tax Incentives
WELFARE STRATEGY	Social Insurance	Mass Education
SOURCE OF ORIGINAL EQUALITY	Fitness to Fate	Innate Capacity
SOURCE OF ULTIMATE INEQUALITY	Natural Hierarchy	Individual Merit
FICTIONAL DEVIL ('DEMONIZED OTHER')	Thomas Gradgrind ('Penny Pincher')	Count Dracula ('Blood Sucker')
REAL DEVIL	Jeremy Bentham	Oscar Wilde

social order: Germany consolidated, France secularised, and the US expanded. The first president of the German Sociological Association, Ferdinand Toennies, christened sociology's founding distinction, *Gemeinschaft* and *Gesellschaft*, as respectively the conservative and the liberal pole out of which this newly integrated conception of society was forged. A legal scholar by training, Toennies regarded this conception as the culmination of a medieval innovation in Roman law.

Until the twelfth century, Roman law recognized two general categories of social life. In the 'natural' mode, property was transmitted through the family (*gens*), an equation of biological reproduction and social succession. But there was also an 'artificial' mode for temporary associations (*socius*), such as joint-stock companies and crusades, which were project-centred and ceased to exist once the project was completed and its profits were distributed to the project's partners. The *Gemeinschaft/Gesellschaft* distinction is grounded in this contrast, which also persists in folk understandings of biologically ac-quired traits as somehow more basic and durable than socially acquired ones. Missing from these two categories was an artificial social entity entitled to perpetual legal protection because its ends transcend those of any or all of its members at any given place and time. In the twelfth century, this entity (*universitas*) was born. It is the source of the paradigmatic objects of social science research. Originally populated by guilds, churches, and, of course, universities, this realm of *universitas* gradually came to include still larger corporate entities like states and firms, the constitution of which was to be central to the sociology of Max Weber.

Considerable significance has been invested in the *universitas* as a distinc-tive expression of humanity. The presence of this legal category testifies to a conception of society that is irreducible to either suprahuman fate or infrahu-man drives—that is, the domains of theology or biology. In this respect, Condorcet and Hegel were only two of the more famous proto-sociologists who identified the 'universal state' with humanity rendered self-conscious. This identification was based not on some misbegotten chauvinism about the French Republic or the German Reich, but on the sheer logic of the concept of *universitas*. Not surprisingly, Toennies had earned his scholarly reputation as the German translator of Thomas Hobbes, who was among the first to exploit this logic for some politically interesting purposes.

Hobbes saw the potential of the *universitas* for self-improvement through the normative regulation of its members. Specifically, he recognized that this process would require the *redistribution* of properties from natural individu-als to the artificial corporate person licensed as a *universitas*. For Hobbes, the fear and force that divide individuals in the state of nature would be alienated and concentrated in his version of *universitas*, the Leviathan state, whose absolute power would then enable the individuals to engage in sustained peaceful associations that would have the long-term consequence of fostering civilization, from which subsequent generations might benefit. The socialist ideals realized in the welfare state may be seen as having carried this logic one step further, as income redistribution aimed to remove the class divisions that emerge unintentionally from the advantage accumulated in post-Leviathan civil associations, which then effectively create a 'civilized' version of the state of nature, as Marx perhaps most vividly recognized. In his more Communist moods, Marx seemed to believe that the proletarian revolution would devolve the Hobbesian sovereign back to the people, who armed with self-consciousness and modern modes of production, would be able to lead a secure and peaceful existence. However, short of that utopian outcome, the threat of the Internal Revenue Service ends up sublimating the threat originally posed by the Leviathan.

No one ever denied that the redistribution of property (understood as both abstract qualities and concrete holdings) entails what economists call 'transaction costs'—that is, the costs involved in bringing about the redistribution. But how to ensure that these costs are borne equitably and in ways that do not overwhelm the transactions they are designed to sustain? A neat feature of the Hobbesian solution—one long associated with Machiavelli—is that a credible threat of force is self-economizing. In other words, the threat works to the extent that it does not need to be acted upon, because prospective targets anticipate its bloody consequences; hence they take pains to avoid conditions that would result in those consequences. Of course, the threat needs to be credible in the first place, which is why Hobbes emphasized the absoluteness of the sovereign's power. Anything short of a complete monopoly of force would invite challenges that would divide the sovereign's energies between securing the conditions for redistribution and the actual redistribution. A normatively desirable redistribution of property may still result—but perhaps with a fraction of the original population. To be sure, this has been an acceptable price to pay for saving Humanity from the more recalcitrant elements of *homo sapiens*—at least according to the revolutionary founders of the first French Republic. Others have been less sure.

In the final quarter of the 19th century, the first professional association of social scientists, the German *Verein für Sozialpolitik*, addressed this problem by proposing a minimal welfare state as the price the rich should pay for tolerating rapid social and economic change without generating civil unrest (Rueschemeyer and van Rossum 1996). In this way, Germany could make a peaceful internal transition to its emergent status as a global imperial player. In the form of Bismarck's social security insurance scheme, conservative paternalism thus made its formal contribution to the realization of socialist ideals, since what had originated as a concession came to be a rallying point for Germany's nascent Social Democratic Party. Nevertheless, Bismarck's scheme did serve to immunize Germany from a Marxist proletarian revolution, whose potential resemblance to the first French Republic frightened partisans on all sides. Moreover, as long as the welfare state provided only the minimum—and not the optimum—for the maintenance of social life, there was little chance that the poor would ever have sufficient leisure to mount a credible organized challenge to the rich. In this respect, Bismarck's welfare state was designed to supplement Ricardo's 'iron law of wages', whereby workers are 'rationally' paid just enough to keep them coming to work the next day.

Whereas the conservatives unwittingly paved the way to socialism in their attempt to maintain order in the face of rapid change, the liberal-inspired promise of greater overall productivity though greater cross-class mobility eventually won the political argument to create more robust welfare states. This argument, popular among Fabian socialists in Britain, was presented as a self-reinforcing 'virtuous circle': The wealth of society as a whole is promoted by everyone doing what they can do best, which means that everyone needs to be given the opportunity to demonstrate what they can do, which in turn will result in greater wealth for society as a whole. This shift in welfare orientation from the past to the future presupposed a different justification for progressive taxation. Whereas Bismarck's welfare initiatives mainly had the rich reward the poor for work well done in keeping them rich, the Fabian welfare state would have the rich make speculative investments on those most likely to maintain or increase their wealth in the future. Accordingly, the welfare state's attention shifted to 'front-loaded' expenditures in preventive medicine and educational equality.

Although the Fabians' more generous sense of welfare came to define 'first world' nations by the third quarter of the 20th century, the strategy has always faced two countervailing forces that have tempted policymakers to return to the biological roots of inheritance: the persistence with which the rich try to reclaim their tax burden and the delay with which welfare beneficiaries improve their life chances. Both potentially wreak havoc on party political campaigns by implicitly raising the question of redistribution's transaction costs. It was against this background of impatience that *eugenics* promised, so to speak, 'socialism on the cheap' (Allen 1998).

The two people most responsible for advancing eugenics as an academically respectable basis for policy in the Anglophone world—Francis Galton and Karl Pearson—were self-styled 'scientific socialists' of the late 19th century (i.e. before Marxists cornered the market on the expression). For Galton and Pearson, the *laissez faire* policies of a so-called Social Darwinist like Herbert Spencer were sociologically naïve because they underestimated the extent to which a single illustrious progenitor could enable successive generations of unproductive offspring to occupy powerful positions. Here the eugenicists took specific aim at the British House of Lords. In a eugenic utopia, election to the upper legislative chamber would be rationalized by examining entire family histories to see which lineages demonstrated consistency or steady improvement across generations. Moreover, on that basis, the eugenicist could expedite the forces of natural selection by providing incentives to increase the reproductive tendencies of the more illustrious lineages and to decrease those of the less illustrious ones.

The 20th century was largely a story of eugenics run amok. To nations faced with an influx of immigrants and mounting costs for public health and education, eugenics promised an easy way out—indeed, at an increasing number of points in the reproductive process, as knowledge of genetic causal mechanisms progressed (King 1999). Early in the century, changes could be induced in reproductive patterns only by either modest incentives (e.g. tax breaks, income subsidies) or brute force (e.g. sterilization, genocide): the one insufficiently compelling and the other too repellent. However, today's eugenicists—now travelling under the guise of 'genetic counsellors'—can intervene at several intermediate stages, including amniocentesis and genetic screening, which are more likely to appeal to a broad moral consensus.

Indeed, following some landmark cases in France, there is now legal precedent for presuming that one has a 'right' not to have been born if those causally proximate to the birth could have reasonably anticipated that he or she would lead a seriously disadvantaged life (Henley 2002). The noteworthy feature of this judgement is its presumption, *à la* Thatcher, that society as such shoulders no special burden for the fate of its members. The judge ruled that the genetic abnormalities called 'disabilities' are not *prima facie* opportunities for socio-legal innovation, as, say, animal rights activists routinely urge on behalf of their constituency. Rather, disabilities are pure liabilities, but ones for which only the disabled person's parents and doctors are responsible.

With this ruling, we have come a long way from the strong welfarist perspective of John Rawls' (1972) 'veil of ignorance', which justified substantial redistribution of wealth on the grounds that if one's own place in society is uncertain, then it is best to allocate resources so that even the worst social position is not so bad. Indeed, for some political philosophers, our increased ability to anticipate the differential outcomes of the genetic lottery provides sufficient grounds for rolling back Rawls altogether.

For example, Hillel Steiner (1998) has swung so far back to libertarianism that he would have tort law absorb most of the state's claims to redistribute benefits and harms. Steiner envisages a world in which a basic knowledge of genetic science and one's own genetic constitution would become integral to citizen education, for which individuals would then be held accountable as a normal part of self-management. For the feminist legal theorist, Roxanne Mykitiuk (2003), this emerging bioliberal regime is simply another step in the march of the post-Keynesian state. Thus, policymakers imagine that as we acquire a more fine-grained understanding of the relationship between our genes and our traits, the state can safely retreat to the regulatory margins of the market, ensuring that biomedical products do what is claimed of them. It is then up to the consumer, provided with such information, to make a decision and endure the consequences.

Ronald Dworkin (2000) has updated Rawls to make a case for socialized insurance against genetic risk, a strategy endorsed by the UK's leading cancer research charity as a basis for public reinvestment in the National Health Service, despite current Labour government policy to devolve healthcare to the private sector (Meek 2002). This reinvention of the welfare state turns on an elementary point of genetic science. Suppose we assume a fixed species or common gene pool—admittedly a 'closed system' that is placed increasingly under strain with progress in biotechnology. Nevertheless, in that ideal case, genetics demonstrates *both* the commonality of possible life chances (i.e. genotypes) *and* the arbitrariness of the particular life chances that are realized in individuals (i.e. phenotypes). Even given clear genetic markers for traits that are agreed to be 'disabilities', the only way to prevent those disabilities from ever arising at all would be to prevent the birth of anyone carrying the relevant markers—even given the unlikelihood that any of the aborted would have led a disabled life. The prenatal terminations proliferated by this approach are called 'false positives' by statisticians and 'errors on the side of caution' (on a mass scale) by everyone else. As a general policy for pre-empting undesirable outcomes, it adumbrates an intolerably risk-averse society. (For example, one landmark French case concerned a relatively *common* disability, Down's Syndrome.) Yet, this policy is proposed as a post-welfarist 'paradise' embraced by not only neo-liberals but also ecologists, who invoke the 'precautionary principle' to similar effect.

At this point, I must comment on a serious rhetorical difficulty concerning the implications of bioliberalism's devolved eugenic sensibility. The contrast between the welfare state and bioliberalism is typically presented in terms of attitudes toward risk: The former supposedly aims to minimize risk, while the latter aims at least to accept risk, if not exactly to maximize it. However, given the ease with which bioliberals pre-empt negative life chances, this way of putting the matter is paradoxical. Although Rawls himself encouraged the view that individuals are naturally risk-averse, the redistributionist strategies of the welfare state in fact *collectivise* risk. In other words, the state enables the reorganization of people so that they are capable of taking *more* risks than they would or could as individuals. As either Spencer or Galton would have seen from their different perspectives, the welfare state's redistribution of resources artificially extends the selection environment to allow for the survival or otherwise unfit individuals—presumably because of the anticipated long term benefit that such individuals would provide for the rest of society. In cases of subsidised education and healthcare to ambitious and clever children from poor homes, the social benefits are palpable within a couple of decades. However, the benefits derived from special educational and health facilities for the disabled depend on more extended notions of humanity.

Martha Nussbaum (2001) has suggested that the policy imagination is recharged by the periodic adoption of what Max Weber would have called a 're-enchanted' view toward so-called 'monstrous births', such that they are not problems to be avoided or liabilities to be minimized—but rather symbolic events from which we learn something deep about what it means to be one of 'us'. Yet, the nature of this 'depth' is far from mysterious. It simply requires interpreting the monstrous birth as an occasion to extend the definition of the human rather than to have the birth excluded for failing to conform to the current definition. (The anthropology of Mary Douglas and the philosophy of science of Imre Lakatos provide interesting precedents for this line of thought: see Bloor 1979; Fuller & Collier 2003: chaps. 5, 7.) Historically speaking, such an attitude has been integral to the distinctive push of Western scientific medicine to regard death—like war, so said Jacques Chirac—as always an admission of failure. The unconditional commitment to the prolonging of human life, no matter the cost, or even the consequences for those whose lives are prolonged, is a secular descendant of the monotheistic concern for the weak and infirm members of *homo sapiens*. In these most vulnerable parties—at least according to Judaism, Christianity, and Islam—lies the human stripped of its worldly power to a form that only God could recognize as 'His' own (Fuller 2000b, 2002b).

The Great Leap Backward from Humanity to
the Politics of Nature

While it is convenient to argue that the concrete failures of socialism and social science explain the great ideological leap backward, an important part of the explanation lies in the diffusion of political interest from the specifically human to a more generic sense of life. No doubt, this reflects the cultural impact of Neo-Darwinism on contemporary political and ethical intuitions. But it also reflects a profound change in political economy. The original defenders of animal rights were urban dwellers like Epicurus, Lucretius, Montaigne, and Bentham, who held no special brief for protecting the natural environment. Indeed, their pro-animal thinking was part of a general strategy of rescuing all sentient beings from captivity in 'the state of nature' (Plender 2001). For them, as for Linnaeus, Lord Monboddo, and Jean-Baptiste Lamarck, the highest compliment one could pay an animal was to say that it was fit for human company. Animal rights came to be absorbed into a general ecological ethic only with the decline of agriculture as a mode of production. Thus, by the time Peter Singer (1981) came to speak of 'expanding the circle' of moral responsibility, he ultimately had the entire planet in his sights—that is the preservation of animal habitats, not simply the incorporation of animals into human society.

I cannot say exactly when animal rights came to be associated with a specifically anti-humanistic sensibility, one that places greater value on wild over domestic animal existence. Nevertheless, the assimilation of animal rights to a global ecological ethic has served to lower *both* the criteria for an adequate human existence (i.e. to the minimization of suffering) *and* the tolerance for individual humans who fail to meet those criteria (i.e. the disabled, the infirm, perhaps even the unwanted). In other words, an extension of rights to animals in general has been accompanied by a restriction of rights to specific classes of humans.

Fuller (2001a) portrays this development as a scientific version of La Rochefoucault's maxim, 'Familiarity breeds contempt'. In effect, animals receive the benefit of the doubt in a global ecological ethic simply because less is known about them. A reified version of this judgement is central to the Aristotelian tradition: Animals are morally neutral in a way that humans are not because the former always realize their lower potential, whereas the latter often do not realize their higher potential. Admittedly, disabled humans are not personally responsible for their failure to realize their potential, but still their lives are valued less when compared to that of able-bodied humans. In light of this lingering Aristotelian sensibility, an unintended long-term value of conducting more research into animals might be that greater familiarity with the grades of animal life will enable similarly nuanced judgements of animals, including perhaps making them liable for their own unrealised potential.

As we have seen, the concept of welfare has been dissipated in two respects. On the one hand, ecologists have wanted to 'expand the moral circle' to cover animal welfare. In a post-socialist period when tax bases are certainly not growing, and are often shrinking, this policy invariably involves spreading welfare provision more thinly among humans. It has resulted in more explicit discussions of tradeoffs in legal coverage and even 'triage' in healthcare. In this context, John Stuart Mill gets his comeuppance for having the temerity to presume that a disabled Socrates (Stephen Hawking?) was worth more than an able-bodied pig. On the other hand, neo-liberals want simply to withdraw state involvement from all but the most basic welfare provision, converting individual tax burdens into added spending power that may be used as individuals see fit.

New developments in genomic-based biotechnology offer comfort to both the ecological and the neo-liberal views of welfare provision. On the one hand, the ontology underlying the new biotechnology stresses a 95%+ genetic overlap between humans and most other animals, creating a presumptive parity of interests and rights. On the other hand, the research agenda of the new biotechnology is oriented toward the identification of specific abnormalities in specific strands of DNA, which ultimately would enable each individual to have a comprehensive understanding of her genetic strengths and weaknesses, so that she can make an 'informed choice' about the degree and kind of healthcare she is likely to need. For a sense of political contrast, an 'old socialist' would read the '95%+' figure as grounds for encouraging xenotransplantation, gene therapy, and animal experimentation—all in aid of maximizing the use of animals to promote human welfare. Moreover, rather than focusing on the uniqueness of each person's DNA, the old socialist would note that they are combinations of elements drawn by chance from a common genetic pool.

A sign that both the ecologists and the neo-liberals have evacuated the ground previously held by the red parties is that the welfare of the most vulnerable members of human society is largely abandoned as an explicit policymaking goal—though both continue to make arguments to the effect that the poor and disabled might benefit indirectly, such as by trickle-down economics or even some 'mercy killing' (especially if the minimization of suffering is taken to be an overriding value). Indeed, there is a tendency for both ecologists and neo-liberals to speak as if the fundamental problems of poverty and immiseration that gave rise to the labour movement and socialist parties have been already more-or-less solved—much as it is often claimed that certain previously widespread diseases like smallpox and polio have now been eradicated. But both sides of the analogy turn out to be empirically flawed and maybe even conceptually confused, if they assume that social progress, once made, is irreversible and hence worthy of benign neglect.

For their part, sociologists have done relatively little to illuminate this rather strange sense of 'living in the future' that characterizes contemporary post-welfarist politics, even as the gap between the rich and the poor within and between countries has arguably increased. Instead, sociologists have fixated on the generalized exposure to risk that the devolution of the welfare state has wrought, and the self-organizing 'lifestyle politics' that have emerged in its wake. It would seem that with the decline of the welfare state has come a phenomenologization of the sociological sensibility, as if the ontology of social structures dissolves right alongside the devolution of state power. I refer here, of course, to the so-called 'risk society' thesis introduced by Ulrich Beck (1992) and popularised in the guise of 'ontological insecurity' by Anthony Giddens (1990). However, this is not quite phenomenology as Alfred Schutz understood it—nor is it politics as anyone normally understands it.

At the dawn of the mass media, Schutz (1964) famously argued that radio gave listeners a false sense of immediacy of events happening far beyond their everyday life experiences, which might embolden them into political intervention. (He was worried about fascist propaganda galvanizing the petty bourgeoisie.) If we replace 'radio' with 'internet', Schutz's reservations would seem to apply to the lifestyle politics associated with, say, the anti-globalization movement. This change of media enables the anti-globalizationists to control the means of knowledge production to a substantial extent, but it also enables them to autonomize their activities from ordinary politics. What is noticeably lacking from this movement—especially when compared with the old labour movement—is sustained engagement with the people on whose behalf the demonstrations are made. Protestors tend not to be members of the classes represented but well-educated, well-meaning people who—by virtue of age, disposable income, or employment situation—can easily transport themselves to the first-world sites where global political and economic oppressors happen to congregate. The actual oppressed are typically too busy working in third-world sweatshops or fearful of local political reprisals to demonstrate for themselves.

To some extent, this lack of sustained engagement already had precedents in the failure of university-based activism in the 1960s and 1970s to touch base with industrial labour, even though much of the academic political rhetoric concerned 'class oppression'. With the 20/20 vision afforded by hindsight, we may say that the more ecological and libertarian features of campus radicalism held little appeal to organized labour, with its generally solidarist strategy for retaining factory jobs. Of course, the jury is out on whether the anti-globalization movement really serves the interests of those they claim to represent. Nevertheless, the movement already displays some distinctive contexts of interaction. The representatives and the represented—the protestors and the oppressed—are usually limited to 'photo-ops' in the broadest sense, ranging from the protestors briefly visiting oppressed habitats in the presence of the cable television news channels to the protestors themselves filming the oppressed to raise consciousness at home.

It is easy to see how such self-appointed representation of others suits a reduction of the politics of humanity to a 'politics of nature'. For example, animal rights activists do not organize animals to revolt against their human oppressors, nor do they necessarily spend much time around animals—though they visit sites of animal captivity, mainly to bring back evidence of their cruelty to the humans who might make a difference to their fate. While this political strategy is perfectly understandable vis-à-vis animals, it should cause the heart of any socialist to sink when applied to humans: *Where are the attempts to persuade the locals that they should organize themselves to revolt against their oppressors?* Of course, in the current political climate, the few such attempts that do occur are regarded as 'treason' and 'terrorism'—indeed, as they were when socialists acted similarly in the 19th century. Yet, the original socialists were not deterred by the threat of state sanction because they believed that the locals could be persuaded of their point-of-view and, crucially, that fact would contribute evidence to the view's correctness. This result, in turn, would embolden the enlarged comradeship to continue spreading the word worldwide.

Here we see one of the many senses in which socialism tried to realize the spirit of Christianity in a secular guise (MacIntyre 1994). Presupposed in the socialist project—at least in this organizational phase before it became the dominant state party of any country—was a sense that one's own faith in the project had to be tested against the unconverted. This gave socialism much of its heroic quality, but it also meant that the doctrine was responsive to the resistance it met from those on whose behalf socialists aspired to speak. In contrast, the anti-globalizationists are essentially a self-appointed emancipatory movement that does not require its subjects to confirm its perspective. Read uncharitably, the anti-globalizationists would appear to be risk-averse or dogmatic in their own sociological horizons. In effect, they have assimilated the plight of oppressed humans to that of the natural environment, whose consent they would also never dream of seeking. In this respect, they engage in a 'dehumanization' of politics—albeit a benevolently inspired one.

Other attempts to provide a post-welfarist grounding for sociology have foundered on the shoals of 'body politics'. In his keynote address to the annual meeting of the British Sociological Association in 2002, Bryan Turner, a founder of the sociology of the body, a popular field speciality, argued for a division of labour within social science to recapture the distinction between a universal human nature and differences among particular societies. Perhaps unsurprisingly, the proposed division was a phenomenologically inspired one—between the universal experience of *pain* and the culturally relative manifestations of *suffering*. For Turner a supposed advantage of this redefinition is that it draws the boundary of the social's domain right at the interface with the natural world. Thus, Turner would extend sociology's remit to cover areas previously ceded to psychology and the biomedical sciences. Unfortunately, this extension comes at the price of attenuating the definition of the 'social' in ways that, once again, give comfort to both ecologists and neo-liberals at the expense of the old left: 'The social' is reducible to a collection of traits possessed by individuals (the neo-liberal turn) and, moreover, these traits are defined such that their possessors need not be humans (the ecological turn). It marks a return to an ontology that sees the difference between 'species', 'race' and 'culture' as matters of degrees, not kinds, and a normative ideal that is fixated on the ideal member of one such group rather than the exemplary collective product that 'humanity' was meant to be.

Conclusion: A New Foundation for
Genetics in the Social Welfare Sciences

No one denies the unprecedented nature of what we know about the genetic constitution of humans and other animals, as well as our capacity for genetic intervention both *in vivo* and *in vitro*. What remains—and will always remain—in doubt is our control over the consequences. Genetics is an irreducibly statistical science. Indeterminacy occurs on at least three levels: interaction effects among genes in a genome, from genotype to phenotype, and the interaction effects between genetic makeup and the environment. In this respect, the very term 'biotechnology' masks a socially significant gap between knowledge and control. Interestingly, at the dawn of the 20th century, when eugenicists learned from the Hardy-Weinberg theorem that most disabilities would remain unexpressed in the individuals carrying the relevant genes, they did not admit defeat for their program of selective breeding. Rather, they intensified their research, as if the indeterminacy were ignorance that could be eliminated through more precise genetic knowledge and invasive genetic technology (Paul 1994: chap. 7). However, as one might expect of any complex phenomenon, this research has succeeded in posing new problems as it solved old ones.

The statistical nature of genetic science provides the best chance for reviving the fortunes of both social science and socialism in the 21st century. But the realization of this future requires a genuine Hegelian 'sublation' of genetics. In other words, the status of genetics as a body of knowledge needs to be reduced before it can be properly incorporated into a renovated conception of 'society'. Specifically, it must come to be seen not as an autonomous, let alone foundational, science but as a 'mere' social technology that can be explained, justified, and applied by a wide variety of theories, ideologies, and policies. Ideally, this involves divesting genetics of its status as a paradigmatic science with a canonical history and fixed location on the intellectual landscape. Indeed, we should aim for the phrase 'genetic engineering' to become a pleonasm. Genetics must become like the economy, which is no longer the preserve of *laissez faire* liberals but a generally recognized and multiply interpretable societal function. However, given the prevalence of what Richard Dawkins (1976) notoriously popularised as the 'gene's eye-view of the world', the public understanding of genetics continues to conjure up the spectre of totalitarian regimes, comparable to the public understanding of political economy, *circa* 1810, which evoked images of dehumanised exchange relations.

The analogy runs deeper, since Dawkins draws—perhaps unwittingly—on the reversal of means and ends that Marx used so effectively in *Capital* to illustrate capitalism's perversion of value. Just as money drives the exchange of commodities, 'selfish genes' use willing organisms to reproduce themselves. In contrast, with renewed sociological vision, genes should not be seen as the prime movers of life but organic by-products of procreation, a means by which people perpetuate several legally sanctioned social formations—most traditionally the family—as they bring the next generation into existence. To be sure, these organic by-products are themselves socially significant as regulators of individuals' bodily functions. Nevertheless, describing the genetic basis of humanity in such ontologically diminished terms draws attention to the subservient role of the gene, which through changes in the constitution of society and extensions in our biomedical capabilities (not least 'cyborganization') may itself come to be transformed, obviated, supplemented, or even replaced.

Moreover, in keeping with a welfarist sensibility, this sociological revaluation of genetics places it squarely in the realm of human endeavour, specifically a product of collective labour that draws indeterminately on a common pool of resources in order to increase society's overall value. Moreover, the value of this product—the offspring—is measured by all the factors that go into its actual production rather than some inherent value of its raw material (as in the extreme bioliberalism of the 'right not to be born' rulings). The relative weighting of these factors and the identity of their bearers are the natural stuff of politics. Indeed, a society's genetic potential is the nearest that nature comes to providing a *res publica*, a focus for public deliberation and collective action. A 'politics of the gene' should be part of an integrated welfare policy that encompasses the pre-natal situation, the conditions of birth and infancy, child-rearing and formal education, as well as preventive, diagnostic, and curative health care. As in debates over taxation, there are many possible points of intervention for influencing an individual's life chances. Each proposes to redistribute the costs and benefits across society rather differently, usually in accordance with some vision of justice. And as in debates over, say, the taxation of inherited wealth, we may look forward to the day when reasonable people disagree over specifically genetic interventions without demonising those whose arguments test the extremes of political possibility. In the end, what matters is the democratic framework for taking these decisions, one that invites the regular examination and possible reversal of standing policies (Fuller 2000a).

It is clear that renewed attention to the concept and processes of redistribution should be central to sociology for the 21st century. In the first place, a property possessed by an individual may be normatively positive or negative, depending on the legal authorization for its transmission. Indeed, there are Biblical grounds for this notion. Biblical literalists concede that the only evil form of transmission is biological reproduction, which grants legitimacy to later generations simply by virtue of being a genetic descendant of Adam, the original sinner. A more sanctified form of transmission requires a formal renunciation of what was evil in this legacy, as in baptism or its secular equivalent, an examination that gives a candidate the opportunity to renounce one's former ignorance or prejudice. Moreover, even if we grant that people are 'by nature' selfish to the point of being prone to use violence to protect their individual inheritance, they may nonetheless improve their sociability simply by the legal transfer of these violent tendencies to the state as executor of their collective inheritance, which is tantamount to maintaining the conditions under which the people remain sociable. The 'arts of citizenship' from military training to regular elections encapsulate this species of political alchemy. Accordingly, potential combatants are compelled to focus on particular activities with clearly demarcated rules of engagement rather than 'taking the law into their hands'.

The reinvention of sociology will also benefit from the mutual recognition of the fundamental equality of individuals that accompanies a redistributionist ethic. 'Equality' here is meant in mainly negative terms, namely, the arbitrariness and potential reversibility of whatever conditions actually differentiate members of a society, be it to one's own advantage or disadvantage. This point may be seen as another way of sublimating the uncertainty that besets *homo sapiens* in a Hobbesian state of nature (e.g. the Rawlsian 'original position') or more positively—following Alasdair MacIntyre (2000)—as identifying humanity with a sense of reciprocity, that is, the capacity for giving and taking. Our achievements are largely due to the collaboration and license of others who neither question our motives nor themselves materially benefit from those achievements. They simply expect that we would act similarly toward them under similar circumstances. Included here are the background institutions that economists say 'minimize transaction costs'. (However, Alvin Gouldner [1973] intriguingly suggested that it may be the *separate* development of the 'giving' and 'taking' phases of reciprocity—that is, beneficence and exploitation—that mark the human.)

Regardless of aetiology, an egalitarian attitude counteracts both complacency about success and fatalism about failure: Informed with a vivid sense that the future may well *not* copy the past, people will endeavour to make their collective efforts exceed whatever they might do individually or in a more socially restricted capacity. The outstanding question that remains is which individuals are eligible for this sort of equality: Is the redistributionist regime limited to only and all those genetically marked as *homo sapiens*? Whereas socialists traditionally answered yes without hesitation, today neo-liberals deny the 'all' and ecologists the 'only' premised in the question. In today's ideological debates over biotechnology, neither neo-liberals nor ecologists speak consistently on behalf of all of humanity, although it is clear that specific humans are likely to benefit from politically realizing one or the other side. Here a renewed socialist sensibility would make a point of *prioritizing* the maintenance and extension of specifically *human* traits, forms, and projects.

In conclusion, I must observe that to compare genetic potential with, say, labour power or inherited wealth is, in an important sense, to render the raw material of our lives banal. Moreover, from a sociological standpoint that regards humanity as a collective project initiated by *homo sapiens*, that is exactly how it should be: Our humanity lies *exclusively* in what we make of our genetic potential, not in the potential itself. In this respect, Aristotelians were right to hold humanity to a higher standard of achievement than animals—but only because we had already achieved so much, not because our raw material was intrinsically better. The task for sociology in the 21st century, then, is to reclaim the ground that the *a posteriori* has lost to the *a priori* in our conception of humanity. For example, what Aristotelians regard as 'virtuous capacities' need to be recovered as 'beneficial consequences'. A telling target for recovery is the 'law of diminishing marginal utility', the fundamental principle of welfare economics, which began life very much inspired by the idea of humanity as a normative project but became a naturalistic account of how humans 'always already' behave.

I earlier noted that John Stuart Mill, despite his links to sociology's founder, Auguste Comte, is conspicuous by his absence from canonical histories of the discipline. Mill originally invoked the law of diminishing marginal utility to demonstrate how liberty and equality could be jointly maximized: If someone possesses a sufficient amount of a good, the overall welfare of society would be increased by transferring any additional amounts to someone who lacks the good. The basic idea is that the resulting compression of the difference in goods would be generously offset by the additional freedom that the transfer's beneficiary would gain to satisfy her wants. Mill interpreted this principle as a policy injunction to redistribute income so that everyone can make the most use of society's resources. He presupposed that economic laws serve as normative correctives to injustices that result from artificial restrictions on the free flow of goods and services that have been backed by generations of legal enforcement. Genetics may provide an opportunity for sociology to return to this Millian sensibility.

However, it is worth recalling that 'economic science' formally broke with 'political economy' when William Stanley Jevons successfully contested Mill's interpretation of the law of diminishing marginal utility in the third quarter of the 19th century (Fuller 2001b). Jevons held that the principle is meant to *represent*, not correct, nature. In that respect, it behaves exactly like a physical law. The appropriate use for the principle, then, is not to decide on policies for correcting injustices but to identify the frame of reference within which one can say that this principle is *already* operating—the invisible hand's implicit reach. From this reinterpretation came the 'positivist' turn that has increasingly marked the history of economics—in particular, a focus on formal models of idealized closed systems (à la Newtonian mechanics) and panglossian explanations for the distribution of resources in actual societies: The urge to redistribute wealth was thus permanently kept in check by the search for hidden redistributions happening elsewhere in the economy. Certain bioliberal tendencies in the social sciences, by making too easy a peace with the emergent forms of biotechnology, come dangerously close to setting us once again on the Jevonian path of least normative resistance, which would in turn only serve to set our disciplines back another 200 years.

References

Allen, Garland (1998). 'Modern Biological Determinism' In M. Fortun and Everett Mendelsohn (eds.), *The Practices of Human Genetics*. Dordrecht: Kluwer.

Beck, Ulrich (1992). *The Risk Society*. London: Sage, pp. 1–24.

Bloor, David (1979). 'Polyhedra and the Abominations of Leviticus'. *British Journal for the History of Science* 13: 254–72.

Dawkins, Richard (1976). *The Selfish Gene*. Oxford: Oxford University Press.

Dawkins, Richard (1982). *The Extended Phenotype*. Oxford: Oxford University Press.

Dworkin, Ronald. (2000). *Sovereign Virtue: The Theory and Practice of Equality*. Cambridge MA: Harvard University Press.

Fuller, Steve. (2000a). *The Governance of Science: Ideology and the Future of the Open Society*. Milton Keynes: Open University Press.

Fuller, Steve. (2000b). "The Coming Biological Challenge to Social Theory and Practice." In J. Eldridge, J. MacInnes, S. Scott, C. Warhurst and A. Witz (eds) *For Sociology: Legacies and Prospects*. York UK: Sociologypress, pp. 174–190.

Fuller, Steve. (2001a). 'The Darwinian Left: A Rhetoric of Realism or Reaction?' *POROI* 1:1 http://inpress.lib.uiowa.edu/poroi/vol2001/fuller2001.html.

Fuller, Steve. (2001b). "Positivism, History of." In Neil Smelser and Paul Baltes (eds) *The International Encyclopedia of Social and Behavioral Sciences*. Oxford: Pergamon, pp. 11821–27.

Fuller, Steve. (2002a). *Knowledge Management Foundations*. Woburn MA: Butterworth-Heinemann.

Fuller, Steve. (2002b). 'Karmic Darwinism: The Emerging Alliance between Science and Religion'. *Tijdschrift voor Filosofie* (Belgium) 64: 697–722.

Fuller, Steve, and James Collier (2003). *Philosophy, Rhetoric, and the End of Knowledge: A New Beginning for Science and Technology Studies*. 2ⁿ edn. (Orig. 1993) Hillsdale NJ: Lawrence Erlbaum Associates.

Giddens, Anthony (1990). *The Consequences of Modernity*. Palo Alto: Stanford University Press.

Gouldner, Alvin. (1973). *For Sociology: Renewal and Critique in Sociology Today*. New York: Basic Books.

Henley, Jon. (2002). 'France Limits the Right of Those Born Disabled to Sue Doctors' *Guardian* (London). 11 January.

King, Desmond. (1999). *In the Name of Liberalism: Illiberal Social Policy in the United States and Britain*. Oxford: Oxford University Press.

Lepenies, Wolf. (1988). *Between Literature and Science*. Cambridge: Cambridge University Press.

MacIntyre, Alasdair. (1994). *Marxism and Christianity*. 2ᵈ edn. (Orig. 1968) London: Duckworth.

MacIntyre, Alasdair. (2000). *Dependent Rational Animals*. London: Duckworth.

Meek, James. (2002). 'Cancer gene tests "will destroy private health"'. *Guardian* (London), 5 August.

Mykitiuk, Roxanne. (2003). "Public Bodies, Private Parts: Genetics in a Post-Keynesian Era" in B. Cossman and J. Fudge eds. *Privatization, Law and the Challenge to Feminism*. Toronto: University of Toronto Press.

Nussbaum, Martha (2001). 'Disabled Lives: Who Cares?' *The New York Review of Books*. 11 January.

Paul, Diane. (1998). *The Politics of Heredity*. Albany: SUNY Press.

Plender, John. (2001). 'Walking with animals, learning new tricks'. *Financial Times* (London), 17/18 March.

Polanyi, Karl. (1944). *The Great Transformation*. Boston: Beacon Press.

Rawls, John. (1972). *A Theory of Justice*. Cambridge MA: Harvard University Press.

Rifkin, Jeremy (2001). 'This is the age of biology'. *Guardian* (London), 28 July.

Rueschemeyer, Dietrich and van Rossum, Ronan. (1996). 'The *Verein für Sozialpolitik* and the Fabian Society: A study in the sociology of policy-relevant knowledge' In D. Rueschemeyer and T. Skocpol (eds.), *States, Social Knowledge and the Origins of Modern Social Policie*s (pp. 117–162) Princeton: Princeton University Press.

Schutz, Alfred (1964). The Well-Informed Citizen: An Essay in the Distribution of Knowledge'. *Collected Papers*, Volume II. (pp. 120–34). Orig. 1932. The Hague: Martinus Nijhoff.

Singer, Peter (1981). *The Expanding Circle: Ethics and Sociobiology*. New York: Farrar, Strauss and Giroux.

Steiner, Hillel (1998). "Silver Spoons and Golden Genes: Talent Differentials and Distributive Justice." In J. Burley (ed.), *The Genetic Revolution and Human Rights*. (pp. 133–50) Oxford: Oxford University Press.

2

Biotechnology, Ethics, and
the Politics of Cloning

Steven Best and Douglas Kellner

> *O, wonder!*
> *How many goodly creatures are there here!*
> *How beauteous mankind is!*
> *O brave new world*
> *That has such people in't.*
> — William Shakespeare, *The Tempest*

> *We're ready to go because we think that the*
> *genie's out of her bottle.*
> —Dr. Panos Zavos

> *Anyone who thinks that things will move slowly*
> *is being very naive.*
> —Lee Silver, *Molecular Biologist*

As we move into a new millennium fraught with terror and danger, a global postmodern condition is unfolding in the midst of rapid evolutionary and social changes co-constructed by science, technology, and the restructuring of global capital. We are quickly morphing into a new biological and social existence that is ever-more mediated and shaped by computers, mass media, and biotechnology, all driven by the logic of capital and a powerful emergent technoscience. In this global context, science is no longer merely an interpretation of the natural and social worlds, rather it has become an active force in changing them and the very nature of life. In an era where life can be created and redesigned in a petri dish, and genetic codes can be edited like a digital text, the distinction between "natural" and "artificial" has become greatly complexified. The new techniques of manipulation call into question existing definitions of life and death, demand a rethinking of fundamental notions of ethics and moral value, and pose unique challenges for democracy.

As technoscience develops by leaps and bounds, and as genetics rapidly advances, the science-industrial complex has come to a point where it is creating new transgenic species and is rushing toward a posthuman culture that unfolds in the increasingly intimate merging of technology and biology. The posthuman involves both new conceptions of the "human" in an age of information and communication, and new modes of existence as flesh merges with steel, circuitry, and genes from other species. Exploiting more animals than ever before, technoscience intensifies research and experimentation into human cloning. This process is accelerated because genetic engineering and cloning are developed for commercial purposes, anticipating enormous profits on the horizon for the biotech industry. Consequently, all natural reality— from microorganisms and plants to animals and human beings—is subject to genetic reconstruction in a commodified "Second Genesis."

At present, the issues of cloning and biotechnology are being heatedly debated in the halls of science, in political circles, among religious communities, throughout academia, and more broadly in the media and public spheres. Not surprisingly, the discourses on biotechnology are polarized. Defenders of biotechnology extol its potential to increase food production and quality, and to cure diseases, endow us with "improved" human traits, and prolong human life. Its critics claim that genetic engineering of food will produce Frankenfoods which pollute the food supply with potentially harmful products; that could devastate the environment, biodiversity, and human life itself; that animal and human cloning will breed monstrosities; that a dangerous new eugenics is on the horizon; and that the manipulation of embryonic stem cells violates the principle of respect for life and destroys a bona fide "human being."

Interestingly, the same dichotomies that have polarized information-technology discourses into one-sided technophobic and technophilic positions are reproduced in debates over biotechnology. Just as we have argued that critical theories of technology are needed to produce more dialectical perspectives that distinguish between positive and negative aspects and effects of information technology (Best and Kellner, 2001), so too would we claim that similar approaches are required to articulate the potentially beneficial and perhaps destructive aspects of biotechnology. Indeed, current debates over cloning and stem cell research suggest powerful contradictions and ambiguities in these phenomena that render one-sided positions superficial and dangerous. Parallels and similar complexities in communication and biotechnology are not surprising given that information technology provides the infrastructure to biotechnology that has been constituted by computer-mediated technologies involved in the Human Genome Project, and, conversely, genetic science is being used to push the power and speed of computers through phenomena such as "gene chips."

As the debates over cloning and stem cell research indicate, issues raised by biotechnology combine research into the genetic sciences, perspectives and contexts articulated by the social sciences, and the ethical and anthropological concerns of philosophy. Consequently, we argue that intervening in the debates over biotechnology require supradisciplinary critical philosophy and social theory to illuminate the problems and their stakes. In addition, debates over cloning and stem cell research raise exceptionally important challenges to bioethics and a democratic politics of communication. Biotechnology is thus a critical flashpoint for ethics and democratic theory and practice. For contemporary biotechnology underscores the need for more widespread knowledge of important scientific issues; participatory debate over science, technology, values, and our very concept of human life; and regulation concerning new developments in the biosciences, which have such high economic, political, and social consequences.

More specifically, we will demonstrate problems with the cloning of animals that for now render the cloning of humans unacceptable. In our view, human cloning constitutes a momentous route to the posthuman, a leap into a new stage of history, with significant and potentially disturbing consequences. We also will take on arguments for and against stem cell research and contend that it contains positive potential for medical advances that should not be blocked by problematic conservative positions. Nonetheless, we believe that the entire realm of biotechnology is fraught with dangers and problems that require careful study and democratic debate. The emerging genomic sciences should thus be undertaken by scientists with a keen sense of responsibility and accountability, and be subject to intense public scrutiny and open discussion. Finally, in the light of the dangers and potentially deadly consequences of biotechnology, we maintain that the positive potential of biotechnology can be realized only in a new context of cultivating new sensibilities toward nature, engaging in ethical and political debate, and participating in political struggles over biotechnology and its effects.

Brave New Barnyard: The Advent of Animal Cloning

> *The idea is to arrive at the ideal animal and
> repeatedly copy it exactly as it is.*
> —Dr. Mark Hardy

From its entrenched standpoint of unqualified human superiority, science typically first targets objects of nature and animals with its analytic gaze and instruments. The current momentous turn toward cloning is largely undertaken by way of animals, although some scientists have already directly focused on cloning human beings (see below). While genetic engineering creates new "transgenic" species by inserting the gene from one species into another, cloning replicates cells to produce identical copies of a host organism by inserting its DNA into an enucleated egg. In a potent combination, genetic engineering and cloning technologies are used together in order, first, to custom design a transgenic animal to suit the needs of science and industry (the distinction is irrevocably blurred) and, second, to mass reproduce the hybrid creation endlessly for profitable peddling in medical and agricultural markets.

Cloning is a return to asexual reproduction and bypasses the caprice of the genetic lottery and random shuffling of genes. It dispenses with the need to inject a gene into thousands of newly fertilized eggs to get a successful result. Rather, much as the printing press replaced the scribe, cloning allows mass reproduction of a devised type, and thus opens genetic engineering to vast commercial possibilities. Life science companies are poised to make billions of dollars in profits, as numerous organizations, universities, and corporations move toward cloning animals and human stem cells, and patenting the methods and results of their research.

To date, science has engineered a myriad of transgenic animals and has cloned sheep, calves, goats, bulls, pigs, mice, and a cat. Though still far from precise, cloning nevertheless has become routine. What's radically new and startling is not cloning itself, since from 1952 scientists have replicated organisms from embryonic cells. Rather, the new techniques of cloning, or "nuclear somatic transfer," from adult mammal body cells constitutes a new form of animal reproduction. These methods accomplish what scientists long considered impossible—reverting adult (specialized) cells to their original (non-specialized) embryonic state where they can be reprogrammed to form a new organism. In effect, this startling process creates the identical twin of the adult that provided the original donor cell. This technique was used first to create Dolly, the first mammal cloned from a cell from an adult animal, and subsequently all of her varied offspring.

Dolly and Her Progeny

Traditionally, scientists considered cloning beyond the reach of human ingenuity. But when Ian Wilmut and his associates from the Roslin Institute near Edinburgh, Scotland, announced their earth-shattering discovery in March 1997, the "impossible" appeared in the form of a sheep named Dolly, and a "natural law" had been broken. Dolly's donor cells came from a six-year-old Finn Dorset Ewe. Wilmut starved mammary cells in a low-nutrient tissue culture where they became quiescent and subject to reprogramming. He then removed the nucleus containing genetic material from an unfertilized egg cell of a second sheep, a Scottish Blackface, and, in a nice Frankenstein touch, fused the two cells with a spark of electricity. After 277 failed attempts, the resulting embryo was then implanted into a third sheep, a surrogate mother who gave birth to Dolly in July 1996.

Many critics said Dolly was either not a real clone or was just a fluke. Yet, less than two years after Dolly's emergence, scientists had cloned numerous species, including mice, pigs, cows, and goats, and had even made clones of clones of clones, producing genetic simulacra in mass batches as Huxley envisioned happening to human beings in *Brave New World* (1958). The commercial possibilities of cloning animals were dramatic and obvious for all to behold. The race was on to patent novel cloning technologies and the transgenic offspring they would engender.

Animals are being designed and bred as living drug and organ factories, as their bodies are disrupted, refashioned, and mutilated to benefit meat and dairy industries. Genetic engineering is employed in biomedical research by infecting animals with diseases that become a part of their genetic make-up and are transmitted to their offspring, as in the case of researchers trying to replicate the effects of cystic fibrosis in sheep. Most infamously, Harvard University, with funding from Du Pont, has patented a mouse—OncoMouse— that has human cancer genes built into its genetic makeup and are expressed in its offspring (see Haraway 1997).

In the booming industry of "pharming" (pharmaceutical farming), animals are genetically modified to secrete therapeutic proteins and medicines in their milk. The first major breakthrough came in January 1998, when Genzyme Transgenics created transgenic cattle named George and Charlie. The result of splicing human genes and bovine cells, they were cloned to make milk that contains human proteins such as the blood-clotting factor needed by hemophiliacs. Co-creator James Robl said, "I look at this as being a major step toward the commercialization of this [cloning] technology."[1]

In early January 2002, the biotech company PPL announced that they had just cloned a litter of pigs which could aid in human organ transplants. On the eve of the publication of an article by another company, Immerge Bio Therapeutics claimed that they had achieved a similar breakthrough.[2] The new process involved creation of the first "knockout" pigs, in which a single gene in pig DNA is deleted to eliminate a protein that is present in pigs which is usually violently rejected by the human immune system. This meant that a big step could be made in the merging of humans and animals, and creating animals as harvest-machines for human organs.

Strolling through the Brave New Barnyard, one can find incredible beings that appear normal, but are genetic satyrs and chimera. Cows generate lactoferrin, a human protein useful for treating infections. Goats manufacture antithrombin III, a human protein that can prevent blood clotting, and serum albumin, which regulates the transfer of fluids in the body. Sheep produce alpha antitrypsin, a drug used to treat cystic fibrosis. Pigs secrete phytase, a bacterial protein that enables them to emit less of the pollutant phosphorous in their manure, and chickens make lysozyme, an antibiotic, in their eggs to keep their own infections down.

"BioSteel" presents an example of the bizarre wonders of genetic technology that points to the erasure of boundaries between animate and inanimate matter, as well as among different species. In producing this substance, scientists have implanted a spider gene into goats, so that their milk produces a super-strong material—BioSteel—that can be used for bulletproof vests, medical supplies, and aerospace and engineering projects. In order to produce vast quantities of BioSteel, Nexia Biotechnologies intend to house thousands of goats in 15 weapons-storage buildings, confining them in small holding pens.[3]

As we see, animals are genetically engineered and cloned to produce a stock of organs for human transplants. Given the severe shortage of human organs, thousands of patients every year languish and die before they can receive a healthy kidney, liver, or heart. Rather than encouraging preventative medicine and finding ways to encourage more organ donations, medical science has turned to xenotransplantation, and has begun breeding herds of animals (with pigs as a favored medium) to be used as organ sources for human transplantation.

Clearly, this is a very hazardous enterprise due to the possibility of animal viruses causing new plagues and diseases in the human population (a danger which exists also in pharmaceutical milk). For many scientists, however, the main concern is that the human body rejects animal organs as foreign and destroys them within minutes. Researchers seek to overcome this problem by genetically modifying the donor organ so that they knock out markers in pig cells and add genes that make their protein surfaces identical to those in humans. Geneticists envision cloning entire herds of altered pigs and other transgenic animals so that an inexhaustible warehouse of organs and tissues would be available for human use. In the process of conducting experiments such as transplanting pig hearts modified with a human gene into the bodies of monkeys, companies such as Imutran have caused horrific suffering, with no evident value to be gained given the crucial differences among species and introducing the danger of new diseases into human populations.[4]

As if billions of animals were not already exploited enough in laboratories, factory farms, and slaughterhouses, genetic engineering and cloning exacerbate the killing and pain with new institutions of confinement and bodily invasion that demand millions and millions more captive bodies. Whereas genetic and cloning technologies in the cases described at least have the potential to benefit human beings, they have also been appropriated by the meat and dairy industries for purposes of increased profit through the exploitation of animals and biotechnology. It's the nightmarish materialization of the H.G. Wells scenario where, in his prophetic 1904 novel *The Food of the Gods*, scientists invent a substance that prompts every living being that consumes it to grow to gargantuan proportions (see Best and Kellner 2001). Having located the genes responsible for regulating growth and metabolism, university and corporate researchers immediately exploited this knowledge for profit. Thus, for the glories of carnivorous consumption, corporations such as MetaMorphix and Cape Aquaculture Technologies have created giant pigs, sheep, cattle, lobsters, and fish that grow faster and larger than the limits set by evolution.

Amidst the surreality of Wellsian gigantism, cattle and dairy industries are engineering and cloning designer animals that are larger, leaner, faster-growing value producers. With synthetic chemicals and DNA alteration, pharmers can produce pigs that mature twice as fast and provide at least twice the normal amount of sows per litter as they eat 25% less feed, and cows that produce at least 40% more milk. Since 1997, at least one country, Japan, has sold cloned beef to its citizens.[5] But there is strong reason to believe that U.S. consumers—already a nation of guinea pigs in their consumption of genetically modified foods—have eaten cloned meat and dairy products. For years, corporations have cloned farmed animals with the express purpose of someday introducing them to the market, and insiders claim many already have been consumed.[6] The National Institute of Science and Technology has provided two companies, Origen Therapeutics of California, and Embrex of North Carolina, with almost $5 million to fund research into factory farming billions of cloned chickens for consumption.[7] With the Food and Drug Administration pondering whether to regulate cloned meat and dairy products, it's a good bet they are many steps behind an industry determined to increase their profits through biotechnology. The future to come seems to be one of cloned humans eating cloned animals.

While anomalies such as self-shearing sheep and broiler chickens with fewer feathers have already been assembled, some macabre visionaries foresee engineering pigs and chickens with flesh that is tender or can be easily microwaved, and chickens that are wingless so they won't need bigger cages. The next step would be to just create and replicate animal's torsos—sheer organ sacks—and dispense with superfluous heads and limbs. In fact, scientists have already created headless embryos of mice and frogs in grotesque manifestations of the kinds of life they can now construct at will.

Clearly, there is nothing genetic engineers will not do to alter or clone an animal. Transgenic "artist" Eduardo Kac, for instance, commissioned scientists at the National Institute of Agronomic Research in France to create Alba, a rabbit that carries a fluorescent protein from a jellyfish and thus glows in the dark. This experiment enabled Mr. Kac to demonstrate his supremely erudite postmodern thesis that "genetic engineering [is] in a social context in which the relationship between the private and public spheres are negotiated."[8] Although millions of healthy animals are euthanized every year in U.S. animal "shelters," corporations are working to clone animals, either to bring them back from the dead, or to prevent them from "dying" (such as in the Missyplicity Project, initiated by the wealthy "owners" of a dog who want to keep her alive indefinitely).[9] Despite alternatives to coping with allergies problems and the dangers with cloning animals, Transgenic Pets LLC. is working to create transgenic cats that are allergen-free.[10] It is time to examine concretely what cloning means for animal existence.

Transgenic Travesties

The agricultural use of genetics and cloning has produced horrible monstrosities. Transgenic animals often are born deformed and suffer from fatal bleeding disorders, arthritis, tumors, stomach ailments, kidney disease, diabetes, inability to nurse and reproduce, behavioral and metabolic disturbances, high mortality rates, and Large Offspring Syndrome. In order to genetically engineer animals for maximal weight and profit, a Maryland team of scientists created the infamous "Beltway pig" afflicted with arthritis, deformities, and respiratory disease. Cows engineered with bovine growth hormone (rBGH) have mastitis, hoof and leg maladies, reproductive problems, numerous abnormalities, and die prematurely. Giant supermice endure tumors, damage to internal organs, and shorter life spans. Numerous animals born from cloning are missing internal organs such as hearts and kidneys. A Maine lab specialized in breeding sick and abnormal mice who go by names such as Fathead, Fidget, Hairless, Dumpy, and Greasy. Similarly, experiments in the genetic engineering of salmon have led to rapid growth and various aberrations and deformities, with some growing up to ten times their normal body weight (see Fox 1999). Cloned cows are ten times more likely to be unhealthy as their natural counterparts. After three years of efforts to clone monkeys, Dr. Tanja Dominko fled in horror from her well-funded Oregon laboratory. Telling cautionary tales of the "gallery of horrors" she experienced, Dominko said that 300 attempts at cloning monkeys produced nothing but freakishly abnormal embryos that contained cells either without chromosomes or with up to nine nuclei.[11]

For Dominko, a "successful" clone Like Dolly is the exception, not the rule. But even Dolly became inexplicably overweight and arthritic, and may have been prematurely aging. In February 2003, suffering from progressive lung disease, poor Dolly was euthanized by her "creators," bringing to a premature end the first experiment with adult animal cloning and raising questions concerning its ethics.

A report from newscientists.com argues that genes are disrupted when cultured in a lab, and this explains why so many cloned animals die or are grossly abnormal. On this account, it is not the cloning or IVF process that is at cause, but the culturing of the stem cells in the lab, creating major difficulties in cloning since so far there is no way around cloning through cultured cells in laboratory conditions.[12]

A team of U.S. scientists at the M.I.T. Whitehead Institute examined 38 cloned mice and learned that even clones which look healthy suffer genetic maladies and scientists found that the mice cloned from embryonic stem cells had abnormalities in the placenta, kidneys, heart, and liver. They feared that the defective gene functioning in clones could, wreak havoc with organs and trigger foul-ups in the brain later in life and that embryonic stem cells are highly unstable.[13] "There are almost no normal clones," study author and MIT biology professor Rudolf Jaenisch, explained. Jaenisch claims that only 1–5% of all cloned animals survive, and even those that survive to birth often have severe abnormalities and die prematurely.[14]

As we argue below, these risks make human cloning a deeply problematic undertaking. Pro-cloning researchers claim that the "glitches" in animal cloning eventually can be worked out. In January 2001, for example, researchers at Texas A&M University and the Roslin Institute claimed to have discovered a gene that causes abnormally large cloned fetuses, a discovery they believe will allow them to predict and prevent this type of mutation. It is conceivable science someday will work out the kinks, but for many critics this assumes that science can master what arguably are inherent uncertainties and unpredictable variables in the expression of genes in a developing organism. A recent study showed that some mouse clones seem to develop normally until an age the equivalent of 30 years for a human being; then there is a spurt of growth and they suddenly become obese.[15] Mark Westhusin, a cloning expert at Texas A&M, points out that the problem is not that of genetic mutation, but of "genetic expression," that genes are inherently unstable and unpredictable in their functioning. Another report indicates that a few misplaced carbon atoms can lead to cloning failures.[16] Thus, small errors in the cloning process could lead to huge disasters, and the prevention of all such "small errors" seems to presume something close to omniscience.

Yet, while most scientists are opposed to cloning human beings (rather than stem cells), and decry it as "unacceptable," few condemn the suffering caused to animals or position animal cloning research itself as morally problematic, and many scientists aggressively defend animal cloning. Quite callously and arbitrarily, for example, Jaenisch proclaims, "You can dispose of these animals, but tell me—what do you do with abnormal humans?"[17] The attitude that animals are disposable is a good indication of the problems inherent in the mechanistic science that still prevails and a symptom of callousness toward human life that worries conservatives.

Despite the claims of its champions, the genetic engineering of animals is a radical departure from natural evolution and traditional forms of animal breeding. Further, human cloning takes biotechnology into a new and, to many, frightening posthuman realm that begins to redesign the human body and genome. Cloning involves manipulation of genes rather than whole organisms. Moreover, scientists engineer change at unprecedented rates, and can create novel beings across species boundaries that previously were unbridgeable. Ours is a world where cloned calves and sheep carry human genes, human embryo cells are merged with enucleated cows' eggs, monkeys and rabbits are bred with jellyfish DNA, a surrogate horse gives birth to a zebra, a dairy cow spawns an endangered gaur, and tiger cubs emerge from the womb of an ordinary housecat.

The ability to clone a desired genetic type brings the animal kingdom into entirely new avenues of exploitation and commercialization. From the new scientific perspective, animals are framed as genetic information that can be edited, transposed, and copied endlessly. Pharming and xenotransplantation build on the system of factory farming that dates from the postwar period and is based on the confinement and intensive management of animals within enclosed buildings that are prison-houses of suffering.

The proclivity of the science-industrial complex to instrumentalize animals as nothing but resources for human use and profit intensifies in an era in which genetic engineering and cloning are perceived as a source of immense profit and power. Still confined for maximal control, animals are no longer seen as whole species, but rather as fragments of genetic information to be manipulated for any purpose.

Weighty ethical and ecological concerns in the new modes of animal appropriation are largely ignored, as animals are still framed in the 17th century Cartesian worldview that views them as nonsentient machines. As Jeremy Rifkin (1997: 35) puts it, "Reducing the animal kingdom to customized, mass-produced replications of specific genotypes is the final articulation of the mechanistic, industrial frame of mind. A world where all life is transformed into engineering standards and made to conform to market values is a dystopian nightmare, and needs to be opposed by every caring and compassionate human being who believes in the intrinsic value of life."[18]

Patenting of genetically modified animals has become a huge industry for multinational corporations and chemical companies. PPL Therapeutics, Genzyme Transgenics, Advanced Cell Technology, and other enterprises are issuing broad patent claims on methods of cloning nonhuman animals. PPL Therapeutics, the company that "invented" Dolly, has applied for the patents and agricultural rights to the production of all genetically altered mammals that could secrete therapeutic proteins in their milk. Nexia Biotechnologies obtained exclusive rights to all results from spider silk research. Patent number 4,736,866 was granted to Du Pont for Oncomouse, which the Patent Office described as a new "composition of matter." Infigen holds a U.S. patent for activating human egg division through any means (mechanical, chemical, or otherwise) in the cloning process.

Certainly, genetics does not augur solely negative developments for animals. Given the reality of dramatic species extinction and loss of biodiversity, scientists are collecting the sperm and eggs of endangered species like the giant panda in order to preserve them in a "frozen zoo," such as exists as San Diego Zoo. It is indeed exciting to ponder the possibilities of a Jurassic Park scenario of reconstructing extinct species (as, for example, scientists recently have uncovered the well-preserved remains of a Tasmanian tiger and a woolly mammoth). In October 2001, European scientists cloned a seemingly healthy mouflon lamb, a member of an endangered species of sheep. In April 2003, ACT produced the first successful interspecies clone when a dairy cow gave birth to a pair of bantengs, a species of wild cattle, cloned from an animal that died over 20 years ago. One of the pair, however, was thereafter euthanized because it was born twice the normal size and was suffering. Currently, working with preserved tissue samples, ACT is working to bring back from extinction the last bucardo mountain goat which was killed by a falling tree in January 2000.[19]

But critics dismiss these efforts as a misguided search for a technofix that distracts focus from the real problem of preserving habitat and biodiversity. Even if animals could be cloned, there is no way to replicate habitats lost forever to chainsaws and bulldozers. Moreover, the behaviors of cloned animals would unavoidably be altered and they would end up in zoos or exploitative entertainment settings where they exist as spectacle and simulacra. Animals raised through interspecies cloning such as the gaur produced by ACT will not have the same disposition as if raised by their own species and so for other reasons will not be less than "real." Additionally, there is the likelihood that genetic engineering and cloning would aggravate biodiversity loss to the extent it creates monolithic superbreeds that could crowd out other species or be easily wiped out by disease. There is also great potential for ecological disaster when new beings enter an environment, and genetically modified organisms are especially unpredictable in their behavior and effects.

Still, cloning may prove a valuable tool in preserving what can be salvaged from the current extinction crisis. Moreover, advances in genetics also may bypass and obviate pharming and xenotransplantation through use of stem cell technologies that clone human cells, tissues, or perhaps even entire organs and limbs from human embryos or an individual's own cells. Successful stem cell technologies could eliminate at once the problem of immune rejection and the need for animals. There is also the intriguing possibility of developing medicines and vaccines in plants, rather than animals, thus producing a safer source of pharmaceuticals and neutraceuticals and sparing animals suffering. None of these promises, however, brighten the dark cloud cloning casts over the animal kingdom, or dispel the dangers of the dramatic alteration of agriculture and human life.

Clones R' Us: The Portent of Human Replication

Human cloning could be done tomorrow.
—Alan Trounson, In Vitro Fertilization
clinician. Monash University

Cloning is inefficient in all species. Expect the same outcome in humans as in other species: late abortions, dead children and surviving but abnormal children.
—Ian Wilmut

Is there any risk too great or any reason too trivial for you not to attempt human cloning?
—Alta Charo, University of Wisconsin bioethicist, speaking to Antinori and Zavos

Thus, the postmodern adventure of the reconstruction of nature begins with the genetic engineering of transgenic animals and the cloning of numerous animal species for agricultural, medical, and "scientific" purposes, while in fact biotechnology is being positioned as a field for prodigious profits. The fate of the human is inseparable from the future of our fellow animal species, as they are the launch pad for the redesign of human nature. With the birth of Dolly, a new wave of animal exploitation arrived, and anxiety grew about a world of cloned humans that scientists said was technically feasible and perhaps inevitable. Ian Wilmut, head of the Roslin Institute team that cloned Dolly, is an example of an animal and stem cell cloning advocate who repudiates human replication. Like Jaenisch and numerous others, Wilmut believes human cloning is unethical, unnecessary, and dangerous, and that the inevitable deformities would be cruel to both the parents and children involved (see Wilmut et al 2000).

Wilmut feels human cloning should not be attempted until there is a quantum leap in cloning technologies, an advance he feels is at least 50 years away. Most of all, Wilmut fears that the drive toward human cloning could cause a backlash against all cloning, and thereby thwart the far more important research into cloning stem cells for therapeutic purposes. For Wilmut, the authentic purpose for biotechnology is to cure disease and improve agriculture. Whatever his intention, however, many scientists and entrepreneurs inspired by the Roslin Institute's work have aggressively pursued the goal of human cloning as the true telos of genomic science. Driven by market demands for clones of infertile people, of those who have lost loved ones, of gays and lesbians who want their own children, of people who want to clone themselves or family members to provide needed organs, and of numerous other client categories, doctors and firms are actively pursuing human cloning.

The Race to Clone Humans

With fame and fortune awaiting the first Cloneumbus to land on the new terrain of posthuman breeding, it is no surprise numerous champions of reproductive cloning have emerged. The first visible human cloning advocate was Richard Seed who shocked the world in 1997 by declaring that he was prepared to clone himself, later appending the project to his wife. Infertility specialists Severino Antinori and Panayiotis Zavos openly announce their intent to clone humans, in defiance of any national law if necessary. The Council for Secular Humanism is a broad coalition of scientists, philosophers, authors, and politicians who decry the influence of religion in the cloning debates and champion the cause of human cloning, as they assure us that cloning will not create any "moral predicaments beyond the capacity of human reason to resolve."[20] The Human Cloning Foundation is an Internet umbrella group for diverse clonistas who see cloning as the best hope for curing infertility and diseases and promoting longevity.[21]

No doubt the most notorious of the clonistas are the Raelins, a wealthy Quebec-based religious cult who believe that alien scientists cloned human beings in space laboratories. In December 2002, Raelins claimed that their "Cloinaid" project had delivered on their promise to produce the first human clone, and that more clones would soon be born. This of course ignited a firestorm of media attention, with Raelin leader Bridgette Boisselier promising to release evidence of the revolutionary breakthough in science. The evidence never materialized, however, leading many to conclude that the entire affair was a sordid hoax all-too eagerly exploited by the media.

One bioethicist estimates that there are currently at least a half dozen laboratories around the world doing human cloning experiments.[22] While cloning human beings is illegal in the U.S., Britain, German, Japan, and elsewhere, in countries such as Asia, Russia, and Brazil it is perfectly legal and human cloning is pursued both openly and clandestinely. In fact, there are at least two known cases where human embryos have been cloned, but the experiment was terminated. According to *Wired* (9.02, February 2001: 128):

In 1988, a scientist working at Advanced Cell Technology in Worcester, Massachusetts took a human somatic cell, inserted it into an enucleated cow egg, and started the cell dividing to prove that oocytes from other species could be used to create human stem cells. He voluntarily stopped the experiment after several cell divisions. A team at Kyung Hee University in South Korea said it created an embryonic adult human clone in 1999 before halting the experiment, though some doubt that any of this really happened. Had either of these embryos been placed in a surrogate mother, we might have seen the first human clone.

In November 2001, ACT created a global sensation with (misleading) reports they had cloned human embryos (see below). While many scientists think human cloning is possible and inevitable, some think it is likely human clones already exist, perhaps in hideous form where they are studied on an island, such as was portrayed in H.G. Wells' *The Island of Dr. Moreau* (see Best and Kellner 2001). The breeding of monstrosities in animal cloning, the pain and suffering produced, and the possibility of assembly-production of animals and humans should give pause to those who want to plunge ahead with human cloning. Animal cloning experiments produced scores of abnormalities and it is highly likely that human cloning would do the same—a possibility more likely given the increased complexity of human beings.

The potential of producing serious human defects raises ethical dilemmas as well as the question of the social responsibility involved in the care of deformed beings produced by human cloning experiments. In April 2003, new studies emerged indicating that cloning humans or other primates may in fact be impossible due to a molecular obstacle preventing cloned cells from properly dividing.[23] Fervent pro-cloners like Antinori and Zavos deny that there are any risks to cloning humans and claim that there is "enough information" to proceed with confidence. If pressed to admit there might be "mistakes," they simply write them off as necessary means to the end of reproductive freedom and medical progress. Ignoring the availability of frozen embryos and existing children for adoption, they claim the "right to reproduce" as crucial for human beings, and argue that this "right"—which in fact does not exist in any social constitution—outweighs any risks to the baby or to society as a whole.

But, at present, what sane person would want to produce a possibly freakish replication of him or herself or a dead loved one? What are the potential health risks to women who would be called upon to give birth to human clones, at least before artificial wombs make women, like men, superfluous to the reproductive process? Who will be responsible for caring for deformed human clones that parents renounce? Is this really an experiment that the human species wants to undertake so that self-centered infertile couples can have their own children (apparently some can only love a child with *their own* DNA), or misinformed narcissists can spawn what they think will be their carbon-copy twins? What happens if human clones breed? What mutations could follow? What might result from long-range tampering with the human genome as a consequence from genetic engineering and cloning?

Furthermore, cloning inevitably involves reproduction of bodily DNA, raising questions of what sorts of minds cloning might produce. What if cloned humans appear to be mentally defective or aberrant as a result of the technology? What might be the long-term costs of the perceived short-term benefits that cloning may produce? Already, scientists are raising the issue of "cognitive deficiencies" in cloned animals and certainly this problem is relevant to the project of human cloning.

In addition, as the TV-series "Dark Angel" illustrates, there is the possibility of a military appropriation of cloning to develop herds of *Übermenschen* (although no two would be exactly alike). Indeed, will commodification of the humane genome, eugenics, designer babies, and genetic discrimination all follow as unavoidable consequences of helping infertile couples and other groups reproduce, or will human cloning become as safe and accepted as in vitro fertilization (IVF), once also a risky and demonized technology? Will developing countries be used as breeding farms for animals and people, constituting another form of global exploitation of the have-nots by the haves? What are the consequences of the commodification of the human genome, and the patenting of stem cells and their research methods?

With so many questions and uncertainties that arise, it is clear that the project of human cloning is being approached in a purely instrumental and mechanistic framework that does not consider the long-term impact on the human genome, social relations, or ecology. Or, if social relations and consequences are considered, likely this is from the perspective of improving the Nordic stock and creating an even deeper cleavage between rich and poor since, without question, only the rich will be able to afford genetically designed and/or cloned babies with superior characteristics. This situation could change if the state sponsors cloning welfare programs or the prices of a "Gen-Rich" (Silver 1998) baby drop like computers, but the wealthy will already have gained a decisive advantage and "democratic cloning" agendas beg the question of the soundness of human cloning in the first place.

Problems with Human Cloning

Thus, we have serious worries about biotechnology not only due to the colonialist history of science and capitalism, the commodification of the life sciences, and how genetic technologies have already been abused for profit and power by corporations like Monsanto and Du Pont, but also because of the reductionistic paradigm informing molecular engineering.[24] Ironically, while biology helped to shape what theorists conceive as a postmodern physics through evolutionary and holistic emphases, the most advanced modes of biological science—genetic engineering and cloning research—have not advanced to the path of holism and complexity (see Best and Kellner, 2001). Rather, biotechnology seems to have regressed to the antiquated errors of atomism, mechanism, determinism, and reductionism. The new technosciences and the outmoded paradigms (Cartesian) and domineering mentalities (Baconian) that informs them generates a volatile mix, and the situation is gravely exacerbated by the commercial imperatives driving research and development, the frenzied "gene rush" toward DNA patenting.

Yet if human cloning technologies follow the path of IVF technologies, they eventually will become widely accepted, even though currently large percentages of U.S. citizens oppose it (90% according to some polls in summer 2001). Alarmingly, scientists and infertility clinics have taken up human cloning technologies all-too-quickly. After the announcement of the birth of Dolly, many were tripping over themselves to announce emphatically that they would never pursue human cloning. Nonetheless, only months later, these same voices began to embrace the project.[25] The demand from people desperate to have babies, or to "resurrect" their loved ones, in conjunction with the massive profits waiting to be made, is too great an allure for corporations to resist. The opportunistic attitude of cloning advocate Panayiotis Zavos is all-too-typical: "Ethics is a wonderful word, but we need to look beyond the ethical issues here. It's not an ethical issue [!]. It's a medical issue. We have a duty here. Some people need this to complete the life cycle, to reproduce."[26]

In his attempt to dispel the ineliminable moral quandaries surrounding cloning, Zavos has confused "need" with desire, and reduced humans to crude reproduction machines. Yet, as his statement shows, defenders of cloning and biotechnology argue for the primacy of individual reproductive rights over potential risks to society as a whole. They believe that science is valuable to the extent that it increases freedom, individuality, and choice, as if embryos were a soft drink and what an "individual" chooses in this case is not of enormous consequence for future humanity, to say nothing of the deformed children who surely will be the guinea pigs of science. Of them, Zavos can only say, "We're ready to face those mishaps…It's part of any price that we pay when we develop new technology."[27]

There are indeed legitimate grounds for fear and loathing about reproductive cloning, but opposing views often are illogical. Standard psychological objections, for example, are poorly grounded. We need not fear Hitler armies assembling because the presumption of this dystopia—genetic determinism—is false and no one can clone the singular experiences and social contexts that in addition to genetics are key constituent features of an individual's make-up. Nor need we fear individuals unable to cope with lack of their own identity since identical twins are able to differentiate themselves from one another relatively well and they are even more genetically similar than clones would be. Nor would society always see cloned humans as freaks, as people no longer consider test-tube babies alien oddities, and there are anywhere from 20,000 to 200,000 such humans existing today (figures vary widely). The physiological and psychological dangers are real, but in time cloning techniques could be perfected so that cloning might be as safe, if not safer than babies born through a genetic throw-of-the-dice, or IVF.

Most fears of human cloning are irrationally rooted in what Leon Kass claims is an intuitive human repulsion—the "yuk" factor—toward something that is seemingly "unnatural" (see Kass 1998 and the critique by Pence 1998b). Intuitions are hardly a sound basis for rooting a critique of technology, especially because perceptions can quickly change from shock to acceptance. Similarly, Francis Fukuyama (2001) argues that reproductive cloning is an assault on human dignity. Fukuyama qualifies his earlier thesis (1992) that society has reached "the end of history" in the sense that liberal capitalism has defeated its main ideological competitors, communism and fascism, and brought moral evolution to its magnificent close. While he does not change the problematic political argument that liberalism is the culmination of human political culture, he describes his profound anxiety that we are entering a "posthuman" stage of history. This era will take off when biotechnology overrides natural limits set on human modification and set us on a dizzying and dangerous path of radical change.

Fukuyama advances an Aristotelian argument that roots ethics and politics in a substantive notion of human nature. Rejecting the "naturalistic fallacy" which claims that "is" cannot be derived from "ought," Fukuyama argues that human nature provides a normative foundation to develop notions of the good life and to address core issues in the debate over biotechnology. His concept of human nature is relatively complex in that it acknowledges a dialectic of nature and culture in shaping human beings and emphasizes that the human species is malleable. But he rejects the idea that human nature is infinitely plastic, arguing that despite dynamic changes in human evolution there are important biological constants that abide transhistorically and cross-culturally. If human beings do not adapt to or flourish under repressive governments, for instance, it is due to elements in their nature that resist being molded in negative ways.[28]

Fukuyama worries, however, that biotechnology has the potential to reshape our nature in negative ways. Biotechnology has distinct political implications in that it could alter liberal democracy and the nature of politics itself by manipulating human personalities, behaviors, and traits. Invoking the dystopia of Huxley's *Brave New World* throughout the book, he fears that human rights and liberal equality is threatened by the spectre of eugenics. Even if germ line engineering never materializes, he observes that genomics, neuropharmacology, and the prolongation of life will transform notions of human equality and give societies new possibilities for manipulating biology and society. His most general fear is that biotechnology will cause us to lose our humanity, "some essential quality that has always underpinned our sense of who we are" (101).[29] With this dehumanization comes a loss of human dignity, some "factor X" that involves the universal human demand for recognition that one person is basically equal to one another. Biotechnology threatens to disrupt complex, long-standing evolutionary processes that we manipulate at our peril. It will undermine key human qualities such as genius or ambition, and eradicate the depth of human experience that is enhanced through struggle and suffering. Biotechnology also threatens to create a new class system based on genetics, and will lead to notions that some individuals inherently are better than others, thereby dissolving liberal democracy.

The state and market could ensure there is full democratization of eugenic technologies, he recognizes, but this would only universalize the other problem of distorting human nature. Not regarding a ban on biotechnology as a plausible goal, he calls for national and international regulation of it. For those who proclaim the genie is out of the bottle, Fukuyama points to past precedents in human history such as with nuclear weapons and energy technologies where humanity has been able to control the spread of powerful technologies.

Essentialist arguments assume the existence of a human species essence that somehow is violated by technological manipulations of the body. From a fluid evolutionary perspective, the concept of species—as something static, changeless, and ontologically sealed from other life forms—has always been suspect as ultimately each "species" is related to every other and all share the same DNA material that enable life to exist on this planet. This not mean, as Fukuyama rightly argues, that there are not species specific characteristics, but it does dispel pre-Darwinian concepts that species are self-enclosed essences.

While other species such as birds and chimpanzees make and use tools, technology has been a major force in the evolution of human intelligence and social life. The human being is a natural being that changes, develops, and evolves through interaction with specific technologies and social conditions. As Marx and Engels observed in their theory of praxis, as we change and shape our world, we change and shape ourselves. Far from something alien to human nature, technology has been part and parcel of the human condition. Although the line between biology and technology has become increasingly blurred, it was never an absolute distinction in the emergence of the hominid line that some 5–8 million years ago evolved into Homo sapiens. While there is nothing about human cloning or genetic alteration to make biotechnology more or less "unnatural" than other technologies, such transformations nonetheless would constitute major new developments that bring about a postbiological mode of human reproduction and a posthuman culture that implodes distinctions among human beings, animals, and machines, as humanity undertakes the project of its own genetic redesign.

Rather than demonizing cloning technologies from a priori essentialist premises that they violate the commands of God or the laws of nature, and are therefore inherently objectionable, we argue that they are better assessed in light of empirical realities of what already has happened with animal cloning, the current commodification of biotechnology, and the consequences that might result from cloning human beings. There is nothing intrinsically wrong with altering "human nature" and, as we have argued, human beings by definition are dynamic self-altering beings. But some changes or mutations are more dramatic and risky than others, and collectively human beings may decide some are safe, ethical, and rational to choose and others are not.

A strong objection against human cloning and genetic engineering technologies is that they could be used to design and mass reproduce desirable traits, bringing about a society organized around rigid social hierarchies and genetic discrimination—as vividly portrayed in the film *Gattaca* (1997). Fukuyama emphasizes this problem and it was, of course, the nightmare of Aldous Huxley, who continued H.G. Wells' speculations on a genetically engineered society and creation of new species. Indeed, with only trivial qualifications, Huxley's *Brave New World* ([1932] [1958a]) of genetic engineering, cloning, laboratory conception, addictive pleasure drugs (soma), entertainment and media spectacles, and intense social engineering has arrived. Huxley thought cloning and genetic engineering were centuries away from realization, but in fact they began to unfold a mere two decades since his writing of *Brave New World* in the early 1930s. Technocapitalism cannot yet, for instance, biologically clone human beings, but it can clone them in a far more effective way—socially. Whereas biological clones would have a mind of their own, since the social world and experiences that conditioned the "original" could not be reproduced, *social cloning* according to a given ideological and functional model is far more controlling. That is why Huxley's sequel work, *Brave New World Revisited* ([1958] 1989b) focused on various modes of psychological conditioning and mind control.

Of course, as Baudrillard argues (2000), cloning is connected as well to the fantasy of immortality, to defeating the life-death cycle. Techno-utopians fantasize about the possibility of cloning one's body, or uploading one's memories into another body or a machine, thereby achieving immortality and alleged continuity of selfhood. The Raelians promote cloning as a chance for "eternal life." In the current social setting, it's no surprise that cryogenics— the freezing of dead human beings in the hope they might be regenerated in the future through medical advances—is a booming global industry.

Defenders of cloning and biotechnology argue that genetic technologies will increase individuality, freedom, and choice, enabling people to design their own children and to alter their own bodies. Already with preimplantation genetic diagnosis, parents can screen out embryos at risk of disease and select those most likely to be healthy, as they also can know in advance the sex of the their child. Soon, parents and doctors might be able to isolate and remove genes that cause obesity, addictions, and a host of fatal illness, as well as to engineer genes that would enhance intelligence, strength, athleticism, physical attractiveness, and other desirable traits.

Along with Lee Silver, Gregory Stock is perhaps the most utopian advocate of germ line engineering (GLE), which, unlike gene therapy, makes potentially permanent changes in the human genome. Cloning is a conservative technology as it simply copies existing genetic information to create a human simulacrum, while GLE is revolutionary in that it alters human genes and makes them susceptible to design. Stock aggressively asserts the positive potential of GLE and believes that it is the next stage in the realization of parent desires to create the best life for their children. Against cyborg champions like Ray Kurzweil (2000), Stock believes that the most important engines of change in the human future will not be computers and implants, but rather genetic manipulation. We will remain largely fleshy beings, but biology will radically change the coding of that flesh. Stock also claims that the dramatic changes GLE will bring are inevitable; history is not a tale of self-restraint, he finds, and change is accelerating all the time. The great promise of GLE, then, is that it will "improve" our genetic assets as it provides us with more choice and freedom: "Human conception is shifting from chance to conscious design" (75).

Stock acknowledges the complexity involved in genetic manipulation, but thinks that through technologies such as artificial chromosomes science can precisely define and control modifications in the human genome. He denies that the charges GLE makes need be permanent modifications in the genome, and therefore ought to be rejected as too dangerous, because he believes the artificial chromosomes can be turned on and off at will. This also allows him to override the objection that parents are wrongly determining physical traits for their children insofar as he believes that children could simply switch them off if they so choose and reclaim their natural heritage. Stock's reliance on a technofix for problems that might arise with complex biological systems is most unconvincing. Quite likely, Stock's intentional evolution will be plagued by unintended consequences. Stock effectively rebuts the argument that GLE will result in the *homogenization* of the human genome, as even if millions of people employ the technology billions will not. But given that advertising models will inevitably influence the kinds of traits future humans will attempt to design, he fails to see that GLE will bring the *trivialization* of humanity as advertising ideologies would become absorbed into the genes themselves.

Currently, the human race stands at a crossroads and must make crucial choices concerning the future of the human, including the issue of GLE. Whatever one's philosophical and ethical conceptions of cloning, it is clear that at present human cloning is unacceptable. Cloning proponents argue that it took hundreds of attempts to develop a test-tube baby and that trial-and-error is simply the scientific method. We need to ask, however, if such costs are legitimate when the benefits are not yet clear. While one might sympathize with couples that fervently desire a child, legions of unwanted children await adoption, and it is difficult to justify the great leap forward to cloning through these kinds of rationale.

Therapeutic v. Reproductive Cloning:
The Debate over Stem-Cell Research

> *It is not unrealistic to say that stem cell research has the potential to revolutionize the practice of medicine.*
> —Dr. Harold Varmus, former NIH director

> *The 20th century was the drug therapy era. The 21st century will be the cell therapy era.*
> —George Daleuy, biologist with the Whitehead Institute for Biomedical Research, Cambridge, Massachusetts

Full-blown human reproductive cloning is problematic for numerous reasons, and we reject it on the grounds that it lacks justification and portends a world of eugenics and genetic discrimination rooted in the creation and replication of desired human types. Yet scientists are also developing a more benign and promising technology of stem cell research, or "therapeutic cloning." The controversy around *embryonic* stem cell research— because it involves using and destroying cells from frozen human embryos—remains one of the key debates of our time, important enough to provoke a major policy crisis for the Bush Administration and to warrant an address to the nation on prime-time TV in August 2001. Rarely do scientific debates erupt into the public forum, and although the technical aspects are difficult and complex, the ethical and medical stakes are clear enough to command a national debate.

In 1998, Dr. James A. Thomson, a developmental biologist at the University of Wisconsin, announced to the scientific world that he had isolated embryonic stem cells, thus portending a new era of "regenerative medicine" based on the renewal and recreation of the body's cells. Stem cells are the primitive master cells of the body that differentiate into functions like skin, bone, nerve, and brain cells (the body produces over 200 cell types). The goal of stem cell research is to program the development of stem cells toward specific functions in order to replace lost or damaged cells, tissues, and organs. Using similar technological breakthroughs such as led to Dolly, stem cell research involves cloning cells from a wide range of human tissue, or very young human embryos (around 5 days of age) and aborted fetal tissues.

In the debates over stem cell research, an important distinction emerged between *adult stem cells* that are derived from blood, bone marrow, fat and other tissues, and *embryonic stem cells* from discarded IVF cultures, aborted fetuses, or embryos created in a lab. While scientists are experimenting with adult stem cells, the current consensus is that embryonic cells are the most pliable and hence have the most regenerative potential. In July 2001, the National Institute of Health issued a report that "Stem cells from adults and embryos both show enormous promise for treating an array of diseases but at this early stage, cells from days-old embryos appear to offer certain key advantages." As Ceci Connolly summarized it: "Embryonic stem cells are more plentiful and therefore easier to extract, can be grown and made to multiply in the laboratory more easily and appear to have the uncanny ability to develop into a much wider array of tissues."[30] In fact, embryonic and adult stem cell research may each contribute to significant medical and health advancement. According to Senator Bill Frist (R-Tenn), the only medical doctor in Congress, an opponent of abortion, and key science advisor to the Bush administration: "because both embryonic and adult stem cell research may contribute to significant medical and health advancement, research on both should be federally funded within a carefully regulated, fully transparent framework that ensures respect for the moral significance of the human embryo."[31]

Scientists argue that therapeutic cloning has tremendous medical potential. Early in life, for example, each individual could have their stem cells frozen to create their own "body repair kit" if they developed a disease or even lost a limb. There would be no organ shortages, no rejection problem, and no need for animal exploitation as the cells would be their own. Although there has of yet been no significant advances in human research, and the results so far confined to animals are not necessarily applicable to human beings, stem cell research nonetheless shows remarkable potential for revolutionary breakthroughs in medicine. Among their achievements with mice, rats, pigs, and fetal monkeys, scientists have directed stem cells to produce insulin, to induce growth of brain cells, and to form new blood vessels in hearts, thereby suggesting immense contributions to curing diabetes, Alzheimer's or Parkinson's, and heart disease.[32] Still, while industries and media often hype the research as producing immanent medical revolutions, many scientists believe breakthroughs in gene therapy and therapeutic cloning are likely decades away and that expectations have been unduly raised.[33]

Another crucial distinction involves using embryonic stem cells from IVF discards and cloning embryos for the explicit sake of research. Whereas Britain allows both kinds of stem cell research, and thus condones embryo cloning for therapeutic purposes, the Bush administration highly restricts the use of IVF stem cell lines and condemns embryonic cloning. Yet many scientists argue that the ideal source of stem cells for regenerative medicine would not only be those derived from IVF embryos, but from embryos cloned from a patient's own cells, as the derived stem cells would be one's own and in theory far less susceptible to rejection. Thus, there is a medical justification for cloning human embryos and embryo cloning will be crucial to regenerative medicine.

On January 22, 2001, Britain became the first country to legalize human embryo cloning, with the proviso, perhaps impossible to enforce, that all clones would have to be destroyed after 14 days of development, and never implanted in a human womb. Britain thus endorsed therapeutic cloning, while banning reproductive cloning.[34] On the whole, Britain seems to have more scientifically advanced and democratic political guidelines and policies on cloning than the U.S. While a ban on human reproductive cloning is pending, therapeutic cloning is allowed under rigorous guidelines. Britain was ahead in the process of IVF since the birth of Louise Brown in England in 1978. Moral philosophers have been debating bioethical issues and there has been much public discussion. Parliament set up an agency on Human Fertilization and Embryology Authority that license fertility clinics and research institutions that study human embryos. The agency has kept detailed statistics of the number of human embryos created, planted and destroyed in fertility clinics.[35] The U.K. is establishing a stem cell bank that would be run as a public resource, in a way similar to the Human Genome Project. Hence, existing stem cell lines and techniques are available to any qualified researcher, and Britain has passed progressive laws banning genetic discrimination and mandating that therapies and medical advances that come out of genetic research will be available to and benefit everyone through its National Health Service.

In the U.S. and elsewhere, many religious groups and hard-core technology critics vituperate against stem cell research as "violating" the "inherent sanctity of life." To be sure, there is an ethical issue at stake in creating embryos for research purposes, or even using IVF cells, as living matter is being used as a means to some end other than its own existence. Clearly, using IVF cells that are going to be destroyed regardless is less objectionable than cloning an embryo for the sake of "harvesting" its cells then terminating it, but many religious groups and conservatives nonetheless vehemently oppose all forms of stem cell research and any manipulation of life, no matter what profound medical consequences may result. "Anyone truly serious about preventing reproductive human cloning must seek to stop the process from the beginning," Leon Kass, later to be Bush's cloning czar, proclaimed before a House judiciary subcommittee in June 2001.[36]

To challenge stem cell research, many conservatives (and some liberals) are recycling philosophical arguments from earlier debates over abortion.[37] The Pope and critics of stem cell research argue that once a sperm and egg are mixed into an embryo, no matter what the medium, there is a human life with all of its rights and sacredness. Others claim that a human life exists only when the embryo is implanted in a mother and has undergone the beginnings of the maturation process. Some medical experts assert that 14 days is the crucial dividing line when a backbone and organs begin to develop, while many pro-choice proponents argue that a fetus itself is not yet fully a human being. These earlier philosophical arguments have been revived in the stem-cell debate to legitimize conflicting scientific and political positions. In the context of stem cell research, religious conservatives repeat the same question-begging argument: (1) a human embryo is a human being; (2) it is wrong to take a human life; (3) therefore, it is wrong to "destroy" an embryo. The most controversial claim of the argument, in premise (1), is either just assumed, or defended through dogmatic claims that "life begins at conception," when, arguably, there is no real conception in a petri dish holding a 5-day-old cell mass.[38]

Ultimately, the debate comes down to the philosophical issue of what constitutes a human being. Opponents of therapeutic human cloning and embryonic stem cell research claim that "conception" takes place when an embryo is produced, even in a petri dish. Critics of this notion of human life argue that an embryo is a merger of sperm and egg that takes place in five or six days and is called a blastocyst, which scientists distinguish from a fetus. Scientists further claim that an embryo only attains fetus-status at around 14 days when it develops a "primitive streak," the beginnings of a backbone. Up until that point, a single embryo can divide into identical twins, and two embryos can merge into one, leading Ronald Green, a Dartmouth bioethicist to conclude: "It is very clear that you cannot speak of a human individual in the first 14 days of development. How can one speak of the presence of an individual soul if the embryo can be split into two or three?"[39]

Clearly, it is difficult to say when human life begins, and claims that it emerges "at conception" are simplistic. So far human life has only been produced from fetuses that mature in the womb of a woman's body, and thus we have trouble conceiving that 5 day-old embryos in a petri dish are human. It also might be pointed out that only about one in eight embryos implanted through IVF achieves fetal status, and few conservative critics worry over the doomed embryos or question the ethics of IVF as a whole, a technology that produces surplus cells for medical research. The fact that embryos typically used for stem cell research are leftover from couples using in vitro fertilization, and are marked for destruction regardless, strongly undercuts the force of the argument against embryonic stem cells.[40]

Indeed, the slippery slope argument beloved by conservatives (the direct and unavoidable path from stem cell research to fetus farms and a society peopled by clones) is easily turned against them. In the age of cloning where possibly any cell can be replicated and turned into an embryo, one might argue that it is unethical even to scrape any skin cells as they too are potential human beings.[41] Silly, perhaps, but this is also an indicator of the surreality of the postmodern adventure. In an amazing alchemy, scientists can directly transform cells of one kind into another. PPL Therapeutics succeeded in transforming a cow's skin cell into a basic stem cell, and then refashioned it as a heart cell. Further, researchers are working on cultivating spermless embryos, studying how to prod unfertilized eggs to grow to produce stem cells.[42] Geron has created heart cells that beat in a petri dish. Clearly, the implications of stem cell research are staggering.

One should not see the use or creation of human embryos for medical resources as a trivial issue, but the debate over therapeutic cloning involves competing values and conceptions of the nature of a human being. This is a conflict between a small clump of cells no bigger than the period at the end of this sentence, and full-fledged human beings in dire medical need. In a conflict between a tiny ball of non-sentient cells or fetuses that would be disposed of regardless, and full-fledged human beings suffering from diseases that lack a cure, most people would reasonably choose the latter category of human persons.

In June 2002, however, an attempt to ban all human cloning, supported by President Bush, was defeated in the U.S. Senate, but then passed by the House in February 2003. Some conservatives are being won over because advocates of embryonic research reject the category of "therapeutic cloning" and even "embryo". The argument is that it is not a question of "cloning," but rather of "somatic cell nuclear transfer" or "regenerative medicine" that works on eggs in a test tube which have not been fertilized by sperm, and thereby cannot be considered research on human embryos. This change in terminology won over some conservatives who were being pressured to support potentially significant medical research, although critics decried the effort as use of "linguistic cloaking devices" and continued their polemic against all cloning.[43]

By March 2003, a broad movement had emerged, however, to undertake embryo stem cell research in the U.S. supported by state legislatures, universities, private foundations, hospitals and corporations.[44] Thus, while many conservatives defend the "sanctity" of embryonic cells, thousands of people continue to suffer and die from Alzheimer's, Parkinson's disease, diabetes, paralysis, and other afflictions. This is a strange position for "pro-life" and "compassionate" conservatives to defend.

The entire moral quandary may be blunted, however, as scientists are now discovering ways to use stem cells derived from umbilical cords, bone marrow, and even fat and brain cells, and have cloned and implanted kidneys in a cow.[45]

Deferring the Brave New World:
Challenges for Ethics and Democracy

> *The enormous collective project of conscious human evolution has begun.*
> —Gregory Stock

By summer of 2001, a technical and esoteric debate over stem cells, confined within the scientific community during the past years, had moved to the headlines to become the forefront of the ongoing science wars—battles over the cultural, ethical, and political implications of science. The scientific debate over stem cell research in large part is a disguised culture war, and conservatives, liberals, and radicals have all jumped into the fray. In our own case, coming from a perspective of critical theory and radical democratic politics, we reject conservative theologies and argue against conflations of religion and the state. Likewise, we question neo-liberal acceptance of corporate capitalism and underscore the implications of the privatization of research and the monopolization of knowledge and patents by huge biotech corporations. In addition, we urge a deeper level of public participation in science debates than do conservatives or liberals and believe that the public can be adequately educated to have meaningful and intelligent input into technical issues such as cloning and stem cell research that have tremendous human and ethical implications.

As we have shown, numerous issues are at stake in the debate over cloning, having to do not only with science, but also with religion, politics, economics, democracy, ethics, and the meaning and nature of human beings and all life forms as they undergo a process of genetic reconstruction. Thus, our goal throughout this paper has been to question the validity of the cloning project, particularly within the context of a global capitalist economy and its profit imperative, a modernist paradigm of reductionism, and a Western sensibility organized around the concept of the domination of nature. Until science is recontextualized within a new holistic paradigm informed by a respect for living processes, by democratic decision making, and by a new ethic toward nature, the genetic sciences on the whole are in the hands of those governed by the imperatives of profit. Moreover, politicians beholden to corporate interests have no grasp of the momentous issues involved, requiring that those interested in democratic politics and progressive social change must educate and involve themselves in the science and politics of biotechnology.

We have already entered a new stage of the postmodern adventure in which animal cloning is highly advanced and human cloning is on the horizon, if not now underway. Perhaps little human clones are already emerging, with failures being discarded, as were the reportedly hundreds of botched attempts to create Louise Brown, the first test-tube baby, in 1978. At this stage, human cloning is indefensible in light of the possibility of monstrosities, dangers to the mother, burdens to society, failure to reach a consensus on the viability and desirability of cloning humans, and the lack of compelling reasons to warrant this fateful move. The case is much different, however, for therapeutic cloning, which is incredibly promising and offers new hope for curing numerous debilitating diseases. But even stem cell research, and the cloning of human embryos, as we have seen, is problematic, in part because it is the logical first step toward reproductive cloning and mass production of desired types, which unavoidably brings about new (genetic) hierarchies and modes of discrimination.

We thus need to discuss the numerous issues involved in the shift to a posthuman, postbiological mode of existence where the boundaries between our bodies and technologies begins to erode as we morph toward a cyborg state. Our technologies are no longer extensions of our bodies, as Marshall McLuhan stated, but rather are intimately merging with our bodies, as we implode with other species through the genetic crossings of transgenic species. In an era of rapid flux, our genotypes, phenotypes, and identities are all mutating. Under the pressure of new philosophies and technological change, the humanist mode of understanding the self as a centered, rational Subject has transformed into new paradigms of communication and intersubjectivity (see Hayles 1999) and information and cybernetics (see Habermas 1979, 1984, 1987).

Despite these shifts, it is imperative that elements of the modern Enlightenment tradition be retained, as it is simultaneously radicalized. Now more than ever, as science embarks on the incredible project of manipulating atoms and genes through nanotechnology, genetic engineering, and cloning, its awesome powers must be measured and tempered through ethical, ecological, and democratic norms in a process of public debate and participation. The walls between "experts" and "laypeople" must be broken down along with the elitist norms that form their foundation. Scientists need to enter dialogical relations with the public to discuss the complexities of cloning and stem cell research, to make their positions clear and accessible, as well as accountable and responsible, while public intellectuals and activists need to become educated in biotechnology in order to engage in debate in the media or public forums on the topics.

Scientists should recognize that their endeavors embody specific biases and value choices, subject them to critical scrutiny, and seek more humane, life-enhancing, and democratic values to guide their work. Respect for nature and life, preserving the natural environment, humane treatment of animals, and serving human needs should be primary values embedded in science. And when these values might conflict, as in the tension between the inherent value of animals and human "needs," the problem must be addressed as sensitively as possible.

This approach is quite unlike how science so far has conducted itself in many areas. Most blatantly, perhaps, scientists, hand in hand with corporations, have prematurely rushed the genetic manipulation of agriculture, animals, and the world's food supply while ignoring important environmental, health, and ethical concerns. Immense power brings enormous responsibility, and it is time for scientists to awaken to this fact and make public accountability integral to their ethos and research. A schizoid modern science that rigidly splits facts from values must give way to a postmodern metascience that grounds the production of knowledge in a social context of dialogue and communication with citizens. The shift from a cold and detached "neutrality" to a participatory understanding of life that deconstructs the modern subject/object dichotomy derails realist claims to unmediated access to the world and opens the door to an empathetic and ecological understanding of nature (see Fox 1983 and Birke and Hubbard 1995).

In addition, scientists need to take up the issue of democratic accountability and ethical responsibility in their work. As Bill Joy argued in a much-discussed *Wired* article in July 2000, uncontrolled genetic technology, artificial intelligence, and nanotechnology could create catastrophic disasters, as well as utopian benefits. Joy's article set off a firestorm of controversy, especially his call for government regulation of new technology and "relinquishment" of development of potentially dangerous new technologies, as he claimed biologists called for in the early days of genetic engineering, when the consequences of the technology were not yet clear.[46] Arguing that scientists must assume responsibility for their productions, Joy warned that humans should be very careful about the technologies they develop, as they may have unforeseen consequences. Joy noted that robotics was producing increasingly intelligent machines that might generate creative robots that could be superior to humans, produce copies of themselves, and assume control of the design and future of humans. Likewise, genetic engineering could create new species, some perhaps dangerous to humans and nature, while nanotechnology might build horrific "engines of destruction" as well as of the "engines of creation" envisioned by Eric Drexler.

Science and technology, however, not only require responsibility and accountability on the part of scientists, but also regulation by government and democratic debate and participation by the public. Publics need to agree on rules and regulations for cloning and stem cell research, and there should be laws, guidelines, and regulatory agencies open to public input and scrutiny. To be rational and informed, citizens must be educated about the complexities of genetic engineering and cloning, a process that can unfold through vehicles such as public forums, teach-ins, and creative use of the broadcast media and Internet. The Internet is a treasure-trove of information, ranging from informative sites such as The Council For Responsible Genetics (www.gene-watch.org/) and The Institute of Science in Society (www.i-sis.org.uk), to lists serves such as hosted by the Sierra Club and various weblogs.

But to publicize and politicize biotechnology issues, social movements will have to take up issues like the cloning and stem cell debate into their public pedagogies and struggles. Movements like the anti-nuclear coalitions and organized struggles against genetically-modified foods have had major successes in educating the public, promoting debate, and influencing legislation and public opinion. It will not do, however, to simply let the market decide what technologies will or will not be allowed, nor should bans be accepted on technologies that can benefit human life. Instead, citizens and those involved in social movements should engage issues of biotechnology and aid in public education and debate.

An intellectual revolution is needed to remedy the deficiencies in the education of both scientists and citizens, such that each can have, in Habermas' framework, "communicative competency" informed by sound value thinking, skills in reasoning, and democratic sensibilities. A Deweyean reconstruction of education would have scientists take more humanities courses and engage ethical and political issues involved in the development and implementation of science and technology, and would have students in other fields take more science and technology courses to become literate in some of the major material and social forces of the epoch. C.P. Snow's "two cultures" provides a challenge for a democratic reconstruction of education to overcome in an increasing scientific and technological age that requires more and better knowledge of science and the humanities.

Critical and self-reflexive scrutiny of scientific means, ends, and procedures should be a crucial part of the enterprise. "Critical," in Haraway's analysis, signifies "evaluative, public, multiactor, multiagenda, oriented to equality and heterogeneous well-being" (Haraway 1997: 95). Indeed, there should be debates concerning precisely what values are incorporated into specific scientific projects and whether these serve legitimate ends and goals. In the case of mapping the human genome, for instance, enormous amounts of money and energy are being spent, but almost no resources are going to educating the public about the ethical implications of having a genome map. The Human Genome Project spent only 3 to 5 percent of its $3 billion budget on legal, ethical, and social issues, and Celera spent even less.[47]

A democratic biopolitics and reconstruction of education would involve the emergence of new perspectives, understandings, sensibilities, values, and paradigms that put in question the assumptions, methods, values, and interpretations of modern sciences, calling for a reconstruction of science.[48] At the same time, as science and technology co-construct each other, and both coevolve in conjunction with capitalist growth, profit, and power imperatives, science is reconstructing—not always for the better—the natural and social worlds as well as our very identities and bodies. There is considerable ambiguity and tension in how science will play out given the different trajectories it can take. Unlike the salvationist promises of the techoscientific ideology and the apocalyptic dystopias of some of its critics, we see the future of science and technology to be entirely ambiguous, contested, and open. For now, the only certainty is that the juggernaut of the genetic revolution is rapidly advancing and that in the name of medical progress animals are being victimized and exploited in new ways, while the replication and re-design of human beings is looming.

The human species is thus at a terribly difficult and complex crossroads. Whatever steps we take, it is imperative we do not leave the decisions to the scientists, anymore than we would to the theologians (or corporate-hired bioethicists for that matter), for their judgment and objectivity is less than perfect, especially for the majority who are employed by biotechnology corporations and have a vested interest in the hastening and patenting of the brave new world of biotechnology.[49] The issues involving genetics are so important that scientific, political, and moral debate must take place squarely within the public sphere. The fate of human beings, animals, and nature hangs in the balance, thus it is imperative that the public become informed on the latest developments and biotechnology and that lively and substantive democratic debate take place concerning the crucial issues raised by the new technosciences.

Notes

1. Cited in Carey Goldberg, and Gina Kolata, "Scientists Announce Births of Cows Cloned in New Way," *The New York Times*. January 21, 1998: A 14. Companies are now preparing to sell milk from cloned cows; see Jennifer Mitol, "Got cloned milk?" abcnews.com, July 16, 2001. For the story of Dolly and animal cloning, see Kolata (1998).

2. See Sheryl Gay Stolberg, "Breakthrough in Pig Cloning Could Aide Organ Transplants" (*New York Times*, Jan. 4, 2001). In July 2002, the Australian government announced draft guidelines that would regulate transplanting animal organs into humans and anticipated research with pig organs translated into humans within two years; see Benjamin Haslem, "Animal-to-human transplants get nod," *The Australian*, July 8, 2002: A1

3. See http://abcnews.go.com/sections/DailyNews/biotechgoats. 000618.html.

4. See Heather Moore, "The Modern-Day Island of Dr, Moreau," http://www.alternet.org/story.html?StoryID=11703, October 12, 2001. For a vivid description of the horrors of animal experimentation, see Singer (1975); for an acute diagnosis of the unscientific nature of vivisection, see Greek and Greek(2000).

5. See "In Test, Japanese Have No Beef With Cloned Beef," http://www.washingtonpost.com/wpsrv/inatl/daily/sept99/japan10.htm. According to one report, it is more accurate to refer to this beef as being produced by "embryo twinning," and not the kind of cloning process that produced Dolly; see "'Cloned' Beef Scare Lacks Meat," http://www.wired.com/news/technology/0,1282,19146,00. html. As just one indicator of the corporate will to clone animals for mass consumption, the National Institute of Science and Technology has donated $4.7 million to two industries to fund research into cloning chickens for food. See "Cloned chickens on the menu," *New Scientist*.com, August 15, 2001.

6. See Heather Moore, "The Modern-Day Island of Dr, Moreau," op. cit., and Sharon Schmickle, "It's what's for dinner: milk and meat from clones," www.startribune. com/stories/462 /868271.html, December 2, 2001.

7. "Clonefarm: Billions of identical chickens could soon be rolling off production lines," www.newscientist.com/hottopics/cloning/cloning.jsp?id=23040300, August 18, 2001.

8. Cited in Heather Moore, "The Modern Day Island of Dr. Moreau," op. cit.

9. The Missyplicity Project boasts a strong code of bioethics; see http://www.missyplicity.com/.

10. See http://www.transgenicpets.com/.

11. "In Cloning, Failure Far Exceeds Success," Gina Kolata, www.nytimes.com/2001/12/11/science/11CLON.html.

12. See "Clones contain hidden DNA damage," www.newscientist.com/news/news.jsp?id=ns9999982; see also the study published in *Science* (July 6, 2001) which discusses why so many clone pregnancies fail and why some cloned animals suffer strange maladies in their hearts, joints, and immune system.

13. "Clone Study Casts Doubt in Stem Cells: Variations in Mice Raise Human Research Issues,"www.washingtonpost.com/ac2/wp-dyn/A23967-2001Jul5?language=printer, July 6, 2001.

14. See "Scientists Warn of Dangers of Human Cloning," www.abcnews.com. See also the commentaries in Gareth Cook, "Scientists say cloning may lead to long-term ills," *The Boston Globe*, July 6, 2001; Steve Connor, "Human cloning 'will never be safe," *Independent*, July 6, 2001; Carolyn Abraham, "Clone creatures carry genetic glitches," July 6, 2001; Connor cites Dolly-cloner Ian Wilmut who noted: "It surely adds yet more evidence that there should be a moratorium against copying people How can anybody take the risk of cloning a baby when its outcome is so unpredictable?"

15. See "Report Says Scientists See Cloning Problems, http://abcnews.go.com/wire.US/reuters200103525_573.html.

16. The Westhusin quote is at abcnews.go.com/cloningflaw010705. htm; the "mis-

placed carbons" quote is in Philip Cohen, "Clone Killer," www.newscientist.com/
news.
17. "Human Clone Moves Sparks Global Outrage," www.smh.com.au, March 11,
2001.
18. Given this attitude, it is no surprise that in September, 2001, Texas A&M University, the same institution working on cloning cats and dogs, showed off newly
cloned pigs, who joined the bulls and goat already cloned by the school, as part of
the "world's first cloned animal fair."
19. See "Back from the Brink: Cloning Endangered Species," Pamela Weintraub,
http://news.bmn.com/hmsbeagle/109/notes/ feature2, August 31, 2001. "Gene Find
No Small Fetus," www.wired.com/news/print/0,1294,41513,00.html
20. For pro-cloning manifestoes, see also www.secularhumanism.org/library/fi/
cloning_declaration_17_3.html; www.humancloning.org and www.reason.com/
biclone.html. For the case against cloning, see articles in the special World Watch
issue "Beyond Cloning" (July/August 2002) and the discussion below.
21. See http://www.humancloning.org/.
22. Investigative reporter Joe Lauria found a secret cloning lab supposedly carrying
out Raelian human cloning experiments, but it appeared abandoned and there are
suspicions that the whole effort was a fraud to exploit a desperate family that
wanted its child cloned; see *London Times*, August 12, 2001. On predictions that
human cloning experiments are already underway, see www.wired.com/wired/
archive/9.02/projectxpr.html).
23. Is human clonign impossible?" http://www.msnbc.com/news/898436,asp?
0cv=CB20.
24. For a discussion of how modern science and capitalism co-evolved in the context
of colonialism, whereby they underpinned each other in the bid to control other
peoples and exploit their knowledges, see Harding (1998).
25. See Gina Kolata, "Human Cloning: Yesterday's Never is Today's Why Not?" *The
New York Times*, December 2, 1997).
26. Cited in Nancy Gibbs, "Baby, "It's You! And You, and You..." *Time*, February,
February 19, 2001: 50. In March 2001, to great media fanfare, Zavos, Israeli
biotechnologist Avi Bin Abraham, and Italian fertility specialist Severino Antinori
announced that the group had signed up more than 600 infertile couples and were
undertaking human cloning experiments to provide them with children; see "Forum on Human Cloning Turns Raucous," *Los Angeles Times* (March 10, 2001).
When Zavos and his partner went to Israel to seek permission to do human
cloning there, ABC News (March 25, 2001) reported that they received the blessing of an old rabbi, but the Israeli justice minister said that he was against cloning
"on moral and ideological grounds." A University of Pennsylvania ethicist said
that Zavos had no medical training, had published no articles in the field, had no
qualifications, and that one of the dangers of cloning was that frauds were operating in the treacherous minefield of human cloning and exploiting people with
false promises. There were also numerous discussions of the failures of animal
cloning that were suggesting that human cloning would be highly hazardous and
disturbing; see Aaron Zitner, "Perpetual Pets, Via Cloning," *Los Angeles Times*
(March 16, 2001), Gina Kolata, "Researchers Find Big Risk of Defect in Cloning
Animals," *New York Times* (March 25, 2001), and the examples that we provide
below.
27. "Brave New World?" http://msnbc.com/news/525661.asp.
28. Once again, Fukuyama's neo-liberal politics are smuggled into his concept of
human nature as he sees no other social system but capitalism to be compatible

with "human nature." His claim that only capitalism can create a political system that does not interfere with "natural patterns of behavior" (14) takes no account of either past cooperative social systems that fostered healthy bonds among people or the destructive aspects of competitive individualism and class structures under capitalism.

29. Fukuyama is not so generous when it comes to deciding the moral status of nonhuman animals. Unlike Darwin, he defines human animals in sharp opposition to all nonhuman animals and posits "a very important qualitative, if not ontological, leap that occurred at some point" (170) in the evolutionary process that led to human beings. Our "factor X" amounts to everything that distinguishes us in "essence" from all other animals. Consequently, Fukuyama defines human dignity as "the idea that there is something unique about the human race that entitles every member of the species to a higher moral status than the rest of the natural world" (160). The nature and moment of the evolutionary "leap" and the concept of dignity that rests on it are left unexplained, as therefore remain crypto-religious notions often embellished with references to God.

30. Ceci Connolly, "Embryo Cells' Promise Cited in NIH Study" (*Washington Post*, July 18, 2001: A01. The NIH notes the preliminary status of the report, the many uncertainties around stem cells, and the need for more research.

31. See www.time.com , July 19, 2001.

32. See "Stem Cells Coaxed To Produce Insulin," http://www.msnbc.com/news/ 607294.asp, "Fetal Stem Cells Boost Brainpower," http://www.msnbc.com/news/ 566735.asp, and "Rebuilding Hearts," http://abcnews.go.com/sections/ GMA/ DrJohnson/ GMA010402Stemcells_dr.Tim.html, and "Early Success Seen with 2nd Type of Stem Cell," www.nytimes.com/2001/07/26/health/genetics/ 26MOUS.html. The experiment with brain cells involved injecting human stem cells from the brains of aborted fetuses into mice, rats, and pigs, thereby imploding species boundaries and demonstrating the versatility of human stem cells. And in February 2003, scientists at the University of Wisconsin announced that they had genetically manipulated human stem cells to provide replacements for specific cells and organs; see "Scientists replace stem cell genes," Reuters (February 10, 2003).

33. One key problem is that scientists as of yet have been unable to get stem cells to grow into the specialized types they seek, rather than clumps of different cells. For an important article that punctures much of the hype surrounding stem cell research, see "A Thick Line Between Theory and Therapy, as Shown With Mice," Gina Kolata, www.nytimes.com/2001/12/18/science/life/18MICE.html.

34. See "Britain Oks Human Embryo Cloning," www.msnbc.com/news520058.asp and Kristen Philipkoski, "U.S. to Clone Brit Policy?," *Wired News*, Jan. 24, 2001. In April, 2001, however, Britain prepared to pass laws criminalizing human cloning, and to make sure that genetic treatment was available to everyone through their national health service. See Marjorie Miller, "Britain Proposes Law Against Cloning of Humans," *Los Angeles Times* (April 20, 2001: A10). After the November 2001 ACT announcement that they had cloned human embryos, however, a loophole was discovered in the law that would allow reproductive cloning despite the fact that the Human Fertilization and Embryology Act sought to ban human cloning. After a High Court judge ruled it was in fact legal to clone embryos, the British House of Lords proposed emergency legislation in late November 2001 to explicitly ban human cloning and have now explicitly banned human reproductive cloning.

35. See Nicholas Wade, "Clearer Guidelines Help Britain to Advance Stem Cell

Work," *New York Times*, August 14, 2001, and Judith Klotzho, "Embryonic victory," *The Guardian*, August 20, 2001.

36. "Cloning Capsized?" *The Scientist* 15[16]:1, August 20, 2001.

37. The philosophical debate over when human life starts is a long-standing one. The Greek philosopher Aristotle choose 40 days into pregnancy, and the 40 day rule was long followed by Jewish and Muslim traditions. The Catholic Church followed this line until 1588 when Pope Sixtus V declared that contraception and abortion were mortal sins; the ruling was reversed, however, 3 years later until 1859 when Pope Gregory XIV brought the church back to the view that the human embryo has a soul and renewed the call for excommunication for abortion at any stage. See Rick Weiss, "Changing Conceptions," *Washington Post*, July 15, 2001: B01.

38. For a thorough critique of attempts to define the "beginning point" of life, see Silver (1998).

39. Cited in Aaron Zitner, "Uncertainty is Thwarting Stem Cell Researchers," *Los Angeles Times*, July 21, 2001: A01.

40. In Britain, "the Human Fertilization and Embryology Authority has reported that some 50,000 babies have been born through in vitro fertilization since 1991, and 294,584 surplus human embryos have been destroyed." While no official records have been kept in the United States, "According to the American Society for Reproductive Medicine, about 100,000 children have been born in the United States by in vitro fertilization, or twice the number in Britain, implying that some 600,000 embryos would have been destroyed if American clinics followed the same five—year storage limit used in Britain. Only a small fraction of the discarded embryos would provide as many stem cells as researchers could use." See Nicholas Wade, "Stem Cell Issue Causes Debate Over the Exact Moment Life Begins," *New York Times*, August 15, 2001.

41. "Adult stem cells found in skin," www.newscientist.com/hottopics/cloning/cloning.jsp?id=ns99991147, August 13, 2001.

42. See "Another Advance for Dolly Cloners," www.wirednews.com/news/print/0.1294.41989.00.html, and Aaron Zitner, "Working On Sperm-less embryos," *Los Angeles Times*, August 12, 2001.

43. See Aaron Zitner, "Cloning Receives a Makeover," *Los Angeles Times*, June 17, 2002: A1 and A13.

44. See Richard Perez-Pena, "Broad Movement is Backing Embryo Stem Cell Research," *New York Times* (March 16, 2003).

45. See "Adult Approach to Stem Cells," http://www.wirednews.com/news/print/0,1294,38892,00.htm; "Need Stem Cells? Its in the Fat," http://www.wired.com/news/print/0,1294,42957,00.html; "Human Fat May Provide Useful Cells," http://www.msnbc.com/news/557256.asp; and Nicholas Wade, "Scientists Make Two Stem Cell Advances," *New York Times* (June 21, 2002). The latter article describes new advances in converting embryonic stem cells into the kind of brain cell that is lost in Parkinson's disease and extracting cells from bone marrow. On the successful cloning and implant of kidneys in a cow, see "Therapeutic Cloning Gets Boost in Implant Study," *Los Angeles Times*, June 3, 2002: A11.

46. See the collection of responses to Joy's article in *Wired* 8.07 (July 2000). Agreeing with Joy that there need to be firm guidelines regulating nanotechnology, the Foresight Institute has written a set of guidelines for its development that take into account problems such as commercialization, unjust distribution of benefits, and potential dangers to the environment. See www.foresight.org/guidelines/

current.html. We encourage such critical dialogue on both the benefits and dangers of new technologies and hope to contribute to these debates with our studies.
47. See www.wired.com/news/0,1294,36886,00.html.
48. On "new science" and "new sensibilities," see Herbert Marcuse (1964 and 1969).
49. For a sharp critique of how bioethicists are bought off and co-opted by corporations in their bid for legitimacy, see "Bioethicists Fall Under Familiar Scrutiny," http://www.nytimes.com/2001/08/02/health/genetics/02BIOE.html.

References

Baudrillard, Jean (2000) *The Vital Illusion.* New York: Columbia University Press.

Best, Steven and Kellner, Douglas (2001) *The Postmodern Adventure: Science, Technology, and Cultural Studies at the Third Millennium.* New York: Guilford Press.

Birke, Linda and Ruth Hubbard (1995) *Reinventing Biology: Respect for Life and the Creation of Knowledge.* Bloomington: Indiana University Press.

Fox, Evelyn (1983) *A Feeling for the Organism: The Life and Work of Barbara McClintock.* (New York: W.H. Freeman and Co.

Fox, Michael W. (1999) Beyond Evolution: The Genetically Altered Future of Plants, Animals, the Earth, and Humans. New York: The Lyons Press.

Fukuyama, Francis (2001) *Our Posthuman Future: Consequences of the Biotechnology Revolution.* New York: Farrar Straus & Giroux.

——— (1992) *The End of History and the Last Man.* New York: Free Press.

Greek, Ray and Greek, Jeanne Swingle (2000) *Sacred Cows and Golden Geese: The Human Cost of Experiments on Animals.* New York: Continuum.

Habermas, Jürgen (1979) *Communication and the Evolution of Society.* Boston: Beacon Press.

——— (1984) *Theory of Communicative Action,* Vol. 1. Boston: Beacon Press.

——— (1987) *Theory of Communicative Action,* Vol. 2. Boston: Beacon Press.

Haraway, Donna (1997) *Modest Witness@Second Millennium. Female Meets Oncomouse.* New York: Routledge.

Harding, Sandra (1998) *Is Science Multicultural? Postcolonialism, Feminism, and Epistemologies.* Bloomington: University of Indiana Press.

Hayles, N. Katherine (1999) *How We Became Posthuman: Virtual Bodies in Cybernetics, Literature, and Informatics.* Chicago: University of Chicago Press.

Huxley, Aldous (1989a) *Brave New World.* New York: Perennial Library.

——— (1989b) *Brave New World Revisited.* New York: Perennial Library.

Kass, Leon (1998) "The Wisdom of Repugnance," in Gregory Pence (ed.) *Flesh of My Flesh: The Ethics of Human Cloning.* Lanham, Maryland: Rowman and Littlefield Publishers. 13–37.

Keller, Evelyn Fox (1983) *A Feeling for the Organism: The Life and Work of Barbara McClintock.* New York: W.H. Freeman and Co.

Kolata, Gina (1998) *Clone. The Road to Dolly and the Path Ahead.* New York: William Morrow.

Kurzweil, Ray (2000) *The Age of Spiritual Machines: When Computers Exceed Human Intelligence.* London: Penguin Books.

Marcuse, Herbert (1964) *One-Dimensional Man.* Boston: Beacon Press.

——— (1969) *An Essay on Liberation.* Boston: Beacon Press.

Pence, Gregory (1998) *Who's Afraid of Human Cloning?* Lanham, Maryland: Rowman and Littlefield.

Rifkin, Jeremy (1998) *The Biotech Century: Harnessing the Gene and Remaking the World*. New York: Tarcher/Putnam.

Silver, Lee (1998) *Remaking Eden: How Genetic Engineering and Cloning Will Transform the American Family*. Bard: New York.

Singer, Peter (1975) *Animal Liberation*. New York: Avon Books.

Stock, Gregory (2002) *Redesigning Humans. Our Inevitable Genetic Future*. Boston and New York: Houghton Hifflin Company.

Wilmut, Ian, Keith Campbell, and Colin Tudge (2000) *The Second Creation: Dolly and the Age of Biological Control*. New York: Farrar, Straus, and Giroux.

3

Becoming Neurochemical Selves

Nikolas Rose

Introduction

How did we become neurochemical selves? How did we come to think about our sadness as a condition called 'depression' caused by a chemical imbalance in the brain and amenable to treatment by drugs that would 'rebalance' these chemicals? How did we come to experience our worries at home and at work as 'generalized anxiety disorder' also caused by a chemical imbalance which can be corrected by drugs? How did we—or at least those of us who live in the United States—come to code children's inattentiveness, difficulties with organizing tasks, fidgetiness, squirming, excessive talkativity and noisiness, impatience and the like as Attention Deficit Hyperactivity Disorder treatable by amphetamines? How did some of us come to understand changes in mood in the last week of the menstrual cycle—depressed mood, anxiety, emotional lability and decreased interest in activities—as premenstrual dysphoric disorder, treatable with a smaller dose of the very same drug that has become so popular in the treatment of 'depression'—fluoxetine hydrochloride? Perhaps some names give a clue. Depression: not so much fluoxetine hydrochloride as Prozac. Generalized Anxiety Disorder: not so much paroxetine as Paxil. ADHD: not methylphenidate or amphetamine/dextroamphetamine but Ritalin and Adderall. Premenstrual dysphoric disorder: not so much fluoxetine hydrochloride (again) but Sarafem. And some more names: Prozac and Sarafem: Eli Lilley. Paxil: GlaxoSmithKline. Ritalin: Novartis (Ciba Geigy). Adderall: Shire-Richmond. In this paper I want to explore the linkages between the reframing of the self, the emergence of these conditions, the development of these drugs, the marketing of these brands and the strategies of the pharmaceutical companies.

These do not just reshape our ways of thinking about and acting upon disorders of thought, mood and conduct. Of course, they have enormous consequences for psychiatry as it is practiced in the psychiatric hospital, for the 'community psychiatric patient,' and in the doctors surgery. But they have also impacted on the workplace and the school, the family and the prison—not to mention the bedroom and the sports field. And this recoding of everyday affects and conducts in terms of their neurochemistry is only one element of a mode widespread mutation in which we in the west, most especially in the United States, have come to understand our minds and selves in terms of our brains and bodies. I have started with neurochemistry: the belief that variations in neurochemistry underlie variations in thought, mood and behaviour, and that these can be modulated with drugs. I might have started with brain imaging: the belief that it is now possible to visualise the activities of the living brain as it thinks, desires, feels happy or sad, loves and fears, and hence to distinguish normality from abnormality at the level of patterns of brain activity. Or I might have started with genomics: claims to have mapped precise sequences of bases in specific chromosomal regions that affect our variations in mood, capacity to control our impulses, the types of mental illness we are susceptible to and our personality. But here, I want to start with the pharmaceuticals themselves.[1]

Psychopharmacological Societies

Over the last half of the twentieth century, health care practices in developed, liberal and democratic societies, notably Europe and the United States became increasingly dependent on commercially produced pharmaceuticals. This is especially true in relation to psychiatry and mental health. We could term these 'psychopharmacological' societies. That is to say, they are societies where the modification of thought, mood and conduct by pharmacological means has become more or less routine. In such societies, in many different contexts, in different ways, in relation to a variety of problems, by doctors, psychiatrists, parents and by ourselves, human subjective capacities have come to be routinely re-shaped by psychiatric drugs.

Whilst attempts at chemical solutions to psychiatric problems have a long history, the modern era begins in the 1950s for it was at the is point that drugs were formulated and marketed that were not merely sedative but claimed to have a specific effect on particular symptoms of certain psychiatric conditions. It is well known that the first widely used psychiatric drug was chlorpromazine, developed from antihistamines by company scientists at the pharmaceutical firm Rhône-Poulenc in the years after the Second World War.[2] Two French psychiatrists, Pierre Deniker and Jean Delay, who administered it to a group of psychotically agitated patients at the Hôpital Sainte-Anne in Paris in 1952, are credited with the discovery of its psychiatric effects. It was taken by Rhône-Poulenc to Canada, and licensed to Smith Kline and French who promoted it heavily in the United States under the name of Thorazine where it spread rapidly through the crowded psychiatric hospitals making them $75m in 1955 alone. It was thought not to be a sedative like barbiturates or chloral, but to act specifically on the symptoms of mental illness. Nonetheless, up to the late 1960s, most psychiatrists thought of it as a general 'tranquillizer'. It was followed by the development of drugs specifically claiming to treat depression and named 'anti-depressants': Geigy's imipramine (Tofranil) was tested by Ronald Kuhn at the Münsterlingen Hospital near Konstanz during the early 1950s and despite the initial lack of enthusiasm—depression was not seen, at that time, as a major psychiatric problem—Tofranil was launched in 1958 and became established as the first 'tricyclic' antidepressant in 1960s—so-called because of its three-ringed chemical structure. It was followed by Merck's tricyclic, amitryptiline (Elavil) in 1961. Over the same period, other drug companies and psychiatrists were experimenting with other drugs—reserpine, isoniazid, iproniazid (Marsalid)—which would eventually give rise to the influential 'serotonin hypothesis of depression' so crucial for the fabrication and marketing of Prozac and its sisters. And, as we shall see, it was also in the 1950s that the pharmaceutical companies developed and marketed drugs for the stresses and strains of everyday life—the compounds that became known as 'tranquillizers'.

Accurate comparative and historical data on psychiatric drug prescribing since the 1950s is not readily available. But some can be found in published sources, and some more is available from commercial organisations that monitor the pharmaceutical industry, notably from the leading organization monitoring the pharmaceutical industry, IMS Health.[3] In this paper, I draw upon these different sources of evidence to illustrate some general trends and patterns. Whilst the interpretation of the detailed figures is subject to many qualifications, and actual numbers should be regarded simply as indicative, they are sufficiently robust for these purposes.

Over the decade from 1990 to 2000, the growth in the value of sales of psychiatric drugs is constant, yet uneven in different regions of the world (Table 3.1):[4]

In South America it has grown by 201.1 percent, in South Africa by 55.9 percent, and in Pakistan by 137.8 percent. In the 'more developed' regions, Japan has grown by 49.6 percent from an initially low base level of sales, in Europe, from a relatively high base, growth has been by 126.1 percent, and growth in the value of sales in the United States been by a phenomenal 638 percent. Within these regions, the value of psychiatric drugs dispensed at pharmacies and hospitals as a proportion of total drugs dispensed in this way varies greatly. At the end of the decade in the United States, sales of prescribed psychiatric drugs amounted to almost $19 billion—almost 18 percent

Table 3.1
Sales of Psychiatric Drugs 1990–2000 in Selected Regions in US Dollars

	1990	1992	1994	1996	1998	2000
USA	2502703	3550709	4841698	6968129	11619747	15203486
Europe	2110420	2689811	2746571	3916055	4421800	4741863
Japan	648050	825424	1094386	1078850	939026	1301840
South America	254148	307091	466861	587906	695702	704153
South Africa	34395	54443	54740	60300	54562	62498
Pakistan	10944	14400	22676	31403	25882	26578

Source: IMS Health

of a total pharmaceutical market of $107 billion,[5] while the market in Japan, at $1.36 billion, amounted to less than 3 percent of a total pharmaceutical market of $49.1 billion.[6]

Of course, these data on the market for prescription drugs and its growth are affected by the relative costs of the drugs, pricing decisions of manufacturers for particular regions, financial regimes in operation in different national health services, and the availability of certain medications on a non-prescription, over-the-counter basis. Hence financial data does not accurately represent changes in the rates of prescribing of these psychiatric drugs. A better indication of this is trends in terms of standard dosage units (see note 2 for an explanation of this measure) (Table 3.2):

These data show that the rising trend in prescription of psychiatric medication from 1990 to 2000 is less marked when measured in standard dosage units. In the more developed regions, the United States shows a growth of 70.1 percent, Europe shows a growth of 26.9 percent, Japan shows a growth of 30.9 percent. In the less developed regions, South America remains remarkably constant with a growth of only 1.6 percent, South Africa shows a growth of 13.1 percent, but the use of prescription drugs in Pakistan grows by 33.4 percent (although from a low base).[7]

This variation in the quantity of drug prescribes is instructive, but we see a rather different pattern when we relate the number of standard doses prescribed in each region (IMS figures) to its population (our data) (Table 3.3).

These figures for the year 2000 show that the annual rates of prescribing psychiatric drugs are actually remarkably similar in the more developed regions—the United States, Europe and Japan—at an average of around 6.5 million standard doses per 100,000 persons. Similarly, the rate of prescribing in the three less developed regions is roughly similar, although it stands at around 12 percent of that in the more developed regions, or around 750 thousand standard doses per 100,000 persons. However, within these figures, there are significant regional variations in the *proportions* of different classes

Table 3.2
Psychiatric Drug Prescribing 1990–2000 in Selected Regions
in Standard Dosage Units (thousands)

	1990	1992	1994	1996	1998	2000
USA	11636094	12879423	14856674	16595893	19390797	19790765
Europe	18705884	19667032	19936563	21795910	22644170	23729807
Japan	6392769	6642150	6810214	7299802	7516007	8366166
South America	3476141	3459499	3311034	3352184	3351119	3532715
South Africa	284097	309715	319443	387332	348032	321181
Pakistan	631188	680381	874609	927253	868879	841957

Source: IMS Health

of psychiatric drugs being prescribed. In the United States, antidepressants form a much higher proportion of psychiatric drugs than any other region, and antipsychotics, hypnotics and sedatives are proportionally low. High proportions of tranquillizer prescribing are shown in Japan, South America and Pakistan, with correlatively low levels of antidepressant prescriptions. The USA is the only region where psychostimulants such as methylphenidate and amphetamine are a significant proportion of the psychiatric drug market, amounting to almost 10 percent in 2000.

What accounts for the high rates of prescribing psychiatric drugs in the 'more developed' regions of Europe, Japan and the United States? And how can the variations in the prescribing of different classes of drugs be explained? In Europe and the United States, the context has been the fundamental transformation of the locus of psychiatric care from the closed world of the asylum to an open psychiatric system. But many specifically pharmaceutical issues have played a key role. The marketing strategies of the companies, the licensing regimes in force in different regions, the availability of over-the-counter medication which does not show in this prescribing data, the relative costs of the drugs and the funding regimes in place, the beliefs of the medical and psychiatric professionals and the demands of the patients and lay public have all played their part. The consequence has been a fundamental shift in the distinctions and relations between mental and psychological health and illness, perhaps even conceptions of personhood itself.

The United Kingdom

Before considering these issues, it is worth pausing to examine the prescribing data in more detail. Thus, for instance, in the UK, between 1960 (when the average number of inpatients in psychiatric hospitals was around 130,000) and 1980 (when this figure had almost halved to around 70,000) the major growth in the psychiatric drug market was in the use of tranquillizers

Table 3.3
Psychiatric Drug Prescribing 1990–2000 in Selected Regions in Standard
Dosage Units (thousands) per 100,000 Population by Drug Class

	USA	Europe	Japan	South America	South Africa	Pakistan
Antidepressants	3165.91	1834.19	883.65	159.72	213.81	86.76
Antipsychotics	655.04	832.19	1432.7	103.93	137.07	72.98
Tranquilizers	1921.33	2249.23	2820.44	471.14	202.67	381.86
Hypnotics and Sedatives	690.16	1553.18	1444.58	123.56	168.79	39.97
Psychostimulants	685.05	36.73	18.03	5.73	14.65	0.63
Total	7117.47	6505.51	6599.4	864.08	736.99	582.2

Source: IMS Health

(both major and minor)—from around 6 million prescriptions per year to around 24 million (Ghodse and Khan, 1988).

Over the following twenty years, the total number of prescription items dispensed in the four main classes of drug used for psychiatric conditions— hypnotics and anxiolytics, antipsychotics (a re-classification of drugs previously classified as 'major tranquillizers' linked to beliefs about their specificity of action) and antidepressants and stimulants, rose from about 34.5 million items to about 44.5 million—a growth of almost 30 percent (Table 3.4).

A decline in prescriptions for hypnotics and anxiolytics of about 32 percent (from about 24.5m prescription items to about 16.5m prescription items per year) was matched by a rise in prescriptions for antidepressants of about 200 percent (from about 7.5m prescription items to around 22m prescription items per year).[8] I will return to the increase in the use of antidepressants later. The small increase in the number of prescriptions dispensed for dexamphetamine and methylphenidate might seem surprising, in view of the contemporary debates about the rise of the use of these drugs for the treatment of Attention Deficit Hyperactivity Disorder. But the overall rise in prescription items dispensed—of about 130 percent—from just over 111 thousand items in 1980 to just over 260 thousand in 2000—disguises the increase in the *quantity* of the drugs being prescribed which has risen almost five-fold, from 6,280,790 standard units in 1980 to 29,358,340 in 2000: almost two thirds of this growth is accounted for by Ritalin which was first introduced to the UK in 1991. The net ingredient cost of these ADHD related drugs rose from £72,970 in 1980 to a staggering £29,358,340 in the year 2000. The total cost of all these classes of psychiatric drugs rose tenfold in the period from 1980 to 2000, from around £50m per annum to around £530m in 2000. However this is broadly consistent with the rising cost of the drug bill generally: expenditure on psychiatric drugs remains at about 8 percent of NHS drug expenditure. This is a point that should be born in mind throughout the paper: the increasing worldwide dependence of health services on commercial pharmaceuticals is not restricted to psychiatric drugs and much of the growth in this sector is in line with that in drugs used for other conditions.

The United States

Data on overall trends in psychiatric drug prescribing in the United States in the period from 1955 to 1980—which would include drugs dispensed in hospitals, by Community Mental Health Centers, and to outpatients in drugstores—is difficult to obtain. It has been estimated that by the mid 1970s more than one fifth of the non-institutionalized population received at least one prescription of psychotropic drugs annually; that in 1977, annual US expenditure on such drugs totalled $850 million; and that in 1974 there were 70 million prescriptions for Valium (diazepam) and Librium (chlordiazepoxide) amounting to 3 billion tablets of Valium and 1 billion tablets of Librium (Brown, 1985: 150). Figures on prescriptions dispensed by drugstores or pharmacies show that the total numbers of prescriptions dispensed in this way actually peaked in the early 1970s, and by 1980 the numbers more or less returned to their1964 levels. This pattern that is largely explained by the rise and fall of the use of minor tranquillizers (Smith, 1991).

The first of the minor tranquillizers, mebrobromate, marketed by Wallace under the name of Miltown, and by Wyeth as Equanil came onto the American market in 1955, amid a welter of favourable publicity about 'happy pills' and 'aspirin for the soul' (my account is derived from Smith, 1991). Demand soon became greater than for any other drug marketed in the USA and around 35 other 'tranquillizers' were brought to market, each claiming to be better than the others. These drugs displaced the barbiturates and other sedatives from their place in the pharmacopoeia, although both doctors and lay people often confused them with chlorpromazine and reserpine, and referred to them all as 'tranquillizers'. By the end of the 1950s, a number of critical reviews were published, arguing that the available studies failed to show that meprobromate was more effective than placebo in treating anxiety; some claimed that, in fact, it was not less toxic than Phenobarbital. In any event, this first generation of minor tranquillizers were themselves soon to be displaced. Librium, developed and marketed by Roche, was the first of the benzodiazepines to come to market, and it soon became the most prescribed drug in the USA. However it soon turned out that it had some undesirable side effects and could cause fits if suddenly discontinued. Valium, also marketed by Roche, displaced Librium from its top spot in 1969 (Shorter, 1997: 319):[9]

Table 3.4

Psychiatric Drug Prescribing (England) 1980–2000: Number of Prescription Items Dispensed (thousands)

Drug Class	1980	1982	1984	1986	1988	1990	1992	1994	1996	1998	2000
Hypnotics and Anxiolytics	24459.81	24373.54	22035.62	21869.8	19641.86	17471.39	16850.61	15969.99	15882.11	16243.85	16463.64
Drugs Used in Psychoses & Related Disorders	2437.826	2350.413	2341.821	2507.537	2771.258	3039.066	3793.038	4273.217	4825.677	5391.665	5873.716
Antidepressant drugs	7369.367	7312.388	6885.619	7029.186	7348.989	8026.669	9914.33	11816.44	14960.61	18424.47	22021.84
Central Nervous System Stimulants	213.109	135.06	80.222	74.667	62.324	64.397	75.713	96.693	153.944	224.074	269.306

Source: Government Statistical Service

By 1970, one woman in five and one man in thirteen was using 'minor tranquilliz-ers and sedatives,' meaning mainly the benzos . . . For the first time, psychiatrists were able to offer their patients a potent drug, unlike the mild Miltown, that did not sedate them . . . The share of psychiatric patients receiving prescriptions in-creased from a quarter of all office visits in 1975 to fully one-half by 1990 (from 25.3 percent to 50.2 percent) With the benzodiazapines as the entering wedge, psychiatry became increasingly a specialty oriented to the provision of medication.

By the mid–1970s, the term Valium was being used generically to mean tranquillizer (Smith, 1991: 12). But, in what was to become a familiar pat-tern, initial professional enthusiasm, public eagerness and glowing reports about efficacy gave way to critical reviews calling for caution and further study. And before long, their were reports of 'overuse' and cries of alarm from some doctors and the press. The manufacturers, supported by many respectable physicians, met theses alarms by arguing that the drugs could, in fact, be used appropriately—the problem could be solved by issuing clear guidelines for prescribing. Nonetheless, in response to publicly expressed concerns, a series of Congressional hearings from 1959 to 1965, and again in the 1970s, considered various aspects of these tranquillizers and other drugs, examining costs, prescribing practices, promotional literature and advertise-ments. In 1962, an Act strengthened the powers of the Food and Drug Ad-ministration in evaluating the safety of drugs and regulating the ways in which they were advertised and promoted. Following this legislation, on several occasions, the FDA required the manufacturers of minor tranquilliz-ers to modify their advertising, labelling and product information. They were instructed to remove the implications that the drugs should be used for man-aging the worries and stresses of everyday life, and to stress the potential dangers of dependence and addiction and the difficulties consequent upon discontinuation. In 1975, the FDA moved the benzodiazapines and meprobromate to its 'schedule IV' which controlled 'refills' or repeat pre-scriptions, and also imposed reporting requirements on pharmacists: predict-ably, prescribing declined (Smith, 1991).

What of other psychiatric drugs over this period? Data on prescriptions filled at pharmacies, even though they do not reflect hospital prescribing, show that while prescriptions for antidepressants rise until 1974 and then stay roughly constant, those for anti-psychotics peak at the same date and then fall slowly. The explanation for this pattern for antipsychotics may lie in the timescale of the acceptance that these drugs, especially when prescribed at high doses over long periods, produced adverse effects—notably the irrevers-ible condition that became known as tardive dyskinesia. In the early years of the use of neuroleptic drugs, psychiatrists tended to assume that so-called extra-pyramidal effects in patients being administered neuroleptic medica-tion—Parkinson like symptoms—were signs that the drugs were working, and hence markers of a therapeutic reaction. This account is derived from

Table 3.5
Psychiatric Drug Prescriptions Filled in US Drugstores 1964–1980

	1964	1966	1968	1970	1972	1974	1976	1978	1980
Antipsychotics	14.3	16.9	17.8	21.9	23.2	25.4	22.2	18.8	18
Antianxiety	45.1	58.8	67.8	83.2	95.1	102.4	96.8	81.1	71.4
Antidepressants	9.5	12.8	16.3	19.8	25	32.3	31.9	29.5	29.9
Stimulants	26.7	26.1	27.2	28.2	11.6	6.5	6.6	4.3	2.4
Sedatives	24.1	23.8	22.1	23.8	20.7	20	19.8	18.3	17.3
Hypnotics	29.4	35.7	33.8	37.5	38.7	29.4	21.8	16.6	13.8
TOTAL*	149.2	173.9	185.1	214.4	214.5	216	191.1	168.6	152.8

* Columns may not add up because of rounding

Source: M. Smith, 1991 drawing on National Prescription Audit, IMS America Ltd. Drugs were reclassified and reorganized by Balter (1975) at the Psychopharmacology research Branch of NIMH for years 1964–73, and by Smith (1991) for subsequent years

Gelman, 1999, and Healy, 2002). Most believed that these effects disappeared when the medication was discontinued, although there were reports from the mid 1950s that Parkinson like symptoms and other effects might persist—in the so-called 'neurotoxic reactions' (Hall, 1956, cited in Gelman, 1999: 31). The syndrome of late onset severe movement abnormalities most noticeable in the mouth, lips and tongue which now known as tardive dyskinesia was actually first described within a few years of the introduction of the neuroleptics (Leonard, 1992: 129).[10] The definitive English language article on neurological complications of the antipsychotics was published in 1961, but there was continuing scepticism from many psychiatrists about the reality of this problem and its relation to drugs (Ayd, 1961). Over the 1960s many leading psychiatrists involved in the developments of psychopharmacology suggested that the dyskinesias could be demonstrated in untreated patients and were actually a sign of the illness or that, in any event, problems without the drugs were worse than those caused by the drugs. But by the late 1960s, the view that long-term treatment might cause a problem was being given authoritative support (Ayd, 1967; Crane, 1968.). The FDA and the American College of Neuropsychopharmacology set up a Task Force which reported in 1973: it acknowledged that tardive dyskinesia could be presumed to result from treatment with antipsychotic drugs. Whilst the condition was "an undesirable but occasionally unavoidable price to be paid for the benefits of prolonged neuroleptic therapy," if possible "neuroleptics should be discontinued at the first sign of tardive dyskinesia. Whilst the unnecessary use of high doses in chronic cases should be minimized" the medications could still "be used with confidence—the overwhelming clinical and objective evidence indicates that a majority of schizophrenic patients" should continue to receive medication (Task Force, 1973). Despite this cautious, vague and generally optimistic tone, the formal professional recognition of the condition and its causation opened the door for legal action. According to David Healy, the first case was in 1974, when SmithKline & French settled a claim for Thorazine induced tardive dyskinesia and it seems that this led to the willingness of the manufacturer to acknowledge the risk of tardive dyskinesia in package inserts (Lennard and Bernstein,1974). Other lawsuits followed, focussing on informed consent, medical negligence, misdiagnosis, violation of civil rights and product liability. The American Psychiatric Association set up a task force chaired by Ross Baldessarini which reported in 1980: it acknowledged in its official summary that in routine neuroleptic drug use over six months to two years, at least 10–20 percent of patients would get more than minimum tardive dyskinesia.

By the 1980s, psychiatrists and the pharmaceutical companies were increasingly involved in litigation. According to Peter Breggin, on 7th October 1983, the official APA newspaper *Psychiatric News* carried the headline 'TARDIVE DYSKINESIA COURT CASES UNDERSCORE IMPORTANCE OF APA REPORT' and reported that two precedent-setting cases had been settled for $76,000 and $1 million, and a headline in the January 1984 issue of *Clinical Psychiatry News* warned its readers to 'EXPECT A FLOOD OF TARDIVE DYSKINESIA MALPRACTICE SUITS' (Breggin 1993: 97, he is citing *Psychiatric News*, 7 October 1983 and *Clinical Psychiatry News*, January 1984). In 1985 the American Psychiatric Association wrote to each of its members to repeat its warning that "at least 10–20 percent of patients in mental hospitals" and at least 40 percent of longer term patients, would get more than minimal signs of tardive dyskinesia, confirmed that children were also at risk, and stated that they were "concerned about the apparent increase of litigation over tardive dyskinesia" (Breggin, 1993: 97). By the end of the decade, tardive dyskinesia lawsuits were on the increase, and, according to *The Psychiatric Times*, out-of-court settlements were averaging $300,000 and jury awards were averaging $1 million. The first 'golden age' of psychopharmaceuticals which had begun with Thorazine (Largactil in Europe) and which saw the development of a host of other antipsychotics: thioridazine (Melleril), haloperidol (Haldol), triflueroperazine (Stelazine) came to an end (Healy, 2002).

But despite the law suits, antipsychotic drugs had become central to the rationale of deinstitutionalization in the United States by the mid-sixties and to the management of the decarcerated—or never incarcerated—population. The gradual acceptance of the reality of tardive dyskinesia, of its prevalence, and of its causation by drug treatment could not reverse the policy or the use of the drugs. A dual strategy took shape. On the one hand, the pharmaceutical industry met with FDA to discuss how to label the propensity of their compounds to cause tardive dyskinesia. On the other hand, the search began for alternative drugs that would not produce such damaging side effects. This track would eventually lead to the marketing of the so-called 'atypical neuroleptics'. But it also underpinned other attempts to engineer so-called 'smart drugs' which could be said to directly target the neurochemical bases of the illness, or at least the symptoms, with the minimum of collateral damage. The first fruit of this line of thinking would be Prozac, soon followed by closely related Selective Serotonin Reuptake Inhibitors. These were apparently 'smart' targeted drugs that seemed to have minimal adverse effects, were safe in overdose, seemed not to be 'addictive' and, so it seemed, did not cause tardive dyskinesia. But it would not be long after the introduction of Prozac and its sisters that these assumptions would be challenged, and the shadow of the law would once more fall over psychopharmacology.

Despite the problems of adverse effects that affected both the minor tranquillizers and the anti-psychotics, the dependence of psychiatry on psychopharmacology was entrenched over the 1980s. Indeed, other legal decisions reinforced the overall push towards psychopharmacology as the treatment of choice for most psychiatric conditions. The famous Osheroff case brought in 1982 involved a claim of malpractice against Chestnut Lodge whose psychodynamic approach was made famous by Hannah Green in *I Never Promised You a Rose Garden* on the grounds that he was denied available psychiatric medication that had proven efficacy. While the case was in fact settled out of court in 1987, and thus did not set a legal precedent, it generated much discussion. It was used to argue that the most valid and convincing evidence of efficacy must be derived from randomised control trials, and that psychotherapies had not passed any equivalent of the scrutiny maintained by the FDA over drugs. From this point on, psychiatrists and psychiatric institutions had to think of the legal consequences whenever they chose *not* to prescribe medication for their patients.

Other changes in the US health care system in the 1980s also contributed to the rise of psychopharmacology. The first of these relates to research and development. The pharmaceutical industry's potion of total US health R&D funding grew from 13 percent in 1980 to 52 percent in 1995. During this same period, despite substantial increases in financial support for health research through the National Institutes of Health, the federal government's share of total health R&D funding dropped from 57 percent to 37 percent. Non-profit organizations contributed 4 percent to health R&D funding and state and local governments added 7 percent (National Center for Health Statistics, 2002: Table 125). When pharmaceutical companies provide a majority of funding for research and development in the US health sector, they clearly have considerable power, not just to determine new product development, but also to shape the very styles of thought which organise responses to mental health and mental illness. Secondly, the funding of health care provision has shifted with the introduction of managed care and the reduction of in-patient treatment. Since 1980, pressure on funding in the health care system, amongst other things, has led to a decline in overall rates of hospitalisation for all conditions by over 30 percent (Popovic and Hall, 1999). Although only 12 percent of the US population is covered by Medicaid, Medicaid patients account for 50 percent of all hospitalisations for schizophrenia and 28 percent of all hospitalisations for depression, and there is great pressure to reduce Medicaid budgets (Elixhauser et al, 1997), 2000). And in the regime of 'managed care', a Health Management Organisation acts as an intermediary between the users of health care services, the funders and the providers. These HMOs are commercial companies whose profits depend upon their success in implementing a range of what are euphemistically termed 'cost-containment techniques'—procedural rules governing the choices of doctors and others, for example by placing strict limits on periods of hospitalisation, refusing to authorise requests by medical staff for extended stay, controlling the drug budget by monitoring prescribing practices in the interests of cost saving and insisting on generic alternatives where available, requiring physicians to adopt a step-care technique in which they begin with the lowest cost treatment and only progress to higher-cost alternatives if these are deemed 'ineffective', delimiting the amount of service, and the type of service, which may be provided for particular conditions. In this context, drug treatment outside hospital becomes the treatment of choice, although short-term, focused, behavioural or cognitive therapy may also be funded, designed to ensure that the patient has the in sight to recognise that he or she is suffering from an illness, and hence to increase the likelihood of compliance with medication.

Thus, perhaps, the current levels of psychiatric drug prescribing in the United States should come as no surprise (Table 3.6).

In the year from July 1999 to June 2000, sales of psychiatric drugs, at ex-manufacturer prices, totalled 15,203,486,000 US dollars (1990: 2,502,703,000). 58.4 percent was for antidepressants (1990: 38.2 percent). 22.8 percent was for antipsychotics (1990: 10.1 percent): the increase in value here presumably arises from the marketing of the so-called atypical antipsychotics since, as we see below, it does not reflect an increase in numbers of these drugs prescribed. 9.3 percent was for tranquillizers (1990: 39.5 percent), 5.5 percent was for hypnotics and sedatives (1990: 9.2 percent) and 3.9 percent was for psychostimulants (1990: 3.0 percent).

Of course, such figures are affected by variations in price, for example the lapse of patents on certain drugs and their availability in generic forms.[11] A more accurate guide to trends is provided by data expressed in terms of the number of standard doses sold (Table 3.7).

Over the decade from 1990–2000 there were two principal contributors to the overall growth in prescribing. Tranquillizers show a 32.5 percent growth over the decade, peaking and falling away after 1998. Antidepressants show a steady growth over the period, amounting to 205 percent overall. Indeed the growth in use of antidepressants may have contributed to the fall off in the use of tranquillizers in the mid–1990s, because it appears that Prozac and the other SSRI drugs were now being prescribed for the treatment of conditions where minor tranquillizers would previously have been given. At the end of the decade, antidepressants were by far the most extensively prescribed psychiatric drug, amounting to around 45 percent of all drug prescribing, with tranquillizers constituting around 27 percent. However, whilst the commonly accepted view is that the growth in the diagnosis of depression is linked, more or less directly, to the availability of the new antidepressants, the figures do not entirely bear that out (Table 3.8).

The SSRI family of antidepressants do show a spectacular rise of over 1300 percent over this period—with final prescribing levels more or less equally split between fluoxetine (Prozac), Sertraline (Zoloft) and Paroxetine (Paxil) though with the newer SNRIs coming up fast. But the traditional antidepressants also show a steady rise, though from a higher base, and by 2001 they still amount to 48 percent of the total antidepressant market. It seems that, however it is treated, what is involved here is the increase in the diagnosis of something called depression, as that which is potentially treatable by antidepressants. Although, as we shall see below, these antidepressants have spread beyond their initial niche, and extended their claims of efficacy to a whole class of relatively new conditions—the anxiety disorders.

It is widely accepted that there is something of an epidemic of Attention deficit Hyperactivity Disorder in the United States. The aggregated data for prescriptions of psychostimulants from 1990 to 2000 (in Table 3.7) thus initially seem surprisingly. This illustrates some of the cautions that need to be used in interpreting this aggregated data, which combines the trends in prescribing in the different drugs within each class. The class of psychostimulants as a whole has shown very little overall growth over this decade, remaining at just under 10 percent of all prescribed psychiatric drugs. But it covers a range of different preparations, not just amphetamines, dexamphetamine, methamphetamine, and methylphenidate—the CNS stimulants used in the treatment of ADHD. Two other groups of drug classed as psychostimulants were prescribed heavily in the United States up until the mid–1990s. The first of these were the amphetamine based drugs that were marketed heavily as anti-obesity drugs up to the mid 1990s, including dexfenfluramine (Adifax; Diomeride; Dipondal; Glypolix; Isomeride; Isomerin; Obesine; Redux; Siran) and fenfluramine. These were removed from the US market around 1997 after evidence of severe adverse effects was finally accepted (Muncie, 2001). The second group of drugs were stimulants based

Table 3.6
Psychiatric drug sales in USA 1990–2000 in US Dollars (thousands)

	1990	1992	1994	1996	1998	2000
Antidepressants	955627	1549877	2709275	4190128	6826620	8883764
Antipsychotics	253469	419886	678855	1106167	2345639	3462159
Tranquillisers	987506	1201197	895356	794615	1255558	1418483
Hypnotics & sedatives	230392	225705	281234	431364	598286	836712
Psychostimulants	75709	154044	276979	445854	593644	602368
Total	2502703	3550709	4841698	6968129	11619747	15203486

Source: IMS Health

on caffeine and epinephrine, such as Viviran, which also disappear from the IMS data in the mid–1990s, as their status changed and they became available over-the-counter. If we consider just the drugs used to treat ADHD, data provided to the US Drug Enforcement Agency by IMS Health show that after increases in the early 1990s, prescriptions for methylphenidate levelled off at about 11 million per year, and those for amphetamines, primarily Adderall (which is an amphetamine-dextroamphetamine mixed salt) increased dramatically since 1996, from about 1.3 million per year to about 6 million per year. Collectively this indicates an increase of prescriptions for ADHD by a factor of 5 in the period 1991 to 1998. Our own IMS data shows that the total number of standard units prescribed rose by almost 800 percent from 1990 to 2000, from around 225 million to around 1,800 million, the early growth being in Methylphenidate—Ritalin—whose dominance has recently been challenged by dexamphetamine—Adderall.

The epidemic of prescribing for ADHD in the United States seems a pretty clear example of a 'culture bound syndrome'. The medications used here are potential drugs of abuse subject to the provisions of Article 16 of the 1971 Convention on Psychotropic Substances, and their manufacture and consumption is monitored by the United Nations Narcotics Control Board, which reports annually. The US Drug Enforcement Administration used UN Narcotics Control Board figures in its congressional testimony in May 2000, to claim that domestic sales of methylphenidate, calculated in kilograms per year, had risen by 500 percent from 1991 to 1999, and those for amphetamine had risen even more sharply, by 2000 percent, although from a lower base (U. S. Drug Enforcement Agency, 2000). Data in the Narcotics Control Board reports for 1995, 1996 and 1998 (Figures 3.11 and 3.12) show the trends for the consumption of methylphenidate and amphetamines in various countries from 1993 to 1998.

Overall, these data show that by the year 2000, around seven million standard doses of psychiatric medication were being prescribed in the United

Table 3.7
Psychiatric Drug Prescribing in USA 1990–2000
in Standard Dosage Units (thousands)

	1990	1992	1994	1996	1998	2000
Antidepressants	2881653	3698308	4764867	5820566	7474836	8195833
Antipsychotics	1104978	1389070	1508067	1482828	1505878	1662413
Tranquillisers	4031476	4335569	5027406	5732952	6719652	5458249
Hypnotics & sedatives	1722688	1688623	1720530	1787488	1695815	1694641
Psycho-stimulants	1895298	1767854	1835805	1772060	1994616	1961087
Total	11636094	12879423	14856674	16595893	19390797	18972223

Source: IMS Health

States per 100,000 population—or an average of around 70 doses per person per year.

Accounting for Psychopharmacology

The patterns of growth in the commercial value of the market for psychopharmaceuticals are clear enough, at least in the United States and the UK, and in Europe more generally. As we have seen earlier, there are broad similarities between overall rates of psychiatric drug prescribing proportional to population size in the USA, Europe and Japan, and broad similarities, although at a much lower level, between the three 'less developed' regions of South Africa, South America and Pakistan.

The most interesting comparator for the UK and the USA is Japan. As we saw earlier, while the overall rate of psychiatric drug prescribing in Japan is broadly similar to that in Europe and the United States, at around 6.6 million SUs per annum per 100,000 population, a far greater proportion of those prescriptions are for tranquillizers and anti-psychotics and less than 15 percent are for antidepressants. Japan seems not to have had the wave of concerns over the benzodiazepines and the traditional neuroleptics that shook psychopharmacology in the West nor does it seem to have experienced the 'epidemic' of depression and anti-depressants (Healy 2002). Indeed fluoxetine hydrochloride was never marketed in Japan, and the first SSRI type drugs (fluvoxamine and paroxetine) did not come on the market until 1999 and 2000. And ADHD is only just being 'discovered' in Japan.

How, then, can we account for the specificity of the UK and USA? The best researched case is that of depression. Of course, the simplest explanation for the remarkable rise in diagnosis of depression and the prescription of antidepressants over the last decade is, first, that that depression is more

Table 3.8
Antidepressant Prescribing in USA 1990–2000
in Standard Dosage Units (thousands)

	1990	1992	1994	1996	1998	2000
SSRI anti-depressants	376,838	569,303	1,422,506	2,246,097	3,279,834	4,390,633
All other anti-depressants	2,504,746	3,128,950	3,342,347	3,574,462	4,194,993	4,080,530
Total anti-depressants	2,881,584	3,698,253	4,764,853	5,820,559	7,474,827	8,471,163

Source: IMS Health

common than has previously been realised, and second that we now have powerful and effective new drug therapies to treat it. The first seems to be the view, for example, of the World Health Organisation, whose 2001 report claimed depression affects over 340 million people worldwide, argued that it is exacerbated by social factors such as an aging population, poverty, unemployment and similar stressors, and predicted "By the year 2020, if current trends for demographic and epidemiological transition continue, the burden of depression will increase to 5.7 percent of the total burden of disease, becoming the second leading cause of DALYs [disability adjusted life years] lost. Worldwide it will be second only to ischemic heart disease for DALYs lost for both sexes. In the developed regions, depression will then be the highest ranking cause of burden of disease" (WHO 2001: 30).

The second is certainly the view, not just of the drug companies and some psychiatrists, but also of some key campaigning groups. Thus by 2001 the National Alliance for the Mentally Ill proclaims mental illness a treatable brain disorder treated with medication just like diabetes is treated with insulin:[12]

Mental illnesses are disorders of the brain that disrupt a person's thinking, feeling, moods, and ability to relate to others. Just as diabetes is a disorder of the pancreas, mental illnesses are disorders of the brain that often result in a diminished capacity for coping with the ordinary demands of life.

Mental illnesses do not discriminate; they affect people of every age, gender, race, religion, or socioeconomic status. Mental illnesses are not the result of personal weakness, lack of character, or poor upbringing. In the United States, *over seven million adults and over five million children and adolescents suffer from a serious, chronic brain disorder.* These illnesses have a great impact on society. *Four of the top ten leading causes of disability are mental illnesses* including major depression, bipolar disorder, schizophrenia and obsessive compulsive disorder, and *the estimated cost of mental health care is over $150 billion per year.* But far more important is the effect untreated mental illness has on the lives of individuals and their loved ones.

Table 3.9
Psychostimulant Prescribing USA 1990–2000
in Standard Dosage Units (thousands)

	1990	1992	1994	1996	1998	2000
Methylphenidate	200516	386574	730923	1064482	1077283	815879
Dexamphetamine	24518	42969	74751	166974	359243	572554
Amphetamine	0	0	3819	18953	168776	394050
Total Psychostimulants	225034	429543	809493	1250409	1605302	1782483

Source: IMS Health

These brain disorders are treatable. As a person with diabetes, takes insulin, most people with serious mental illness need medication to help control symptoms. Supportive counseling, self-help groups, housing, vocational rehabilitation, income assistance and other community services can also provide support and stability, contributing to recovery.

And it says of depression:[13]

Whatever the specific causes of depression, scientific research has firmly established that major depression is a biological brain disorder.

Norepinephrine, serotonin, and dopamine are three neurotransmitters (chemical messengers that transmit electrical signals between brain cells) thought to be involved with major depression. Scientists believe that if there is a chemical imbalance in these neurotransmitters, then clinical states of depression result. Antidepressant medications work by increasing the availability of neurotransmitters or by changing the sensitivity of the receptors for these chemical messengers.

Scientists have also found evidence of a genetic predisposition to major depression. There is an increased risk for developing depression when there is a family history of the illness. Not everyone with a genetic predisposition develops depression, but some people probably have a biological make-up that leaves them particularly vulnerable to developing depression. Life events, such as the death of a loved one, a major loss or change, chronic stress, and alcohol and drug abuse, may trigger episodes of depression. Some illnesses and some medications may also trigger depressive episodes. It is also important to note that many depressive episodes occur spontaneously and are not triggered by a life crisis, physical illness, or other risks.

In both the UK and the USA, campaigns to 'recognise depression' operate in these terms: arguing that depression is an illness, often inherited in the form of increased susceptibility and triggered by life events, that it is often untreated, and that drugs form the first line of treatment—for example in the recent Defeat Depression in the UK. This view of the biochemical basis of, and treatability of, depression has also been popularised in a number of autobiographical accounts by well-known public figures: for example, *Dark-*

Table 3.10
Calculated Daily Consumption of Methylphenidate
(Defined Daily Doses) per 1000 Inhabitants in
Selected Regions

	1993–1995	1994–1996	1996–1998
USA	2.49	3.14	3.42
Canada	1.32	1.58	2.03
Israel	0.3	0.54	0.35
Australia	0.33	0.51	0.67
UK and NI	*	0.49	0.33
New Zealand	0.22	0.39	0.81
Norway	0.22	0.17	0.4
Chile	0.1	0.16	*
South Africa	*	0.12	*

Source: UN Narcotics Control Board, 1997, 1998, 2000

* = figure not available

ness Visible by William Styron, or *The Noonday Demon* by Andrew Solomon (Styron, 1991, Solomon, 2001).

Most of those who have explored this rise are not satisfied with such a 'realist' account. There is certainly convincing epidemiological evidence that such factors as poor housing, poverty, unemployment or precarious and stressful working conditions are associated with increased levels of psychiatric morbidity. But these factors do not seem sufficient to account for such a rapid

Table 3.11
Calculated Daily Consumption of Amphetamine
(Defined Daily Doses) per 1000 Inhabitants in
Selected Regions

	1993–1995	1994–1996	1996–1998
USA	1.62	1.19	1.82
Canada	0.16	0.2	0.26
Israel	*	*	*
Australia	0.44	0.74	1.01
UK and NI	0.31	0.72	0.17
New Zealand	*	*	*
Norway	*	*	
Chile	*	*	0.42
South Africa	*	*	*
Iceland	0.16	0.38	0.2
Sweden	0.07	0.08	*

Source: UN Narcotics Control Board, 1997, 1998, 2000

* = figure not available

Table 3.12
Proportions of Psychiatric Drugs Prescribed in Various Regions in 2000,
Expressed as Percentage of Total Prescribing of Standard Dosage Units per
100,000 population

	USA	Europe	Japan	South America	South Africa	Pakistan
Antidepressants	44.5	28.2	13.4	18.5	29.0	14.9
Antipsychotics	9.2	12.8	21.7	12.0	18.6	12.5
Tranquillisers	27.0	34.6	42.7	54.5	27.5	65.6
Hypnotics and Sedatives	9.7	23.9	21.9	14.3	22.9	6.9
Psycho-stimulants	9.6	0.6	0.3	0.7	2.0	0.1
Total	100.0	100.0	100.0	100.0	100.0	100.0

Source: IMS Health

increase in diagnosis and prescription, even if it was accepted that contemporary social conditions were more pathogenic than those that preceded them. Older sociological explanations that linked the rise of mental disorders to general features of social organization have fallen out of fashion—for example, the suggestion that urban life generates neurasthenia or that capitalism isolates individuals and hence places strains on them that lead to mental breakdown—with the possible exception of feminist accounts in terms of patriarchy. Alain Ehrenberg has recently suggested that the very shape of depression is the reciprocal of the new conceptions of individuality that have emerged in modern societies (Ehrenberg, 2000). At the start of the twentieth century, he argues, the norm of individuality was founded on guilt, and hence the exemplary experience of pathology what that of neurosis. But in societies that celebrates individual responsibility and personal initiative, the reciprocal of that norm of active self-fulfilment is depression, now largely defined as a pathology involving the lack of energy, an inability to perform the tasks required for work or relations with others. Whilst such a global cultural account is unconvincing, it is certainly the case that the shape and incidence of the pathology of depression in western developed nations can only be understood in relation to contemporary conceptions of the self involving the obligation of freedom: responsibility, choice and active self-fulfilment. The continual incitements to action, to choice, to self-realisation and self improvement act as a norm in relation to which individuals govern themselves and are governed by others, and against which differences are judged as pathologies.

But other factors also need to be addressed. First, no doubt, these developments are related to the increasing salience of health to the aspirations and ethics of the wealthy west, the readiness of those who live in such cultures to define their problems and their solutions in terms of health and illness, and the tendency for contemporary understandings of health and illness to be posed largely in terms of treatable bodily malfunctions. Second, they are undoubtedly linked to a more profound transformation in personhood. The sense of ourselves as 'psychological' individuals that developed across the twentieth century—beings inhabited by a deep internal space shaped by biography and experience, the source of our individuality and the locus of our discontents—is being supplemented or displaced by what I have termed 'somatic individuality' (Novas and Rose, 2000). By somatic individuality, I mean the tendency to define key aspects of ones individuality in bodily terms, that is to say to think of oneself as 'embodied', and to understand that body in the language of contemporary biomedicine. To be a 'somatic' individual, in this sense, is to code one's hopes and fears in terms of this biomedical body, and to try to reform, cure or improve oneself by acting on that body. At one end of the spectrum this involved reshaping the visible body, through diet, exercise, and tattooing. At the other end, it involves understanding troubles and desires in terms of the interior 'organic' functioning of the body, and seeking to reshape that—usually by pharmacological interventions. Whilst discontents might previously have been mapped onto a psychological space—the space of neurosis, repression, psychological trauma—they are now mapped upon the body itself, or one particular organ of the body—the brain.

This is not the place to explore the processes that have led to such discontents and their treatments being understood in this way—premised on the belief that the brain itself is the crucial locus of the disorder and the target of the treatment. However it is possible to consider one limited aspect of this, which concerns the reshaping of particular kinds of experiences as mental disorders amenable to pharmacological treatment. Most notable, here, is the way in which many pathologies of the active, responsible, choosing self have come to be seen as depression, and depression itself has come to be linked with anxiety disorders—in particular generalized anxiety disorder, social anxiety disorder, panic disorder, obsessive compulsive disorder and post traumatic stress disorder.[14] This involves a co-production of the disease, the diagnosis and the treatment. This can be seen in the strategies of psychiatrists, of health care professionals, of some support and anti-stigma groups, but most significantly of the pharmaceutical companies themselves. The earliest (and most quoted) example of this co-production of disorder and treatment concerns depression. Frank Ayd had undertaken one of the key clinical trials for Merck, which filed the first patent for the use of amitryptiline as an antidepressant. Ayd's book of 1961, *Recognizing the Depressed Patient* argued that much depression was unrecognized, but that it did not require a psychiatrist for its diagnosis—it "could be diagnosed on general medical wards and in primary care offices" (Healy, 1997: 76). Merck bought up 50,000 copies of Frank Ayd's book (Ayd, 1961) and distributed it worldwide. As Healy argues, Merck not only sold amitryptiline, it sold a new idea of what depression was and how it could be diagnosed and treated. From this point on it appeared that there was an untapped market for antidepressant drugs outside hospitals. There was also an audience for the idea that the certain drugs specifically targeted the neurochemical basis of depression, and pharmaceutical companies invested funds in research to develop antidepressants,. Rating scales to identify depression were developed (notably the Hamilton depression scale); these generated new norms of depression which were not only used to test the efficacy of drugs, but also changed the shape of the disorder itself. Across the 1960s depression became linked to levels of secretion and reuptake of brain amines in the synapses—gradually coming to focus on serotonin. The serotonin hypothesis of depression was formulated, and despite its obvious scientific inadequacies, it became the basis of drug development leading to the SSRIs and the basis of a new way of thinking about variations in mood in terms of levels of brain chemicals that penetrated deeply into the imagination of medical practitioners and into popular accounts of depression.

The central presupposition, perhaps more significant than any individual drug, was that of *specificity*. This presupposition was actually three sided. First, it was premised on the neuroscientific belief that these drugs could, and ideally should have a specificity of target. Second, it was premised on the clinical belief that doctors or patients could specifically diagnose each array of changes in mood, will, desire, affect as a discrete condition. Third, it was based on the neuroscientific belief that specific configurations in neurotransmitter systems underlay specific moods, desires, and affect. The three presupposition were then mapped onto one another. Thus the iconic status of Prozac arose less from its greater efficacy in treating clinical depression, than from the belief that it was first 'smart drug', in which a molecule was designed with a shape that would enable it specifically to lock into identified receptor sites in the serotonin system—hence affecting only the specific symptoms being targeted and having a low 'side effect profile'. And, on the other hand, its status was confirmed by clinical reports and popular accounts such as those given by Peter Kramer to Elizabeth Wurtzel of the specific psychological transformations wrought by the drug. These presuppositions have fuelled an industry of commentary—utopian or dystopian—on cosmetic psychopharmacology and the possibilities of reshaping our human nature at will, most recently from Gregory Stock on the and former side and Francis Fukuyama on the latter (Stock, 2002; Fukuyama, 2002). However, as neurochemical and pharmacological research proceeded, the simple belief that there was one kind of receptor for each neurotransmitter was shown to be wrong—in the case of serotonin there were at least seven 'families' of 5HT receptors and most had several subtypes. This might have proved fatal for this explanatory regime, but it did not. It was now argued that each of these subtypes of receptors had a specific function, that anomalies in each type were related to specific psychiatric symptoms, and that they could be ameliorated by drugs designed specifically to affect them.

The premises of specificity were central to the vigorous campaigns that the pharmaceutical companies mounted to marker their products to physicians. Take this advertisement for Lustral (sertraline) published in the *British Journal of Psychiatry* in 1991:

On the one hand, the specific advantages of the molecule in question, sertraline, are stressed—its selectivity, effectiveness, low side-effects, low dependency, compliance and simplicity. On the other that assemblage of virtues is condensed into a simple brand name—Lustral—manufactured by Pfizer (marketed as Zoloft in the USA) with its smiley image and rising sun logo.

Or consider this advertisement for Prozac published in the *American Journal of Psychiatry* in 1995.

"The Prozac promise" to the doctor and his or her patient is to deliver the "therapeutic triad" of convenience, confidence and compliance. But one can note here the increased space in he advertisement devoted to adverse events. This may have something to do with the fact that in Autumn 1994, the first lawsuit against Prozac reached the courtroom in Louisville, concerning Joseph Wesbecker who some five years earlier, shortly after being prescribed Prozac, had shot 28 people at the printing plant where he worked, killing 8 before shooting himself. This case brought longstanding concerns about adverse effects of these drugs into the public domain—concerns about increases in agitation (akathesia) and suicidal ideation in a small but significant number of those administered Prozac which had led the German licensing authorities to insist upon product warning in 1984 before they would issue a licence. As the first generation of the drugs goes out of patent, the manufacturers are also fighting against a shoal of analogous cases. Thus in June 2001, court in Cheyenne, ordered GlaxoSmithKline to pay $6.4m (£4.7m) to the family of Donald Schell who shot his wife, daughter and granddaughter and then killed himself—two days after his GP prescribed Paxil (paroxetine, known as Seroxat in Europe) for depression. The jury decided that the drug was 80 percent responsible for the deaths. And two weeks earlier, in May 2001, an Australian judge ruled that having been prescribed sertraline—Zoloft—which is Australia's most widely used antidepressant—caused David Hawkins to murder his wife and attempt to kill himself: "I am satisfied that but for the Zoloft he had taken he would not have strangled his wife" (Justice Barry O'Keefe).[15] And, if that were not enough, criticisms are now mounting of the difficulties

Figure 3.1
Lustral: "The choice is simple—with bright prospects in mind" *British Journal of Psychiatry*, 1991

of withdrawing from this medication—not dependency as is often suggested, but the severe and unpleasant physical effects—pains, sweating, nausea and much more—which occur when patients who have been taking these drugs for a while cease to take them—no doubt caused by the fact that the molecules act very widely in the body, and the artificial raising of the levels by the drugs leads to a down regulation of the bodies own production of, or sensitivity to the molecules in question.[16]

Recall that Prozac was initially marketed as a specific for mild to moderate depression, but was soon surrounded by claims that it was much more versatile, acting, for example, on eating disorders, obsessive compulsive disorder and even low self-esteem. For some, this questioned the very distinctions and classifications on which modern American psychiatric medicine rests. For a belief in the reciprocal specificity of disorders and drug action implies that the drugs, and the span and limits of their efficacy, should determine the criteria for inclusion in, and the boundaries around, mental disorders. But, more immediately, this diversity of classifications provides a key marketing opportunity. Companies seek to diversify their products and niche market them, either by making minor modifications to produce new molecules, or by licensing their existing drugs as specifics for particular DSM IV diagnostic categories. The best example here concerns the anxiety disorders Social Anxiety Disorder, Panic Disorder and Generalized Anxiety Disorder and their relation, in the first instance, with one particular brand—Paxil owned by GlaxoSmithKline. Let me focus on Generalized Anxiety Disorder (GAD).

As recently as 1987, the section on prevalence of this disorder (coded 300.02) in the third, revised edition of the Diagnostic and Statistical Manual of the American Psychiatric Association said "When other disorders that could account for the anxiety symptoms are ruled out [they previously stipulated that the disorder should not be diagnosed if the worry and anxiety occurs during a mood disorder or a psychotic disorder, for example], the disorder is not commonly diagnosed in clinical samples" (APA, 1987: 252). By the publication of DSM IV, in 1994, the same section read "In a community sample, the lifelong prevalence rate for Generalized Anxiety Disorder was approximately 3 percent, and the lifetime prevalence rate was 5 percent. In anxiety disorder clinics, approximately 12 percent of the individuals present with Generalized Anxiety Disorder" (APA, 1994). In this move, GAD was reframed: the diagnosis could now co-exist with mood disorders, and could be separated out from the general class of mood disorders. The clinical trials of Paxil in the treatment of GAD thus enabled it to be advertised as a specific treatment for this condition, and hence the disorder could be freed, in its public representations at least, from depression. And once it could stand as a diagnosis without subsumption into the class of depression, its prevalence could be recalculated. By April 2001, when GlaxoSmithKline announced that the US Food and Drug Administration (FDA) had approved Paxil for the treatment of GAD—the first SSRI approved for this disorder in the US—it was widely being claimed that GAD affected "more than 10 million Americans, 60 percent of whom are women".[17]

In fact, Paxil had been widely used "off label" for the treatment of GAD before being specifically licensed for the condition. Licensing is significant, however, because it allows marketing for the licensed indication. Hence, as soon as the licence was issued in the Spring of 2001, GlaxoSmithKline en-

Figure 3.2
The Prozac Promise
American Journal of Psychiatry, 1995

gaged in a marketing campaign in the US. What was characteristic about this campaign is that it marketed, not so much the drug, Paxil, as the disease, GAD. Whilst the USA is one of the few countries that allow 'direct to consumer' advertising of prescription drugs—which has grown into a $2.5 billion a year industry since drug advertising legislation was relaxed in 1997— it is not the only country where "disease mongering" has become a key marketing tactic.[18] As Ray Moynihan and others have recently pointed out, this process involves alliances are formed between drug companies anxious to market a product for a particular condition, biosocial groups organised by and for those who suffer from a condition thought to be of that type, and doctors eager to diagnose under-diagnosed problems (Moynihan, Heath and Henry, 2002; Moynihan, 2003). Disease awareness campaigns, directly or indirectly funded by the pharmaceutical company who have the patent for the treatment, point to the misery cause by the apparent symptoms of this undiagnosed or untreated condition, and interpret available data so as to maximise beliefs about prevalence. They aim to draw the attention of lay persons and medical practitioners to the existence of the disease and the availability of treatment, shaping their fears and anxieties into a clinical form. These often involve the use of public relations firms to place stories in the media, providing victims who will tell their stories and supplying experts who will explain them in terms of the new disorder. Amongst the examples given by Moynihan et al.—which include baldness and Propecia, erectile dysfunction and Viagra, irritable bowel syndrome and Lotronex, and Pfizer's promotion of the new disease entity of 'female sexual dysfunction'—is the promotion by Roche of its antidepressant Auroxix (moclobemide) for the treatment of social phobia in Australia in 1997. This involved the use of the public relations company to place stories in the press, an alliance with a patients group called the Obsessive Compulsive and Anxiety Disorders Federation of Victoria, funding a large conference on social phobia, and promoting maximal estimates of prevalence. These are not covert tactics—as a quick glance at the Practical Guides published on the Web by the magazine Pharmaceutical Marketing will show.[19]

"Paxil ® . . . Your life is waiting" announces the Paxil website, proclaiming Paxil to be the first and only FDA-approved SSRI for GAD—a site which helpfully provides a Self-Test for the condition with encouragement to consult a healthcare practitioner who can make the diagnosis.[20] And consider the text of a "direct to consumer" television advertisement for Paxil in the United States in October 2001 (Figure 3.3).

Here is how the action of Paxil is described to physicians in the information issued by the manufacturers:[21]

> The antidepressant action of paroxetine . . . its efficacy in the treatment of social anxiety disorder . . . obsessive compulsive disorder [OCD], and panic disorder [PD]) is presumed to be linked to potentiation of serotonergic activity in the central

Figure 3.3
Paxil: "The real story about chronic anxiety"
US Television, October 2000

Female Character 1:

I'm always thinking something terrible is going to happen, I can't handle it

Female Character 2:

You know, your worst fears, the what ifs ... I can't control it, and I'm always worrying about everything

Female character 3:

Its like a tape in your mind, it just goes over and over... I just always thought I was a worrier

Caption

THE REAL STORY ABOUT CHRONIC ANXIETY

Male character:

Its like I never get a chance to relax. At work I'm tense about stuff at home. At home I'm tense about stuff at work

Female narrator

If you are one of the millions of people who live with uncontrollable worry, anxiety and several of these symptoms....

Symptoms roll across the screen:

WORRY ... ANXIETY ... MUSCLE TENSION ... FATIGUE ... IRRITABILITY ... RESLESSNESS ... SLEEP DISTURBANCE ... LACK OF CONCENTRATION

you could be suffering from Generalized Anxiety Disorder and a chemical imbalance could be to blame.

PAXIL works to correct this imbalance to relieve anxiety.

IMAGES OF PREVIOUS CHARACTERS, NOW HAPPY AND PLAYING WITH CHILDREN, WASHING CAR ETC. WHILST NARRATOR RUSHES THOUGH LIST OF SIDE EFFECTS

Prescription Paxil is not for everyone...

Tell your doctor what medicines you are taking.... Side effects may include decreased appetite, dry mouth, sweating, nausea, constipation, sexual side effects, tremor or sleepiness. Paxil is not habit forming

Female character 1:

I'm not bogged down by worry anymore, I feel like me again, I feel like myself

nervous system resulting from inhibition of neuronal reuptake of serotonin (5-hydroxy-tryptamine, 5-HT). Studies at clinically relevant doses in humans have demonstrated that paroxetine blocks the uptake of serotonin into human platelets. In vitro studies in animals also suggest that paroxetine is a potent and highly selective inhibitor of neuronal serotonin reuptake and has only very weak effects on norepinephrine and dopamine neuronal reuptake. In vitro radioligand binding studies indicate that paroxetine has little affinity for muscarinic, alpha1-, alpha2-, beta-adrenergic-, dopamine (D2)-, 5-HT1-, 5-HT2—and histamine (H1)-receptors; antagonism of muscarinic, histaminergic and alpha1-adrenergic receptors has been associated with various anticholinergic, sedative and cardiovascular effects for other psychotropic drugs

Thus these rather general and fuzzy new disorders such as OCD and PD are connected up to a whole style of molecular argumentation designed to emphasise the specificity of the neurochemical basis of the diagnosis and the mode of action of the drug. This new style of thought is thus simultaneously pharmacological and commercial. Drugs are developed, promoted, tested, licensed and marketed for the treatment of particular DSM IV diagnostic classifications. Disease, drug and treatment thus each support one another though an account at the level of molecular neuroscience.

As an SSRI drug for the treatment of depression, Paxil had arrived relatively late on the scene. But nonetheless the rate of increase in prescribing in the US kept pace with the brand leaders, and by 2001, as it succeeded in linking itself to the treatment of the anxiety disorders, it achieved a market share about equal to Pfizer's Zoloft and Lilley's Prozac.

Other drug manufacturers rushed to trial and re-licence their own antidepressants so that they could promote them as treatments for GAD and the other related anxiety disorders—Wyeth with Venlafaxine XF, Pfizer with Zoloft—or to patent and licence new molecules specifically for this diagnosis. Pfizer's bought the rights to Pagoclone from Indevus Pharmaceuticals, but returned them in June 2002 when the results of its clinical trials failed to show levels of efficacy significantly above placebo—Indevus stocks dropped by 65 percent on the day of the announcement and Pfizer concentrated their efforts on their own drug Pregabalin.[22] Shareholder value and clinical value appear inextricably entangled.

These links and relays between classification of disorders, marketing disorders and testing, licensing and promoting psychopharmaceuticals have recently come in for much criticism. Many leading figures in American—and worldwide—psychiatry act as consultants for the pharmaceutical companies, rely upon them for funds for their research, are involved in trialling, testing and evaluating their products, are on the committees responsible for revising and updating diagnostic criteria, advise the licensing authorities on the acceptability and risk of drugs, and indeed have financial interests and shares in the companies themselves.[23] Take Professor Kenneth Blum as an example chosen more or less at random. Blum is the author of numerous articles that claim to find associations between the genes responsible for various aspects of the neurotransmitter systems—such as dopamine D2 receptors and dopamine transporters—and particular DSM IV pathologies especially those related to substance dependency and various forms of 'compulsive' behaviour. The newsletter of Secular Organizations for Sobriety—an organization providing a non-religious alternative to "Twelve Step" recovery programs—provides us with a helpful biography.[24] Blum, a member of the Advisor Board of this organization, is considered an international authority in neuropsychopharmacology and genetics, has published over three hundred articles on neuropsychopharmacogenetics and is a full professor of Pharmacology at the

Table 3.13
SSRI and Related Drug Prescribing USA 1990–2000
in Standard Dosage Units (thousands)

	1990	1992	1994	1996	1998	2000
Fluoxetine	376,838	467,930	701,917	899,534	1,189,953	1,189,269
Sertraline	0	101,373	404,276	648,518	872,492	1,079,613
Paroxetine	0	0	217,031	416,941	720,579	923,311
Venlafaxine	0	0	98,872	225,008	322,234	538,695
Citalopram	0	0	0	0	25,128	420,724
Mirtazapine	0	0	0	5,466	66,616	146,152
Fluvoxamine	0	0	410	50,630	82,832	92,869
Total SSRI anti-depressants	376,838	569,303	1,422,506	2,246,097	3,279,834	4,390,633

Source: IMS Health

University of Texas Health Science Center, San Antonio. He chairs scientific conferences worldwide including two Gordon Alcohol Research Conferences (1978, 1982), and is currently the chairman of the first Gordon Research Conference on Psychogenetics. But he is also the managing director of 1899 Limited Liability Corporation a Virginia biotechnology firm, Scientific Advisor for Zig Ziglar Corporation, and Chief Executive Officer of Pharmacogenomics Inc. Pharmacogenomics Inc. is a wholly owned subsidiary of ACADIA Pharmaceuticals which specialises in genomics-based drug discovery and tries to link genomic and chemical information to generate gene-specific small molecule drugs with improved side effect profiles for neuropsychiatric and related disorders, and is commercializing this pipeline through licensing and discovery collaborations with pharmaceutical partners.

Conclusions

By the 1990s a fundamental shift had occurred in psychiatric thought and practice. No matter that there was little firm evidence to link variations in neurotransmitter functioning to symptoms of depression or any other mental disorder in the living brains of unmedicated patients—although many researchers are seeking such evidence and occasional papers announce that it has been found. And no matter that most of the new smart drugs are no more effective than their dirty predecessors for moderate or severe depression—they are favoured because they are claimed to be safer, and to have fewer 'unwanted effects'. A way of thinking has taken shape, and a growing proportion of psychiatrists find it difficult to think otherwise. In this way of thinking, all explanations of mental pathology must 'pass through' the brain and its neurochemistry—neurones, synapses, membranes, receptors, ion channels, neurotransmitters, enzymes . . . Diagnosis is now thought to be most accurate when it can link symptoms to anomalies in one or more of these elements. And the fabrication and action of psychiatric drugs is conceived in these terms. Not that biographical effects are ruled out, but biography— family stress, sexual abuse—has effects through its impact on this brain. Environment plays its part, but unemployment, poverty and the like have their effects only through impacting upon this brain. And experiences play their part—substance abuse or trauma for example—but once again, through their impact on this neurochemical brain. A few decades ago, such claims would have seemed extraordinarily bold—for many medico-psychiatric researchers and practitioners, they now seem 'only common sense'.

And, in the same movement, psychiatry has become big business. One of the criticisms of the private madhouses before the spread of public asylums was that they were generating what was termed 'a trade in lunacy' in which profit was to be made by incarceration—leading to all manner of corruption (Parry Jones, 1972). No one made enormous sums out of public psychiatry in the nineteenth century, or indeed up until the middle of the twentieth. One of the eugenic arguments in Nazi Germany was that the care of the psychiatric ill was an enormous drain on the public purse (Burleigh, 1994). Of course, as we all know, in the second half of the twentieth century, psychotherapy and counselling became big business. But psychiatry itself—in the mental hospitals, the clinics, the GPs surgeries and the private psychiatric consulting room—also became a huge and profitable market for the pharmaceutical industry. Only the large pharmaceutics companies can now afford the risk capital involved in developing, trialling and licensing of a new psychiatric drug. And because contemporary psychiatry is so much the outcome of developments in psychopharmacology, this means that these commercial decisions are actually shaping the patterns of psychiatric thought at a very fundamental level. The factories of the pharmaceutical companies are the key laboratories for psychiatric innovation, and the psychiatric laboratory has, in a very real sense, become part of the psychopharmacological factory. Many of these large multinational conglomerates make a considerable proportion of their income from the marketing of psychiatric drugs, and their success, or failure, in attracting market share is key to maintaining the shareholder value of the company. Paul Rabinow's assessment of the new life sciences is especially apt for psychiatry—the quest for truth is no longer sufficient to mobilise the production of psychiatric knowledge—health—or rather, the profit to be made from promising health—has become the prime motive force in generating what counts for our knowledge of mental ill health (Rabinow, 1996). Nonetheless, but from another perspective the developments in psychiatric drug use are merely one dimension of a new set of relations between ideas of health and illness, practices of treatment and prevention of bodily malfunctions, and commercially driven innovation, marketing and competition for profits and shareholder value. Where Foucault analysed biopolitics, we now must analyse bioeconomics and bioethics, for human capital is now to be understood in a rather literal sense—in terms of the new linkages between the politics, economics and ethics of life itself.

Of course, to identify this new medico-industrial complex and to point to its power is not to critique it. In a situation where only investment of capital on a large scale is capable of producing new therapeutic agents, such linkages of health and profitability might well be the inescapable condition for the creation of effective drugs. But the consequences of many of the developments we have charted here cannot be reduced to a debate about efficacy, as if illness, treatment and cure were independent of one another. We have seen that, in certain key respects, the most widely prescribed of the new generation of psychiatric drugs treat conditions whose borders are fuzzy, whose coherence and very existence as illness or disorders are matters of dispute, and which are not so much intended to 'cure' a specific transformation from a normal to a pathological state as to modify the ways in which vicissitudes in the life of the recipient are experienced, lived and understood. The best selling drugs these days are not those that treat acute illnesses, but those that are prescribed chronically. These include Lipitor for the lowering of blood lipid levels thought to predispose to heart attack and stroke; Premarin for the treatment of the effects of the menopause in particular its effects on sexuality; Atenolol and Norvasc for the long term management of high blood pressure; Prilosec for the treatment of Gastroesophageal Reflux Disease and heartburn. As for psychiatric drugs in the top twenty most prescribed drugs in the USA in 2001, Xanax is 10th—it is a benzodiazepine used for the management of anxiety disorders—and two of the SSRIs we have discussed here—Zoloft (sertraline) and Paxil (paroxetine)—are in 14th and 15th place.[25] These are the drugs most amenable to the extension and reshaping of the boundaries of disease and 'treatability'. They promise a power to reshape life pharmaceutically that extends way beyond what we previously understood as illness. Not just Premarin and its sisters, but previous generations of pharmaceuticals for contraception, have rewritten the norms of reproduction—its timetables, its kinship relations. Premarin and other forms of hormone replacement treatment have rewritten the norms of female ageing. Drugs such as Alazopram are rewriting the norms of social interaction. So the capitalisation of the power to treat intensifies the redefinition of that which is amenable to correction or modification. This is not simply blurring the borders between normality and pathology, or widening the net of pathology. We are seeing an enhancement in our capacities to adjust and readjust our somatic existence according to the exigencies of the life to which we aspire.

As is well known, Gilles Deleuze (1995) has suggested that contemporary societies are no longer disciplinary, in the sense identified by Foucault—they are societies of control. Where discipline sought to fabricate individuals whose capacities and forms of conduct were indelibly and permanently inscribed into the soul—in home, school or factory—today control is continuous and integral to all activities and practices of existence. In the field of health, the active and responsible citizen must engage in a constant monitoring of health, a constant work of modulation, adjustment, improvement in response to the changing requirements of the practices of his or her mode of everyday life. These new self-technologies do not seek to return a pathological or problematic individual to a fixed norm of civilised conduct through a once-off programme of normalisation. Rather, they oblige the individual to engage in constant risk management, and to act continually on him or herself to minimise risks by reshaping diet, lifestyle and now, by means of pharmaceuticals, the body itself. The new neurochemical self is flexible and can be reconfigured in a way that blurs the boundaries between cure, normalisation, and the enhancement of capacities. And these pharmaceuticals offer the promise of the calculated modification and augmentation of specific aspects of self-hood through acts of choice.

Psychiatric drugs today are conceived, designed, disseminated in the search for biovalue. But they are entangled with certain conceptions of what humans are or should be—that is to say, specific norms, values, judgements internalised in very idea of these drugs. An ethics is engineered into the molecular make up of these drugs, and the drugs themselves embody and incite particular forms of life in which the 'real me' is both 'natural' and to be produced. The significance of the emergence of treatments for mental ill health lies not only in their specific effects, but also in the way in which they reshape the ways in which both experts and lay people see, interpret, speak about and understand their world. Hence the growing market for non-prescription products that claim to enhance serotonin levels in the brain—in health food shops and of course on the internet. A cascade of claims are made that everything from chocolate to exercise makes you feel good because it 'enhances serotonin levels'. It seems that individuals themselves are beginning to recode their moods and their ills in terms of the functioning of their brain chemicals, and to act upon themselves in the light of this belief. Psychoanalysis brought into existence a whole new way of understanding ourselves—in terms of the unconscious, repression, neuroses, the Oedipus complex, and, of course, the theme of the centrality of sexuality to our psychic life. So it makes sense to ask whether general practitioners, psychiatrists and other mental health practitioners are beginning to see the problems their clients and patients experience in terms of this simplistic model of mental ill health as a disorder of neurotransmitters. To see in this way is to imagine the disorder as residing within the individual brain and its processes, and to see psychiatric drugs as a first line intervention, not merely for symptom relief but as specific treatments for these neurochemical anomalies. If we are experiencing a 'neurochemical' reshaping of personhood', the social and ethical implications for the twenty first century will be profound. For these drugs are becoming central to the ways in which our conduct is problematized and governed, by others, and by ourselves—to the continuous work of modulation of our capacities that is the life's work of the contemporary biological citizen.

Notes

1. In this paper, I draw upon data collected by myself and Mariam Fraser for our study 'The Age of Serotonin', funded by the Wellcome Trust Programme in Biomedical Ethics based in the Department of Sociology at Goldsmiths College, University of London. Thanks to our researcher, Angelique Praat, for her work on the collection and analysis of some of this material. Like all who investigate this area, my work follows lines of enquiry first opened up by David Healy, and my argument is indebted to his work. I also draw upon a survey commissioned for that study from IMS Health, detailed in footnote 2 below, and would like to thank Robin Keat, Pete Stephens and Ian Webster of IMS in particular for their help and advice data.

2. The best historical work on the development of psychopharmacology has been done by David Healy, and I draw extensively on this here: notably The Antidepressant Era, Harvard University Press, 1997; I would also like to thank him for letting me see The Creation of Psychopharmacology, Harvard University Press, 2002, in manuscript.

3. For the UK, it is possible to obtain roughly consistent figures for the period commencing in 1980 by the Government Statistical Service and they kindly provided us with a breakdown of their data, which we use in this analysis.

   For drugs that are listed in the schedules of the UN Convention on Psychotropic Substances of 1971—hallucinogens, stimulants, depressants and some analgesics that have medical and scientific uses but can also be drugs of abuse—international comparative data is published annually in the reports on psychotropic substances of the International Narcotics Control Board Now available on line at http://www.incb.org/.

   However, these data do not include most antidepressants or antipsychotic drugs: for that, one has to go to commercial organizations providing data to the drug companies themselves.

   To access this data, we commissioned a customised study from IMS Health based on the data that they compile from over 120 countries, and includes, for the countries chosen, drugs prescribed in hospital and sold through retail outlets. These data provided the basis for calculations made by our team, and IMS has no responsibility for these or our interpretations. The regions chosen for this study are USA, Japan, Europe (UK, Germany, France, Spain, Italy, Belgium, Austria, Finland, Ireland, Luxembourg, Netherlands, Portugal, Greece), South America (Argentina, Brazil, Mexico, Colombia, Peru, Uruguay, Venezuela), South Africa (data for other countries in Sub-Saharan Africa was not available) and Pakistan (12 year data for India was not available).

   Our principle comparative measure is the Standard Dosage Unit (SU). SUs are determined by taking the number of counting units sold divided by the standard unit factor which is the smallest common dose of a product form as defined by IMS Health. For example, for oral solid forms the standard unit factor is one tablet or capsule whereas for syrup forms the standard unit factor is one teaspoon (5 ml) and injectable forms it is one ampoule or vial. This is the best available measure for comparative purposes, but it is far from perfect. For example a 30 day pack of a product given 4 times a day will contribute 120 SUs for each pack sold whereas a similar pack of a once daily product will contribute only 30 SUs. Many more products now have once daily dosing regimes than in the past. In such circumstances SU analyses can make it appear that the market has collapsed even though the days of treatment will have remained constant or increased. There are therefore some risks to using SUs for comparative purposes over the time periods and the regions reported here, and where these are of particular relevance we have tried to supplement SUs with other measures. Dates shown are calendar years except for the two most recent years—for technical reasons arising from IMS data techniques, 1999 covers the four quarters from July 1999 to June 2000, and 2000 covers the four quarters from July 2000 to June 2001. Prices refer to total sales ex-manufacturer (not retail prices) in US dollars at the exchange rate at the date in question. Figures credited to IMS Health are based on that report, but the analysis, charts and figures are our own. Some drugs used to treat psychiatric conditions, such as the anti-convulsants, are not included, as most prescriptions for such drugs are for non-psychiatric conditions.

4. Of course, data on medications obtained on a prescription basis are obviously rather limited, as they show prescribing practices rather than consumption practices and we know that consumers often do not take all, or any, of the drugs they are prescribed. And aggregated data conceals significant variations.

5. For technical reasons, to do with a change in counting methods, these figures refer to the period for the twelve months to July 2000.

6. Figures from IMS Health.

7. Of course, even these data are affected by national policies, as they refer to drugs obtained on prescription, not those available over-the-counter (OTC)—hence if a drug or group of drugs moves from prescription status to OTC status, it ceases to appear in the figures.

8. Earlier comparable figures are not available. Note that the data up to 1990 are not consistent with data from 1991 onwards. Figures for 1980–90 are based on fees and on a sample of 1 in 200 prescriptions dispensed by community pharmacists and appliance contractors only. Figures for 1991 onwards are based on items and cover all prescriptions dispensed by community pharmacists, appliance contractors dispensing doctors and prescriptions submitted by prescribing doctors for items personally administered.

9. For the 1970 figures, Shorter uses Parry et al., 1973: 769–783; 775. For the later figures he uses data from the National Center for Health Statistics Vital and Health Statistics in various years.

10. Leonard claims that the first report was by Schoneker within five years of the introduction of the neuroleptics.

11. Also it should be noted that in 2000 alone, US prescription drug sales increased by 14.7 percent. New products and changes in utilization accounted for a 10.8 percent increase in drug expenditure while price inflation accounted for 3.8 percent (IMS America, 2000).

12. http://www.nami.org/illness/whatis.html, 12.8.02

124   Biotechnology: Between Commerce and Civil Society

13. http://www.nami.org/helpline/depress.htm, 12.8.02
14. We have already seen that anxiety, not depression, has been until recently the exemplary pathology in Japan. DSM IV distinguishes Mood Disorders, which include the major depressive disorders, from Anxiety Disorders. Of course, the SSRI drugs were not marketed in the first instance for major depression or bipolar disorder, but for mild to moderate depression, and it is in this fuzzy area that the new links between depression and anxiety are being established. Whilst marketing strategies tend to avoid coding the anxiety disorders as forms of depression, psychiatrists themselves tend to see them as closely linked conditions.
15. Quoted at http://www.antidepressantsfacts.com/David-John-Hawkins.htm
16. A 1997 review of these effects can be found on the website of the American Society of Consultant Pharamcisits http://www.ascp.com/public/pubs/tcp/1997/oct/ssri.html, 12.8.02
17. On the Doctor's Guide website, http://www.pslgroup.com/dg/1f8182.htm, 12.8.02.
18. Cassels, Alan (2002) 'The drug companies' latest marketing tactic: "disease awareness" pitch—a new licence to expand drug sales', at http://www.policyalternatives.ca/publications/articles/article315.html, 12.8..02
19. http://www.pmlive.com/pharm_market/prac_guides.cfm, 12.8.02
20. http://www.paxil.com/index.html, 12.8.02.
21. http://www.rxlist.com/cgi/generic/parox_cp.htm, 12.8.02.
22. http://biz.yahoo.com/bw/020607/72033_2.html: 15.8.02; http://www.biospace.com/ccis/news_story.cfm?StoryID=8819419&full=1: 15.8.02.
23. Healy 1997; see also the resignation letter of leading American social psychiatrist from 'The American Psychopharmaceutical Association: Lauren Mosher, Resignation letter to APA, 1998: at http://www.oikos.org/mosher.htm, 12.8.02
24. http://www.cfiwest.org/sos/newsletter/about.htm, 12.8.02.
25. Listed on the Rx List at http://www.rxlist.com/top200.htm; with the end of its patent and the proliferation of alternative formulations of fluoxetine, Prozac has slipped well down the list.

References

American Psychiatric Association (1987) *Diagnostic and Statistical Manual of Mental Disorders*, Third Edition, Revised (DSM-III-R). New York: American Psychiatric Association.
———1994) *Diagnostic and Statistical Manual of Mental Disorders*, Fourth Edition. New York: American Psychiatric Association.
Ayd, Frank J. (1961) *Recognizing the depressed patient; with essentials of management and treatment..* New York: Grune & Stratton
———(1967) 'Persistent dyskinesia: a neurological complication of major tranquilizers,' *Medical Science*, 18: 32.
Breggin, Peter (1993) *Toxic Psychiatry*. London: Fontana
Brown, Phil (1985) *The transfer of care : psychiatric deinstitutionalization and its aftermath*. Boston: Routledge & Kegan Paul.
Burleigh, Michael (1994) *Death and Deliverance*. Cambridge: Cambridge University Press.
Crane, George E. (1968) 'Tardive dyskinesia in patients treated with major neuroleptics: a review of the literature,' *American Journal of Psychiatry*, 124 (February Supplement): 40.

Deleuze, Gilles (1995) 'Postscript to 'Societies of Control,' in Deleuze, *Negotiations*, translated by M. Joughin. New York: Columbia University Press.

Ehrenberg, Alain (2000) *La Fatigue d'etre soi*. Paris: Odile Jacob.

Elixhauser, A, Yu, K, Steiner, C, Bierman, A. S (1997). *Hospitalization in the United States: Healthcare Cost & Utilization Project* (HCUP) Fact Book No. 1. Rockville, MD: Agency for Healthcare Research and Quality. (Also available at http://www.ahrq.gov/data/hcup/factbk1/)

Fukuyama, Francis (2002) *Our Posthuman Future*: Consequences of the Biotechnology Revolution. New York: Farrar Straus Giroux.

Gelman, Sheldon (1999) *Medicating Schizophrenia*: A History. New Brunswick: Rutgers University Press.

Ghodse, Hamid and Khan, Inayat, eds. (1988) *Psychoactive drugs*. improving prescribing practices. Meeting on the training of health care professionals in rational prescribing. Geneva: World Health Organisation.

Hall, Robert A. et al. (1956) 'Neurotoxic reactions resulting from chlorpromazine administration,' *Journal of the American Medical Association*, 161: 214–217.

Healy, David (1997) *The Antidepressant Era*. Cambridge, MA: Harvard University Press.

———(2002) *The Creation of Psychopharmacology*. Cambridge, MA: Harvard University Press.

International Narcotics Control Board (1997, 1998, 2000) *Report of the International Narcotics Control Board for various years*. New York: United Nations Publications.

Leonard, Brian E. (1992) *Fundamentals of Psychopharmacology*. Chichester: Wiley.

Lennard, Henry L. and Bernstein, Arnold (1974) 'Perspectives on the New Psychoactive Drug Technology,' in *Social Aspects of the Medical Use of Psychotropic Drugs*, ed. Ruth Cooperstock. Toronto: Addiction Research Foundation.

Moynihan, Ray, Heath, Iona and Henry, David (2002) 'Selling sickness: the pharmaceutical industry and disease mongering'. *British Medical Journal*, 321, 886–890.

Moynihan, Ray (2003) 'The making of a disease: female sexual dysfunction', *British Medical Journal*, 326, 45–47.

National Center for Health Statistics (2002) *Health, United States, 2002*. Hyattsville, MD: National Center for Health Statistics (also available at "http://www.cdc.gov/nchs/products/pubs/pubd/hus/02hustop.htm" http://www.cdc.gov/nchs/products/pubs/pubd/hus/02hustop.htm)

Novas, Carlos and Rose, Nikolas (2000) 'Genetic risk and the birth of the somatic individual,' *Economy and Society*, 29, 4: 485–513.

Parry, Hugh J. et al. (1973) 'National patterns of psychotherapeutic drug use,' *Archives of General Psychiatry*, 28: 769–783.

Parry Jones, William (1972) *The Trade in Lunacy*, London: Routledge.

Popovic, J. R, and Hall, M. J. (1999) *National Hospital Discharge Survey, Advance data from health and vital statistics*, no.319. Hyattsville, MD: National Center for Health Statistics.

Rabinow, Paul (1996) *Severing the Ties*: Fragmentation and Dignity in Late Modernity, in Essays on the Anthropology of Reason. Princeton: Princeton University Press.

Shorter, E. (1997). *A History of Psychiatry*. London: Wiley,

Smith, Micky (1991) *A Social History of the Minor Tranquilizers*. Binghampton, NY: Pharmaceutical Products Press.

Solomon, Andrew (2001) *The Noonday Demon. an anatomy of depression*. London: Chatto and Windus.

Stock, Gregory (2002) *Redesigning Humans*: our inevitable genetic future. Boston: Houghton Mifflin.
Styron, William (1991) *Darkness Visible. a memoir of madness*. London: Cape
Task Force (1973) 'A special report,' *Archives of General Psychiatry*, 28: 463.
World Health Organisation (2001) *The World Health Report 2001*: Mental Health: New Understanding, New Hope. Geneva: World Health Organisation

Part II

Biotechnology, Commerce and Civil Society: The Social Construction of Biotechnology

Introduction

Frederick H. Buttel

The title of this anthology, "Biotechnology: Between Commerce, and Civil Society," is consistent with the fact that the expression "biotechnology" is widely understood to pertain to a broad range of "new genetic technologies," to be applied in a diversity of sectors such as agriculture, health care, chemicals, environmental control, and so on. In practice, however, social research on biotechnology policy and politics tends to be highly sector-specific. The papers by Javier Lezaun and Anne Kerr demonstrate the sectoral specificity of the literatures on agricultural and biomedical technologies by virtue of the fact that they do not have one literature citation in common. The Priest and Ten Eyck paper does so as well by showing the dramatic differences in media framing of agrofood versus biomedical technologies in both the U.S. and Europe.

There are clearly some sound reasons why the issues involved in agricultural and biomedical biotechnologies are implicitly seen as being distinct ones. Agriculture and biomedicine, while both are primordial realms, are socially and biologically quite different. In agriculture, the most fundamental commercial vector of biotechnology is the seed, and the basic biology of the seed—the fact that this key input is multiplied (rather than consumed) during the production process—is the key constraint on private R&D. Private firms thus must introduce their innovations in the form of hybrids (which are essentially a "biological patent"; Kloppenburg, 1988), or else implement draconian practices for protecting their innovations as depicted in Lezaun's paper. The massive constraint posed by the biological reality that one seed becomes many in the agricultural production process is what has made "terminator" technology (also known as genetic use restriction technologies, or GURTs) so attractive—and, in some sense, so necessary—for private accumulation in agricultural biotechnology. Commercialization of biomedical biotechnologies must, to be sure, deal with biological constraints, but these constraints are not nearly as fundamental or formidable as the biological constraints to commercialization of agrofood biotechnologies. There are a number of actual or potential commercial vectors for biomedical biotechnology: pharmaceuticals, genetic fingerprinting and analysis, gene therapy, diagnostics, therapeutic cloning, and so on. The fact that the biological constraints on commercialization of agrofood and biomedical biotechnologies are so distinct is one of the major reasons why the 1980s trend toward creation of integrated agricultural and pharmaceutical "life science" companies firms had been almost completely reversed by the turn of the twenty-first century (Tait et al., 2002). In the early 2000s, biotechnological R&D in the health care sector is performed by one set of corporations (chiefly, pharmaceutical companies), while agrofood biotechnology R&D is performed by a largely separate group of firms.

The Priest and Ten Eyck paper provides an empirical window on another profound difference between the agrofood and biomedical biotechnology sectors. Priest and Ten Eyck show that in both the U.S. and Europe, medical biotechnologies are much more likely to be framed by the media in "progressive" terms than are agrofood biotechnologies. Similarly, agrofood biotechnologies are much more likely to be framed in terms of being a "runaway technology," or opening "Pandora's Box," than are medical biotechnologies. Indeed, one of the useful contributions of the Priest and Ten Eyck paper their demonstration of the fact the agrofood versus medical referent of stories is more important than country/continent (U.S. versus Europe) of the media outlet in explaining variations in media accounts of biotechnology. Their paper is a useful antidote to the conventional wisdom (e.g., Marks, Kalaitzandonakes, and Zakharova, 2002) that there are dramatic differences between the U.S. and European press in the mix of positive and negative coverage of biotechnology (especially agrofood biotechnologies) and that European resistance to GM foods is largely driven by negative press coverage.

Further, Kerr's paper shows that the major issues in biomedical biotechnology tend to revolve around the cost of, equity in access to, and discrimination in the application of the new genetics to health care. By contrast, in agrofood biotechnology, consumer-citizen access issues are far less important than consumer-citizen choice issues, such as GM food labeling, and environmental and health risk concerns. "Citizen access" in agrofood biotechnology is, more often than not, a matter of consumers being able to *avoid*—rather than being able to achieve—exposure to biotechnology genetically modified food products.

There is thus a definite logic to the fact that the literatures on agrofood and biomedical biotechnologies have been developed in relative isolation and in different directions. In my commentary on the three papers, however, I want to direct attention to the fact that these sectoral differences notwithstanding, there are indeed some *general issues* raised by the relations among biotechnology, commerce, and civil society. Each of these common issues is raised— sometimes explicitly, sometimes implicitly—in the three papers.

The Lezaun and Kerr papers both show the enormous role played by patent systems in shaping the nature of biotechnology R&D. The *Monsanto v. Schmeiser* decision depicted by Lezaun was based in substantial measure on the degree to which the U.S. patent system permits broad patents and can call forth extraordinary patent enforcement measures (Monsanto's "gene police"). The judge's decision in *Monsanto v. Schmeiser* essentially involved a judgment that the scope of protection is sufficiently broad that the natural occurrence of genetic "spread" and the replication of the Roundup resistance (EPSPS) gene in a farmer's field constituted farmer infringement of the Monsanto patent. Kerr likewise stresses the influence of the U.S. patent system by way of its having made possible the patenting of "raw" genetic information through the Human Genome Project.

The issue of patent breadth has been raised particularly forcefully by the fact that the Wisconsin Alumni Research Foundation (WARF), the non-profit intellectual property arm of my university, was granted a stem-cell patent of what can now be seen as being of extraordinarily broad scope, including the five original cell lines developed by University of Wisconsin scientist James Thompson as well as the laboratory methods used to produce them. WARF licensed the patent to Geron Corporation in the late 1990s under terms that might have inadvertently given Geron a virtual proprietary lock on future stem-cell technology. It was only due to Geron's slow pace of commercialization—and to subsequent court action by WARF that resulted in the licensing agreement being voided—that WARF was able to re-assert control over the stem-cell patent and preserve space for public R&D in stem-cell technology development (Shulman, 2001).

The U.S. patent system also involves considerable latitude to submit successful applications for patent protection on traditional landrace varieties. In one of the most egregious examples of this, Texas-based RiceTec, Inc. obtained a U.S. patent on Basmati-style rice varieties that were essentially the same material traditionally grown by Indian peasants. Such a patent seems difficult to reconcile with the novelty criterion that is presumably the bedrock of industrial patenting practice.[1]

The enormous sums of money invested in agrofood (and biomedical) technologies and the resulting rush to commercialization have created a climate of U.S. Patent and Trademark Office permissiveness in granting both broad patents and patents that are questionable on novelty grounds. U.S. PTO practices have also contributed to the nature of the TRIPS portion of the Uruguay Round Agreement on Agriculture which has served to extend the international reach of U.S. patenting practices to countries such as Canada (where the *Schmeiser* case was decided). It should be noted in this regard that the European Union's patent practices have been and continue to be more restrictive than those of the U.S. At the same time, international competition and the resulting pressures being brought to bear by European companies on the EU are creating a climate within which the EU is likely to move in the direction of American practices (Economic Policy Committee, 2002). Whether the European Union's patenting practices (currently a stronger emphasis on novelty, a greater cost of patent applications, and less encouragement of university patenting than in the U.S.) are harmonized with those of the United States, or whether current practices are maintained, will have a great deal to do with the kinds of technologies that are developed and commercialized in the two regions.

A second commonality across these two papers is the importance of discursive framing and discursive struggles in biotechnology policymaking in the agrofood and biomedical sectors. Kerr, for example, highlights "the role of enlightened experts, who variously employ their social conscience and objective expertise in negotiating decision-making in the clinical and policy realms." Kerr notes that this "enlightened stance" involves a certain sensitivity on the part of clinicians to issues of access and discrimination, but this stance is just as often employed to deflect criticism of the clinical and policy decisions made in the realm of genetic services. The context of Priest and Ten Eyck's comparative analysis of media framing of biotechnology issues in the European and U.S. press is basically the question of whether media portrayals of these technologies would serve to favor proponents' or opponents' claims. Lezaun does not deal directly with discursive struggles in agrofood biotechnology, except when he makes the crucial observation that the *Schmeiser* case, which on its face seemed prejudicial to Monsanto because of its having derived from the company's "gene police" practices, became very highly publicized by the anti-biotechnology NGO community as an example of unethical corporate behavior.

A final commonality between the two sectors that is worth stressing concerns the timing of public input into decision-making about new genetic technologies. Kerr mentions specifically that public input and debate are almost always confined to periods when particular technologies, such as gene therapy regimes, are in substantial measure already in place, either at or nearing commercial development. Lezaun does not make this argument directly, but one might note that Kerr's observation is equally true in the agrofood arena. The fact that public input rarely occurs before products or technologies are well into the commercialization pipeline is understandable, since there are practical difficulties of scrutinizing technologies before they reach tangible commercial form. At the same time it is worth noting that public input may be more effective if it is brought to bear when technologies are in embryonic form and when there still remain options for designs of final products or services.

I will conclude by mentioning that there is one other crucial commonality—the current state of (and alternatives for) the division of labor between public research and private R&D—that unfortunately was not addressed by Lezaun, Kerr, or Priest and Ten Eyck. In both biomedicine and agriculture, it is of crucial importance whether the role of universities is directed mainly at pursuit of public-goods-generating and/or orphan technologies, or alternatively whether universities are structured mainly as institutions that undertake discovery of fundamental knowledge to be transferred as an input into private sector R&D. The division of labor between public and private R&D is related to the patenting/proprietary protection issue noted earlier; broad patents and public policy encouragement of university patenting (as in the U.S.' Bayh-Dole Act of 1980), for example, tend to steer public research toward commercially attractive areas and result in patented rather than public-domain knowledges. In addition, a whole host of other policies (such as university conflict of interest rules and relative salary levels of university and industry scientists) affect the public-private division of labor. Ultimately, the key public policy issue in biotechnology and other areas of high-technology R&D will be how to deal with the realities of corporate control of R&D in early twenty-first century economies while maintaining the legitimate interests of state and civil society in academic autonomy.

Note

1. Note, however, that in 2001, as a result of litigation and complaints by the Indian government, the U.S. Patent Examiner changed the title of RiceTec's patent (by omitting the term Basmati) and limited patent coverage to a few varieties on which RiceTec had performed significant varietal development research.

References

Economic Policy Committee (2002) *Report on Research and Development*. Brussels: Council of the European Union.

Kloppenburg, Jack, Jr. (1998) *First the Seed*. New York: Cambridge University Press.

Marks, Leonie A., Nicholas Kalaitzandonakes, and Lucy Zakharova (2002) "On the media roller coaster: Will biotech foods finish the ride?" *Choices* (American Agricultural Economics Association) (Spring) 6–10.

Shulman, Seth (2001) "Owning the future: The morphing patent problem," *Technology Review* 104 (November):33–34

Tait, Joyce, Joanna Chataway, and David Wield (2002) "The life science industry sector: Evolution of agro-biotechnology in Europe," *Science and Public Policy* 29:253–258.

4

Pollution and the Use of Patents: A Reading of Monsanto v. Schmeiser

Javier Lezaun

Detectives in the Field

On August 18, 1997, detective Wayne Derbyshire, of the firm Robinson Investigations, visited several farms in the rural municipality of Bayne, Saskatchewan. Mr. Derbyshire was investigating reports of unlicensed planting of Roundup Ready canola in the area on behalf of Monsanto Corporation. Monsanto was trying to sniff out farmers who were growing its transgenic herbicide-tolerant canola without having signed the company's Technology Use Agreement (TUA). Any farmer who had obtained the seed through fraudulent means (so-called 'brownbagging') would be guilty of avoiding the 'technology fee' that the company charges for the genetically modified seed.[1] Since 1995, when Roundup Ready canola was first commercialized in Canada, Monsanto had established different surveillance mechanisms to uncover illicit uses of the technology, either by contract-holders who may have conducted some of the activities prohibited under the TUA (such as saving seed from the previous harvest, or providing it to anyone for replanting or seed development), or by non-contract holders (individuals who should not have gotten access to Monsanto's genes to begin with). One of these mechanisms was an anonymous call line, where farmers could report suspected cases of patent infringement. The company had recently contracted with Robinson Investigations to track down these tips, and conduct 'random audits' of farmers throughout Saskatchewan. The business was promising—Robinson Investigation's business, that is. The firm had put five detectives to work on the Monsanto assignment in 1996 (when approximately 50,000 acres of Roundup Ready canola were grown by some 600 farmers in Canada), but the operation soon expanded. By 2000, when almost 5 million acres of genetically modified herbicide-tolerant canola (or 40% of the total Canadian harvest) were being grown, Robinson Investigations would be employing close to 30 detectives to carry out 'blitzes' on suspect Saskatchewan farmers.[2]

One of the farmers Mr. Derbyshire visited that day in August was Percy Schmeiser, a resident and former Mayor of the town of Bruno. Having failed to obtain permission to enter Schmeiser's land, Mr. Derbyshire drove around some of his fields and took samples of canola along the roads. After collecting the pods of several plants, Mr. Derbyshire put them in separate, sealed bags, which he then labeled with Schmeiser's name, the date, and a sample number. For the next three days the bags were kept in Mr. Derbyshire's freezer, until, on August 27, they were sent by courier to the office of Robinson Investigations in Saskatoon. Mike Robinson, president of the firm and a former Royal Canadian Mounted Police officer, forwarded the samples to a Monsanto manager, who then removed the seeds from the pods, put the seeds in envelopes, and sent them to the Crop Science Department of the University of Saskatchewan where grow-out tests could be conducted. There, four seeds from each of the envelopes were planted and, after germination, sprayed with Roundup herbicide. Almost all of the seedlings survived. This evidence was used by Monsanto to file a lawsuit against Percy Schmeiser for infringement of the Patent No. 1,313,830 awarded to Monsanto for the invention of 'glyphosate resistant plants' capable of tolerating Monsanto's Roundup herbicide.[3]

Robinson Investigations detectives and Monsanto employees collected additional samples of Percy Schmeiser's canola throughout 1998 and 1999 (using on one occasion a court order to gain access to his land). Through these collections they hoped to produce further proof of the presence of Monsanto's canola in his fields. Mr. Schmeiser, however, claimed that the seed he had planted in 1997 was conventional seed, selected and saved from his previous harvest. In fact, Mr. Schmeiser pointed out, he had not purchased any commercial seed since 1993. He had never bought any transgenic varieties, and had had no contact with Monsanto salespersons whatsoever. When the case reached the court, Mr. Schmeiser and his lawyer challenged the validity of the samples and of the tests conducted by the prosecution. Their case, however, hinged on different sort of argument. Throughout the hearings, and later in several appeals, Schmeiser and his lawyer argued that even if genetically modified canola plants containing Monsanto's patented genes were present in his fields, this was due to "contamination." This contamination could have been caused, Schmeiser argued, either by pollen, blown into his fields or carried by insects from nearby crops of Roundup Ready canola, or by seed spilt from trucks and harvesting machinery driving by his fields. When in August of 1999 the parties failed to reach an out-of-court settlement, Percy Schmeiser launched his own lawsuit against Monsanto, accusing the corporation of libel, illegal trespassing, and the contamination of his fields with transgenic canola. Not only that—since Monsanto's seed had been allowed to spread and self-replicate out of control, Percy Schmeiser's lawyers argued that the company had waived any original property rights, and that the courts should declare void the company's intellectual property rights.

Patents and Pollution

In the last two decades, patents have been used an instrument for the construction and allocation of property rights over bioengineered products, but the practical relationship between patents and living organisms has been plagued by a multitude of complex legal questions. In the 1980 decision *Diamond v. Chakrabarty*, the U.S. Supreme Court declared man-made living organisms—in fact, "everything under the sun that is made by man"—as patentable subject matter, and pointed out that "the relevant distinction" established by Thomas Jefferson (and later reaffirmed by Congress) in the Patent Act, "was not between living and inanimate things, but between products of nature, whether living or not, and human-made inventions."[4] While asserting the traditional distinction between nature and invention, the Supreme Court placed modified organisms (in the particular case of Chakrabarty, bacteria produced through cell fusion) in the sphere of the invention.[5] This kind of boundary-work is typical of the legal system. As Sheila Jasanoff has pointed out, "the law is called upon to fix the leaky walls between the worlds we construe as social and natural, to recreate normative order when previous understandings have been stretched to the fraying point" (Jasanoff 1995: 161). The courts do so by dichotomizing the spectrum of entities into natural and artificial, and ascribing ambiguous objects to one of the two categories.

Monsanto v. Schmeiser represents yet another case where the ability of the courts to reenact a legitimate separation between natural and social worlds—thereby delimiting a non-natural realm in which property rights may apply—is challenged and stretched to a new limit, both by the specifics of the case and by the particular political and economic circumstances surrounding it. Canola is, after all, an utterly artificial organism that "never existed in nature," clothed in a multitude of intellectual property rights.[6] Its germplasm was developed over time by public institutions, and belongs to the public domain, but specific varieties are protected by Plant Breeders' Rights legislation, while the transgenic genes incorporated through genetic engineering have been patented by transnational corporations.[7] Sorting this multitude of claims into neatly separated distinctions—natural versus social, public versus private—requires a great deal of legal and rhetorical work. Established boundaries can be made to appear highly precarious. Canola is, moreover, an outcrossing organism; some refer to it as a "promiscuous" plant. With the help of wind, water, bees and other animals, it excels at releasing its genes into the environment, often to large distances. Some refer to it as a "promiscuous" plant; in fact, it is nothing but a highly capable weed.[8] Each plant produces thousands of small and smooth seeds that are extremely easy to spill during farming operations or transportation. Consequently, the mobility of canola genes often disrupts another set of boundaries: the physical lines separating different plots of lands, the buffer zones between roads and fields, the borders between public and private spaces. Schmeiser, after all, accused the Robinson detectives of having trespassed on his land in their search for samples, and he often claimed that his "property rights" over anything growing on his land were being violated by Monsanto's lawsuit. When patented genes cross property limits, two forms of ownership rights collide. Does the legal protection granted to biotechnology firms accompany the movement of their proprietary genes? One more quality of these transgenic organisms adds further complexity to this scenario. Proprietary genes are eminently detectable. Precisely because they are well-characterized and contain a known insert, one can follow and trace their movement in new detail. This allowed Monsanto to present quantitative data on the presence of Roundup Ready canola in Schmeiser's fields. The feasibility of testing due to the availability of marker genes has increased the awareness of 'gene flow.' In fact it has turned 'gene flow' into an object of scientific inquiry, and the new knowledge about the distances and degree of pollen and seed dispersal has challenged previous practices of transgenic crop management.[9]

Monsanto v. Schmeiser has been presented as a sort of 'David versus Goliath' story for the movement against genetically modified crops, by posing a charismatic farmer against a powerful multinational corporation, while for biotechnology firms it offered a test of the extension of intellectual property rights in real agricultural conditions. Percy Schmeiser became an international celebrity. He travelled throughout the world to publicize the plight of farmers who defend their traditional right to plant and reuse seed against biotechnology companies' aggressive patent protection strategies. Many factors conspired to make this a case of international relevance. The international campaign against Monsanto and other promoters of agricultural biotechnology also made the case as an occasion to battle corporate control of the seed supply. The fact that it was a patent infringement case meant that it had to be tried by a Federal Court.[10] The case was widely covered by the national and international press, and was scheduled to be heard at the Federal Court in Ottawa in June 2000.

Monsanto v. Schmeiser is the most prominent case pitting claims of 'genetic pollution' against the validity of patents over genetically engineered organisms, and the precariousness of the hold of patents over living matter. In recent years, 'pollution claims' have played a central role in the struggle to define the system of control for agricultural biotechnology, and with the *Monsanto v. Schmeiser* case some of those claims reached the courts. These claims challenge the patentability of transgenic organisms by pointing to the inability of the holders of the intellectual property rights to control the spread and transfer of 'their' genes. If we take pollution to mean, in its most basic sense, "matter out of place," in the case of this new 'genetic pollution' we are dealing with genes out of place (Douglas 1996). And similarly to other pollution contexts, 'genetic pollution' refers to the likelihood of a disruption of existing categories and distinctions, a disruption that in this case is caused by gene flow. The fundamental implication of this theory of pollution is that the movement of genes effectively challenges the ability to distinguish between, and to keep apart, conventional and modified products, and to separate different kinds of bioengineered organisms. In *Monsanto v. Schmeiser* pollution interferes with some of conditions on which intellectual property rights have traditionally been justified. Pollution is, thus, a state of things—either an accepted condition or the probability of its occurrence—that interferes with existing institutional arrangements for the protection of the seed as a commodity.

This paper interrogates this relationship between pollution and patentability by analyzing how arguments regarding genetic pollution play out in legal cases impinging upon the legal protection of genetic patents. *Monsanto v. Schmeiser* offers a landmark example of the rhetoric and reasoning through which property rights over the seed are being contested. The April 2001 ruling produced by Justice Andrew MacKay, of the Canadian Federal Court in Saskatoon, suggests some of the ways in which the legal system might eventually re-stabilize patents in relation to genetic pollution. Whether this particular legal fix to the problem of genetic pollution will prevail in the face of multiplying challenges is a matter that will have to be resolved in the near future.

The Nexus of Control: The Seed as Commodity

The seed lies at the intersection of the laboratory and the market, as it is the material vehicle through which new genes enter the realm of commercial agriculture. Control over the seed is thus essential to any regulatory effort to police and regulate agricultural biotechnology. As Jack Kloppenburg points out in his history of the privatization of plant breeding, the seed is the critical point of control in agricultural and food production: "the seed is the endpoint of research and development process, and it is in that form that the new plant variety becomes a commercial product" (Kloppenburg 1988: 201). This basic fact has only been reinforced in the age of agricultural biotechnology. Transformations at the molecular level can only become commercial realities if and when embedded in the seed. "Insofar as biotechnology permits specific and detailed "reprogramming" of the genetic code," Kloppenburg argues, "*the seed, as embodied information, becomes the nexus of control over the determination and shape of the entire crop production process*" (Kloppenburg 1988: 201). But this link between the laboratory and the market has to be sustained, and to do so a certain chain of custody must be preserved. Purity of the seed is a prerequisite for, as well as the outcome of, the successive linkages between the laboratory and the production field. Once the seed reaches the market, proprietary control is the condition for the capitalization of the research process and the continuing commodification of the product. Indeed, control over the seed means today its constitution and appropriation as a commodity, as an object of trade and of private accumulation. An increasingly concentrated seed industry develops and commercializes new varieties, which are then protected through patenting and must be purchased by the farmer as an external input of agricultural and food production.

Traditionally, two elements of the biopolitics of seed production have prevented its full commodification. One is primarily biological: seed is both end product and means of production, grain to be commercialized *and* self-replicating organism. In other words, with each crop farmers traditionally reproduced their means of production. They could save part of the crop and use it as seed for the next harvest, thereby limiting the role of seed as a vehicle for capitalist accumulation (Kloppenburg 1988: 11). The second element is primarily historical and institutional. The technical capacity to produce new plant varieties through breeding and selection of suitable genes has historically been controlled by institutions, like Land Grant universities in the United States, whose mandate is to promote the public good rather than private profit.

The commodification of the seed is, thus, the result of the undoing of both these elements. First, technical transformations in plant breeding have turned the seed into a vehicle of capital accumulation by eliminating the biological barriers to privatization. The key innovation was the development of hybrid corn in the 1930s, and the subsequent development of hybridization techniques for other crops. Hybrid varieties often produce higher yield, but are "economically sterile" (Berlan and Lewontin 1986). Seed saved from hybrid crops will produce increasingly lower yields: a hybrid variety is the (first) cross of two inbred, homozygous parents, and its offspring will be increasingly heterozygous and its yield uneven. The economic sterility of hybrid seed prevents the generalized saving and replanting of seed from the previous crop, or at least makes the replanting of this seed increasingly unprofitable.

The farmer is thereby pushed to purchase new seed for every new planting. By breaking the biological link between seed and grain, hybridization operates "the fission of the identity of the seed as product and as means of production" (Kloppenburg 1988: 11). Thanks to hybridization, a viable private seed industry came into being in the United States in the second half of the twentieth century. This industry could rely on stable, yearly sales of new hybrid varieties. Private seed companies, however, still had to compete with a strong public system of plant breeding. The great success of the industry has been precisely to define a new division of labor between public and private plant breeders: while private breeders oversaw the development of commercial varieties, public plant breeding programs were limited to doing 'basic research.'

Two other parallel processes were part and parcel of the constitution of the seed as a commodity. First, production of commercial seed became an increasingly complex technoscientific enterprise. This is obvious in the age of molecular biology and genetic engineering, but it became already evident with the development of hybrid varieties. The costs—in capital, labour, knowledge and time—of developing and maintaining the purity of new high-yield varieties soon increased exponentially. The outcome was the progressive exclusion of the farmer from the production of seed, the negation of his or her role as an autonomous plant breeder. The farmer became then the day-to-day manager of operations that are coordinated and supervised by private seed companies. The second element is eminently legal, and concerns the recognition and protection of private proprietary rights over the seed. First with the 1970 Plant Variety Protection Act, and then with the extension of patentability to plant and plant elements by the U.S. Supreme Court decision on *Diamond v. Chakrabarty* in 1980, a regime of proprietary rights over the seed came into being in the United States, and was later extended internationally. The commodification of the seed, its patentability and the regime of property rights that go with it, has recently come under a new sort of challenge, which, as this paper argues, can be understood as the multiplication, in and outside the courts, of pollution claims.

The Uses of Patents

When Monsanto decided to bring Percy Schmeiser to court, it sought protection of its property rights under the Canadian Patent Act. Schmeiser was accused of having infringed Patent No. 1,313,830, known through the hearings as "the '830 patent." The text of the '830 Patent describes as the object of invention "a method of genetically transforming plant cells which causes the cells and plants regenerated therefrom to become resistant to glyphosate and the herbicidal salts thereof." The "claims of the invention" of the patent include over forty elements, all of them variations of the two key items: a chimeric plant gene—the EPSPS gene that confers resistance to glyphosate—and the glyphosate-resistant oilseed rape cell comprising the chimeric plant gene (quoted in MacKay 2001: par. 20).

Plant genes and cells can be protected under two different statutes in Canada, as in the United States: the plant variety protection laws (in the case of Canada, the Plant Breeders' Rights Act of 1990) and the patent utility law (the Canadian Patent Act of 1985). The differences between these two kinds of legal protection are crucial for the distribution of rights and control over genes and organisms, and can be best described with the example of the U.S. legislation. In the United States, the 1970 Plant Variety Protection Act (PVPA) basically extended to sexually reproducing species the rights that had been granted in 1930 by the Plant Patent Act to breeders of asexually reproducing organisms.[11] The 1970 Act represented a crucial boost to private plant breeders and seed merchants, but it also aimed to safeguard farmers' right to save and plant seed from previous harvests, by limiting the scope of proprietary rights over plant genes.

A different, broader form of protection for seed came into being following the 1980 decision on the patentability of living matter in *Diamond v. Chakrabarty*.[12] Nevertheless, the compatibility of plant variety protection and the new patent statutes was at first unclear, and for several years the U.S. Patent and Trademark Office consistently rejected patents on plants or plant components, arguing that these were preempted by the very existence of the PVPA—which, the Office argued, specifically restricted the kinds of protection that could be extended to plants, implicitly excluding patents. In a 1985 decision (*Ex parte Hibberd*), the United States Patent Office Board of Appeals and Interferences decided to recognize patent rights over tissue culture, seed, and whole plants, thereby significantly broadening the range of protection extended to plant germplasm. In October of 2001 (*J. E. M. Ag Supply Inc v. Pioneer Hi-Bred*), the U.S. Supreme Court upheld the Board of Appeals and Interferences's decision in *Ex parte Hibberd*, and explicitly recognized patent protection to sexually reproducing plant varieties.

A key difference between a plant variety protection certificate and a patent is that, whereas the former allows for protection of a single property claim over the plant variety as an indivisible whole, a patent can be granted over different plants belonging to the same variety, and to various components of a single plant. That is, a patent can authorize control over genes, cells, tissue cultures, or seed, as well as over the entire plant. This is particularly relevant as new genetic engineering techniques permit transformations at new level of the organism. "The ability to make multiple claims," Kloppenburg points out, "significantly broadens the protection afforded the invention. It also permits the licensing of particular components—e.g., a gene for herbicide tolerance— for use by third parties. Because genetic engineering in plants is geared to transformations at the cellular and molecular levels, utility patents provide a significant advantage over [Plant Variety Protection] certificates, which can provide property rights only in the whole organism" (Kloppenburg 1988: 263–264). The Canadian Patent Act is somewhat more restrictive that its U.S. equivalent: under Canadian law only *genes*—neither other plant components, nor the plant as a whole—can be subject to patenting.

The other fundamental difference between plant variety protection and patent statutes is that the former often recognized, albeit in a limited fashion, the farmer's right to save seed from his or her harvest for replanting. Patents, however,, while patents explicitly preclude this possibility. Section 42 of the Canadian Patent Act gives the patentee, and not the frmer, "the exclusive right, privilege and liberty of making, constructing and using the invention and selling it to others to be used."[13]

The case of *Monsanto v. Schmeiser* was therefore from the point of view of the plaintiffs a pure patent infringement case. The issues to be determined were solely the validity of Monsanto's patent over the genes carrying the glyphosate tolerance trait, and whether Percy Schmeiser had indeed committed a violation or infringement of this patent. Of the multitude of interrelated aspects and decisions involved in *Monsanto v. Schmeiser*, two deserve particular attention here: the dispute over whether the presence of glyphosate-tolerant canola plants in Percy Schmeiser's fields constituted "use" of Monsanto's patented genes and cells, and the question of whether the manner in which those genes arrived to Schmeiser's fields affects in any way the validity of Monsanto's proprietary claims and the definition of the defendant's actions as infringement. Both issues were fought out around particular understandings of 'genetic pollution'—of the agency of natural and human actors, and of the controllability of genes and agricultural practices.

The first line of defense in Percy Schmeiser's argument was that Monsanto's patent should not be considered valid, because, among other reasons:

> The alleged invention . . . is self-propagating and can spread without human intervention; the patent was obtained for an illicit purpose of creating a noxious plant that would spread by natural means to the lands of innocent parties so as to entrap them with nuisance patent infringement claims (Defense 2000).

The second claims was that Percy Schmeiser had never intended to use Monsanto's invention. According to the defendant's account, after spraying Roundup herbicide around some telephone poles in 1997, Schmeiser discovered that some of the canola plants near the road had survived. Monsanto would later argue that the 1998 harvest contained up to 98% of herbicide-tolerant plants. What happened between 1997 and 1998 was the object of contention. Schmeiser claimed that his fields had been contaminated by Monsanto's genes in the first place, and that the spread of the contamination in the following year was likely an effect of cross-pollination. He declared never to have knowingly saved and planted glyphosate-tolerant seed. Proof of this, he argued, was the fact that he never used glyphosate herbicides to spray his crops, and thereby failed to make use of the benefits of Roundup Ready plants. He had been saving his own seed for decades, to improve the quality of his canola through selection. In an interview, Schmeiser described the events leading up to the trial:

> Right after they filed the lawsuit they went after me and said that I had done these things. I stood up to Monsanto and said no. My wife and I knew that we were using our own seed. If it was now contaminated with Monsanto's Roundup Ready, then they had actually destroyed 50 years of my work. So we decided to fight Monsanto. It eventually went to pretrial and in those hearings Monsanto admitted they had no record that anyone had ever said to them that I had obtained a seed illegally. But they said it didn't matter, the fact that there was some GMO seed on my land—no matter how it got there—meant that I was guilty of infringing on their patent (ACRES 2002).

Monsanto tried to demonstrate that the amount of herbicide-tolerant canola in Schmeiser's fields could only be explained as a result of a purposeful action on his part—the planting of illegally obtained commercial seed—and not as an effect of natural causes. Monsanto's lawyers first argued that Percy Schmeiser had obtained Monsanto seed through 'brownbagging,' probably from another farmer in the area, but the company later dropped this accusation, and argued that Schmeiser had used as seed the plants that survived the Roundup spraying in 1997. Several witnesses for the prosecution argued that neither seed dispersal nor pollen-mediated gene flow could account for, under normal conditions, the proportion of herbicide-tolerant plants in Percy Schmeiser's fields. Keith Downey, considered 'the inventor of canola,' testified at the court that the chances of contamination producing such a high presence of herbicide-tolerant plants in a field of conventional canola were minimal, and that, consequently, "the Roundup tolerant plants observed growing in [Schmeiser's] field must have arisen from a crop planted with Roundup Ready pedigreed seed and not from outcrossing."[14] Barry Hertz, professor of mechanical engineering at the University of Saskatchewan, and an expert in road vehicle aerodynamics, argued that seeds being blown off trucks could not have flown the 16.8 meters separating the road from the limit of Schmeiser's canola crops. A number of experts were called by the prosecution to validate the test results. Robinson Investigations employees, for instance, defended the legality of the samples taken, while Monsanto researchers presnted data backing their analytical results. Percy Schmeiser's lawyers, on the other hand, offered alternative tests demonstrating a lower level of contamination in his fields, which were more consistent with the hypothesis of 'gene flow.'

These are important, yet typical claims and counter-claims in legal disputes involving genetic testing. 'Chains of custody' are often scrutinized, and alternative statistical models are presented to interpret the analytical results.[15] In this respect *Monsanto v. Schmeiser* is not all that different from, say, the O. J. Simpson trial. What makes our case interesting from the point of view of the proprietary control of genes is the fact that all these disputes over the scientific assessment of gene flow and the technical results of testing became largely marginal to the resolution of the case.

Justice MacKay ruled that both the origin of the glyphosate-tolerant plants *and* the intentions of Percy Schmeiser were immaterial to a decision on the issue of patent infringement. On the first issue, Justice MacKay argued that "the source of the Roundup resistant canola in the defendants' 1997 crop is really not significant for the resolution of the issue of infringement which relates to the 1998 crop." It did not matter, then, whether the plants were there due to pollen-mediated gene flow, seed dispersal, or 'brownbagging' of commercial seed. Similarly, the 'real' intentions of the defendant were irrelevant to the issue of infringement. It is precisely this immateriality that makes patents such a powerful resource for the protection of property rights. "Mere use, however unintentional," Martin Phillipson points out in regard to the Schmeiser case, "is sufficient to render an individual liable for prosecution" (Phillipson 2001). According to the accepted legal doctrine, "infringement occurs when *the essence* of the invention is *taken*."[16] 'Taking' is here understood as 'using.' Simple "possession" of a plant containing the patented gene, for instance, should not be sufficient cause of infringement. What the Canadian Patent Act grants and recognizes is, after all, "the exclusive right, privilege and liberty of making, constructing and using the invention and selling it to others to be used," and, as a result, it is on the definition of *use* that the issue of infringement hinges.

But how is "use" to be defined? *Monsanto v. Schmeiser* demonstrates that use can only be defined in relation to, and together with, a particular construction of what "the essence" of Monsanto's invention is. And, far from being set once and forever in the patent certificate, both elements—use and essence—are challenged and must be renegotiated in the context of disputed claims over 'genetic pollution.'

The defense's argument hinged on an extension of the definition of what constitutes an invention: invention must encompass not only the genes and cells—the specific "claims of invention" listed in a patent certificate—but also the human and social practices with which these were associated. Percy Schmeiser, this argument goes, had not taken the essence of Monsanto's invention, simply because he had not used glyphosate herbicides on his fields. And it was the defense's contention that there is no use of the patented gene without use of the herbicide to which the gene confers tolerance:

To grow canola is not to use the gene. This is because the gene does not cause canola to grow. The invention has not utility unless a farmer is spraying his canola with Roundup intending it to survive. Only then is he using the gene technology patented by Monsanto. (. . .) If the object of the patent was to protect a component which made a plant grow better, merely growing canola may constitute "use" of Monsanto's invention. But Monsanto's invention does not cause the plant to grow. The gene is merely an accidental and non-essential part of the plant (Defense 2000, par. 146 & 156).

Consequently, the defense argued, "the invention will be used if a grower applies Roundup to his canola after it has reached the leaf stage. In this case he is utilizing the invention, i.e. a gene which gives a plant glyphosate-resistance. If he is not applying Roundup in this manner, he is not using the gene. No infringement has occurred" (Defense 2000: par. 157).

In his ruling, Justice MacKay emphasized that the issue to be determined was indeed whether Schmeiser had used the patented genes—neither where these genes had come from, nor the intention of the farmer. The discussions on the paths that could have led Monsanto's genes to his fields was inconsequential, and Justice MacKay specified some of the (immaterial) ways in which this could have happened:

> Thus a farmer whose field contains seed or plants originating from seed spilled into them, or blown as seed, in swaths from a neighbour's land or even growing from germination by pollen carried into his field from elsewhere by insects, birds, or by the wind, may own the seed or plants on his land even if he did not set about to plant them. He does not, however, own the right to the use of the patented gene, or of the seed or plant containing the patented gene or cell. (MacKay 2001: par. 91)

It was this "right to use" that was protected under the '830 patent. But should "use" be defined by the application of the product to which the gene construct confers resistance—glyphosate—as the defense argued? Or can the invention be separated, for the purposes of patentability, from the agricultural product and practices to which it is commonly and by genetic design linked? In his resolution Justice MacKay thought "use" should be understood solely on the basis of the genes' agency. Once again, what the farmer did or did not do was inessential. "In my opinion," he argued, "whether or not that crop was sprayed with Roundup during its growing period is not important. Growth of the seed, reproducing of the patented gene and cell, and sale of the harvested crop constitutes taking the essence of the Plaintiff's invention, using it, without permission. In so doing the defendants infringed upon the patent interests of the plaintiffs" (MacKay 2001: par. 123).

Note here that Justice MacKay's description of what constitutes 'use' does not include terms commonly used to describe farmers' actions, verbs like "planting," "sowing," or "harvesting." Significantly, two of the three elements in his definition—the "*growth of the seed*" and "*the reproducing*" of genes and cells—do not necessarily describe purposeful human actions. As embedded in the seed, patented genes are able to spread through the air and replicate, germinate and grow, outside human control. In Justice MacKay's opinion, any of these processes would constitute 'use' of the patented gene.

Let us note also that this particular view of rights and control is presented in an argumentative structure that stresses the agency of non-human actors and that disregards the purpose or intention of human actions. The allocation of degrees and forms of agency to the different actors involved in the Schmeiser case—genes, farmers, wind, seeds, inspectors, insects—is a central rhetorical resource, and it is a flexible one too. For instance, at key moments in its argument the defense stressed the role of the farmer's agency (the alleged intentions and purposes, or lack thereof, of Percy Schmeiser's actions) and of Roundup spraying to define what "using" a patent means. In so doing it tried to downplay the specific agency of genes. But at other points in the trial, the defense was similarly able to emphasize the role of genes as independent actors, particularly when the controllability of genetic pollution was concerned. To describe Percy Schmeiser's helplessness in the face of gene transfer, or Monsanto's loss of control over genes and the proprietary rights that accompany them, the defense would depict genes as actors capable of moving at free will, or even of making 'decisions': "Monsanto has not property interests in its gene," the defense argued, "only intellectual property rights. It certainly does not own canola seed, or canola plants *this gene has decided to incorporate itself into*" (Defense 2000: par. 161; my emphasis). In this somewhat awkward but telling linguistic construct, the gene appears to be an uncontrollable actor, one who moves and wanders around freely, and whose incorporation into organisms is beyond the control of the patent holder. It is the gene's 'decision' that determines where it ends up.[17] Surely, the defense argued, proprietary rights cannot follow this self-replicating actor wherever it goes . . . The point here is that when it comes to proprietary claims over living matter, defense and accusation lawyers can smoothly move from sophisticated social constructivism (e.g. the patented object is only given meaning by the purposeful actions of human agents) to straightforward naturalism; from anthropomorphic natural actors to abstract "natural functions." From this fluid combination of argumentative strategies and flexible use of alternative rhetorical repertoires, however, the court must produce a clear boundary between the natural and social worlds.

In its appeal, the defense did return to the critical meaning of "using a patent," to challenge Justice MacKay's ruling. If the Patent Act grants the patent holder "the exclusive right . . . of making, constructing and using the invention and selling it to others to be used," use could only be meaningfully defined, according to Schmeiser's lawyers, as "commercial exploitation," a form of activity exclusively human and explicitly purposeful. In fact, as the defense pointed out, the French version of the Act uses the verb 'exploiter' (and not, say, 'utiliser,' 'employer,' or 'se server de') as the appropriate equivalent for the English 'using.' The shared meaning of these two terms was that of "beneficial, commercial or exploitive use." It was this meaning that should prevail in the patent infringement case, a meaning that would "conform to the commercial nature of patent rights" (Defense 2001: par. 99). An interpretation of use along these terms would likely reduce the chances of Percy Schmeiser being found in infringement of the patent. Since no court evidence showed he had used glyphosate-based herbicides on his canola plants, there was no proof that he had "exploited" the patented genes. "The essence of the invention," the defense contended, "was not its physical existence, but its novel utility; and the essence of the Respondent's [Monsanto's] monopoly rights was not possession, *but commercial use or exploitation*. Because there was no finding that Mr. Schmeiser sprayed the 1998 canola crops with a glyphosate-based herbicide such as Roundup, *thus exploiting the patented genes*, the Appellants did not infringe the Patent" (Defense 2001: par. 100).

The ultimate argument behind the defense's challenge to Justice MacKay's definition of use—"growth of the seed, reproducing the patented gene and cell, and sale of the harvested crop"—was that it failed to limit infringement to situations caused by human agency, and human agency alone. "Commercial exploitation" would be a much more unambiguous term in this respect. In contrast, Justice MacKay had confused human and natural forms of agency, and had extended patent rights to both. The Justice's definition of use, the defense argued, "suggests that the scope of Monsanto's patent extended beyond the resistance of the gene to glyphosate herbicides and included the natural functions of canola seed—that is their capacity, once they are embedded in the soil, to grow into a plant and reproduce. Such a view ignores both the legal principle that patents are to protect *inventions*—works that are innovative, novel and useful—and the fact that canola itself is not man-made" (Defense 2001: par. 79).

The defense thus showed irritation at what it considered an unclear delimitation of 'natural functions' and man-made processes, that produced a hybrid definition of use and unfairly extended Monsanto's proprietary rights. Roundup Ready canola may be a man-made object, a product of human ingenuity that deserves patent protection. But it undoubtedly has—or maintains—"natural functions," and these should not be allowed to define the meaning of use, and, by extension, the applicability of property rights.[18] The defense is thus trying to establish here a distinction between, on the one hand, canola—if not a natural plant itself, at least a plant still possessing 'natural functions'—and, on the other hand, Monsanto's proprietary genes and cells. Monsanto's patent should only apply, the argument goes, to those activities and processes determined by the presence of the proprietary genes—voluntary planting of Roundup

Ready canola *together with* the spraying of glyphosate herbicide, for in-stance—and not to those caused by characteristics that both conventional and genetically modified canola plants would have in common as 'naturally' occurring organisms.

In a certain sense, however, Justice MacKay does not confuse natural and man-made processes, but simply extends and universalizes the latter. A radi-cal interpretation of his decision would pick up on his implication that that a patented object can have no "natural functions" whatsoever, at least not when growing on a private plot of land. Justice MacKay argued that, since the canola plants were growing on his land, Percy Schmeiser "knew or ought to have known" that they were Roundup tolerant. Thus, once established patents seem to eliminate nature as a meaningful sort of agency and an effective source of legitimation. They do so by allowing the interpretation of any event or occurrence in terms of human rights and obligations—as a process over which humans or corporations (i.e. Monsanto) hold proprietary rights, or as events over which humans (i.e. Percy Schmeiser) ought to possess knowledge and exert responsibility.

Pollution and 'Confusion'

As discussed thus far, the gene's agency and the corporation's control were central to the arguments in the trial. Percy Schmeiser's lawyers also presented the case as one concerning the "admixture of goods," and thereby tried to draw on the law of intermixture and on the jurisprudence bearing on the limitations, or forfeiture, of propriety rights caused by the commingling of goods. There is a substantial body of legal precedent that explicitly relates property claims to the ability to trace and identify goods that have entered into new mixes or combinations, and ultimately it was in this doctrine that Schmeiser's lawyers hoped to find support for their claims (MacCormack 1990: 32–59).

The origins of the legal doctrine on admixture can be traced back to the principles of *confusio* and *commixtio* in Roman Law. Originally, Roman Law used *commixtio* to characterize dry mixtures, and *confusio* to define wet mixtures; but the difference underlying these categories—a distinction that has been maintained in modern jurisprudence—is that between admixtures where the different goods maintain their separate identities and can be identi-fied as such (*commixtio*), and, on the other hand, situations where goods can no longer be separated or distinguished from each other (*confusio*). Parris summarizes these distinctions of Roman Law as follows:

> *Confusio* dealt with the position where goods were so combined as to be insepa-rable: the admixture of two liquids, or where A's purple was used for dyeing B's

garment. *Commixtio* . . . was where there was the admixture of the chattels of two owners in such a way that they could readily be separated (Parris 1986:89).[19]

Roman Law used these notions to determine and allocate entitlements to property over such admixtures. In general, it established that in cases where goods or substances have been commingled and cannot be separated or distinguished, and when such admixture occurs by accident or agreement, the resulting good would be common property of the involved parties, and their shares in the new object would be proportional to those of the original goods (Vaines 1957: 312–313). Common law coincides with this interpretation, but diverges from Roman Law in how to deal with cases where the intermixture is due to the *purposeful* action of only one of the parties involved, against the will of the other. This divergence of Roman and Common Law is described by Blackstone in a classic passage in his commentaries on English Common Law:

> But if one willfully intermixes his money, corn, or hay, with that of another man, without his approbation or knowledge, or casts gold in like manner into another's melting-pot or crucible, the civil law, though it gives the sole property of the whole to him who has not interfered in the mixture, yet allows a satisfaction to the other for what he has so improvidently lost. But our law, to guard against fraud, allows no remedy [to the guilty party] in such a case; but gives the entire property, without any account, to him, whose original dominion is invaded, and endeavoured to be rendered uncertain, without his own consent (Blackstone 1962 [1766], p. 405).

The defense lawyers, in quoting the above passage omitted the reference to Civil Law (and the satisfaction to the party responsible for the *confusio* that it allows), claimed that Schmeiser's domain had indeed been rendered "uncertain" by the uncontrolled transfer of Monsanto's genes into his canola fields, and consequently demanded that the property of this domain be granted to Percy Schmeiser, and to him alone. The situation, the defense argued, was the same as in the 1811 case of *Colwill v. Reeves*, where the court decided that, "if a man puts into my bag, in which before there is some corn, the whole is mine, because it is impossible to distinguish what was mine for what is his."[20]

The question remains: what sort of agency provokes pollution? For Common Law only allocates unrestricted property over the admixture if one of the parties is found guilty of "willfully intermixing" the other's domain. Otherwise, if confusio is brought about by an 'accident' or by agreement, both Civil and Common Law agree that the resulting domain becomes the common property of the affected parties. In that case, Percy Schmeiser and Monsanto would have to share the property of the canola crops. If the law of intermixture were to be applied, then, and if the defense were to sustain the argument that Monsanto had no rights to damages whatsoever, pollution would have to be construed not as an accident, nor as an act of nature, but as the direct result of Monsanto's willful action.

In the defense's argument, this matter is framed as one of agents—patented genes—not being controlled by their proprietor—Monsanto. Monsanto was guilty of rendering Schmeiser's domain 'uncertain' by its inability or lack of interest in effectively controlling the movement and transfer of its patented genes in the environment. In fact, the defense argued, this lack of control carried with it the abrogation of whatever rights over the Roundup Ready genes Monsanto may have been awarded. In other words, failure to contain and control gene flow should be cause for the loss of whatever property rights Monsanto possessed over the gene:

> Had [Monsanto] maintained control over its invention, it may have maintained its exclusive rights. However, inventions do not usually spread themselves around. They do not normally replicate and invade the property and lands of others . . . Any exclusive rights Monsanto may have had to its invention were lost when it lost control over the spread of its invention. Surely, the exclusive right to possess such an invention cannot be maintained if the spread of the invention cannot be controlled. The unconfined and uncontrolled release into the environment is an act by Monsanto completely inconsistent with its exclusive rights. It cannot on the one hand unleash self-propagating matter uncontrolled into the environment and then claim exclusivity wherever it invades. It can, by this, be taken by its conduct to have waived its statutory rights (Defense 2000, par. 170).

The defense invoked and extended to this situation the 'stray bull' precedent: if a stray bull trespasses on another's property and impregnates his cows, the progeny of those cows will belong exclusively to the cows' owner. Similarly, Schmeiser's lawyers argued, if the Monsanto genes had pollinated Mr. Schmeiser's plants, or if Monsanto seed had found its way to his fields, it would be fair to argue that property of the resulting plants would belong completely to Mr. Schmeiser. The defense presented the 'stray bull' case as one literally concerning the propagation of genes, and drew the inevitable analogy of Monsanto's genes 'trespassing' on Schmeiser's fields and 'impregnating' his canola plants.[21]

How did the court respond to this set of arguments? As we have seen, Justice MacKay's argument hinged, first and foremost, on a broad understanding of "use." In MacKay's decision "use" was in a certain sense restricted, by decoupling it from the application of Roundup herbicide and the prescribed practices of farmers. "Use" concerns the genes that are the object of the patent, and those genes alone, and does not concern practices or products associated with the expression of those genes. But, on the other hand, the meaning of "use" was expanded by the combination—one could say admixture—of human and non-human actions and forms of agency: the "growth of the seed," the reproduction of genes and cells, the placement on the market of the resulting crop . . . any and all one of these actions would constitute use and therefore infringement of the patent. As we have argued, the first two elements of the definition can be construed as natural processes brought about by gene flow, whereas the third one, "sale of the harvested crop," did not necessarily entail the commercialization of the crop for the particular economic benefit that the patent is intended to accrue. The fact that Percy Schmeiser had not used glyphosate herbicide on his canola crops, and had thereby failed to benefit explicitly from the presence of the EPSPS gene, was inconsequential, in Justice MacKay's determination of infringement.

When it came to the relevance of pollution and control for property rights, Justice MacKay adopted a narrow definition of the case at hand. The situation could not be presented as an admixture of goods, he argued, for Monsanto "does have ownership in its patented gene and cell and pursuant to the [Patent] Act it has the exclusive use of its invention," and this mere fact "distinguishes this case from others on which the defendants rely," most notably those involving 'stray bulls' and other similarly unwelcome spreaders of undesired pollution (MacKay 2001, paragraph 93).

With respect to the defense's argument that lack of control over the spread and replication of the gene constitutes an abrogation of the patent, Justice MacKay argued that Monsanto did in fact endeavor to control the dissemination of its proprietary genes and the plants in which it is contained. The Technology Use Agreement that it forced farmers to sign was itself evidence of this endeavor, for the goal of the contract is precisely to limit the number of users and the kinds of uses of the technology, and therefore to control the spread of the patented object. Together with the continuous inspections and audits of farmers thought to be growing the genetically modified canola without authorization, and the "volunteer control policy" (under which Monsanto assists in the removal of unwanted Roundup Ready canola plants), these activities were proof, in Justice MacKay opinion, that "the plaintiffs undertook a variety of measures designed to control the unwanted spread of canola containing their patented gene and cell" (MacKay 2001: par. 97).[22] It was on the basis of this reasoning that Justice MacKay decided that Monsanto's patent had been infringed, and that Percy Schmeiser should pay damages to Monsanto.[23]

Conclusion: Legal Containment

Outside the court, Justice MacKay's ruling was widely seen as a precedent for future cases involving patent protection and genetic pollution, and different groups reacted accordingly. The biotechnology industry hailed the judgment as a landmark decision in the protection of seed patent rights against farmers' unlicensed use of proprietary genes. Monsanto, on the other hand, was keen on downplaying the relevance of the decision for farmers beyond the specifics of the case, trying to allay fears of more aggressive 'gene police' actions. "It is important," Trish Jordan, Manager of Public and Industry Affairs for Monsanto Canada argued, "that this case does not get hauled up for the world to say, ok, now this means this. For us it has been one case, one individual, one particular situation, and every situation is going to be different."[24] For environmental groups and some farmers' organizations, the judgment was an international scandal, for, in their opinion, it made farmers responsible for the effects of genetic pollution. The Rural Advancement Foundation International (RAFI) compared the case to "unsafe sex": "it's like saying that Monsanto's technology is spreading a sexually transmitted disease but everyone else has to wear a condom" (RAFI 2001). Or as Terry Boehm, of the Saskatchewan National Farmers Union puts it:

> The question for farmers and the broader public is if a patented gene is self-replicating and indeed promiscuous when released into the environment, how can they be found to be in violation of a patent, particularly when it finds its way uninvited into their crops and/or seed? This gene pollution places the burden on those very people who do not want it and do not seek it. (. . .) Would it not be incumbent on Monsanto to extract its gene from the plant or seed contaminated with its presence and then return the undamaged plant and seed to the farmer. This obviously is not practical but it begs the question, is Monsanto's patent practical? (Boehm 2003).

Among critics of agricultural biotechnology, Justice MacKay's ruling only strengthened the opposition to Monsanto's patent protection practices, and multiplied the charges of genetic pollution in and outside the courts. Organic farmers in Saskatchewan decided to launch a lawsuit against Monsanto and Aventis, accusing them of endangering their certification as organic producers by releasing genetically modified genes into the environment.[25] Growing organic canola, they argued, had become impossible in Western Canada due to the high level of background genetic contamination in the region. The goal of the lawsuit is not only to define liability and demand compensation for the damages inflicted on organic farmer, but also to use the experience with transgenic canola to obtain an injunction barring the introduction of genetically modified wheat in Canada.[26] The controllability of transgenic canola and the coexistence of genetically modified and conventional crops, moreover, remain a contentious policy question in the debate over agricultural biotechnology. Genetically modified canola with multiple resistance to a variety of herbicides—a result of cross-pollination in the field—has been found in different areas of Canada, and official reports have warned about widespread contamination of the seed supply, going back to the nurseries where plant breeders develop new varieties. "There is no such a thing as containment. (. . .) There is no such a thing as pure seed, it is all contaminated," Schmeiser points out, because the transgenic canola "doesn't know a boundary."[27] In the meantime, batches of conventional canola imported into Europe have repeatedly been found to contain genetically modified varieties, and plant breeders have been forced to move seed production out of Western Canada, looking for countries where the stringent purity thresholds can be maintained. All in all, the practical ability to control canola crops, and to maintain the necessary separations in agricultural production and trade is still very much under challenge, regardless of the rule of the Canadian Federal Court.

In fact, Justice MacKay's curious decision in the Schmeiser case managed to side-step these issues altogether. Pollution as a practical problem, and as an object of intense scientific controversies, was ultimately deemed irrelevant to the Court's reasoning, and to patent infringement cases more generally. This form of *legal containment* is achieved through a unique understanding of what "using a patent" means. As Justice MacKay argued, the origin of Monsanto's genes, and the causes that brought them to Schmeiser's fields, are aspects that bear no relevance on the decision. Following his argument to its ultimate conclusions, one discovers that patents leave no room for pollution as a *natural* phenomenon—for they define the genes' 'natural functions' as within the domain of infringement.

Monsanto v. Schmeiser is, however, only the beginning of a long battle, as similar legal cases multiply throughout the world (Phillipson 2001). Schmeiser's case will soon be heard by the Canadian Supreme Court, which may decide to address some of the matters of principle involved in the case, including the patentability of what Schmeiser and his lawyers often refer to as "life-giving forms." Here as in other cases, the fundamental issue is whether biotechnology patent holders will in the future be found liable for the consequences that the self-replication of their inventions might bring about. In short, whether intellectual property rights will carry with them new control obligations. Or whether, in the face of increasingly unmanageable genetic pollution, the courts will extend the meaning of patents and the limits of patent protection, to cover processes not necessarily under human control. Alternatively, they may discover that patents and traditional understandings of intellectual property rights cannot fully contain some of the legal and social implications of self-replicating life forms.

Notes

1. Monsanto charges C$15 per acre of Roundup Ready canola. This is in contrast to other crops, where the fee is applied directly to the seed bought from the seed dealers, and the farmer pays per bag of seed. In the case of canola, thus, the relationship between Monsanto and the farmer is unmediated.

2. "Monsanto Sleuth Suspected 'Brown Bag' Sale of Seed: Company Lawyers Wrap Up Case Against Bruno-Area Farmer," *The Saskatoon StarPhoenix/Regina Leader-Post*, June 13, 2000.

3. This description is based on the court proceedings of Monsanto Canada Inc. and Monsanto Company *versus* Percy Schmeiser and Schmeiser Enterprises Ltd. See also Justice W. Andrew MacKay's judgement (MacKay 2001). Most of these documents are available from Percy Schmeiser's website: http://www. percyschmeiser.com.

4. Diamond v. Chakrabarty, 447 U.S. 303 (1980), 313.

5. Invention is intertwined with notions of authorship that legitimize the award of exclusive rights over products of "human ingenuity," whereas 'pure nature' comes to be defined in opposition to invention, as that that has no author. For a treatment of authorship in intellectual property rights disputes see Boyle (1996).

6. The ancestor of canola, rapeseed, was used mostly as a source of lubricant oil during the Second World War. When in the 1950s scientists discovered that its oil contained high levels of eicosenoic and erucic fatty acids, and that these acids presented a potential hazard to human health, Canadian plant breeders developed a variety of oilseed rape with a low level of saturated fat and named it canola. As Justice MacKay was to argue in his decision on the Percy Schmeiser case, canola is "a great Canadian success story." In fact, the term canola is simply a combination of 'Canada' and 'oil.' Canola seed contains a high proportion (approximately 40%) of oil, which is used for human consumption or in processed foods. The protein-rich meal left after crushing the seed is generally used for livestock feeding. Since the 1960s, most of the canola grown for human consumption in Europe and North America is of the "double low" kind: low erucic acid content in the oil, and low glucosinolate content in the meal. Canola is thus, technically speaking, a brand name. The term describes a certain oil quality, which can be legally applied to some members of the *Brassica* family only. The term, however, is commonly used as a general noun, to describe particular varieties of oilseed rape. See Organisation for Economic Co-Operation and Development (1997). The statement that canola "never existed in nature" is from Dr. Wilf Keller, Director of Research at the Plant Biotechnology Institute, National Research Council, in Saskatoon. He was interviewed for the 'Canola Wars' project of the Division of Media and Technology of the University of Saskatchewan, 2002.

7. For more details on the political history of canola, see Busch et al (1994) and Kneen (1992).

8. OCDE (1997: 16). The European Union has been the source of much of the recent research on gene flow from oilseed rape (or canola), prompted by the local need to regulate the coexistence of transgenic and conventional crops. See for instance, European Environment Agency (2002) and Joint Research Centre (2002). For an analysis of the emergence of 'gene flow' as an object of regulatory science, particularly in relation to canola varieties, see Bonneuil *et al* (2002).

9. Particularly in the production of certified seed. It appears now that the traditional isolation distances established by the OECD Seed Schemes to manage the production of seed with a sufficient degree of purity will not be sufficient to limit the presence of transgenic types in conventional seed, to the degree required in certain markets (i.e. European Union)..

10. "I wish it would have been held under Provincial Court," Schmeiser would argue at some point, "where I could have had a jury with farmers who understand what farming is all about." See ACRES (2002: p. 28).

11. It is interesting to note here that one of the reasons why the U.S. Congress refused to extend protection to sexually propagated species back in 1930 was the lack of genetic stability of these organisms, due to the genetic drift between generations. As Kloppenburg points out, the Department of Agriculture thought at the time that this fact "would present insurmountable difficulties in enforcement of the act." (Kloppenburg 1988: 133). In a certain sense, the discussion anticipated the issue of 'genetic pollution,' and the patentability of cross-pollinated varieties more generally. The Senate Report on the 1930 Plant Patent Act noted that "All such plants must be asexually reproduced in order to have their identity preserved. This is necessary since seedlings either of chance or self-pollenization from any of these would not preserve the character of the individual." The Senate explained the limitation of the statute on the basis of "a practical situation": the loss of 'genetic identity' of the offspring of sexually propagating varieties. S. Report No. 315, 71st Congress, 2nd Session, 3 (1930) (Quoted in U.S. Supreme Court, JE.M Ag Supply v. Pioneer Hi-Bred, October 2001).

12. Diamond v. Chakrabarty, 447 U.S. 303 (1980), 313.

13. Canadian Patent Act, s. 42.

14. "Farmer's Story Lack Credibility, Says Scientist," *The Western Producer*, June 15, 2000.

15. See Halfton (1998) and Jasanoff (1998) for an analysis of the role of these issues in DNA identification cases.

16. *Lishman v. Erom Roche* Inc, 1996. My emphasis.

17. A vision of the gene that contrasts with of the ideology of controllability and precision often associated with genetic engineering.

18. In a certain way, the defense's argument resembles that of *Moore vs. Regents of the University of California* (1990). In that landmark decision the California Supreme Court held that researchers at the University of California Medical Center could maintain a patent over cell lines derived from John Moore's spleen. Once of the reasons offered by the Court was, in opposition to "naturally occurring" cells the cell line is the expression of "an inventive effort." The implication is that no such patent would have been granted over naturally occurring organisms or processes. Moore v. Regents of the University of California, 5 Cal. 3d 120 (Cal. 1990).

19. The other two relevant principles of Roman Law, which were however not invoked by the defenders in the Schmeiser case, are *accessio*, when something of trifling value is added to a more substantial good, and *specificatio*, where a good or entity of a new species is created out of goods belonging to other parties.

20. Colwill v. Reeves (1811), 2 Camp. 575 (Book of Authorities, Tab 17), p. 576.

21. Another well-established paradigm that the defense's argument can be compared to is the theory of negligence used in cases concerning pesticide drift. As John Mandler points out, summarizing the doctrine, "in cases where a pesticide is known to be especially dangerous to the specific nearby crops, or where the sprayer had knowledge of shifting winds, applicators have been held liable for damages under negligence theory" (Mandler 2000). In this case, however, the defense is not simply trying to obtain damages, but to argue that uncontrolled release of a living organism represents loss of patent rights. That is, that negligence in the containment of a self-replicating organism invalidates the patent in the first place. Mandler argues that this line of argumentation could be potentially damaging to seed companies dealing with cases of pollen-mediated gene flow. "While a seed company could argue that cross pollination due to pollen drift is

outside of the control of the parties and uncontrollable given the many agronomic and environmental factors at play, it will be difficult to establish that such crop pollination was unforeseeable."

22. According to Monsanto, between 1996 and 2002 they received less than thirty calls from farmers requesting the removal of volunteer Roundup Ready canola plants.

23. After an appeal process, the amount was finally set in C$19,832.

24. Interviewed for the 'Canola Wars' project of the Division of Media and Technology of the University of Saskatchewan, 2002.

25. Statement of Claim between Larry Hoffman and Dale Beaudoin (Plaintiffs) and Monsanto Canada and Aventis CropScience Canada (Defendants).

26. Interview with Marc Loiselle, Saskatchewan Organic Directorate, Vonda, Saskatchewan. 9 June 2003. One important legal point brought up by this lawsuit, and still to be resolved, is whether the definition of organic farmers as a 'class,' capable of launching a class action suit against the biotechnology industry, is warranted.

27. Interview with Percy Schmeiser, Bruno, Saskatchewan. 9 June 2003.

References

ACRES (2002) "Facing Down Goliath: One Farmer's Battle with a GM Giant" *ACRES*, January 2002, Vol. 32, No. 1.

Berlan, Jean-Pierre and Richard Lewontin (1986) "The political economy of hybrid corn" *Monthly Review* 38:3.

Blackstone, William (1962) [1766] *Commentaries on the Laws of England*, Volume II, Chapter XXVI, "Of Title to Things Personal by Occupancy." Boston: Bacon Press.

Boehm, Terry (2003) "The Politics of Biotechnology—The Politics of Food." Paper obtained from the author.

Bonneuil, C., Marris, C & Pierre-Benoît Joly (2002) "Epistemic cultures, public controversy and the reframing of GMOs' risk expertise and research in France." Paper presented at the meeting of the European Association for the Study of Science and Technology (EASST), York, July 31-August 3, 2002.

Boyle, Jams (1996) Shamans, Software, & Spleens: Law and the Construction of The Information Society. Cambridge: Harvard University Press.

Busch, L., Gunter, V., Mentele, T., Tachikawa, M., & Keiko Tanaka (1994) "Socializing Nature: Technoscience and the Transformation of Rapeseed into Canola" *Crop Science* 34, no. 3.

Defense (2000) Trial Brief on Behalf of the Defendants, Percy Schmeiser and Schmeiser Enterprises Ltd, Federal Court—Trial Division, Court File No. T–1593–98.

Defense (2001) Memorandum of Fact and Law of the Appellants, Percy Schmeiser and Schmeiser Enterprises Ltd. Federal Court of Appeal, Court File No. A–367–01. December 2001

Douglas, Mary (1996) [1966] *Purity and Danger: An Analysis of the Concepts of Pollution and Taboo*. London and New York: Routledge.

European Environmental Agency (2002) *Genetically Modified Organisms (GMOs): The significance of gene flow through pollen transfer*. Environmental issue report, No. 28.

Halfton, Saul (1998) "Collecting, Testing and Convincing: Forensic DNA Experts in the Courts" *Social Studies of Science* 28/5–6 (October-December 1998) 801–828.

Jasanoff, Sheila (1995) *Science At The Bar: Law, Science, and Technology in America.* Cambridge: Harvard University Press.

Jasanoff, Sheila (1998) "The Eye of Everyman: Witnessing DNA in the Simpson Trial" *Social Studies of Science*, 28/5–6, 1998; pp. 713–740.

Joint Research Centre (2002) *Scenarios for co-existence of genetically modified, conventional and organic crops in European agriculture.* Institute for Prospective Technological Studies, Sevilla: Spain.

Kloppenburg, Jack (1988) *First the Seed: The Political Economy of Plant Breeding, 1492–2000.* Cambridge: Cambridge University Press.

Kneen, Brewster (1992) *The Rape of Canola,* Toronto: NC Press.

McCormack, Gerard (1990) *Reservation of Title.* London: Sweet & Maxwell.

MacKay, Andrew (2001) Reasons for Judgement, 2001 FCT 256. Docket: T–1–1593–98. Federal Court of Canada. Ottawa: March 29, 2001.

Mandler, John P. (2000) "Liability exposure to seed companies from adventitious GMO pollination due to pollen drift resulting in cross pollination or outcrossing" Faegre & Benson LLP.

Organisation for Economic Co-Operation and Development (OECD) (1997) *Consensus Document on the Biology of Brassica Napus L. (Oilseed Rape)* Series on Harmonization of Regulatory Oversight in Biotechnology No. 7, Paris.

Phillipson, Martin (2001) "Agricultural law: containing the GM revolution" *Biotechnology and Development Monitor*, No. 48, December 2001.

Rural Advancement Foundation International (RAFI) (2001) *"Monsanto vs. Percy Schmeiser*: No Corporate Liability for Unsafe Sex and Bioserfdom" April 2001.

Vaines, J. Crossley (1957) *Personal Property.* London: Butterworth & Co.

5

Genetics and Citizenship

Anne Kerr

Introduction

In recent years social scientists have become particularly interested in the implications of the new genetics for citizenship and personhood (Finkler, 2000; Novas and Rose, 2000; Parsons and Atkinson, 1993; Petersen and Bunton, 2002; Robertson, 2001; Rose, 1999, 2001). The focus of much of this work is on the implications of developments in pre-symptomatic testing for a range of increasingly complex genetic disorders. The wider ramifications of new clinical practices for people's sense of identity and autonomy are the subjects of considerable empirical analysis (Finkler, 2000; Hallowell, 1999; Cox and McKellin, 1999; Novas and Rose, 2000; Parsons and Atkinson, 1992; 1993; Polzer et al, 2002; Rapp, 2000). This is matched by a more theoretically-driven emphasis on transformations in 'new genetic citizenship' (Petersen and Bunton, 2002), exemplified by the work of Nikolas Rose and Paul Rabinow. Both authors reject comparisons between the new genetics and eugenics (Rose, 1999, 2001; Rabinow, 1996, 1999a & b), on the grounds that, in the words of Rose, 'our very biological life itself has entered the domain of decision and choice' (Rose, 2001, 22, see also Rabinow, 1996). Rose argues that a contemporary 'logic of control' is enacted through the ethics of the genetic counselling session and the registries and databases of the risk society. Individual susceptibility and individual choice are at the core of these logics, alongside complex and fragmentary notion of genes and their functions (Rose, 2001). New forms of biosociality (Rabinow, 1996), such as patient support groups (Rabeharisoa & Callon, 2002), alongside the disintegration of clear notions of expertise (and indeed illness), are thought to be important contributors to contemporary biopolitics in the clinic and beyond. As Andrew Webster, the director of the ESRC's Innovative Health Technologies Programme has noted, contemporary innovations are not simply extending the medical repertoire and the instruments available to it but are *transforming* it. In addition these innovations are changing our understanding of health, illness and disease, so redefining health, medicine and the body (Webster, 2002, 446).

This renegotiation of citizenship is taking place at a time when there is also increasing emphasis upon public involvement in policy-making about genetics (Barns et al, 2000; Davison et al, 1997; Kerr and Cunningham-Burley, 2000). This form of active citizenship is often invoked by genetic policy makers and their critics in both radical and patient support groups. As Petersen and Bunton (2002) have noted, individual autonomy and a consensual society (exemplified in the work of Habermas) are key priorities for all of these groups.

The emphasis on the scale and pace of change in both of these forms of new genetic citizenship chimes with public discourse of high profile geneticists, who often emphasise the pace and scale of change in genetic knowledge and practice through rhetoric such as 'the genetics revolution,' 'frontiers' in genetics medicine, or even the 'new genetics'. As Van Dijck has noted, this optimistic discourse has a history of its own, beginning in the 1950s, separating genetics from its tainted predecessor of eugenics (Van Dijck, 1998; see also Kerr et al, 1998c). Professional elitism and autocracy are also said to have transformed into relations of partnership with patients and publics and transparent, accountable practices. Transformation is also a powerful commercial discourse that underlines the novelty and desirability of new genetic treatments and diagnostic technologies, highlighting their powers to predict and cure genetic disorders that were previously taken for granted.

Noteworthy research programmes that address the social and ethical dimensions of the new genetics, at the behest of a range of corporate, medical and social research agencies, also highlight transformations in and around the new genetics. For example, the UK's Economic and Social Research Council's Innovative Health Technologies Programme (co-funded by the MRC and GlaxoSmithKline)[1] and the Wellcome Trust's Medicine in Society Programme,[2] both stress, in the words of the Wellcome Trust, the 'breathtaking' pace of discovery in the life sciences and the 'unprecedented questions' this poses for society.

Without denying that new technologies, notions of personhood and forms of politics associated with genetics are dynamic and complex, I want to query this prevailing emphasis on transformation. Although it is important to reject simplistic parallels between the eugenics of the past and the genetics of the present, there is a danger that this focus on transformations is resulting in less attention being paid to the static and reactionary aspects of the 'new' genetics and its wider social context, particularly the ways in which autonomy, participation and uncertainty might be undermined by new developments in genetic testing, screening and public consultation. Genetic information which is presented in certain terms, genetic counselling which is explicitly directive, and elitist and antidemocratic aspects of policy-making about genetics are less likely to be considered when transformations are privileged (for exceptions see Petersen and Bunton, 2002; Kerr and Shakespeare, 2002; Paul, 1992; Williams et al, 2002a & b). The more established and routine forms of antenatal screening and the traditional format of patient support groups (funded and in many cases managed by other larger groups which are dominated by medical professionals) are also less likely to be interrogated when newer forms of presymptomatic testing and web-based support groups are fore grounded (Novas and Rose, 2001; Polzer et al, 2002; Rabinow, 1996, 1999a & b). Professional discourses of responsibility and choice, such as the ways in which they might articulate a sense of their obligation to dominate and control genetic counselling sessions and policy-making, are also being overlooked in studies that focus on the *impact* of new genetic technologies on patients.[3]

The new genetics necessarily involves a range of competing discourses and practices as professionals negotiate the 'jurisdictional boundaries' (Abbott, 1988) between their work and that of the more established medical and scientific domains, in the context of fears about repetition of the past excesses of eugenics. In this paper I will explore some of the tensions around new genetic citizenship as it is articulated in professional discourses and practices in the clinic and wider policy making networks, focusing in particular upon changes and continuities between past and present. I am especially interested in professional discussions about rights and responsibilities in the clinic, but also in the wider discourse of public involvement in policy-making about genetics. I will also draw on empirical studies of professional practice to illustrate some of the continuities between past and present that tend to be overlooked by scholars whose work is framed by a focus on transformation. I am interested in what models of citizenship are being privileged in these discussions and examples. Following Turner (2001), I am not looking for a static set of rights and responsibilities, but treating citizenship as a set of inter-linked processes of inclusion and exclusion of individuals based on the allocation of entitlements, obligations and immunities, which depend upon notions of their contribution to society.

Citizenship and the Patient

Patients' rights and responsibilities are frequently addressed in professional and policy discourses about genetic testing and screening. Genetic counselling is repeatedly cast as non-directive in these accounts and explicitly contrasted with eugenics (Paul, 1992; Petersen, 1999; Kenen, 1997). The burgeoning body of psychosocial literature about the factors involved in people's decision to take a genetic test has further intensified genetic counsellors' reflexivity about the purpose and outcomes of the counselling process (e.g. Biesecker and Peters, 2001; see also Rapp, 2000, Pilnick, 2002). Rejecting an earlier focus on 'barriers to communication', counselling is now conceived by some as a 'psycho educational process' (Biesecker and Peters, 2001), which involves negotiation over the meanings and consequences of genetic knowledge.

Individual choice nevertheless remains an important ideal in much of the discourse of professional and patient organisations concerned with genetic services (Cunningham-Burley and Kerr, 1999; Shakespeare, 1999; Kerr and Shakespeare, 2002). Patient's autonomy and their rights to information are privileged above professional's role in advising and guiding their clients (Clarke 1991; Kerr et al, 1997, 1998c; Lippman, 1992; Petersen, 1999). This is linked to an emphasis on patients' entitlements to access to genetic services, in contrast to their obligations to use them. There are considerable tensions between professionals about the amount of information and indeed advice which is provided during genetic counselling sessions and the circumstances under which this information should be shared with relatives (see Clarke 1991 as an example). In certain circumstances professionals also express significant ambivalence about their 'neutrality', given that clients maybe actively seeking advice and guidance (Williams, Alderson and Farsides, 2002a & b). The discourse of individual choice is nevertheless often presented as a reason to expand genetic service provision beyond the select few, in the interests of equity of access. Genetics services are thereby cast as another 'consumer issue' (Davison et al, 1997; Henn, 2000; Kerr and Shakespeare, 2002; Lupton, 1997).

The privileging of 'informed consent' to the donation of DNA for research purposes can also be related to the expansion of DNA databases. Informed consent forms are explicitly constructed to limit the entitlements of clients to financial gain from patents taken out on the basis of research involving their DNA and to secure consent for future uses without further consultation. Such 'presumed' consent is designed to enable potential donors to consider and then renounce their entitlement to participate in decision-making about future uses of their DNA, and, in so doing, underline the entitlement of clinicians to make these decisions. As data banking moves onto a larger scale, this increasingly applies to publics rather than patients in the traditional sense, as I go on to discuss shortly.

Professional's emphasis on patient choice does not necessarily subsume patients' sense of obligations to participate in testing and to encourage their families to do the same. Clinicians need not be explicit in fostering participation as 'at-risk consciousness', given that this is already well established (Robertson, 2001; Petersen, 1998; Rose, 1990). As Hallowell and others have documented, there are also other less explicit ways in which the testing agenda is shaped by clinicians in terms of the information they provide, the alternatives that are offered and the ways in which they portray responsible and positive health behaviour (Hallowell, 1999a & b; Burke and Kolker, 1994; Rapp, 2000; Marteau, 1989). This generates obligations on the part of clients to engage in testing. The structural arrangements for screening provision also shape people's experiences, as they are translated into everyday practice in the clinic. These are moral technologies that prompt self-disciplining behaviour (Adelsward and Sachs 1998, quoted in Robertson, 2001).

We must also recognise that guidance is not always an anathema to genetic counsellors or, indeed, their clients. In certain circumstances, clinicians and scientists do argue that it is appropriate for the clinician to advise clients to take a genetic test (Kerr et al, 1997; Marteau et al, 1993, 1994), particularly when the client is perceived to be in a high-risk group. The advice given to men who are seeking fertility treatment because of a form of infertility linked to Cystic Fibrosis (CF) is one such example (Kerr, 2000). There is evidence that these men and their partners are sometimes 'strongly advised' to take a genetic test for CF in some clinics (ibid.). Not all professionals stop short at mandatory counselling. Some even advocate mandatory testing when both partners are known to have one or two CF mutations. For example, in a review article about pre-implantation genetic diagnosis where CF and Congenital Bilateral Absence of the Vas Deferens (CBAVD) are discussed, one group of clinicians and scientists from Belgium wrote,

> Couples in which the men have CBAVD and the women carry a CF mutation might have children presenting CF [through IVF]. Mutation screening in both partners and counselling about their risk of having a CF or CBAVD child is *mandatory* for these couples. When both partners are carriers of CF mutations, pre-implantation diagnosis can eventually be carried out in order to transfer unaffected or carrier embryos (Liu et al, 1996, 533, my emphasis).

Hallowell (1999) has also found that, in the context of non-reproductive decision making, for example around breast cancer genetics, advice is quite acceptable to some clients and their counsellors, given that self-surveillance is a standardised medical response to at-risk individuals. Marteau's work with colleagues also shows quite clearly that pregnant women are often advised to participate in reproductive screening during pregnancy (Marteau et al, 1992, 1993).

These examples of professional guidance and client's sense of obligations to participate in genetic testing and screening, alongside the expansion of genetic services, cut across other stresses on patient autonomy and immunity from coercion, thus undermining any fundamental transformations in the form or function of genetic counselling in the era of the new genetics. Far from being unique to the contemporary period, these tensions have long been a feature of genetic counselling, and can be found throughout the history of eugenics (see Kerr and Shakespeare, 2002 for further details).

There are also reasons to doubt that genetic knowledge has fundamentally changed so that it is now presented and interpreted in relative terms, especially in the case of more routine types of antenatal or postnatal screening (see, for example, Parsons and Atkinson, 1993; Rapp, 2000). Uncertainty in genetic knowledge is neither universal nor inevitable. Notwithstanding uncertainties in the case of predictive tests for so-called 'single gene' disorders like Huntington Disease, professionals advise their clients that not inheriting the gene means *they will not get the disease* and, in the vast majority of cases, inheriting the gene means they will. Certainty and uncertainty are negotiated anew in each clinical and research context. This is well illustrated from a quote from an interview with a leading geneticist in the CF field,

> The single gene disease, it's never single, and it's not only CF [where that is the case], it's a more global process. Most . . . so-called single gene disease are not [single] if you look carefully and learn how to detect less typical cases . . . you just widen the spectrum. . . . there are some cases that we will have a problem with classifying . . . [But] we have not abandoned classes or categories for practical reasons . . . [in] the medical setting you have to deal with the certain description of disease for diagnosis. You have your criteria and then you decide if somebody has the disease or not.[4]

Although this tension between certainty and uncertainty cannot determine how clients will interpret and engage with genetic knowledge in their own terms, it nevertheless establishes an important frame of reference that is likely to colour their interpretation and subsequent use of this knowledge.

It is also worth noting that clinicians' influence can extend beyond the bounds of the clinic, to the establishment and agenda of many patient support groups. This is not a crude ploy to control the medical agenda and limit patients' power, rather it is one of the ways in which some clinicians and scientists act out their sense of responsibility for the care and treatment of people with the condition in which they have an interest. A good example of this is the UK CF Trust and the (now disbanded) Association of CF Adults. This adult association was set up during the 1980s by several people with CF, including one medical student, after prompting from the director of the CF Trust.[5] As more adults survived and began to take on a more influential role in the Trust, lobbying the NHS for better services for example, there was less of a need for the Association to continue, as their priorities merged with those of the mainstream Trust. But the Trust did not transform into a patient-led organisation. Medical experts continue to dominate the membership of important committees, particularly where research funding and public education are concerned. It remains the case that other influential patient groups, such as the UK Genetics Interest Group (GIG), are far from grass-roots organisations of people affected by genetic conditions. GIG works closely with the medical and scientific establishment to support genetic research and expansion of services.

Citizenship and the Public

When one turns to consider citizenship in its broader sense of participation in policy-making, there are similar trends to those outlined above. In the UK influential bodies like the Royal Society, the Human Genetics Commission and the Wellcome Trust have moved away from the so-called 'deficit model' of public understanding of science in recent years, instead favouring public engagement, transparency and dialogue. However, public education remains an important goal of policy makers and professionals concerned with the social and ethical implications of genetics. For example, the Royal Society Science in Society Programme,[6] the BBC's Gene Story initiative,[7] and Café Scientifique meetings[8] all have a strong educational element.

This focus on education is, in part, an outcome of geneticists' and other scientists' sense of social responsibility, as is their pledge to the veracity of their work in public (Kerr et al, 1997; 1998c). A recent example of this is Michael Rutter's presidential address at the Society for Research in Child Development (SRCD), where he argued against misleading hype and 'scientific evangelism' about susceptibility genes involved in personality and behaviour (Rutter, 2001). Dean Hamer's public position on the dangers of the so-called 'gay gene' reinforcing homophobia, and the condemnation of reproductive cloning by Ian Wilmut (the scientist who 'cloned' Dolly the sheep) are other good examples of this professional gatekeeping. More generally, genetics professionals' are engaged in collaborative research to promote ethical practices. An excellent example of this is the Cardiff Genetics and Society Research Group co-ordinated by Angus Clarke, which works in collaboration with a range of social scientists and legal scholars to study patient understandings of genetic risk, evaluate the ethical aspects of genetic services, and engage with the implications of genetic knowledge for insurance.

Notwithstanding these geneticists' greater commitment to public engagement, it still remains the case that policy making and public commentary about the ethics of genetics continue to be dominated by medical and scientific experts. As Irwin has commented, the terms of policy agendas about genetics are pre-framed rather than open and they assume the inevitability of technological development and commercial benefit from that development (Irwin, 2001). There is also a tendency to concentrate upon the publics' views about the implications of technologies rather than research and development priorities. In this sense the public's role as citizens is more reactive than active, as Irwin puts it (ibid.). The focus of public consultation exercises is often narrowed to concentrate on technical possibilities and their specific implications for legislation, rather than wider concerns about stigma against people with disabilities, for example. The tendency to focus on technicalities, such as the wording of informed consent forms, also reflects a focus on the entitlements of individual patients as opposed to those of the wider community.

As Petersen and Bunton (2002) and others such as Dunkerley and Glasner (1998) have commented, this framing of members of the publics' entitlements to participation in genetic policy-making can at times slip into a sense of their obligations to participate. The public are supposed to engage in 'informed debate' in order to stem the potential for abuse of genetic information. Yet, as has been argued above, there are few routes for members of the public to influence the types of research and legislation that are developed.

This slippage towards the public's obligations for policy-engagement is mirrored in other recent developments in the area of genetic donation, such as the proposed UK Biomedical Population Collection, or UK Biobank as it is known. UK Biobank will involve half a million UK citizens between the ages of 45 and 64 years. Although the exact details of the study are as yet unclear, recruitment of research subjects is expected to take place through General Practitioners. The Wellcome Trust is one of the key organisations involved in UK Biobank. They are very aware that the success of UK Biobank is dependent upon public goodwill. This explains the distinct air of confidence building in their recent efforts at public consultation on the subject. This is evident the following statement, taken from the protocol for the collection, published in 2001,

> The research has shown that there was little existing knowledge of the proposal but that it was accepted in principle. However, there was significant misunderstanding and misinformation about genetics research. The research had underlined the importance of good communication with participants and getting informed consent to what is proposed. It was also important that the proposed resource should be owned by the public sector. Oversight by an independent body would reassure the public that the data were being managed and used in the public interest (Wellcome Trust, 2001, 1).

The protocol even defines 'citizen's role' in UK Biobank, as one of self—surveillance and information provision to clinicians (although doubts were expressed about citizen's competency or willingness to engage in these tasks).

A more recent Wellcome consultation exercise continued to stress citizen involvement in Biobank. A study by People Science and Policy Ltd dismissed some participants' scepticism about the need to conduct research into an area where a lot is already known about genes and disease, and claimed that there was little evidence of concern about the use of this information to study genes involved in behaviours or personality, findings largely at odds with other research in this area (e.g. Kerr et al, 1998b). The report also drew conclusions such as 'Taking part must be made as easy as possible. People may look for excuses to justify their inertia.'[9]

On the one hand, citizens' obligations are apparently being extended beyond the arena of diagnostic testing for 'at risk' individuals and beyond the obligations of informed citizenry, to obligations to participate in wide-scale genetic surveillance. On the other hand, professionals' entitlement to control the processes of ethical scrutiny and judgement of these initiatives remains.

Medical expertise is also crucial to the regulation and ownership of genetic knowledge and products more broadly. As Abraham and Lewis have argued,

> While there is an undeniable growth in the number of people with medical expertise working for consumer organizations as employees, consultants and advisors, our analysis indicates that there is an even more systematic and widespread growth in the extent to which medical experts are bound into an industry-regulator alliance within the European drug approval process . . . More significantly, the limited concessions made to consumerist demands have been far outweighed by the measures taken to accommodate the trade interests of the pharmaceutical industry (Abraham and Lewis, 2002, 83).

This alliance between government, science and capital is also apparent when gene patenting is concerned. Prior to the simultaneous publication of the draft genomes by the Human Genome Project (HGP) and Celera in 2000, the HGP's head, Francis Collins, talked about patenting in an interview with CNN, where he noted the importance of balancing the interests of producers and the public in such a way as to recognise ownership of novel products and therefore encourage research and development in genomics, and to protect the public interest by preventing ownership of so-called 'raw' genetic information, which would stifle research.[10] This emphasis on balancing public and private interests presaged the subsequent emphasis on partnership or synergy between the private and public sectors in the genomics field. Notwithstanding the emphasis of high profile campaigns like that of Sir John Sulston and the Wellcome Trust against the 'privatisation' of public knowledge, the mutual priorities of the public and private sectors means they are frequently cast as 'partners', sharing medical expertise and commercial ownership of public data in the public interest. For example, the UK Medical Research Council recently purchased access to Celera's database, on the ground that it would allow UK scientists to maintain their 'competitive edge.'[11]

A similar discourse is likely to emerge with respect to the Myriad patent on BRCA1 and 2 and the use of breast cancer genetic tests by the UK NHS.

Despite protests by high profile geneticists like Martin Bobrow and organisations such as the Clinical Genetics Society, and contestation of the European patent by a range of scientific organisations and member nations, the UK Department of Health is poised to organise a deal with Myriad which is expected to honour the patent. Even patients' organisations that are part of the policy networks around genetics, such as the Genetics Interest Group, try to engage with and promote the interests of industry in areas like tissue banking. In these discussions, the public's interests (to better drugs and diagnostic tests) are to be secured through the entitlements of the private sector to own genetic knowledge and the public's obligation to facilitate this by co-operating with research.

It would, however, be wrong to imply that support for gene patenting and the model of 'genetic citizenship' it aligns with, are monolithic. There is considerable opposition to the gene patent system, which suggests a competing model of citizenship also exists. For example, the large majority of members of the public who took part in a survey conducted by MORI on behalf of the UK Human Genetics Commission expressed opposition to private ownership of genetic information on the grounds that it would undermine research and service provision.[12] The HGC, and more recently the UK Nuffield Council on Bioethics, have also expressed concern about the proliferation of patents, on the grounds that this will harm the public good by restricting access to a full range of genetic services and stifling competition in the development of new tests and therapies. Here it is the public's entitlement to genetic services and professionals' and government's obligations to produce them that are cast as outweighing capital's entitlements to ownership.

Discussion

These models of genetic citizenship involve several processes of mediation between the obligations, immunities and entitlements of professionals, clients and publics where the production, application and regulation of genetic information are concerned. Professionals' responsibilities for knowledge provision and advice or guidance are not fixed, but dependant on the socio-political context, from the inter-personal context of the counselling situation, to the wider political economy of international research collaboration. In many cases professionals have adopted the role of enlightened experts, who variously deploy their social conscience and objective expertise in negotiating decision-making in the clinical and policy realms. This enlightened stance involves considerable reflexivity about their practices and motives, so much so that reflexive practice has become an important outcome of genetic counselling, alongside the actual decision of the client. The remit of professionals is also extending beyond the clinic, as links are forged with other members of the policy networks around genetics, including social scientists. Where once professionals were involved in spearheading the eugenic cause through public education campaigns, their role today is often one of abuse prevention, as eugenics of the past comes to symbolise the worst of professional elitism and dominance.

There are, of course, considerable tensions around the extent and deployment of professionals' expertise and responsibility, and that of clients and publics, whose own involvement in decision making in the clinical and policy arenas is also contested. These tensions are not unique to the contemporary period, but they are undoubtedly more prominent in public and professional discourses than they were in the past, partly because of the ongoing negotiation of the boundary between the eugenics of the past and contemporary genetics.

Tensions notwithstanding, professional's entitlements and patient's or public's obligations continue to be privileged in these models of genetic citizenship, now, as in the past. Obligations and entitlements with respect to citizenship are distributed on the basis on people's contributions to society. It seems that contributions on the basis of scientific and medical expertise and capital are still highly valued in contrast to those based on lived experiences of disease and disability, reproductive and caring labour and community involvement. Decision-making about the allocation of resources to fund research and services, and about the appropriate regulatory mechanisms to oversee them, is still dominated by professional scientists, and allied professionals with a similarly technocratic outlook, alongside government and industry representatives. All of these groups share an interest in economic gain, as well as intellectual kudos, values that mediate their definition of the 'public good' that genetics is supposed to serve. The obligations of professionals and funding-bodies tend to be constructed in such a way that they compliment rather than undermine this corral of entitlements. Obligations to standardisation, equity of service, and informed consent compliment professionals' entitlements to control their research agendas, and to act as service regulators. Similarly, the entitlements of clients and publics are often cast in terms of quality services, information, and choice, rather than active involvement in decisions about *limiting* service provision. It seems that patients and publics entitlements are often narrowly expressed in relation to their role as citizen-consumers of already existing services.

The discourse of individual entitlement to genetic services and genetic choices readily translates into a discourse of individual obligation to participate in self-surveillance. The same slippage between entitlements and obligations can be found in the area of reproductive screening, as the policy agenda of cost reduction is translated into the clinical arena of risk assessment and the cascade of intervention. Recent trends towards the centralisation of surveillance through population DNA banking further exacerbate this gulf between professional entitlements and patient obligations, as the public good of donation is stressed, alongside the ethics of informed consent, in the campaign to recruit participants. This parallels recent developments in policy-making where the discourse of the rights of the publics to 'engage' with policy-making form a thin veneer over an underlying message of public responsibility for forestalling eugenics.

Although genetics is now framed within the twin discourses of health and individual choice, and the obligations of patients and publics are more muted than those of the past, just as the entitlements of governments and professionals are more constrained, there are parallels between past and present models of genetic citizenship that it would be wrong to ignore. Professionals still take the lead role in determining policies about genetic research and services and patients/publics still bear responsibility for eliminating hereditary disease. This is now achieved through individual health and reproductive management and the donation of DNA to research projects, rather than state-sponsored coercion, so in that sense responsibility has been devolved, but professionals continue to oversee and co-ordinate this process of devolution. The balance between entitlements and obligations remains weighted in terms of professional entitlement and patient or public obligations and the slippage around patient and professional entitlements, obligations and immunities supports this weighting.

An appreciation of these aspects of professional discourse and practice adds another dimension to work on genetic and citizenship which runs counter to the conclusions of other studies which tends to highlight novel gene technologies and their role in transforming patients' experiences of health and their bodies. It suggests that more attention ought to be paid to the wider aspects of the distribution of obligations and entitlements amongst professionals, clients and publics where the new genetics is concerned. The flexibilities of genetic citizenship are particularly interesting, especially the slippage from entitlements to obligations that are associated with the prevailing emphasis on the contemporary citizen-consumer. The variations and contradictions in professionals' discourses and practices should also be subject to further critical reflection.

This suggests that we ought to be cautious about demands for individuals' rights to genetic choices and citizens' rights to involvement in policy making about genetics, given the obligations that the language of entitlement can mask. This is particularly important when socially excluded groups are concerned. Their rights not to make genetic choices, and not to participate in 'public debates' that are of little interest or importance in the context of their everyday lives, are being overlooked. This is part of a broader trend to devolved governance of and by genetics, as opposed to government of genetics through state regulation. Given the history of eugenics it is understandable that the State is viewed with suspicion. But circumventing government can also foster discrimination and elitism, given its potential to undermine elected representatives' responsibilities to the people. A thoroughgoing understanding of transformations in genetic citizenship requires that we consider its paradoxes.

Notes

1. see http://www.york.ac.uk/res/iht/
2. http://www.wellcome.ac.uk/en/1/mismis.html.
3. For some examples where this is not the case see Atkinson et al, 2002; Burke and Kolker, 1992; Kerr et al, 1997, 1998, Cunningham-Burley and Kerr, 1999, Hallowell, 1999, Lippman, 1992, Marteau et al, 1993, 1994, Petersen, 1999, Rapp, 2000; Williams, 2002a&b.
4. Interview with Julian Zielenski, as part of Wellcome Trust History of Medicine Project: A Social History of Cystic Fibrosis (1997–2002).
5. Interview with Sarah Walters, as part of Wellcome Trust History of Medicine Project: A Social History of Cystic Fibrosis (1997–2002).
6. http://www.royalsoc.ac.uk/templates/scienceinsociety/index.cfm
7. http://www.bbc.co.uk/genes/
8. http://www.cafescientifique.org/
9. http://www.wellcome.ac.uk/en/images/biobankuktrust_5973.pdf
10. http://www.cnn.com/SPECIALS/2000/genome/story/interviews/collins.html
11. http://www.mrc.ac.uk/index/public_interest/public-topical_issues/public-celera_genomics_database.htm
12. http://www.hgc.gov.uk/business_publications_morigeneticattitudes.pdf

References

Abbott, Andrew (1988) *System of Professions*. Chicago: University of Chicago Press.

Abraham, John and Graham Lewis (2002) "Citizenship, Medical Expertise and the Capitalist Regulatory State in Europe," *Sociology* 36 (1): 67–88.

Adelsward, V. and L. Sachs (1998) "Risk discourse: Recontextualisation of numerical values in clinical practice," *Text* 18 (2): 191–201.

Barns, Ian, Renato Schibeci, Aidan Davison, and Robyn Shaw (2000) "'What Do You Think About Genetic Medicine?' Facilitating Sociable Public Discourse on Developments in the New Genetics," *Science, Technology and Human Values* 25 (3): 283–308.

Biesecker B. B. and K. F. Peters KF (2001) "Process studies in genetic counseling: Peering into the black box," *American Journal of Medical Genetics* 106 (3): 191–198.

Burke, B. Meredith and Aliza Kolker (1994) "Directiveness in prenatal genetic counseling," *Women and Health* 22 (1): 31–53.

Clarke, Angus (1991) "Is non-directive genetic counselling possible?" *Lancet*, 338 (8773): 998–1000.

Cox, Sue and William McKellin (1999) "There's this thing in our family: predictive testing and the construction of risk for Huntington's Disease," in *Sociological*

Perspectives on the New Genetics, Peter Conrad and Jon Gabe (eds.). Oxford: Blackwell Publishers, 622–46.

Cunningham-Burley, Sarah and Anne Kerr (1999) "Defining the "social": towards an understanding of scientific and medical discourses on the social aspects of the new genetics," *Sociology of Health and Illness* 21 (5): 647–668.

Davison, A., Barns, I., Schibeci, R. (1997) "Problematic Publics: A critical Review of Surveys of Public Attitudes to Biotechnology," *Science, Technology and Human Values* 22 (3): 317–348.

Dunkerley, David and Glasner, Peter (1998) "Empowering the public? Citizens' juries and the new genetic technologies," *Critical Public Health* 8 (3): 181–192.

Finkler, Kaja (2000) *Experiencing the New Genetics: Family and Kinship on the Medical Frontier.* Philadelphia: University of Pennsylvania Press.

Hallowell, Nina (1999a) "Advising on the management of genetic risk: offering choice or prescribing action?" *Health Risk and Society* 1 (3): 267–80.

——— (1999b) "Doing the right thing: genetic risk and responsibility," in *Sociological Perspectives on the New Genetics,* Conrad, Peter and Jon Gabe (eds) Oxford: Blackwell Publishers, 97–120.

Henn, W. (2000) "Consumerism in prenatal diagnosis," *Journal of Medical Ethics* 26 (6): 444–446.

Irwin, Alan (2001) "Constructing the scientific citizen: science and democracy in the biosciences," *Public Understanding of Science* 10 (1): 1–18.

Kenen, Regina (1997) "Opportunities and impediments for a consolidating and expanding profession: genetic counselling in the United States," *Social Science and Medicine* 45 (9): 377–1386.

Kerr, Anne (2000) "(Re)Constructing Genetic Disease: the clinical continuum between cystic fibrosis and male infertility," *Social Studies of Science* 30 (6): 847–94.

Kerr, Anne and Sarah Cunningham-Burley (2000) "On Ambivalence and Risk: Reflexive Modernity and the New Human Genetics," *Sociology* 34 (2): 283–304.

Kerr, Anne and Tom Shakespeare (2002) *Genetic Politics: From Eugenics to Genome.* Cheltenham: New Clarion Press.

Kerr, Anne, Sarah Cunningham-Burley and Amanda Amos (1998b) "Drawing the Line: An Analysis of Lay People's Discussions about the New Human Genetics," *Public Understanding of Science* 7 (2): 113–133.

——— (1998c) "Eugenics and the New Human Genetics in Britain: Examining Contemporary Professionals' Accounts," *Science, Technology and Human Values* 23 (2): 175–198.

——— (1997) "The New Genetics: Professionals' Discursive Boundaries," *Sociological Review* 45 (2): 279–303.

Lippman, Abby (1992) "Prenatal genetic testing and genetic screening: constructing needs and reinforcing inequalities," *American Journal of Law and Medicine* 17 (1&2): 15–50.

Liu, J., W. Lissens, P. Devroey, I. Liebars and A. Van Steirtegham (1996) "Cystic Fibrosis, Duchenne muscular dystrophy and preimplantation genetic diagnosis," *Human Reproduction Update* 2 (6): 531–39.

Lupton, Deborah (1997) "Consumerism, reflexivity and the medical encounter," *Social Science and Medicine* 45 (3): 373–381.

Marteau, Theresa (1989) "Framing of information: its influence upon decisions of doctors and patients," *British Journal of Social Psychology* 28 (1): 89–94.

Marteau, T., Drake, H., and Bobrow, M. (1994) "Counseling following diagnosis of foetal abnormality: the differing approaches of obstetricians, clinical geneticists, and genetic nurses," *Journal of Medical Genetics* 31 (10): 863–867.

Marteau, T., Plenicar, M., and Kidd, J. (1993) "Obstetricians presenting amniocentesis to pregnant women: practice observed," *Journal of Reproductive and Infant Psychology* 11 (1): 3–10.

Novas Carlos and Nikolas Rose (2000) "Genetic risk and the birth of the somatic individual," *Economy and Society* 29 (4): 484–513.

Parsons, Evelyn and Paul Atkinson (1993) "Genetic Risk and Reproduction," *Sociological Review* 41 (4) : 679–706.

——— (1992) "Lay Constructions of Genetic Risk," *Sociology of Health and Illness* 14 (4) : 439–455.

Paul, Diane (1992) "Eugenic anxieties, social realities and political choices," *Social Research* 59 (3) : 663–683.

Petersen, Alan and Robin Bunton (2002) *The New Genetics and the Public's Health.* London: Routledge.

Petersen, Alan (1999) "Counselling the genetically 'at-risk': a critique of 'non-directiveness'," *Health Risk and Society* 1 (3) : 253–266.

——— (1998) "The new genetics and the politics of public health," *Critical Public Health* 8 (1): 59–71.

Pilnick, Alison (2002) "There are no rights and wrongs in these situations: identifying interactional difficulties in genetic counselling," *Sociology of Health and Illness* 25 (1): 66–88.

Polzer ,Jessica, Shawna L. Mercer and Vivek Goel (2002) "Blood is thicker than water: genetic testing as citizenship through familial obligation and the management of risk," *Critical Public Health* 12 (2): 153–168.

Press, N. and Browner, C. H. (1997) "Why women say yes to prenatal diagnosis," *Social Science and Medicine* 45 (7) : 976–989.

Rabeharisoa, V. and Callon, M. (2002) "The involvement of patients' associations in research," *International Social Science Journal* 54 (171): 57–67.

Rabinow, Paul (1996) "Artificiality and Enlightenment: from sociobiology to biosociality," in *Essays on the Anthropology of Reason.* Princeton: Princeton University Press.

——— 1999a 'Severing the Ties: Fragmentation and Redemption in Late Modernity,' in *The Anthropology of Science and Technology.* D. Hess, & L. Layne (eds.). Greenwich, CT: JAI Press 169–187.

——— 1999b *French DNA: Trouble in Purgatory.* Chicago: The University of Chicago Press.

Rapp, Rayna (2000) *Testing Women, Testing the Fetus, The Social Impact of Amniocentesis in America.* London: Routledge.

Robertson, Ann (2001) "Biotechnology, political rationality and discourses on health risk," *Health* 5 (3): 293–309.

Rose, Nikolas (1990) *Governing the soul: the shaping of the private self.* London: Routledge.

——— (1999) *Powers of Freedom: Reframing Political Thought.* Cambridge: Cambridge University Press.

——— (2001) "The politics of life itself," *Theory Culture and Society* 18 (6): 1–30.

Rutter, Michael (2001) *Nature, Nurture, and Development: From Evangelism through Science towards Policy and Practice,* Society for Research in Child Development Presidential Address, Institute of Psychaitry, London, 30 May 2001.

Shakespeare, Tom (1999) "Losing the plot'? Medical and activist discourses of contemporary genetics and disability," *Sociology of Health and Illness* 21 (5): 669–688.

Turner, Bryan (2001) "The erosion of citizenship," *British Journal of Sociology* 52 (2): 189–209.

Van Dijck, Jose (1998) *Imagenation: Popular Images of Genetics.* London: MacMillan.
Webster, Andrew (2002) "Innovative health technologies and the social: redefining health, medicine and the body," *Current Sociology* 50 (3): 443–58.
Wellcome Trust (2001) *Report of the UK Population Biomedical Collection Protocol development workshop*, Royal College of Physicians, London, 17 April 2001.
Williams, Clare, Patricia Alderson and Bobbie Farsides (2002a) " 'Drawing the line' in prenatal screening and testing: health practitioners' discussions," *Health, Risk and Society* 4 (1) : 61–75.
———— (2002b) "Is nondirectiveness possible within the context of antenatal screening and testing?" *Social Science and Medicine* 54 (5) : 339–347.

6

Peril or Promise: News Media Framing of the Biotechnology Debate in Europe and the U.S.

Susanna Hornig Priest and Toby Ten Eyck

Any possibility of a broad democratic debate in modern society concerning technology or science, other than those confined to elite circles, is dependent on the mass media. While science and technology policy is imagined to have great influence over the course of people's lives, these influences are rarely obvious in the short term. Everyday people have many other, often more immediate, daily concerns, and they do not necessarily have many other sources of expert information or interpretation for these issues. For these reasons it is very likely that the power of media to influence public opinion is stronger for science and technology issues than for other questions. Media messages do not dictate public opinion; readers and viewers exercise considerable power in their selection and interpretation of messages. But messages influence the opinion climate in which individuals see themselves as being situated. This, in turn, has consequences for shaping the course of public debate.

For example, while the direct effects of mass media messages on public opinion are often misunderstood (and greatly exaggerated), their ability to set the agenda for popular debate is very well documented (see, e.g, McCombs and Shaw 1972; Iyengar and Kinder 1987; Dearing and Rogers 1996). Media can also frame debate by defining issues in certain ways, and they represent particular points of view as legitimate while marginalizing others. These indirect effects certainly do not fully determine opinions nor entirely constrain debate; media audiences are active rather than passive and not always so easily manipulated by the whims of reporters or the sources they quote (Priest 1995). But on the other hand media framing and legitimization effects undoubtedly contribute to the formation of an opinion climate in which public debate on certain issues can be discouraged or even suppressed while attention is focused on others, and some actors and positions are taken more seriously than others.

The ability of media to suggest which issues are important and to create a sense of how others feel about them are thus indirect but nontrivial forms of influence. People are quite unlikely to form strong opinions about technical issues they have never heard about, for one thing. And the sense people have about what others are thinking—what is expert opinion, what opinions belong only to a marginalized minority, what are the opinions of other people like them, and so on—is also an important factor. Opinion formation is dependent on what people understand the opinions of others to be. We quickly position ourselves along an imagined opinion continuum in crystallizing our own thinking and in projecting how others might react.

Further, people's willingness to speak out—as postulated by Noelle-Neumann's (1993) "spiral of silence" theory—is especially subject to being influenced by perceptions as to what others think, specifically what dominant or mainstream opinion is perceived to be. If people do not believe others share their opinions or that they may be ostracized for holding particular opinions, their points of view are less likely to expressed and thus can have less of an influence on the course of public discussion.

Activists can impact others through direct persuasion, though that is typically not enough. It is important that a dissenting message is publicized by the news media—that the rhetoric of a group of people with a particular, especially a non-mainstream, opinion, is made available for public reflection. This has the effect of extending the range of public debate; it is easy to imagine people reorienting themselves on a revised public opinion continuum and projecting a different reaction from others as a result of learning about oppositional views. Activist groups know this; public protests are a means to gain entrance to the public sphere (via media coverage) that is often deemed worth the risk some legitimacy could be lost in the process, depending on the nature of the coverage. Conversely, the expressed opinions of corporate and governmental leaders—those that represent the existing power structure in society—define the mainstream backdrop against which dissent will be illuminated.

In Western democracies the role of the media is generally seen as providing balanced discussion of important issues, the kind of discussion everyday people need to make up their minds about the issues of the day. However, news traditions vary across localities. U.S. news organizations in particular— even though some of them are thought of as more liberal or more conversative—are expected to be "objective" in their reporting. News stories are not supposed to reflect or even reveal the point of view of the reporter or his/her organization. This is arguably less true in much of Europe, where particular publications or programs/channels are more often and more strongly identified with particular political positions. Both the U.S. and European presses (to use the term broadly to encompass broadcast as well as print media) are expected to inform public debate. However, it may be that some European populations have available (from media accounts) a broader range of legitimized opinion from which to construct an imagined opinion scale. While this is not necessarily a direct result of differences in how the media operate, it is also apparent that certain voices (e.g., environmentalist voices) are more likely to be regarded as legitimate or mainstream in Europe than in the U.S. This may be very important for opinion formation in regard to biotechnology (Priest et al., in press).

In general, is it possible to identify which interests the media serve? Scholars often see media as instruments of social control, despite media organizations' perceptions of themselves as fulfilling a "watchdog" role. "Objectivity" may be a defensible ethic on the grounds of the media's role in democracies, but it is also necessarily a mythical standard in practice; choices about which issues to emphasize, how to define them, which sources to treat as legitimate cannot be made "objectively" but reflect judgment and values. In addition, news media are highly dependent on official cooperation in the form of information provision and general facilitation of news gathering. Despite the common expectation that in democracies the media will have an adversarial relationship to government, media still cannot do their jobs without government support, even where this support consists largely of no more than tacit cooperation.

Further, in Western capitalist democracies news media operations are generally owned by corporations (with some exceptions where the broadcast system is publicly owned), often large corporations who have interests and investments in other areas, and for this reason—especially in the U.S.—the media are regularly accused by scholars of reflecting a pro-corporate, proestablishment point of view. This is true despite journalism's general reputation for "liberalism." This is a bias inherent in the dependence of the institutions of journalism on both official sources and substantial financial interests.

In other words, generally speaking, there are strong reasons to suppose that media in the U.S. and other democratic capitalistic systems tend to overemphasize mainstream, large-organization points of view, whether governmental or corporate. And this point has also been made specifically for science and technology reporting, which often adopts a "booster" orientation; see Gandy's (1982) discussion of information subsidies, or Nelkin's (1995) discussion of the media's role in "selling" science.

The media's legitimization role takes on new and very special significance in discussions of scientific truthtelling; reporters' errors in such cases—e.g., in their assumption of the invincibility of the U.S. space shuttle program before the Challenger explosion, or of the validity of cold fusion theory as announced by two Utah scientists in 1989—also receive considerable post hoc attention. The media are often criticized for distorting or exaggerating many risks (see, e.g., Kasperson and Kasperson 1996) and for inducing negative public reactions in all cases of technology-based controversies (Mazur 1981). Especially in the absence of clear and present evidence of either malfeasance or catastrophe, journalists who report risks are subject to accusations of being scaremongers. But in cases like the Challenger disaster or Pons and Fleishman's claims about "discovering" cold fusion processes, media are also blamed for ignoring risks and uncertainties that—after the fact—seem glaring, as though better reporting could have prevented the Challenger disaster or establish more quickly than the scientific community that Pons and Fleishman's conclusions were not entirely credible. This form of criticism also has the effect of serving mainstream interests to the extent the media can thus be made scapegoats for technological and scientific failures.

This is good context for understanding the issues underlying an analysis of media framing of the biotechnology controversy with respect to the media's role in facilitating democratic debate. For biotechnology, despite years of "booster" coverage of the investment opportunities and potential social benefits of genetic engineering, the human genome project, and other miracles of modern life science, the scientific mainstream remains concerned that the news media have overemphasized and inappropriately legitimized opposition points of view. This does not seem to be borne out by available evidence regarding news coverage of biotech in the U.S. or Europe.

Even in the case of cloning, where coverage reached an intensity that was probably unprecedented for any science-related story, serious criticism in the U.S. press was short-lived and rather quickly set aside in favor of stories that marveled at pseudoscientific attempts to duplicate individual humans. Even some bona fide research efforts, such as the Texas A&M University "Missiplicity" project that (despite its otherwise legitimate scientific purposes) was funded by someone wishing to clone their beloved pet dog, effectively helped to marginalize the whole subject by relegating it to crackpot status.

Meanwhile, reports of research suggesting negative effects from biotechnology—from concerns about escaping modified fish outcompeting wild species to the potential harm to Monarch butterflies from engineered crops to the genetic cross-contamination of Mexican maize—regularly set off criticism that the news media have overstated the significance of what are perceived by biotech boosters as at most mild "glitches," small dark clouds on an otherwise sunny horizon. Even those critical reports that are made by credentialed scientists seem to engender this kind of controversy, as though journalists should exercise a more active gatekeeping function over what constitutes legitimate science. This seems rather a lot to ask. It also illustrates the extent to which some of us seem to have come to expect journalism to exercise a social control function vis-à-vis the definition of scientific, as well as social, legitimacy.

Below, we present data from a multinational and multiyear study of elite newspaper coverage of biotechnology in the U.S. and Europe that serves to define the more general patterns in how the media frame these issues on either side of the Atlantic.

Media Framing in the U.S. and Europe

The analysis and interpretation that follows is based on content analyses of newspapers from 14 European countries (Austria, Denmark, Finland, France, Germany, Greece, Italy, The Netherlands, Norway, Poland, Portugal, Sweden, Switzerland, the United Kingdom), Canada, and the U.S. It should be noted that coordinating and training even a small group of researchers within one country can be difficult, and this has been exacerbated by including groups from 16 different countries. While efforts were made to increase intercoder reliability across countries, some discrepancies are inevitable. At the same time, we feel that the following discussion is a reasonable reflection of elite newspaper coverage within each of these countries.[1]

Researchers in each country were asked to code articles from those newspapers that believed to be national opinion leaders. In the U.S., for example, *The New York Times* and *Washington Post* were used, while in the U.K., researchers used *The Times* for 1973 to 1987 and the *Independent* from 1987 to 1999. French researchers used *Le Monde*, while in Germany, *Der Spiegel* and *Frankfurter Allgemeine Zeitung* were used (see Gaskell and Bauer 2001 for more details). The number of articles coded in each country differed, relative to the total number of articles focused on genetic issues. The coding scheme used for these analyses stemmed from Gamson and Modigliani's (1989) work on nuclear power in which framing was a key variable in understanding how media coverage was presenting the issues. Other variables such as placement, length of article, sources quoted or referenced, issue being discussed, benefits and risks presented, and use of metaphors were also coded.

Given our focus here on processes of legitimation, we decided that the framing data would give the best indication of how issues related to genetics were being presented to the general public in each country. Eight frames were developed to help categorize the articles. These included (1) progress—includes discussions of how the technology is an extension of science or a debate over its efficiency and effectiveness; (2) economic—includes discussions of financial developments around new drugs and crops; (3) ethical—

encompasses concerns with the role of humans in developing new species, the role of the church in these debates, and so forth; (4) Pandora's Box—presents arguments that if this kind of technology is released into the environment it will only bring evil; (5) runaway technology—presents contentions that if this technology is started humans will not be able to stop or control it; (6) nature/nurture—reflects concerns with designer babies and other species of animals and plants; (7) public accountability—asks the question, if something goes wrong, who will be responsible?; and (8) globalization—asks questions regarding dependency of some nations on those nations where the technology is being developed. Given discourse on the transatlantic divide (e.g., Gaskell and Bauer 2001), one may assume that it is only the U.S. and Canada where biotechnology and other genetic topics are being framed as progressive. In fact, the progressive frame is one of the top three frames in every nation, though this ranges from a low of 12 percent in Denmark to a high of 67 percent in Portugal. In eleven of the sixteen countries, the progressive framing was the most used frame. Use of this frame averaged 37 percent across Europe, 39 percent in Canada, and 63 percent in the U.S.

The second most used frame was public accountability, followed by economic prospects. The mention of risks and benefits for each of these frames shows how reporting was legitimizing genetic technology. When progressive framing is used, 58 percent of the articles mentioned that a benefit was either likely or very likely, though only 8 percent of these articles mentioned that a risk was likely or very likely. For the public accountability frame, the respective percentages mentioning benefits or risks are 24 percent and 33 percent, and for economic prospects they are 48 percent and 16 percent. While public accountability is typically a negative frame, the difference between discussions of benefits and risks is much smaller than for the progress and economic prospect frames.

While the progress frame is the most significant across all countries, it is not equally distributed across issues. In Europe, for example, nearly 60 percent of articles dealing with medical issues used the progressive frame, while only about 30 percent of the agriculture/food articles used the progressive frame. In Canada, just over 63 percent of the medical articles were framed as progressive, and 36 percent of the agriculture/food articles. In the U.S., 51 percent of the articles with food themes were written as progressive, while 65 percent of medical articles fell under the progressive theme. All of these differences are statistically significant at the .01 level.

Some correlation is apparent between these media trends and public acceptance of agriculture/food versus medical applications of genetic technologies; in all countries studied there is more public support for medical biotechnology than for agriculture/food applications. It is not our intention to overinterpret this relationship, as few agree as to what extent media discourse might be a reflection of public opinion (or, vice versa, its source). In addition, it would be difficult to discern whether these attitudes represent support for medical biotechnology per se, or for new developments in medical research more generally. What is interesting to note is the seemingly deeper resonance for medical technologies being considered progressive as compared to food and agriculture applications, and the fact that this difference clearly exists on both sides of the Atlantic. This persistent pattern seems to overshadow observed differences between Europe and the U.S. in either general attitudes or general patterns in media framing vis-à-vis biotechnology as a whole.

To further explore this generalization, we analyzed two of the more damaging frames—runaway technology and Pandora's Box. In Europe, over 11 percent of the food articles used the Pandora's Box frame, and just over 4 percent used the runaway frame. For medicine, the Pandora's Box was only used in just over 3 percent of the articles, and the runaway frame was used less than 2 percent of the time. In Canada, no medical articles were framed as runaway technology, and Pandora's Box was used in less than 3 percent of the articles. For food, on the other hand, the Pandora's Box frame was used in 15 percent of the articles, though runaway technology was used for just over 3 percent of the articles. Finally, in the U.S., the Pandora's Box frame was used in 8 percent of the food articles, but only 3 percent of the medical articles, while the runaway technology frame was used for over 9 percent of the food articles and just over 2 percent of the medical articles. The major discrepancies in this matrix are within countries in terms of the treatment of food and medical technologies, not between the countries. While we must again stress that these discrepancies cannot be described as "causes" of opinion differences, they certainly reflect and resonate with such differences.

These issue framings also draw attention to the processes of legitimation that occur within the pages of newspapers. According to Blumer (1971), a topic does not become a social issue until it is carried within a public arena. Blumer was mainly concerned with social problems, but the applicability of his assertion can easily be extended. Biotechnology, genetic engineering, and other issues related to genetics have all become part of both the mainstream news and popular culture (e.g., *Jurassic Park*, *The X-Men*), as well as the science-based literature. Surveys of public knowledge concerning genetics still show gaps in awareness of these issues, though this does not necessarily reflect a lack of publicly available discourse. These issues have become legitimate in the sense that they are seen as needing space or attention in a highly valued public arena—the mass media—which has a limited carrying capacity.

The legitimation process involves more than just issues; it also reflects back reciprocally on the legitimacy of sources. In an analysis of 2720 articles from the U.S. appearing in *The New York Times* and *Washington Post* between 1971 and 2000, scientists were more likely to be attached to progressive frames than were government officials. This connection between scientists and progress frames legitimizes biotech, but it also invites readers to conclude that science and scientists are about moving ahead, and that the enterprise of science (as it relates to biotechnology and genetics) is evolutionary and beneficial. Recent surveys (see Corrado 2001) have shown that the U.S. public tends to rate scientists as high on levels of trust, making them persuasive as information sources. At the same time, the U.S. public tends to rate the mass media low on the same scales, though we would argue that many people in the U.S. only hear from scientists when they are quoted in the news.

In addition to scientists and government officials, reporters used corporate spokespersons, activist groups, opinion polls, and financial advisers (including stock markets) to make sense of the genetic revolution. Few of these groups shared the same amount of media spotlight as scientists and government officials, and none were as likely to be attached to the progressive frame as scientists. This is true in both North America and Europe, where, once again, there seem to be as many differences within countries with regards to framing as between them.

Media Coverage and the Public Sphere

Continuities in framing between leading U.S. and European papers suggest that we cannot attribute differences in opinion between U.S. and European populations exclusively to media treatment. However, subtler differences between the structures of media systems in Europe and the U.S. are not reflected in content analysis that is limited to a handful of elite publications and may be very important for understanding the character of public debate in the context of media reports on both sides of the Atlantic.

While there is some indication that news media in much of Western Europe are headed toward a U.S. model in which "objectivity" rather than analysis is emphasized, the concept of press freedom and the press's appropriate role in society is different in the U.S. and Europe. U.S. Press law is different, for one thing (Picard 2003). And historically, for reasons of political history and economics as well as cultural tradition, the European system has produced papers more clearly identifiable with particular political positions than has the U.S. system, in which domination by Associated Press wire stories has created a relatively homogeneous news system across the 50 states. (AP domination often extends to the agenda in television news reports as well.)

It is quite possible, therefore, that diversity of opinion is much more visible and more encouraged in press accounts in Europe as opposed to the U.S., despite the fact that in many ways U.S. law seems more adamantly protective of journalistic freedom. This hypothesis would go a long way toward explaining why the actual differences between U.S. and European opinion—while they are definitely real—are rather less striking than casual perusal of news on both continents would suggest. Yet leading elite papers in both areas are still dominated by similar interpretations of biotechnology issues.

In addition, studies of mainstream U.S. papers may further mask the existence of diversity of perspective in that local news accounts of biotech-related controversy may not achieve national attention at all (Priest and Ten Eyck, in press). The U.S. is a nation of fifty states and countless communities that are geographically and ethnically diverse. Stories about local events—especially controversies related to agriculture, which are going to be seen as less compelling to the audiences in major urban centers that produce the elite publications most often studied—only become nationally prominent on rare occasions.

The same dynamics likely characterize the European press, and this may also help explain the apparent commonalities in news framing, even while more diversity of perspective may well characterize the national news in many European countries than in the U.S. In other words, studying the news as reported in leading national U.S. papers may suggest a monolithic view that is not representative of broad public opinion and not reflective of "mundane" local controversy. Studying the news as reported in leading European papers may give somewhat the same impression, although the availability of competing national papers in many European countries nevertheless may make dissent more visible to well-read citizens, whereas in the U.S. the range of opinion legitimized in the news is likely to be more limited. This remains a subject for further research, as the logistical and measurement problems associated with characterizing news content across different nations are formidable.

It also seems highly likely that some voices are more likely to be portrayed as legitimate "players" on the public political stage, as well, and this also differs in different national cultures. This is not just a news phenomenon but reflects differences in political culture. A number of European countries have active environmental ("Green") parties, for example, who are recognized as legitimate political forces operating in mainstream arenas rather than "fringe" groups that are more easily dismissed. The U.S. does not, at this time, although such a movement may be growing. Inevitably, news coverage will reflect these differences in political culture. Dissenting voices can be represented as voices that count or as voices that do not, and this representation takes place in ways too subtle to reflect in most large-scale content studies.

In short, the superficial similarity in news frames between European and U.S. elite papers goes a long way toward undermining the assertion that opinion differences here are a simple function of news accounts. However, it is important not to take this line of reasoning too far, because the European press may well tend to legitimize certain opposition points of view and/or make them more visible in comparison to the more relentlessly mainstream national press in the U.S. While it would be naïve to suppose that public opinion differences are so easily manipulated or created, it would also be naïve to suppose that news accounts make no contribution to the political culture in each case. In the U.S., only a handful of national media exist and these are largely dominated by the Associated Press agenda (and heavily influenced on technical issues by information subsidies from mainstream institutions such as large corporations and research universities). While the more elite papers in much of Europe no doubt reflect similar dynamics, the likely generally greater prominence and legitimacy of dissenting views may well have contributed to more vigorous and open public debate on questions related to biotechnology.

U.S. researchers often assume that opinion differences between the U.S. and Europe on biotechnology-related issues are attributable to differences in knowledge of the science involved, implicating journalism in another, less direct way.[2] While there is a relationship, it is a weak one (Priest 2001; Priest et al., in press). Rather, in cases of public controversy citizens engage in a process of making choices among competing voices and claims, and those choices are influenced by their relative trust of the claimsmakers. Research continues on whether a "spiral of silence" (Noelle-Neumann 1993) might have existed for dissent over biotechnology within the U.S. that made the appearance of European objections particularly unexpected.

What does the future hold for biotechnology and the media in the public sphere? If the "hype" over cloning had any longterm impact on U.S. public opinion, it may well have been the diminution of a silence spiral and the reframing of debate over biotechnology to encompass ethics. Other research-ers have presented evidence of a late–1990s turn toward the critical in U.S. coverage, a turn that may foreshadow further public attention to risk, ethics, accountability, and other associated controversies on the U.S. side of the Atlantic (Nisbet and Lewenstein 2001). A critical turn in the media may not change U.S. opinion, but it is also quite plausible that these trends will at least make U.S. dissent less invisible. Others have argued that media imagery may serve an important symbolic function by facilitating public thinking about a new technology, without necessarily determining public attitudes, and that the intensity of media attention will naturally diminish once the technol-ogy becomes a more familiar one (Wagner et al., 2002); this progression may turn out to describe the European picture for biotechnology. Either way, some degree of public opinion convergence across the Atlantic might possibly be in the offing.

Notes

1. Collection of the comparative media data reported in this chapter was conducted by an international team working under the leadership and coordination of George Gaskell and Martin Bauer of the London School of Economics, with funding by the European Commission. In Canada, this work was conducted by Edna Einsiedel of the University of Calgary. The work of the U.S. researchers who wrote this chapter (and that of the other non-E.U. teams) was independently funded. The authors of this chapter received funding for their work on this project from Texas A&M University, Michigan State University, and the National Science Foundation, Ethics and Values Studies program.
2. Many observers have speculated that the explanation for differences in acceptance of food biotechnology between U.S. and European populations stems from cultural differences in attitudes toward food; however, we know of no specific empirical evidence that would serve to prove or disprove this hypothesis, however intriguing.

References

Blumer, Herbert (1971) "Social Problems as Collective Behavior." *Social Problems* 18:298–305.

Corrado, Michael (2001) "Trust in Scientists: Recent research reveals that more people trust scientists to tell the truth than may have been suggested." Available at http://www.mori.com/pubinfo/pdf/trust.pdf.

Dearing, James W. and Everett M. Rogers (1996) *Agenda-Setting*. Thousand Oaks, CA: Sage.

Iyengar, Shanto and Donald R. Kinder (1987) News that Matters: Television and American Opinion. University of Chicago Press.

Gamson, William A. and Andre Modigliani (1989) "Media Discourse and Public Opinion on Nuclear Power: A constructionist approach." *American Journal of Sociology* 95:1–37.

Gandy, Oscar H. (1982) *Beyond Agenda-Setting: Information Subsidies and Public Policy*. Norwood, NJ: Ablex.

Gaskell, George and Martin W. Bauer (eds.) (2001) *Biotechnology, 1996–2000*. London, UK: Science Museum.

Kasperson, Roger E., and Jeanne X. Kasperson (1996) "The Social Amplification and Attenuation of Risk." *Annals of the American Academy of Political and Social Sciences* 545: 95–105.

Mazur, Allen (1981) "Media Coverage and Public Opinion on Scientific Controversies." *Journal of Communication* 31(2): 106–115.

McCombs, Maxwell E. and Donald L. Shaw (1972) "The Agenda-setting Function of Mass Media." *Public Opinion Quarterly* 36 (2), pp. 176–187.

Nelkin, Dorothy (1995) *Selling Science: How the Press Covers Science and Technology*. (2ⁿ Ed.) N.Y.: W. H. Freeman.

Nisbet, Matt, and Bruce V. Lewenstein (2001) "A Comparison of U.S. Media Coverage of Biotechnology with Public Perceptions of Genetic Engineering 1995–1999." Paper presented to the International Public Communication of Science and Technology Conference, Geneva, Switzerland, February 103.

Noelle-Neumann, Elisabeth (1993) *The Spiral of Silence (2ⁿ ed.)*. Chicago: University of Chicago Press.

Picard, Robert G. (2003) "Press Freedom in Europe." Pp. 7–23 *in* Kwadwo Anokwa, Carolyn A. Lin, and Michael B. Salwen, eds. *International Communication: Concepts and Cases.*

Priest, Susanna Hornig (1995) "Information Equity, Public Understanding of Science, and the Biotechnology Debate." *Journal of Communication* 45(1): 39–54.

Priest, Susanna Hornig (2001) "Misplaced Faith: Communication Variables as Predictors of Encouragement for Biotechnology Development." *Science Communication* 23(2): 97–110.

Priest, Susanna Hornig, Hans Bonfadelli, and Maria Rusanen (in press) "The 'Trust Gap' Hypothesis: Predicting Support for Biotechnology Across National Cultures as a Function of Trust in Actors." *Risk Analysis.*

Priest, Susanna Hornig, and Toby Ten Eyck (in press) *In* Sandra Braman, ed. *Biotechnology and Communication: The Meta-Technologies of Information.* Lawrence Erlbaum.

Wagner, Wolfgang, Nicole Kronberger, and Franz Seifert (2002) Collective symbolic coping with new technology: Knowledge, images and public discourse. *British Journal of Social Psychology* 41: 323–343.

Part III

Major Societal Institutions and Biotechnology: The Law, the State, and the Economy

Introduction

Martin Schulte

In his paper Alexander Somek deals, in particular, with the *moral* problems of genetic testing and genetic discrimination. He considers genetic testing as the nightmarish vision of a world in which people are classified, in every conceivable respect, pursuant to genetic patterns. For him this reveals something deeply disturbing about the *moral* beliefs that we incalculate, beliefs reflecting the prevailing market mentality, a result of a particular strand of modern political liberalism. In particular, biotechnology threatens to remove an element which has made "ignorance" from within the market mentality acceptable thus far. For Alexander Somek, this is a misnomer for "tolerance", which is eroded as the success of testing technologies rises. In effect, bio-technological knowledge removes tolerance, it is tolerance-subverting. In the long run, the element of solidarity that has made the market mentality politically sustainable is being lost in this process. Therefore, genetic discrimination is not about our genes, but about the *moral* bankruptcy of the market mentality.

This raises the question how legal practice and legal dogmatics deal with these serious moral problems of genetic testing. From their perspective genetic testing scarcely seems to be a problem of legislation. Quite the opposite! Everyone has a constitutional right (right of personality) to both, namely genetic knowledge and genetic ignorance. But, considering the real compulsion of the technological progress it is really a problem of rights enforcement. Nevertheless the latest reform proposals await new legislative initiatives: non-negotiable rules guaranteeing real parity between the partners to a contract; a comprehensive legislative act on genetic screening; a new prohibition of the distinction with regard to genetic discrimination in Art. 3 Paragraph 3 of the German Basic Law. Insurance companies shall not be allowed to request, to accept, or to make use of genetic testing. In a similar manner this is valid for labour law (Lege, 2003: 764 ff., 771).

From a sociological theory of law qua an external description of the legal system as a self-describing system (Schulte. . . .), the state of affairs sketched above demonstrates mutual irritability between legal philosophy, legal

189

dogmatics and legal practice as internal descriptions of the legal system. Legal philosophy represents itself as the discipline that reflects on and discusses the questions of fundamental juridical principles and general problems in a philosophical manner. With regard to genetic testing, this is valid for the basic legal principles of equality, solidarity and tolerance as Alexander Somek has pointed out very clearly. In this way, legal philosophy aims at a conceptual definition of the identity of the legal system in contrast to its environment, by, *inter alia,* making observations about the legitimation of the validity of positive law (e.g. legitimation by giving reasons). Owing to their cognitive openness on the one hand and their operative closure on the other, legal dogmatics and legal practice operate on the basis of their programmes, following the code of legal/illegal. Thus, legal practice is bound to produce decisions following the universal code of legal/illegal and the standards of decision-making programmes (e.g. constitution). Legal dogmatics, however, creates normative draft versions of the legal system, in particular, the legislator, by making juridico-political suggestions on the further development of valid law. In this context the proposal of a constitutional amendment concerning genetic discrimination, as outlined above, is at the same time an expression of a structural coupling of the legal and political system (Luhmann, 1993: 470). In this way, the legal and the political system make an important contribution to the management of the moral problems connected with genetic testing. This is something the economic system may not welcome, but as a result of its operative closure, which characterizes all social systems, the economic system will make the next decision on the basis of its universal code (payment/no payment). No more and no less!

The paper of Steven Vallas, Daniel Kleinman, Abby Kinchy and Raul Necochea provides a number of interesting and important observations on the way academic and industrial scientists working in the field of biotechnological research construe the value of their work (for further details see Kleinman/ Vallas, 2001: 451–492). In their opinion, many academic researchers do not feel compelled to offer any moral justification of their research, instead taking for granted their autonomy vis-à-vis societal needs. When moral claims are made, these are often merely strategic gestures made in order to secure funding for research that continues without clearly intersecting with social needs. However, industrial scientists differ from this pattern in several respects. Many of them have been attracted to research positions in industry precisely because these positions offer an opportunity directly respond to urgent medical and social needs. For Steven Vallas and his co-authors, the rhetorical strategy of the academic researchers constructs an intellectually and politically indefensible opposition between the sacred and the pure on the one hand (university science) and the profane and impure on the other (industrial pursuits generally). Against this background, their paper suggests that in the face of the ongoing transformation of the economy and, with it, the university, the academic researcher needs to develop a distinct vision of the role of his work and its contribution to the public good (e.g. arguments regarding their contribution to the richness of human culture, adding to our understanding of the universe; adding to the common knowledge; contributing to the education of future citizens). To put it in a nutshell: Commercialization of Science or a "Scientification" of the economy? That's the question!

First of all, let us follow some reflections of Peter Weingart in his latest book on the relationship between science, politics, economics and mass media in the knowledge society, entitled "The Hour of Truth?". I agree with him when he stresses the fact that the close relationship between science and economics is by no means an altogether new phenomenon of our times. The foundation of my university, the Technical University of Dresden in 1828, is an outstanding example here. "Commercialization of knowledge or science" takes for granted the theoretical distinction between science and economics. Therefore the "blurring of the boundaries" is a popular way of speaking while remaining analytically diffuse (Weingart, 2001: 196 f.). The crucial point, however, is the commercialization of knowledge by means of intellectual property law, e.g. patent law.

This leads directly to a second remark. Property, protected by intellectual property law, functions as the structural coupling of the economic and the legal system (Luhmann, 1993: 455). Free communication of knowledge on the one hand and protection of property rights on the other are represented by the distinction between invention and discovery. But it's this very distinction that proves to be highly controversial in the national and international law of biotechnology. Art. 3 and 5 of the Directive 98/44/EC of the European Parliament and of the Council of 6 July 1998 on the legal protection of biotechnological inventions (Official Journal L 213, 30/07/1998 P. 0013–0021) make this more obvious. Art. 3 reads: "For the purpose of this directive, inventions which are new, which involve an inventive step and which are susceptible of industrial application shall be patentable even if they concern a product consisting biological material or a process by means of which biological material is produced, processed or used. Biological material which is isolated from its natural environment or produced by means of a technical process may be the subject of an invention even if it previously occurred in nature." However, the mere description of a hitherto unknown biological substance, e.g. a gene or a partial sequence of genes, proves to be a discovery but is not an invention. Against this background, reason 23 of the above-mentioned directive remains vague: "Whereas a mere DNA sequence without indication of a function does not contain any technical information and is therefore not a patentable invention.". On the one hand, it's entirely possible that the isolation of a DNA sequence is subject to a technical doctrine, on the other, the requested description of the biological function of the DNA sequence is, as well, only a discovery of something already existing in nature. Therefore, the directive does not answer the crucial question, namely, what is it that makes a DNA sequence a patentable invention (Lege, 2003: 795 ff.). Furthermore, this makes obvious that a "blurring of the boundaries" is indeed an appropriate way of speaking with regard to the distinction of invention and discovery in intellectual property law – indeed, a problem of global dimensions, for the European and the American standards for patentability differ fundamentally (Weingart, 2001: 228).

Finally, in his paper Herbert Gottweis describes new strategies in bio-politics that combine technologies of risk and of uncertainty shaping a space of governance in which practices of individual self-control connect with imperatives of political-institutional decision-making. To this extent I agree with him. However, my agreement does not extend to his remark concerning the role and importance of laws and regulations in this process: "Laws and regulations lose importance in the shaping of medical and scientific developments. Instead, new institutionalizations of conversation, confession and negotiation rituals become increasingly central government technologies." And "While institutional politics has become deeply involved in the reflection of such issues, the debate has also clearly moved beyond the realm of legislatures and ethics institutions."

While the risk-problematic has already been discussed in sociology for some time, and a "sociology of risk" has been established (e.g. Japp, 2000), the career of "risk" as a legal concept has become familiar only in the last decade (e.g. Di Fabio, 1994). In the meantime, however, a juridico-conceptual approach has been developed that seeks to steer issues on how knowledge, lack of knowledge, and uncertain knowledge are to be handled in the law (from a sociological perspective see Stehr, 2003). Nowadays administrative law of risk management is regarded as a classical field within the public law, of ever greater importance.

Therefore, it is true to say that the law as such, also in the modern field of bio-politics, has not lost its significance. The latest news on legislative initiatives concerning biotechnologically changed or cloned animals in Great Britain and the United States make this more obvious. In addition, the decisive argument of science in this context is the expression of consumers' trust in these new technological developments. In the wake of such modern developments as bio-politics, however, it is possible that the law appears in a somewhat different light. Still, the legal system is able to irritate the political system. This is valid for the field of bio-politics, too. The constitutional right of human dignity as the structural coupling of the legal system and the political system is an outstanding example.

References

Di Fabio, Udo (1994) *Risikoentscheidungen im Rechtsstaat.* Zum Wandel der Dogmatik im öffentlichen Recht, insbesondere am Beispiel der Arzneimittelüberwachung. Tübingen: J.C.B. Mohr (Paul Siebeck).

Japp, Klaus (2000) *Risiko.* Bielefeld: Transskript.

Kleinman, Daniel Lee and Vallas, Steven P. (2001) Science, capitalism, and the rise of the "knowledge worker": The changing structure of knowledge production in the United States, *Theory and Society* 30: 451–492.

Lege, Joachim (2003) Das Recht der Bio-und Gentechnik, in: Martin Schulte (ed.), Handbuch des Technikrechts. Heidelberg: Springer Verlag: 669–805.

Luhmann, Niklas (1993) *Das Recht der Gesellschaft.* Frankfurt am Main: Suhrkamp.

Schulte, Martin (2003) The Use of Knowledge in the Legal System: The Relationship Between Scientific Expertise and Legal Decisions, in: Nico Stehr (ed.), *The Governance of Knowledge.* New Brunswick, NJ: Transaction Publishers.

Stehr, Nico (2003) *Wissenspolitik.* Frankfurt am Main: Suhrkamp.

Weingart, Peter (2001) *Die Stunde der Wahrheit? Zum Verhältnis der Wissenschaft zu Politik, Wirtschaft und Medien in der Wissensgesellschaft.* Weilerswist: Velbrück Wissenschaft.

7

This is About Ourselves: Or, What Makes Genetic Discrimination Interesting

Alexander Somek

Exploring the Obvious

The title of my paper is more or less self-explanatory. I think that, from a normative angle, genetic discrimination is interesting because it is about ourselves.

It may not be self-explanatory, though, that genetic discrimination and one of its concomitant techniques, genetic testing,[1] are "interesting" also as a matter of social fact. Over the past decade, genetic discrimination has attracted a good deal of attention, not just by the general public (see Miller 2000: 232–233; Reilly 1999: 106–107), but also by legal experts working in the field of insurance and employment law. The *social fact* that genetic discrimination is interesting is thus reflected in an abundant and ever growing body of legal literature, which is conspicuous by the repetitiveness of arguments reflecting the pertinent pros and cons. I shall return to these below.

The incessant spin off of legal commentary is, in my opinion, indicative of the very reason that makes genetic discrimination interesting. Genetic discrimination receives so much attention for it appears to be, paradoxically, *the most rational* and, at the same time, *the most invidious form* of discrimination. This is not to say that where genetic discrimination is concerned one arrives necessarily at two contradictory legal statements. It is not the case that, within legal systems, genetic testing is at one and the same time permissible and forbidden; rather, legal thought and legal regulations reflect, most often, an *uneasiness* as to how to respond to new technologies and their promise to underpin the long-standing social practice of taking into account, in the allocation of resources, the physical and mental conditions of persons.[2]

In what follows, I would like to explore the *normative conundrum*, which is reflected in this uneasiness. Genetic discrimination is rational behaviour for it is based on knowledge which is widely believed to disclose what people are really like. Not infrequently, "genes" are referred to as if they were the scripts determining human life (Lewontin 1993). At the same time, genetic information is perceived to be potentially threatening because these scripts are attributed the power to reveal something about the nature of persons (Pagnattaro 2001: 140; Pickens 1998: 161). If there is anything special about our genes, from a sociological perspective, then it is the potential to make known, possibly, the naked truth about our present condition and our future destiny (Lewontin 2000: 137). Exposure to this truth and, in particular, to the mere purport of such truth, are regarded as potentially disruptive of the fabric of society and to the meaning of individual lives (Epstein 1994: 10).

The dissemination of knowledge revealing our true (or purportedly true) nature is met with deep and widespread indignation. There may be a simple reason for that. As autonomous beings we would be bereft of control to determine what is known, or even falsely believed, about us by others or even ourselves. Our (partial) control about what can be known about ourselves is an essential key to gaining and preserving access to social co-operation (Epstein 1978). It is feared, thus, by some that the unbridled use of genetic testing might result in the social exclusion of those who are likely to be deemed biologically inferior (Kaufmann 1999: 401–4). More precisely, the major concern expressed in the literature is that genetic discrimination may leave a class of people "virtually unemployable and uninsurable" (Gostin 1991: 142). This prospect is taken to be quite real.

Legal Validity

So far I have spoken only loosely about legal thought, legal discourse and "the law". A brief remark may be in order, however, explaining that there is an essential continuity between legal discourse and what we take to be valid legal norms.

The legal system can be understood as the "grammar" (in the sense employed by Wittgenstein 2001: §§ 90, 496) underlying the articulation of a special type of reason for action (Somek & Forgó 1996). Conceiving of the law in such a way suggests that it is, essentially, a bounded but variable set of linguistic practices. Admission to such practices enables the participants to formulate normative beliefs offered in defence of coercion. In a post-positivist situation, legal validity, that is, the meaning of claims about right course of action, are essentially drawn on the basis of trade offs between arguments from morality and arguments from efficiency (Somek 1998). This is not to deny that "sources" of law play a singularly important role in such arguments, nevertheless, the relevance of sources is mediated through other considerations. In other words, the meaning of statutes or precedents is constructed from the perspective of competing "policy" arguments.

I take this to be a very elementary understanding of the law (see also Kennedy 1998). It loses its apparent triviality, however, when it is contrasted with the belief, widely held among legal academics, that the law is a system of rules and principles. Such an understanding of the law is derivative of a specific self-simplification (Luhmann 1984: 89) of the legal system. It can be traced back to the pedestrian view, hinted at above, that the justification of coercion turns on the existence of "sources" for valid legal norms. Rules and principles are constructs made for the presentation of reasons for action as if the sole point of legal justification consisted in an application of one or the other rule or principle. This self-simplification renders obscure that the reference to sources is embedded in a whole grammar of justification. I mention this merely to explain that a description of the law on genetic discrimination would be fatally incomplete if the discourses feeding into statements concerning legal validity were not taken into account.

What Genetic Discrimination Is

Genetic discrimination is commonly defined as "discrimination against an individual or against members of that individual's family because of real or perceived differences from the 'normal' genotype" (Billings et al. 1992; Gridley 2001: 974). This definition may well be too narrow. Broadly understood, genetic discrimination may arise whenever a distinction is made between individuals on the basis of differences in their genetic endowment.

The narrower definition is usually encountered in the legal context, which may be owing to its relevance for the application of the Americans With Disabilities Act (ADA). In the latter context, and in other cases of anti-discrimination legislation, however, the use of an even narrower definition may be appropriate. It specifies genetic discrimination as "discrimination against persons in good health who a test indicates may become ill" (Reilly 1999: 107). Thus understood, genetic discrimination emerges from perceiving a person as a "time-bomb" with regard to the onset of a disease (from this perspective, analogies to HIV are drawn in the literature; Miller 2000: 242–245). At the same time, this definition is very broad for it does not distinguish genetic conditions from other bodily states, such as a viral infection which causes a future disease.

It should be noted, too, that genetic discrimination need not necessarily be based upon genetic testing. Genetic discrimination may also take place on the ground of information obtained from a person's medical record or the medical history of his or her family. The forced sterilisation of persons with mental disabilities in the 1920s is a case in point (see Buck v. Bell, 274 U.S. 200 [1927]). "Genetic" knowledge has been and still can be obtained from several other sources. Diver and Cohen emphasise correctly that a great deal about a person's genetic inheritance can be gleaned "from direct physical observation, medical examinations and tests, a personal medical history, a family medical history, and the like" (Diver & Cohen 2001: 1452). If what presumably is "in the genes" were all that mattered to the ongoing debate there would be little reason to believe that the use of information obtained from direct testing is more disquieting than knowledge obtained from other sources.[3]

Apparently, the growing fear of genetic discrimination is not ungrounded (Billings et al. 1992). On the basis of genetic information employers may avoid hiring persons who in their opinion are likely to take sick leaves or to retire early (for this would help to avoid additional transaction costs involved in recruiting and training). Likewise, insurance providers, in particular inasmuch as health insurance or life insurance are concerned, are expected to readjust their schedule of rates according to knowledge collected about predispositions for a disease (Clayton 2000: 135). Most lawyers and legal scholars believe that there is evidence suggesting that the practice of genetic screening is on the rise.[4] Both sympathetic and critical commentators predict that with the progress of modern biotechnology genetic testing will be more widely used by employers and insurers in the future (Miller 2000: 235), and that it would be an illusion to believe that genetic test information would be erased from medical records or kept undisclosed (Reilly 1999: 129). If anything can be said at the moment, it is true that the *potential* for genetic screening is increasing (Hudson et al. 1995; Miller 1998; Reilly 1999: 113–7; Hall 1999; Rachinsky 2000: 576–7).

Legal Discourse

I have pointed out above that legal statements are arrived at on the basis of broader considerations of the moral and economic merits of public policy. Such considerations reflect "jurisprudential perspectives" that can be brought to bear on a normative question. With regard to the permissible use of genetic testing, at least two perspectives can be distinguished (see also Gaulding 1995: 1647, 1674–5).

Why Genetic Discrimination is Good

To begin with, there is the camp of those supporting genetic testing as a reliable means of enhancing efficiency in the underwriting and rating of insurance contracts on the one hand and in the allocation of jobs on the other (Epstein 1994; Diver & Cohen 2001). The basic jurisprudential point of view betrays a libertarian creed.It is a wellspring of arguments in favour of genetic discrimination.

From this perspective, insurance, also health insurance, is available on the basis of a private deal. The insurer assumes the insured's risk in exchange of a premium, which is equal to the expected loss, that is, the size of the possible loss multiplied by its probability (Gaulding 1995: 1651). Clearly, the amount of the premium paid depends on the probability and the gravity of the risk insured and on the pool of insured available for the insurer. The more accurately the insurance policy fits the risk of the insured, the better the policy works for those whose risks are comparatively lower than the risks of others. Actuarial adjustment of insurance policies according to fine-tuned classifications of risks is not just in the interest of the insurer, it is also in the individual interest of the insured. A classification system that is optimally fine-tuned with regard to different risks is presumably also fair, for it requires from each insured to pay only that amount of premium that approximates as closely as possible his or her expected loss.

For private health insurance contracts, it is argued that a more discriminate use of information helps both insurers and insured to obtain policies that can be delivered by competitive markets. One of the major problems encountered in this context is that of pre-empting adverse selection (Epstein 1994: 13–15). Adverse selection means that an insurance policy invites underwriting by those with a high potential of risk that is unknown to the insurer. Without safeguards against adverse selection insurers are likely to end up with the group of potential customers that is least preferred by them. Insurers respond to this problem through the use of distinctions in the process of underwriting, and through measures affecting rating and co-insurance. Genetic testing promises to make information about an important set of facts available that is needed by insurers to determine differential ratings matching corresponding risk (in any event, so long as pre-diagnostic risks are concerned). Owing to the information obtained from genetic testing, insurers would be in a position to classify risks more accurately and "thus [to] equate the price of coverage to its value" (Diver & Cohen 2001: 1465). Likewise, insurance seekers with a more favourable genetic profile could benefit from lower risks related to their genotype.

Indeed, the most powerful arguments in favour of genetic testing which are offered from this perspective, draw on current techniques used to come to grips with adverse selection problems. Present insurance practice deals with these problems through the use of medical underwriting (that is, checks before signing the contract), exclusion of pre-existing conditions, deductibles, and coinsurance. If genetic information were available only to the potentially insured and not to the insurer, adverse selection problems would be severely exacerbated (Epstein 1994: 10). There would be great incentives for persons with elevated risks to join an insurance pool composed of others who are in a lower risk category. What is more, pre-existing condition exclusion and coinsurance provisions would turn out to be "impotent weapons to combat the allocative distortions caused by adverse selection" (Diver & Cohen 2001: 1466–7). Without having recourse to genetic testing, insurers would be unable to prove asymptomatic pre-dispositions. Coinsurance provisions are likely to be completely ineffectual to handle emergent distortions of adequate risk classifications.

As a consequence of informational asymmetry, Diver and Cohen argue, the insurance market might develop in either of two directions (2001: 1467). On the one hand, an equilibrium might ensue that will be marked by "massive misclassification and mispricing of risk, with attendant invisible cross-subsidies and deadweight losses" (ibid.). The market could drift into a direction in which coverage would be either so severely restricted in its scope or so expensive that it would be either useless or unavailable to the vast majority of potential buyers. The other scenario, developed by Diver and Cohen, is even worse. The market, the authors contend, could even collapse, thereby leaving a large segment of the population without any access to insurance at all. As high-risk individuals will attempt to obtain coverage at standards rates, "their better-endowed neighbours will flee from subsidising" with the result that the individual health insurance market will go down in a "death spiral" (ibid.: 1457).

Legal prohibitions on the use of genetic testing would therefore give rise to enormous losses in aggregate welfare (Epstein 1994: 20–21), in particular, they would dampen or asphyxiate the therapeutic and ameliorative benefits following from widespread genetic screening. The paternalistic impulse of protective legislation would "envelop market actors in a shroud of enforced genetic ignorance" (Diver & Cohen 2001: 1454).

When it comes to employment, similar arguments are made with regard to the efficiency losses caused by the adoption of rigid anti-discrimination policies. Employers would not be in a position, then, to take into account how certain pre-dispositions to develop an illness may adversely affect future job performance. In addition, hiring and firing an unproductive or unqualified worker is a costly affair. Reliance on past employment history or on monitoring mechanisms involve uncertainty and increase costs. Against this background, genetic testing seems to hold out the promise to facilitate a selection of workers who, as it were, will be running of themselves. As Diver and Cohen argue (ibid.: 1461): "Monitoring and corrective action require investment in supervision, and often require changes in production design and scheduling. In the meantime, the underperforming worker inflicts on the organisation both demoralisation costs and the opportunity costs of foregone output. For these reasons it is almost always in the employer's interest to establish better ex ante screening mechanisms so as to select workers who will require less supervision and corrective action." Efficiency gains, the argument continues, should not be limited to the process of employee selection. In the long run, genetic monitoring would give rise to productivity gains (ibid.: 1462). Through the use of knowledge linking genotype and job-performance, workers could—again, as if the were perfect robots—rotate among jobs until a perfect or near perfect fit in the relation of genetic potential and task execution would be attained. Safety risks could be reduced, waste of resources by unqualified workers avoided etc (ibid.: 1464). All in all, genetic testing is likely to improve the quality of predictions concerning the two determinants of job performance, namely, intensity and quality of effort (id.: 1461).

Why Genetic Discrimination is Bad

Advocates of genetic discrimination are rare. Most commentators take it for granted that distinctions made among persons on the basis of genetic information are inherently suspect from the perspective of the equality principle. They think that the use and dissemination of genetic information is likely to result in imposing a disadvantage on persons on the ground of characteristics that are by definition beyond their control (Dworkin 2001: 436). For example, insurers have a strong interest in treating a genetic predisposition as a pre-existing condition and to exempt it from coverage (Gostin 1991: 136 reminds the reader of the fact that insurers began testing for HIV and regard HIV as an uninsurable condition). But this would be manifestly unfair since there is nothing that a person can do to avoid being affected by such a pre-disposition. The positions in the literature vary, nonetheless, with respect to the degree to which the differentiation between, and the use of, classifiers is deemed offensive. At any rate, a less pronounced and a more pronounced position can be made out.

According to the *less pronounced position*, employers and insurers *may* legitimately resort to genetic information for the purpose of designing efficient insurance policies provided that the factors taken into account are causally connected to the risk measured, controllable and not associated with historical instances of invidious discrimination (Gaulding 1995: 1676). Some classifications, therefore, may not be used as proxies for genetic conditions, in particular when their use is invidious in light of past discrimination against a certain group. This means that racial or sexual classifiers, if used as proxies for some genetic trait, ought be regarded as highly suspicious. Interestingly, it is also understood that genetic traits *per se* are not invidious since they are not intertwined with a "history" of discrimination.

The distinction between historically burdened categories on the one hand and "clean" classifications according to genetic traits on the other is difficult to sustain. If there had ever been a rational pretence for practices of "invidious" discrimination, then race and sex were playing the role of mere proxies for purportedly "real" biological differences. Therefore, the less pronounced position severely underestimates the discriminatory potential that resides in the evaluation of human nature as such.

Consequently, the *more pronounced* position dismisses the special emphasis on race and gender as too narrowly drawn. This is in line with legislation by American states that restricts the use of genetic information regardless of a link to traditionally invidious categories. The more pronounced position, however, encounters a difficulty of its own. One cannot ban all use of genetic information for the knowledge collected about us in appraisals of our fitness for social co-operation allows genetic information to pass as (potential) truth about persons. Our moral thinking is so replete with assumptions about "innate abilities" and "factors beyond our control" that the latent biological determinism (Lewontin 2000: 4–5), which is manifest in the practice and perception of genetic testing, merely hits home the bias of common morality.

Facing this difficulty, defenders of the more pronounced position are inclined to find genetic testing acceptable in some instances and to dismiss them in others, depending on the type of interest affected. Abraham (1999), for example, draws a distinction between health insurance on the one hand and life insurance on the other by pointing to the following differences: adverse selection problems and asymmetry of information are more severe when it comes to the buying of life insurance (id.: 126). In the United States, most health insurance is sold on a group basis through large employers without individual underwriting. Since there is, under these circumstances, almost no individual selection, there are consequently scarcely any adverse selection problems. Health insurance is also substantially different from other types of insurance. It is the major means of allocating the basic good of health care to everyone on equal terms.[5]

These differences notwithstanding, there is agreement, though, that the availability of genetic information could give rise to widespread irrational behaviour. Persons carrying certain genetic pre-dispositions, even if recessive, are likely to be treated as if they suffered from a contagious disease. Anti-discrimination norms seem to offer a promising remedy here. Moreover, protection from irrational behaviour should also be granted at least as long as scientific records are far from complete. Abraham argues that it would be unfair to use the little that is known to the disadvantage of those about whose genetic condition data have been collected. Absent more encompassing information about the genome of humankind it would be unfair to apply to them what is fortuitously known about them (Abraham 1999: 128). Finally, there is hardly any individual underwriting in large group health insurance. Prohibitions on the use of genetic information prevent disadvantaging of a small number of employees with individual or small-group coverage.

Legislation

Needless to add that these two jurisprudential positions are reflected in legal policy choices. The type of action of taken by legal policy is basically twofold. One is general, the other is context-specific. The general response has left its trace in European soft law, that is, law that need not but may be permissibly treated as binding law. The context-specific response is characteristic, in particular, of the situation in the United States.

Europe

The most straightforward response, exceeding even the anti-discriminatory zeal of the more pronounced position, can be found in the Convention for the Protection of Human Rights and Dignity of the Human Being With Regard to the Application of Biology and Medicine.[6] It was adopted by the Council of Europe in 1997. As an international instrument, the Convention imposes on the signatory states an obligation to bring national laws in line with the principles laid down in the Convention. This obligation extends also to state intervention into private dealings.

Article 11 of the Convention, which is relevant to our discussion, prohibits "any form of discrimination against a person on grounds of his or her genetic heritage". Indeed, this prohibition is intended to sweep so broadly as to rule out any kind of genetic discrimination with the exception of the permissible use of test results for health purposes. This exception is laid down in Article 12 of the Convention.[7] From both provisions follows, prima facie at any rate, that any discrimination or discrimination with regard to long-term employability is strictly forbidden (see the Explanatory Report on the Convention, http://conventions.coe.int/treaty/en/Reports/Html/164.htm: para. 74–77).

The Convention aside, European data protection laws and various statutes regulating health care provide for direct or indirect protection from genetic discrimination (Schwartz 1997: 407). Only rarely, the issues raised by modern biotechnology are addressed in one consolidated statute. My home country, Austria, is an exception to this rule. The Austrian "Genetic Technology Law" (*Gentechnikgesetz:* BGBl. Nr. 510/1994) contains a provision saying that employers and insurers are prohibited from asking for genetic tests. In addition, even the voluntary submission of such tests by individuals is forbidden (section 67 of the *Gentechnikgesetz).* This rule is intended to preclude that others feel obligated to avail themselves over test information, too—a clear endorsement of "genetic privacy". Other countries adopted different regimes, though. The United Kingdom, for example, makes it permissible for members of certain risk groups to present genetic tests showing that they are personally exempt from the risk (See http://www.doh.gov.uk/hgac/papers/papers_b.htm).

United States—in General

The regulatory regime of the United States is characterised by a high degree of tentativeness. The laws do not amount to a coherent and systematic response to the challenges posed by genetic discrimination, rather, they are more like erratic inroads made into an unfolding practice (Reilly 1995: 971–2; Rothenberg et al. 1997: 1755–7).

The regulatory regime is composed of several pieces of federal and state legislation, and of extensions of already established anti-discrimination principles to new situations (Zindorf 2001; Pickens 1998; Taylor 2001). Indeed, wanting a coherent response from the federal level,[8] it is not unlikely that more and more states might step in to compensate for what is perceived to be a deficit of regulation (Kaufmann 1999: 436). More often than not, however, the spectacle created through the "taking of action" by legislatures might be more important than the solving of problems. As Reilly observes, since most of the laws enacted by states lack a clear definition of "genetic disorder" it is difficult to make out the type of problems the laws purport to solve (Reilly 1999: 111).

Several states adopted legislation restricting the use of genetic information, mostly by health insurers,[9] to varying degrees (Rothenberg 1995; Annas 1995; Reilly 1997: 375–6; 1999: 121). The laws range from a total protection from genetic testing proper (this does *not* exclude, however, inferring genetic information form medical records or family history; Reilly 1999: 122) to restrictions on the use of test results (Kaufmann 1999: 433–4; Miller 1998: 192–3). Currently half of the states have some form of legislation that in varying degrees prohibits genetic discrimination (Reilly 1999: 123). California Law, for example, prohibits employers from discriminating against individuals based on medical conditions. Under this law, the definition of medical conditions includes genetic characteristics (Zindorf 2001: 716).

If Reilly is correct, then the new laws adopted by the states "may be most relevant to a fraction of the population that is unlikely to need them" (1999: 122). Some of the statutes pertain to individually underwritten health insurance, a segment of contracts that is steadily declining mostly because of the high cost of such policies.

Under Federal Law, state insurance law supersedes federal insurance laws unless Congress provides otherwise. Currently, the only federal law prohibiting genetic discrimination in health insurance is the Health Insurance Portability and Accountability Act of 1996 ("HIPAA"), which only applies to employer-based and commercially issued group health insurance (see http://www.cms.hhs.gov/hipaa). This protection is particularly important considering that most American workers receive their health insurance from their job and need protection from discrimination on genetic grounds as they move from one job to another (Miller 2000: 255–6; Reilly 1999: 125). The Act expressly rules out that in group insurance plans eligibility for, or termination of, coverage is made dependent on "genetic information". The Act restricts the extent to which employment-based group health insurance plans can exclude coverage for pre-existing conditions and rules out that genetic predispositions be counted among them (Diver & Cohen 2001: 1449–50). Therefore, susceptibility to genetic disorders alone may not be treated as a pre-existing condition for which coverage can be denied.[10] Since the Act extends only protection to those who are members of an employment-based group insurance plan it does not encompass one third of American workers who are not protected by such plans, such as persons buying insurance on the market or the unemployed.[11]

Employment, nevertheless, is the major context in which genetic discrimination is submitted to the rigors of federal legislation. The major seats of legislation are Title VII of the Civil Rights Act of 1964, the Americans with Disabilities Act of 1990 ("ADA"), the Rehabilitation Act of 1973, Federal Executive Order 13145 and, when it comes to banning the use genetic test results to the disadvantage of workers, also the Occupational Safety and Health Act ("OSHA"; see Kaufmann 1999: 425–9).

In the following I shall provide a brief overview of only the most important pieces of federal legislation.

United States—in Particular

Title VII of the Civil Rights Act is applicable where an employer discriminates on the ground of genetic factors that are linked to a "racial" disposition (Kaufmann 1999: 418–24; Rachinsky 2000: 588–90; Taylor 2001: 59–61; Miller 2000: 247–51). Where a genetic trait is correlated with ethnicity ("race"), any discrimination against this trait can be subject to Title VII scrutiny. Most genetic traits, however, are not race specific and therefore only rarely fall within the ambit of Title VII protections (Zindorf 2001: 710). Nevertheless, the conduct of an employer may conflict with Title VII if discrimination on the ground of a genetic trait, even though neutral on its face, disparately impacts on one specific group (for sickle-anaemia testing, see Gostin 1991: 138–9) for the protection against discrimination also extends to cases of indirect discrimination.

At this point in time it is not entirely clear whether the Supreme Court will accept the claim made by the Equal Employment Opportunity Commission (EEOC) that genetic discrimination would in principle also fall under the protection of the Americans with Disabilities Act of 1988 ("ADA").[12] The point of the ADA is to protect persons with impairments from discrimination provided that they are qualified for the performance of a job.[13] A prima facie case of discrimination can be established by the plaintiff by showing that (a) he or she is disabled, (b) otherwise qualified for employment or an associated benefit, and that (c) he or she was excluded from employment or from receiving a benefit only on the basis of his or her disability (Gridley 2001: 982).

The ADA does not explicitly recognise genetic discrimination as a protected category. Under the ADA a "disability" is characterised by either of the following, not mutually exclusive, conditions ("prongs"), namely, first, a physical or mental impairment that substantially limits one or more of the major life activities of the individual, second, a record of such impairment, or, third, being regarded as having such an impairment. According to most scholars, the third prong of this test, which introduces the "being regarded as disabled" condition, should be extended to victims of genetic discrimination (Zindorf 2001: 711–2; Gostin 1991: 123–6). Consequently, individuals ought to be protected from any discrimination "on the basis of a genetic predisposition to illness, disease, or other disorder, even if the disability has not yet manifested" (Miller 2000: 139). In the eyes of their potential or actual employers, persons with pre-dispositions are "healthy ill" or "at risk" (Gostin 1991: 124 note 83). Not infrequently, however, the inclusion of pre—or asymptomatic persons may be even justified under the first prong of the test by drawing an analogy to the extension of protection to HIV positive persons that was brought about by the Supreme Court in Bragdon v. Abbott (524 U.S. 641; see Miller 2000: 242–4).

Affording persons with genetic pre-dispositions for an illness protection under the ADA is also the position of the EEOC. In 1995 it laid down a guideline saying that it would interpret the ADA such as to include pre-symptomatic individuals with a genetic pre-disposition for a disabling condition (2 U.S. EEOC, Compliance Manual, Order 915.002 at 902–945; Miller 2000: 239; Diver & Cohen 2001: 1450). This interpretation, even though it can be used as persuasive authority (Miller 2000: 241), is not binding on the courts. However, even if the EEOC were to prevail with this interpretation, it should be noted that the protection from discrimination afforded by the ADA has its limits (Diver & Cohen 2001: 1450–1). The Act requires employers only to make "reasonable accommodations" in bringing disabled persons into a position to perform a job. At the "pre-placement stage", that is, after a conditional offer of employment has been made (42 U.S.C. § 12112(c)(2)(A); drug testing, though, is not considered a medical examination), employers may obtain or use information about a prospective employee's medical condition or history (on additional conditions, see Kaufmann 1999: 407–8). According to the EEOC, however, a person to whom a job offer has been made that is withdrawn as a consequence of a test, should be covered under the anti-discrimination protections of the ADA. In the EEOC guideline the example is used of a healthy woman about whom the employer learns, after an conditional offer has been made, that she harbours a gene that increases her risk of colon cancer. Withdrawing the job offer would amount, in the eyes of the EEOC, to a violation of the ADA (2 U.S. EEOC, Compliance Manual, Order 915002, 902–945 [1995]). If as a consequence of this policy an employer were to suffer from decreased output or additional medical costs then this should be regarded as the appropriate normative consequence of the implementation of anti-discrimination policy (Gostin 1991: 134).

On the basis of the EEOC guideline, President Clinton issued Executive Order 13145, which is also known under the name of "Genetic Executive Order" (Executive Order 13145, To Prohibit Discrimination in Federal Employment Based on Genetic Information, 65 Fed. Reg. 6875 [2000]). It prohibits federal employers from requiring or requesting genetic information (tests) as a condition for employment or promotion or for the purpose of classifying current employees. This Executive Order also requires that in the case of any genetic testing, which is permissible after a conditional job-offer has been made,[14] the results are kept confidential and separate from personnel files (Zindorf 2001: 713–4; Miller 2000: 250). Section 501 of the Rehabilitation Act gives federal employees the power to enforce violations of Executive Order 13145.

What Makes It Interesting

Anti-discrimination law purports to regulate the limits drawn for the unequal treatment of persons on the basis of, in this case, genetic information that has been obtained about them. In drawing a line for the permissible use of classifications it does *not* impose an outright prohibition. Anti-discrimination law, thus understood, implicitly endorses the view that genetic knowledge may *legitimately* be taken into account in appraising the sameness or difference of persons. Even without genetic testing a great deal of information is in circulation that appears to reveal something "natural" about us. Diver and Cohen are right, therefore, in asking the following question (2001: 1451): "Do prohibitions on the use of genetic information include restrictions on references to such characteristics as intelligence, or aggressiveness, or obesity that appear to have genetic, as well as environmental, roots?" In a sense, then, we are always and already subject to genetically based classifications and this is not considered irrational if it they are applied in an appropriate way.

But what makes, then, genetic discrimination and genetic testing, in particular, so potentially invidious? The relevant reasons are more difficult to pin down than one might expect at the outset. In the remaining sections of this article I would like to distinguish three such reasons.

Rationality

According to the first reason, the availability and widespread circulation of genetic information is likely to give a free rein to *irrational behaviour*. People ought to be protected from the influence of prejudice and stereotypes. In most legal writings the fear of stigmatisation (Clinton 1997: 1951) is presented as the fear of exposure to attitudes that are not based on a rational appraisal of a person's capabilities.[15] Accordingly, most often the concerns raised in the literature affect the inappropriate use of genetic knowledge (for an exception questioning the reliablity of genetic tests, see http://www.aclu.org./issues/worker/gdfactsheet.html [last visited July 2002]). Clients that have been identified as carrying a predisposition are at risk of being treated as if they were already ill. Asymptomatic individuals that have been positively tested with Chorea Huntington, cystic fibrosis, colon cancer or other conditions will most likely be earmarked with the stigma of illness before the actual onset of the disease. Fear of stigmatisation will discourage individuals to enjoy the benefits of genetic screening, which may in turn engender adverse consequences for their health (Miller 2000: 234–5).[16]

The literature reveals, however, that more than the mere irrationality and the interference of stereotypes is at stake here. The normative belief expressed implicitly in the literature is that genetic knowledge should not be relevant when it comes to granting access to work and work-related social benefits, such as health insurance. In other words, the claim is that having a fair share of social primary goods should not be made dependent on what nature has written into our genes.

Responsibility

The second reason complements the first by introducing the dimension of responsibility. Genetic discrimination would be tantamount to holding persons *responsible* for conditions that are, by definition, beyond their control.

The problem with the second reason is that it sweeps too broadly, not because of its propensity to include a too wide range of circumstances into the set of circumstances beyond our control but because of its application of the notion of responsibility to the allocation of resources. It is ludicrous to think that if a role in a movie or play is given to the more handsome of two candidates, the one who is denied the job is held responsible by the employer for his lesser attractiveness (Hurley 2002). The responsibility reason, if it is applicable at all, has to be formulated in the form of the question of whether those who have lost out, at least in some respect, in the lottery of nature are themselves responsible for making *special efforts* to avoid the social disadvantages associated with "genetic imperfection". Formulated from the reverse perspective, the question is—and this is *the* question of "luck egalitarianism" (Anderson 1999: 289–92, 295–308)—whether society has a responsibility to indemnify people, at any rate partly, against the ill luck that they suffer in the lottery of nature.

I understand that this question is implicitly answered in the affirmative by those who are concerned about the social exclusion of the genetically feeble. But, interestingly, indemnification against the strikes of ill luck is by no means an uncontested principle of law, not even of anti-discrimination law. In a legal context, the second reason has to be presented, therefore, by those who endorse it, in the guise of the first. Preventing the social exclusion of the genetically unlucky needs to be advocated as if it were a matter of combating irrational behaviour. I cannot explain here in which respect this can be observed for the application of the "third prong" of the ADA (on the three prongs see above p. 13).

The Market Mentality

The third reason is in my opinion the most important one. It says that the growth of genetic discrimination threatens to unleash the potential of the market mentality to dissipate the elements of solidarity on which social cooperation—in a market economy—has been resting so far. This daunting prospect affects deeply how we conceive of ourselves as members of society.

According to the market mentality, which finds a most articulate expression in the political philosophy of modern liberalism (e.g. Dworkin 2001), the use of the distinction between innate endowments on the one hand and personal ambitions on the other is a permanent feature of common morality (ibid.: 323–4). With respect to our endowments our lives can be better or worse without any fault of our own. For example, we attribute the success of the successful, in part, to their greater natural beauty or their ample natural gifts. We are inclined to believe that to a non-negligible extent the distinctions of social class reside in our genes (Lewontin 2000: 35). This way of thinking is coherent with considering ourselves *burdened* with having to *respond*, reasonably, to our possible ill luck in the lottery of nature.[17] It reflects the fact that in a market economy we impose on ourselves, collectively and unwittingly, an *individual* responsibility for responding accurately to the value of our endowments. Put in simple terms, we are determined to view one another as the trustees of a random set of talents (Singer 1993: 87).

It is the prudence with which we act in this capacity that we are held to be responsible for, whereas endowments are a matter of luck.

In their actual operation, markets fail to distinguish between these two domains. In a market society external resources are allocated regardless of individual responsibility. Moral desert is not, and certainly not the prevalent, mechanism of allocation (Nozick 1972: 158–9). There is, hence, a remarkable asymmetry in the relation of how we conceive of ourselves as managers of our human resources and the way in which markets respond to our endowments by attaching prizes to them. Markets do not take into account whether or not we are responsible for the low exchange value of our talents. From the perspective of political liberalism, therefore, the existence of markets can only be reconciled with our moral beliefs if some institutional arrangements can be found making markets more *sensitive* to the distinction between choice and circumstance—or ambition and endowment, respectively.

The market mentality responds to this challenge with reference to the existence of *market-correcting markets*. They allow for a transformation of "brute luck" into "option luck" (Dworkin 2001: 73). Anyone can buy insurance against incidents of bad luck. Health insurance, unemployment insurance etc. offer market-based responses to the moral indifference of markets (interestingly, such market correcting markets, such as insurance markets, aggravate the burdens of individual responsibility since their sheer existence makes us responsible for responding to self-perceived hazards). This is the way in which social solidarity is recognised and acknowledged from within the confines of the market mentality and its attendant liberal social model (Esping-Andersen 1990: 43). In fact, it is the only way in which the meaning of solidarity is accessible from its perspective (this is also manifest in the jurisprudence of the European Court of Justice, see Case C–218/00, Cisal di Battistello Venanzio & C. Sas v. Istituto nazionale per l'assicurazione [2002] ECR I–691). For this reason, the fundamentally solidaristic elements built into social life present themselves as problems of permissible or impermissible "cross-subsidisation", tolerable or intolerable adverse selection or acceptable or unacceptable freeloading (Diver & Cohen 2001: 1472–3).

Against this background, it is transparent why genetic discrimination is so awfully interesting in the context of insurance and employment contracts. Once our ill luck in the draw is known, insurance is no longer available to us. We find ourselves, in effect, bereft of the power to respond responsibly to the market's indifference toward individual responsibility. Genetic testing threatens to eliminate "option luck" as a means of organising solidarity through the creation of market-correcting markets. This explains the conundrum that I have identified at the outset of this article. From the perspective of market behaviour genetic discrimination is rational. From the perspective of the distinction between choice and circumstance it is invidious, for it undercuts any market-based solution that could be adopted to rectify the moral indifference of markets.

Conclusion

We should not be dumbfounded by the allures of technological progress. We should not falsely attribute the prospective horrors of genetic discrimination to the availability of testing. The disquieting aspects of modern technology bear the imprints of normativity (Reilly 1999). My conjecture is that the nightmarish vision of a world in which people are comprehensively classified according to genetic patterns reveals something deeply disturbing about the *moral* beliefs that are inculcated into us by the prevailing market mentality. Thus understood, fear of genetic discrimination is an instance of *social reflexivity*. Society is implicitly reflecting upon itself through the moral sentiments of its members.

Even though some authors are rightly suspicious of what they call "genetic exceptionalism" (Friedman Ross 2001; Lazzarini 2001; Zindorf 2001: 722), it cannot be denied that there is indeed something special about modern biotechnology. It threatens to remove an element which has made the market mentality acceptable so far. From its own perspective, this element is addressed as "ignorance". Ignorance, however, is a misnomer for the *tolerance* that has been inherent, heretofore, in employment and insurance contracts. Within a certain range, people were allowed to come as they are. With an eye to Polanyi, it can be said that owing to their "embeddedness" in tolerance, labour (and insurance) markets have been socially acceptable (Polanyi 2001). Until now.

With the rise of testing technologies this tolerance is eroding. The advent of new knowledge gives rise to a dialectical process in whose course tolerance is not just misrepresented as ignorance but also in jeopardy of being eliminated from the basic terms of social cooperation. In effect, indirectly, biotechnological knowledge removes tolerance. It is tolerance-subverting.

What is being lost in this process is the *solidaristic* element that has survived the ascent of the market mentality and that has made it politically sustainable. Genetic discrimination is not about genes. It is about social disintegration. We find ourselves exposed to reifications that make us increasingly susceptible to well-known practices of "mismeasure" (Gould 1981). It is an open question how we are going to live together after solidaristic relationships will have been broken up by the moral caricatures of a knowledge-based economy.[18]

Notes

1. For a definition of genetic testing, see Watson (1999: 92): "The analysis of human DNA, RNA, chromosomes, proteins, and certain metabolites in order to detect heritable disease-related genotypes, mutations, phenotypes, or karyotypes for clinical purposes. Such purposes include predicting disease, identifying carriers, establishing prenatal and clinical diagnosis or prognosis, and monitoring, as well as carrier, prenatal and newborn screening, but they exclude tests conducted purely for research. Tests for metabolites are covered only when they are undertaken with high probability that an excess or deficiency of the metabolite indicates the presence of heritable mutations in single genes." It should be clear, though, from the outset that there are several ways of gauging genetic information. It can be inferred from the results of a physical examination or from studying the medial history of a family.

2. If genetic discrimination is deemed unfair, at any rate in principle, it should be noted that this unfairness is already part of our life (Dworkin 2001: 434). For a further elaboration of this point see p. \h 18.

3. Staying at the level of conceptual preliminaries at the moment, a further distinction can be made. Depending on the stage of an employment or insurance relationship, genetic *screening* and genetic *monitoring* can be distinguished. The purpose of genetic screening is to determine whether an applicant for a job or an insurance policy carries some genetic predisposition for a disease or illness. Employers used as early as in the 1970ies genetic screening to identify African-Americans who carry the gene mutation for sickle-cell anaemia. Those with positive test results were denied employment. Screening may also be used, however, to detect susceptibility for the onset of a certain disease under specific environmental conditions. Genetic monitoring, on the other hand, is meant to determine whether an individual's genetic make-up has changed owing to exposure to certain environmental conditions or hazardous substances. See National Human Genome Research Institute, 'Genetic Information and the Workplace', http://www.nhgri.nih.gov/HGP/Reports/genetics_workplace.html (last visited July 2002).

4. This goes back to surveys published, such as the one by Billings et al. 1992. See also 'Genetic Information and the Workplace' http://www.nhgri.nih.gov/HGP/Reports/genetics_workplace.html (last visited July 2002); Kathy L. Hudson et al. 'Genetic Discrimination and Health Insurance', http://www.vhl.org/newsletter/vhl1996/96aqinsu.htm (last visited July 2002).

5. A public-funding argument against genetic testing is adduced by Buchanan et al. (2001: 262): "Unless something is done to eliminate the threat of widespread genetic discrimination in employment and insurance, the chief public justification for using tax monies to finance the Human Genome Project and related genetic research will be discredited. That justification was that public monies were to be used to benefit the public. If the knowledge that this infusion of public funds produces is systematically used to the disadvantage of citizens at higher genetic risk for certain diseases, then it cannot be said, without serious qualification, that these public funds are being used to benefit the public."

6. See http://conventions.coe.int/treaty/en/treaties/html/164.htm.

7. Article 12 of the Convention reads as follows: "Tests which are predictive of genetic diseases or which serve either to identify the subject as a carrier of a gene responsible for a disease or to detect a genetic predisposition or susceptibility to a

disease may be performed only for health purposes or for scientific research linked to health purposes, and subject to appropriate counselling."

8. Piecemeal, and almost exclusively employment-related legislation goes back, in part, to the 1970ies, in which efforts were made to combat the racism implicit in the testing of the pre-condition for sickle-cell anaemia. See the National Sickle Cell Anaemia Control Act, 42 U.S.C. § 300b (1976). The Act was repealed in 1981. It withheld federal funding from states unless sickle cell testing was deemed voluntarily. See Gridley (2001: 975); on the perceived need for a more coherent response from the federal level, see Rachinsky (2000).

9. Within the realm of insurance, current state laws focus primarily on health insurance. Only twelve states have adopted legislation that protects employees from genetic discrimination in the workplace. See 'Genetic Discrimination in the Workplace Fact Sheet' http://www.aclu.org./issues/worker/gdfactsheet.html (last visited July 2002). For an overview of existing state legislation, see Reilly (1997).

10. Generally, genetic information by itself cannot constitute a pre-existing condition. There is a serious restriction, however, to the application of this rule. Employers who transfer from one group insurance plan to another are not protected by the pre-existing condition exclusion if they have a break of coverage of more than sixty-two days. This is to the detriment of those workers who experience more prolonged periods in which they are between jobs. See Clayton (2000: 135–136).

11. Nevertheless, the HIPAA is regarded as an important legislative advance in the effort to diminish genetic discrimination in health insurance. See Reilly (1999: 125) and Clayton (2000: 135). She points out (ibid. 135–136), however, that the HIPAA leaves a gap that is detrimental to the employment-based voluntary health-insurance system in the United States: Once an insurer finds out that one employee covered by a group insurance plan is at high risk of developing a disease or incurable illness, the insurer still maintains the right to raise the rates charged to the employer and to exclude some interventions from coverage. Employers might decide then to stop offering health insurance.

12. In other words, it is not clear as of yet whether or not the courts will determine that the ADA prohibits employers from discrimination on the basis of a diagnosed, but asymptomatic, genetic condition or trait. See Miller (2000: 239). Most commentators think that, in this context, a genetic disposition to contract a certain disease or to develop a certain illness is tantamount to a disability for the purposes of the ADA. See, for example, Miller (2000: 238–47); Gridley (2001: 976); Kaufmann (1999: 404–14); but see also Rachinsky (2000: 590–93). For a first analysis of the applicability of the ADA to cases of genetic discrimination, see Gostin (1991: 120–35).

13. Title I of the ADA prohibits discrimination on the ground of disability by employers with fifteen or more employees. It states that "no covered entity shall discriminate against a qualified individual with a disability because of the disability [...] in regard to job application procedures, the hiring, advancement, or discharge of employees, employee compensation, job training, and other terms, conditions, and privileges of employment" (42 U.S.C. § 12112 [a]). A "qualified" person must be capable of meeting all the performance and eligibility criteria for a certain position. See 42 U.S.C. §§ 12112(b)(b) and 12131(2).

14. According to Miller (2002: 250–1) "information obtained under this exception may be disclosed only to medical personnel involved in or responsible for determining whether further tests are needed".

15. This is, as it were, the foundational myth of the American belief in the efficacy

and appropriateness of anti-discrimination law: its power "to replace reflexive actions based upon irrational fears, speculation, stereotypes or pernicious mythologies, with carefully reasoned judgements based upon well established scientific information" (Gostin 1991: 129).

16. This has to do, in part, with the lack of data protection in the United States. A survey reported that persons refrain from taking genetic tests because they fear that the results may be disclosed to their employer.

17. One of the more disquieting developments is that as the likelihood increases that genetic information becomes readily accessible to would-be patients, responsibility is shifted on the individual to take precautions. This is part of the transformation of brute luck into option luck. Once alternatives are available, the responsibility of individuals increases. One is responsible for one's genetic record.

18. For helpful comments on a first draft of this paper I would like to thank Elisabeth Holzleithner, Gerhard Luf and Viktor Mayer-Schönberger. Remaining errors are, of course, attributable to my genes.

References

Abraham, Kenneth S. (1999) "Understanding Prohibitions Against Genetic Discrimination in Insurance" 40 *Jurimetrics Journal* 123–128.

Anderson, Elisabeth (1999) "What Is The Point of Equality?" 109 *Ethics* 287–337.

Annas, George J., et al (1995) *The Genetic Privacy Act and Commentary.* Boston: Health Law Department, BU School of Public Health.

Billings, Paul R. et al. (1992) "Discrimination as a Consequence of Genetic Testing" 50 *American Journal of Human Genetics* 476–482.

Buchanan, Alan & Brock, Dan W. & Daniels, Norman & Wikler, Daniel (2001) *From Chance to Choice. Genetics and Justice.* Cambridge: Cambridge University Press.

Clinton, William Jefferson (1997) "Preface" 276 *Science* 1951.

Diver, Colin S. & Cohen, Jane Maslow (2001) "Genophobia: What is Wrong With Genetic Discrimination" 149 *University of Pennsylvania Law Review* 1439–1482.

Dworkin, Ronald (2001) *Sovereign Virtue. The Theory and Practice of Equality.* Cambridge, Mass. & London: Harvard University Press.

Clayton, Ellen Wright (2000) "Comments on Philip R. Reilly's 'Genetic Discrimination'" 3 *Journal of Health Care Law and Policy* 134–139.

Epstein, Richard A. (1978) "Privacy, Property Rights, and Misrepresentation" 12 *Georgia Law Review* 455.

——— (1994) "The Legal Regulation of Genetic Discrimination: Old Responses to New Technology" 74 *Boston University Law Review* 1–23.

Esping-Andersen, Gøsta (1990) *The Three Worlds of Welfare Capitalism.* Princeton: Princeton University Press

Friedman Ross, Lainie (2001) "Genetic Exceptionalism vs. Paradigm Shift: Lessons from HIV" 29 *Journal of Law, Medicine and Ethics* 141–148.

Gaulding, Jill (1995) "Race, Sex, and Genetic Discrimination in Insurance: What's Fair?" 80 *Cornell Law Review* 1646–1694.

Gostin, Larry (1991) "Genetic Discrimination: The Use of Genetically Based Diagnostic and Prognostic Tests by Employers and Insurers" 17 *American Journal of Law and Medicine* 109–144.

Gould, Steven Jay (1981) *The Mismeasure of Man.* New York & London: Norton.

Gridley, Deborah (2001) "Genetic Testing Under the ADA: A Case for Protection from Employment Discrimination" 89 *Georgetown Law Journal* 973–999.

Hall, Mark (1999) "Legal Rules and Industry Norms: The Impact Restricting Health Insurers' Use of Genetic Information" 40 *Journal of Jurimetrics* 93.

Hudson, Kathy L. et al. (1995) "Genetic Discrimination and Health Insurance: An Urgent Need for Reform" 270 *Science* 391–392.

Hurley, Susan (2002) "Roemer on Responsibility and Equality" 21 *Law and Philosophy* 39–64.

Kaufmann, Melinda B. (1999) "Genetic Discrimination in the Workplace: An Overview of Existing Protections" 30 *Loyola University of Chicago Law Journal* 393–438.

Kennedy, Duncan (1998) *A Critique of Adjudication. Fin de siècle.* Cambridge, Mass.: Harvard University Press.

Lapham, E. Virginia et al. (1996) "Genetic Discrimination: Perspectives of Consumers" 274 *Science* 621–624.

Lazzarini, Zita (2001) "What Lessons Can We Learn from the Exceptionalism Debate (Finally)?" 29 *Journal of Law, Medicine and Ethics* 149–151.

Lewontin, R. C. (1993) *The Doctrine of DNA. Biology as Ideology.* London: Penguin Books.

——— (2000) *It Ain't Necessarily So. The Dream of the Human Genome and Other Illusions.* New York: New York Review Books.

Luhmann, Niklas (1994) *Soziale Systeme. Grundriss einer allgemeinen Theorie.* Frankfurt/Main: Suhrkamp.

Miller, Paul Steven (1998) "Genetic Discrimination in the Workplace" 26 *Journal of Law, Medicine and Ethics* 189–197.

——— (2000) "Is There a Pink Slip in My Genes? Genetic Discrimination in the Workplace" 3 *Journal of Health Care Law and Policy* 225–265.

Nozick, Robert (1972) *Anarchy, State, and Utopia.* New York: Basic Books.

Pagnattaro, Marisa Anne (2001) "Genetic Discrimination and the Workplace: Employee's Right to Privacy v. Employer's Need to Know" 39 *American Business Law Journal* 139–185.

Pickens, Kourtney L. (1998) "Don't Judge Me By My Genes: A Survey of Federal Genetic Discrimination Legislation" 34 *Tulsa Law Journal* 161–181.

Polanyi, Michael (2001) *The Great Transformation. The Political and Economic Origins of Our Time.* new ed., Boston: Beacon Press.

Rachinsky, Tara (2000) "Genetic Testing: Toward a Comprehensive Policy to Prevent Genetic Discrimination in the Workplace" 2 *University of Pennsylvania Journal of Labour and Employment Law* 575–598.

Reilly, Philip R. (1995) "Genetics and the Law" In W.T. Reich (ed.), *Encyclopaedia of Bioethics.* rev. ed. New York: Simon & Schuster, vol. 2, 967–976.

——— (1997) "Laws to Regulate the Use of Genetic Information" In Mark A. Rothstein (ed.), *Genetic Secrets. Protecting Privacy and Confidentiality in the Genetic Era.* New Haven & London: Yale University Press 369–391.

——— (1999) "Genetic Discrimination" In C. Long (ed.) *Genetic Testing and the Use of Information.* Washington: AEI Press 106–133.

Rothenberg, Karen H. (1995) "Genetic Information and Health Insurance: State Legislative Approaches" 23 *Journal of Law, Medicine and Ethics* 312–319.

Rothenberg, Karen, et al. (1997) "Genetic Information and the Workplace: Legislative Approaches und Policy Challenges" 275 *Science* 1755–1757.

Schwartz, Paul M. (1997) "European Data Protection Law and Medical Privacy" In M. A. Rothstein (ed.) *Genetic Secrets. Protecting Privacy and Confidentiality in the Genetic Era.* New Haven & London: Yale University Press 392–417.

Singer, Peter (1993) *Practical Ethics*. 2d ed., Cambridge: Cambridge University Press.

Somek, Alexander & Forgó, Nikolaus (1996) *Nachpositivistisches Rechtsdenken. Form und Inhalt des positiven Rechts*. Vienna: WUV-Universitätsverlag.

Somek, Alexander (1998) "Gesetzesbindung als Problem der Demokratie" 6 *Journal für Rechtspolitik* 41–62.

Taylor, Jennifer R. (2001) "Mixing the Gene Pool And the Labour Pool: Protecting Workers from Genetic Discrimination in Employment" 20 *Temple Environmental Law and Technology Journal* 51–72.

Watson, Michael S. (1999) "The Regulation of Genetic Testing" In C. Long (ed.) *Genetic Testing and the Use of Information*. Washington: AEI Press. 89–105.

Wittgenstein, Ludwig (2001) *Philosophische Untersuchungen*. 3d. ed. Oxford: Blackwell's.

Zindorf, Natalie E. (2001) "Discrimination in the 21st Century: Protecting the Privacy of Genetic Information in Employment and Insurance" 36 *Tulsa Law Journal* 703–726

8

The Culture of Science in Industry and Academia: How Biotechnologists View Science and the Public Good[1]

Steven P. Vallas, Daniel Kleinman, Abby Kinchy,
and Raul Necochea

Introduction

In recent years, dramatic changes have taken place in the linkages that exist among scientific research, private corporations, and state economic policy throughout much of the advanced capitalist world (Slaughter and Leslie 1997). These changes seem particularly apparent in the USA, where the post-war "social contract" between science and society has largely come undone (see Brooks 1993; Byerly and Pielke 1995). That social contract guaranteed academic scientists support for "basic" research, largely conducted in university settings; in return, scientists were expected to contribute, in the long run, to the social and economic well-being of the society. Now, with the end of the Cold War and the rise of the "knowledge economy" (Brint 2001), the outlines of a new agreement have begun to emerge, with policymakers viewing universities in a quite different light. Increasingly, they have approached scientific research in terms of its potential contribution to the competitiveness of the US economy. Implied in this shift is a significant redrawing of the boundaries between science and capitalism, and between the university and for-profit establishments (Owen-Smith 2003). Although these developments raise vital questions about the organizational imperatives that are likely to shape the pursuit of knowledge within the decades to come, they remain as-yet poorly understood.

Elsewhere, in the effort to understand this institutional reconfiguration, we have argued that a process of "asymmetrical convergence" is underway in which the boundaries between previously distinct organizational fields are beginning to collapse (see Kleinman and Vallas 2001). Basing our analysis on a wide array of secondary sources, we held that, as universities and corporations interact with increasing frequency, their internal structures and practices grow increasingly isomorphic. Organizational logics previously unique to industry have increasingly been imported into academia, *and vice versa*. Thus, in their effort to attract scientific talent and to establish their reputations, biotechnology firms have found it useful to adopt academic conventions that have not traditionally been found within industry (e.g., support for journal publication, intellectual exchanges, and provision for basic or "curiosity-driven" research). At the same time, academic institutions increasingly foster entrepreneurial management practices (e.g. stressing external funding as a criterion of faculty evaluation, or using quantitative measures of faculty productivity), suitably redefined to make them more palatable to the professoriate. These reconfigurations, we contend, have generated new structures of knowledge production that defy inherited normative traditions and give rise to anomalies, contradictions, and ironies that have yet to be understood (Leicht and Fennell 1998).

Our earlier work suggests that universities, once viewed as sites that cultivated a spirit of collegiality among relatively autonomous scientists, increasingly compel scientists to respond to the demands of the commercial world, whether by conducting research with market potential or by engaging in the race for the accumulation of revenues. At the same time, many high tech firms have brought a more cooperative or collegial orientation to bear upon their commercial goals, providing scientists with a measure of autonomy from managerial pressures that many academics now seldom enjoy. Ironically enough, the resources needed to support academic norms –the most sophisticated equipment, the most generous budgets, the greatest freedom from revenue generation — are now likely to be found within the capitalist firm. We believe that these changes are likely to have multiple implications. For example, they seem likely to introduce salient tensions and contradictions into the organizational logics that inform scientific research in both academica and in industry, engendering expanding levels of uncertainty and ongoing debate. They are also sure to recast the professional socialization of young scientists, prompting many to rethink traditional prestige hierarchies and career preferences they have inherited from the past (Leicht and Fennell 1998).

Seeking to disentangle these complex and contradictory developments, we set out to explore the rise of asymmetrical convergence more fully. Drawing on semi-structured interviews with an array of workers employed in both academic and industrial biotechnology laboratories, we have addressed a number of questions concerning the newly evolving knowledge regime (Jin 2001).

How does the diffusion of organizational logics alter the cultural milieux in which US scientists are employed? In what ways and through what processes do norms and practices come to circulate across institutional domains? And, most important for our purposes here, how might the meanings and representations of science currently held by scientists themselves affect the institutional changes currently underway?

Sociologists of science have hardly ignored the latter question (cf. Dubinskas 1988; Rabinow 1996; Hackett 1990, 2001; Gieryn 1983, 1999; Hilgartner 2000). Yet not since the work of Marcson (1960) and Kornhauser (1962) have researchers compared the values and perceptions that obtain among bench scientists employed in both academic and industrial contexts. Seeking to fill this gap, we explore the meanings that scientists attach to their everyday work and the symbolic representations they construct. Put differently, we ask how academic and industrial scientists themselves view the shifting boundary between "curiosity-driven" and applied or commercial research. In so doing, our aim is not so much to test hypotheses or to develop causal models. Rather, we view our work as an exercise in theory construction, using qualitative methods to develop a fuller understanding of institutional processes whose contours are only now beginning to become clear.

Toward this end, we have conducted semi-structured interviews with a broadly representative sample of biologists in molecular biological-related fields (N=88) employed in two different geographic regions within the USA: the Route 128 area adjoining Boston and the San Francisco Bay Area in California. Half of our interviews were conducted with academic scientists, administrators, and support personnel, while the other half were undertaken with a parallel group of respondents employed at twelve for-profit biotechnology firms in the same geographic locales. Interviews, ranging in length from forty-five minutes to nearly two hours, were taped and transcribed. Themes addressed in the interviews ranged widely, encompassing aspects of the scientists' work situations, their attitudes toward their research and their employers, perceptions of the organizational culture and social relations they encountered at work, and the ways in which the normative environment affected the distribution of opportunity among particular subgroups of scientists.

To gain a deeper understanding of the normative environment in which our respondents were employed, we interviewed multiple respondents at each research site, focusing on respondents who held varying positions within each organization's hierarchy. Thus within academia, we interviewed not only professors of varying ranks, but also postdoctoral fellows, graduate students, and technicians at their laboratories. We also interviewed administrators, to understand their orientation toward the academic units they oversee. Within the biotech firms, our interviewing focused on respondents who held jobs ranging from technician and research associate up through lab leaders (Ph.D. scientists) and research directors. We also interviewed executives in finance and human resources. The resulting data enable us to explore the textured and fine-grained accounts provided by academic and industrial research personnel in two important centers of biotechnology research.

Although there is variation within and across the two sectors, several themes stand out brightly. First, in what we believe represents an historical shift, the academic scientists we interviewed only occasionally alluded to the public goods their work might provide. Rather than stressing the social benefits that ultimately accrue from support for basic research, the academic scientists we interviewed tended to employ a rhetoric of intellectual fascination and discovery, in which the value of their research ultimately rested on its personal interest and cognitive appeal. Indeed, when academic scientists *did* allude to the public benefits of their work, they often did so in the most highly tendentious or strategic of ways. To a significant extent, our interviews provide an image of university scientists as a set of isolated, competitive, and self-interested actors who seem largely unconcerned with social needs external to their own fields.

Second, and ironically perhaps, it is the scientists *in private industry* who stress the moral or social benefits that flow from their research. Especially in the smaller biotech firms, scientists seem much more clearly driven by the need to address urgent social needs. This outlook, which seems imbued with clear moral or pragmatic themes, rejects the empty, status-oriented abstractions in which academic science is often caught. It derives particular moral force by construing university scientists as an aloof, quasi-aristocratic group that is largely unconcerned with the public good. Using such rhetoric, scientists in industry are able to imbue themselves with an aura of universality that (at least on the face of it) academic science typically lacks. Clearly, this pattern marks a dramatic and ironic shift from the social contract for science that emerged from World War II. Then, relatively autonomous disinterested academic scientists were able to appear as the protectors of the public good, while corporate researchers were portrayed as driven by narrower and more self-interested motives (Kleinman 1995).

In assessing this evidence, we conclude that the representations provided by many of our industrial scientist interviewees present an implicit action-critique of university science that ought to prompt academics to re-examine the inherited justifications on which scientific detachment stands. Especially given the increasing interpenetration of the academy and industry, the traditional defense of scientific autonomy — the search for knowledge as an end in itself — is easily portrayed as merely another exercise in the accumulation of capital (in this case, its academic variant). In other words, science stands revealed as an *illusio*, or game, whose self-interested practices attract less and less support (Bourdieu 1977, 1984). In making this argument, we do not mean to add to anti-intellectual attacks on the place of science in modern life. Nor do we mean to endorse the logic governing the capitalist economy. Rather, we suggest that *if scientists are to have a hand in shaping the institutional shifts currently under way, traditional defenses of scientific autonomy will need to evolve in ways that place a stronger emphasis on the public benefits that accrue from scientific research.* In our conclusion we offer some suggestions toward this end.

The chapter is organized into three sections. We begin by describing the social contract for science that emerged from World War II, exploring how science was represented in the wake of that contract. In this section, we also discuss the transformation of that contract and the process of asymmetrical convergence that we detect. Second, we present our findings with regard to the representations of scientific research we unearthed among life scientists and support personnel in both academic and industrial domains. The paper concludes by weighing the efficacy of the rhetorics we have observed and then offering some critical commentary and suggestions on the limits of traditional academic defenses of scientific autonomy.

A Social Contract for Science

World War II marked a turning point for the funding of science in the United States. During the War, the federal government became a massive patron of university-based science, and as the end of the War came into sight, members of Congress and scientists centrally involved in the war effort increasingly debated how science should be funded in peacetime. Populists favored the creation of a government agency that would link scientific research directly to economic development. Elite scientists, and their business supporters, led by Vannevar Bush, favored creation of an agency that would fund basic research undertaken in US universities. Basic science, as described in Bush's report, *Science—The Endless Frontier,* was research "performed without thought of practical ends." It was investigation that would "result in general knowledge and an understanding of nature and its laws" (Bush 1945: 18). Why should taxpayers support such research? Because, according to Bush and his colleagues, this kind of study by academic scientists would ultimately promote the national welfare by leading to improved national security and economic growth. Basic investigations, according to the Bush report, would create "the fund from which the practical applications of knowledge must be drawn" (1945: 19).

The Bush doctrine ultimately became institutionalized in the US National Science Foundation and became the basis of what has since come to be known as the social contract for science. For nearly five decades, it was used by scientists and administrators to justify federal funding of university science. That this justification was not, however, transparently valid is evidenced by its reassertion regularly across these decades (cf. Kleinman and Solovey 1995). From government reports to newspaper articles, supporters of the postwar social contract argued that the government should support basic science in universities because this would ultimately provide US citizens with better health, a higher standard of living and a more secure society.

The changing economic environment of the 1980s in the US put the social contract for science under threat. As the US faced a so-called crisis of competitiveness, and as federal fiscal difficulties arose, leaders in business and politics called for government funding of science that had clear economic relevance (Kleinman 1995: 178–188). A rhetoric that pointed to a link between basic research and economic health was no longer good enough. Legislators promoted mechanisms that would facilitate closer interaction and cooperation between industry and academia. Congress, for example, passed legislation that gave universities control over intellectual property created with the benefit of federal funding (the Bayh-Dole Act of 1980) and provided support for research centers that promoted university-industry collaboration (Slaughter and Leslie 1997).

It is in this context that many expected universities to take on a central and unambiguous role in promoting economic development. Indeed, to some extent this has happened — a development that some critics have bemoaned (cf. Shenk 1999). But this transformation of the economic landscape has not led to a straightforward collapse of the wall between industry and academia. Instead, it seems to be reconfiguring that distinction in complex and often ironic ways. As we argue in another context (Kleinman and Vallas 2001), academic institutions have come to adopt codes and practices previously associated with the corporate domain (such as an *entrepreneurial* orientation to academic research and an increasingly proprietary view of knowledge). At the same time, knowledge intensive corporations are adopting *collegial* forms of corporate control traditionally associated with universities (e.g., embracing the norm of journal publication and hosting academic-style seminars and talks).

But if we were to assume a straightforward transfer of codes across domains where the university took on industrial norms and industry adapted academic codes, we might very well expect many in industry to argue for the centrality of basic research and indeed to support such work, while academic scientists advocated the virtues of economically relevant research. Such notions notwithstanding, our data present a much more complicated portrait of an environment in flux, where old and new logics commingle and where contradictions and ironies abound.

We begin our discussion by presenting our findings with respect to our academic respondents, and then discuss patterns found among their counterparts in private industry. Although we do address the organizational structures and work situations of these scientists, our primary interest here lies with the meanings and rhetorical practices found among each group. As we shall see, there are important differences across the two sectors that represent significant variations from the pattern that has existed within the recent past.

Representations of Science in Industry and Academia

Interest without Introspection: The Meaning of Academic Research

There can be little doubt that the academic institutions we studied are indeed encountering growing pressures to conduct practical research with clear commercial significance. One indication of this trend appeared when several academic respondents related noteworthy incidents in which commercial and academic norms seemed to collide. These incidents—in which partnering efforts foundered over non-disclosure agreements and provisions governing intellectual property — became symbolic events for several respondents, signaling to them that traditional academic norms were increasingly besieged. A further indication emerged in the rhetoric produced by administrators, which clearly indicated the path down which their institutions needed to move. Said one Dean:

> We are not given the privilege any longer of doing research just because we're curious about an answer . . . Because nowadays I think it's absolutely critical that we justify the use of taxpayer money based upon the fact that it has some potential to have impact on people. I don't know whether or not the committees that are evaluating people for promotion and tenure are now beginning to understand that they must take into consideration numbers of patents, numbers of companies, the commercialization and the impact of that on the economy of the area. But I'm assuming that if we're going to encourage that, which I know we are, that that will start to become part of the equation, if it isn't already.

Referring to institutional changes at his university, another dean used an industrial metaphor to clarify his institution's role in the new economy:

> Right now as a university we're going through a fairly [major] search and re-evaluation of who we are and what we do, and how well we're doing it in view of budget cuts, how we should react, and what I've tried to convince my colleagues is that *it would be reasonable to think of a university as a manufacturer of capital goods. We manufacture minds*, ideas, patents in some cases, and these are the capital goods that industries are built around, and I think if you view yourself as a manufacturer of capital goods, then your success is actually having your capital goods placed in a production environment somewhere, so we build students, they go off, they get jobs, they do great stuff. That's really what we're for. If we get money back from industry, then that would be really a very nice thing but for it to

be more of a one-way street, um that might seem fair, is probably fair. That's why we're here [emphasis added].

A further indication of the rise of entrepreneurial norms and practices was evident in the observations of several graduate students, whose career choices were shaped by the commercial pressures they watched their advisors face. Said one graduate student:

> I don't see myself running my own lab, I mean not in a place like this at least, a huge university. [Here, success depends on] how much data you turn out, how much your publications [are worth] . . . , how much money you get. So that's not something I want to do.

This student was inclined to seek a position in a liberal arts college, thus escaping the entrepreneurial pressures his advisor had to shoulder. A second graduate student went even further, making a choice that we find especially revealing:

> I don't think I could ever be a PI because . . . I don't think I could lead a lab. I would not want the responsibility of being in control of directing an entire research effort, and being in control of other people's lives in terms of funding. I mean . . . if you're a PI and you can't get funding then you can't pay your graduate students and you can't pay people that are relying on you. I think maybe in industry I could hopefully get into a position where I wouldn't have to be in such authority.

Note the irony here: this second student was inclined to pursue a career *in industry*, precisely to *avoid* the entrepreneurial or managerial logic that seemed to engulf her own professors. Instances like these (which we term "ironic inversions") were indicative of the cross-cutting normative pressures to which biotechnologists were repeatedly exposed.

If academic institutions are indeed encountering growing entrepreneurial pressures, the question is how faculty have responded to these trends, and how they construe the meaning and value of their research. Although the limited size of our sample renders it difficult to estimate the prevalence of each variety of response, our research did unearth several clear patterns of response among academic scientists. Our findings here, which closely track those of Owen-Smith and Powell (2001), give rise to the following observations.

One outlook arose among academic scientists who enthusiastically embraced the pursuit of alliances and partnerships between industry and academia. This view was epitomized by a senior faculty member at an elite institution in the Boston area who had personally sought to further such ties and had made substantial headway in this respect.

> My experience with companies has been generally very positive, that it's been mutually beneficial. It's helped the lab [and] helped develop things, and in fact has

led to important drugs that have been very beneficial to society . . . Some things that we've done have led to really important commercial [products] . . . .[E]arly in my lab, we developed a lot of recombinant DNA technology that formed the basis of many biotech companies, and later we worked on signaling pathways that are involved in chain regulation and that led to drugs that are now in the clinic for cancer. So we didn't start out by trying to find a drug that we could treat cancer with but the discoveries that we made opened the opportunity to do that.

This view was clearly a minority view among our respondents.

A second outlook, only somewhat more commonly held, was found among faculty who seemed to accommodate the commercial trend, acknowledging in measured terms a place for industry within certain bounds, providing that an appropriate 'balance' could be found. Said one assistant professor in the Boston area:

I think that in moderation, *all* of it [both basic and commercially relevant research] should be done. I mean it's kind of silly to say that the only kind of science that [should] happen is if you really do it basically. I mean that's very silly. At the same time, the other extreme of doing research only for, completely for applied, is also I think too restrictive, so I think . . . you should really be able to have a moderation where you allow partnership but perhaps, you know, keep track of it so that their financial interests and so on don't conflict.

A doctoral student from California made a related point: "I think there's definitely room for both [basic and applied research]. I don't think they're diametrically opposed to each other, and people waste a lot of energy saying they are."

A third position that was most commonly and insistently drawn by our respondents, involves what might be called an *anti-utilitarian* outlook. This perspective seeks to reaffirm the traditional conception of detached university research. This outlook warrants particular attention, not only because of its predominance among our respondents, but also because it rests on an argument that has figured prominently in ongoing academic and administrative debates.

The coordinates of this anti-utilitarian outlook were apparent in a number of ways. First, when describing how they decided to study a particular problem or why they do the work they do, its adherents seemed to feel little or no obligation to provide any social or moral justification for their work. Topics were chosen, according to several respondents, simply because they held a measure of intellectual fascination for the scientist involved –an inclination that often implied an assertion of the autonomous and insulated nature of the university. What emerged among many of these faculty members was a sense of entitlement, indicative of their assumption that admission to the academic domain relieves the scientist of any moral obligation to connect his or her research to any manifest social need.

This point was evident when academic scientists alluded merely to the intellectual pleasures and personal rewards of scientific questions which they found it "fascinating" to pursue. A doctoral candidate at a Bay Area university told us that she pays no attention to applied research because "I happen to not be interested in [or see] anything worthwhile where marketing is concerned. So I happen to look down on that as something that I never want to do because of my lack of interest." Likewise, a professor at another west coast university said simply that "what I work on is what is of interest to me." A postdoctoral fellow at a Massachusetts university argued that it is important in academia for scientists like himself to be able to "do whatever you want." And a scientist at a prominent Boston university articulated this view most boldly:

> With regard to whether you, anyone has some obligation to make their research useful, I think that's silly. If people want to make money, they can make money and, and, if they want to, if they want to feel like they're curing diseases or helping mankind, they can cure diseases and help mankind. That's a different thing from saying that somebody who is interested in basic questions has some obligation to make that information useful. Your obligation as a basic scientist is to make your information available. It's to publish what you do, not to just amuse yourself and then not publish anything. You have an obligation to make the results of your research available to the broader scientific community. Whether other people use it or not is their business.

Adherents of this anti-utilitarian outlook often made derisive references to the profit-oriented ethos of industrial science, depicting the latter as lacking merit on both technical and intellectual grounds. One respondent referred to the biotech firms she knew as mere "data mills" that commonly conducted shoddy and mindless research:

> It seems to me that in those companies there's the rare person who is really interested in . . . understanding how something works and developing [it] in what we would call the right way. Something that would . . . be able to withstand peer review in a competitive grant panel for instance, and also the research would be able to result in publications . . . in high level peer review journals . . . . Most of the people in the companies are so goal-oriented. . . . What they want to know is how many samples can you process, how fast can you do it, and how cheaply can you do it for us? So they seem to be, at least the ones I've talked to seem to be much more sort of data mills, and . . . I haven't found it particularly . . . intellectually stimulating.

Scientists who hold these views often legitimated their research on purely intellectual grounds. For them, the virtue of curiosity-driven research seemed so firmly institutionalized, so self-evident, that they often seemed to resist any obligation to justify their research or connect it to wider social needs. Indeed, when academic scientists *did* justify their research on these grounds, such efforts were often merely strategic or *rhetorical* in their nature –that is, mere "framing" exercises performed on instrumental grounds. Thus, when we asked a Massachusetts professor whether his research was driven more by basic or by applied pursuits, he answered in the following way:

> I would say it's very "basic," about as basic as you can get. [Laughs] Although it's funded by the NIH and *officially* . . . the grant proposals and everything always have at the beginning part [comments], basically where you make, establish the medical relevance . . . But . . . *realistically,* I mean, we work on studying cell biology in yeast . . . which is obviously quite distant from humans . . . .[I]n order to get NIH funding uh one cannot just simply say 'I am studying this problem because it fascinates me' [laughs] . . . So the, the applicability and so forth already gets built in.

Such rhetorical gestures occasionally occurred in contexts involving interaction with members of the public. Thus, one respondent admitted that she was often compelled to speak of diseases when explaining her research to lay audiences, even though her research is, in truth, far removed from applied issues:

> I often have to resort to talking about human diseases like Alzheimer's to try and justify what I'm doing to someone that I'm sitting next to on an airplane, which indicates to me that what we're doing is pretty basic. I don't know if I see many direct practical applications, especially if you're working in a plant model organism.

Here, too, an applied connection is made largely to justify research conducted for decidedly non-applied ends.

The foregoing observations do not exhaust the ways in which our academic respondents portrayed the meaning and the value of their work. One additional and highly exceptional outlook was found among three of our respondents, who did view the significance of their research in terms of its ability to engage broader social needs. This outlook –essentially, a problematic of engagement to be discussed more fully below—was held by respondents whose careers seemed exceptional in important respects. For example, one of the strongest defenders of engaged or applied science was born and educated in the developing world, and was attracted to a department that rewarded "social mission" practices. The following exchange is revealing:

> *Interviewer (AK)*: What made you decide to pursue a career in the university as opposed to industry?
>
> *Scientist in a Boston area university*: Um passion for teaching, um one. Second I felt having my roots in India if I, even though income-wise it's not you know . . . it's a struggle . . . I felt [the] university's the only place where my teaching and research all can be connected. But more importantly, *how that can be helpful to society*, particularly to developing countries. So I felt this is where I have the freedom to do what I like . . . And I don't think anywhere else I would get this opportunity.

A second adherent to this engaged problematic also stressed the value of linking scientific research to particular social needs. As this graduate student explains, she sees herself as quite distinct from the other academics in science she knows:

> Most of my colleagues aren't very interested or aware of how what we do impacts society very much. It's like 'As long as [regulatory bodies] don't make decisions that get in the way of our research, I don't really care' . . . Like, it's just not something that my colleagues think about. And I think that's unfortunate, because we're the ones that actually know the information [laughs].

This latter respondent believed so strongly in the need to address the social impacts of science that she felt compelled to *leave* science, instead pursuing a career in science policy. These cases were clear exceptions to the norm that prevailed among the respondents in our study, for whom social issues or the ethical concerns of regulatory bodies held little explicit significance at all.

These data allow us to draw a number of preliminary observations. Although academic scientists respond in varying ways to the rise of entrepreneurial pressures, allusions to any eventual linkage between basic and applied science – the social benefits promised by the postwar social contract — were conspicuous by their near absence. When a rhetoric of linkage is invoked, such actions are often taken to secure the resources needed to pursue research defined along entirely different lines. Perhaps because the postwar contract has been so deeply institutionalized, the predominant sentiment was one that took for granted, as the scientist's birthright, the license to pursue research that is personally fascinating or intriguing. As we show further below, these symbolic constructs are not only sharply distinct from, but also less cogent or efficacious, than the rhetoric found among scientists employed in biotechnology firms.

Markets and Morality: The Value of Science in Industry

It can hardly be surprising that industry-based respondents often stressed economic or commercial imperatives as an important feature of the scientific research their firms conduct. Said one scientist at a small start-up firm, "We have to survive. If you spend your time and money on academic science we will be going belly-up soon. Right?" Respondents who stressed such commercial concerns often referred to the need to turn a profit, to supply markets, and to "get product out the door" –language that would be familiar to applied researchers or designers working for any large corporation. For these respondents, however, the scientific activities in which they were engaged often held meanings far beyond the logic of profit generation. Indeed, even when they spoke of such economic concerns, these respondents emphasized the social and moral contributions their work provides, articulating a connection between science and the surrounding society much more fully than our academic respondents managed to do.

In interviews probing scientists' work attitudes and career choices, what emerged most prominently was an orientation toward science that can best be described as a *moral-pragmatic* outlook, in which scientists are attracted to their research precisely because of its ability to address the public's medical needs. Respondents here embrace the idea of *using* science as a practical and benevolent force with which to provide urgently needed therapeutics (vaccines, drugs, and biogenetic treatments). Indeed, many respondents found this aspect of their jobs enormously compelling. One respondent, the director of a Boston-area biotechnology company explained her career path by remarking quite simply: "I wanted to see my research applied to clinical studies, to you know, to make medicine for people." Another respondent from a Boston-area firm said that what he liked about his job is the ability to watch one's "product move its way through, to grow a company that has the ability to drive multiple products, to make clinical trials, and then hopefully some day to [get to] the market place so that you can treat patients that have some pretty tough diseases."

Often, this moral-pragmatic orientation was framed in ways that made critical allusions to academic conventions. In such cases, purely academic scientists were portrayed as either out of touch with practical social needs or else consumed by a self-absorbed concern for the accumulation of prestige. Thus, one respondent who was strongly attached to the morally benevolent nature of her work made the following comments about university-based science:

> . . . if you go into an academic lab that has no ties to industry at all, no influence, [you] go into a lab that does something like [mentions species of flatworms] [that's] a fantastic organism for, you know, natural genetics and everything. But the common man is just not going to understand why are we spending umpteen million dollars on breeding worms [laughs] . . . [Y]ou know, a lot of academics don't work for a lot of money, and they believe that the research that they do is purely for the betterment of mankind yada yada yada. [But really] um a lot of their reward is how many times they get their name published in a paper and I'm going to tell you, the egos are immense.

She was hardly alone in making this attribution. A senior scientist at a different Bay Area firm compared her own academic and industrial experiences in the following way:

> . . . I felt very isolated at . . . [names a university-affiliated institute]. I was the head of my own group, which was great, but you're kind of an island, and here there are *real* problems and it's not just a matter of you know getting a paper out or getting a grant. You know, *real* issues that have to be addressed and so it's a lot more concrete in terms of what the goals are . . . Because you're working with

> people who care about it and um, you know, you see where it makes a differ-
> ence . . . .

The idea here is that research in industrial settings generates social benefits
("it makes a difference") in ways that are typically lacking in university
research. Indeed, despite its lofty status, the latter often amounts to little more
than the accumulation of career accolades that hold a tenuous connection to
the "real problems" that society actually confronts.

Commentary on the shortcomings of the academic milieu took other forms
as well. One scientist at a large biotech firm in the Bay area voiced sharp
frustration with the merely rhetorical allusion to medical needs that academic
scientists so often make:

> in academia you sort of do this hand waving and 'this could pertain to cancer'
> when you write your grants, and here I think that you're held accountable to be
> closer to the clinic . . . I mean, I think it's a real luxury to come up with a hypoth-
> esis and be able to walk in the lab and test it, and science is just a really exciting
> area to be in. It always has been and even now, you know, it's getting more
> attention from the community and it's more clear now how science really impacts
> on society and it affects diseases [especially] as you begin to see more and more
> drugs come on to the market. And for me, coming to a company made possible
> doing, doing something to really help patients . . . .

Some of our industrial respondents applied these sorts of distinctions to
employees within their own firms. One scientist at a start-up firm in the
Boston area distinguished between those of her co-workers who are "only
fighting for themselves," whom she saw as quite different from the others
who were "real team players." Ironically, as she explains, the more competitive, self-seeking scientists were those with an academic orientation:

> I think some of us are more academia oriented, which means that they are only
> trying to save their asses because they're only fighting for themselves, versus the
> real team players that really share any and every type of information. And there are
> both sides in the company.

In this case, barriers to the sharing of information arose from an "academic"
concern with self-advancement. Ironically, the *corporate* outlook was viewed
as far more collectivist or collaborative in its orientation.

At times, this moral-pragmatic orientation emerged as a distinct orientation in its own right. Yet more often, it was alloyed with other symbolic
elements, creating powerful ideological ensembles that took varying forms
(Lamont 1992; Vallas 2001). One such form arose among scientists whose
comments in effect brought together themes that were simultaneously moral
and intellectual in their nature. Respondents here emphasized the *intellectual*
value of the knowledge that biotechnology firms provide, which they felt was
at least as cogent and meritorious as anything that academics can provide:

You know, we want to be successful scientists and we're, in many ways I would say, academics at heart and we know that you know when you're excited about what you do, you want to tell people about it and you want to get their ideas and so you have to be open and if you're not talking to people on the outside, you get you know kind of stuck in one way of thinking. It's just, I mean it's just part of the whole scientific process . . . If you're not publishing, if you're not going to conferences, then of course you're, you're not a real scientist.

This man, a senior scientist at a large Bay Area firm, spoke with resentment about what might be termed "the traditional view of industrial science," which, as one respondent put it, sees the latter in terms of "Turn the crank, let's, you know, make a molecule but not care about what we're understanding." He is at pains to point out that he *is* a "real scientist" whose work does indeed generate valuable knowledge.

This combination of moral and intellectual elements was apparent in remarks made by several other respondents, who likewise noted that what they enjoyed most about their jobs in industrial settings was their ability to do "real science" on matters that have important social and economic consequences. Said the director of science at a prominent biotech firm in the Bay Area, combining moral and intellectual elements in one brief statement:

I think the fact that you're working on a therapeutic is extremely exciting and I like to think that you can affect so many lives that way is, is um, is kind of humbling. [Also,] the exciting thing about [this company] is really *the science*. I have looked around you know at other companies and there's just you know no other company that has the amount of creative work on so many different fronts so that's what's fun about this place.

In precisely the same vein, the chief scientific officer at a Boston biotech firm alluded to the "strong passion for basic science" he and his fellow scientists brought to bear on their search for new applications of gene therapy.

This confluence of moral and intellectual themes was not the only ideological ensemble that emerged in our interviews with workers in the biotechnology industry. A second, parallel combination occurred where moral themes were fused with *market* considerations, generating an outlook that views the industry's profit orientation as providing an incentive for firms to address the public's most pressing medical needs. This fusion of morality and market considerations was especially apparent among senior personnel in industry – particularly those who had risen to executive positions. Thus, one CEO at a small biotech firm in Boston explained his choice of a career in industry as opposed to academia in the following terms:

I had this view that capitalism in general is one of the most powerful social forces, not just economic, but social forces in our society. And so, you know, being able to work within that type of infrastructure would allow me to do more in terms of influencing people and actually making for a better society than working in academia.

Here, the market is viewed as a mechanism for morally benevolent work. A similar yet in some ways distinct fusion of markets and morally benevolent work is apparent in the following remarks made by a vice president at a large firm in the Bay Area:

> [S]ometimes what drives you is the potential of the market, so the dollar does drive you to some extent . . . If you know that you can come up with a treatment for Parkinson's Disease and you know that big bucks are at the end . . . [you do it]. We're choosing to [pursue research in cell therapy] because we think the research is so, um, compelling that it's going to be worth it in the long run for the people, you know. But, you know, the path that we're going, once we've made that decision, is based on the diseases that have the biggest market for us. We're in the business to succeed. So [the company is] around to get the products out there to, to come up with the treatments for the patients.

In this case, the extent of the market and the profits to be made are transformed, in a peculiar sort of alchemy, into a measure of the benefits which the firm is able to provide. Such an approach is, of course, convenient for the firms involved, yet it is a potentially potent discursive strategy at one and the same time.

Not all of our respondents shared in this tendency to identify market mechanisms with moral benevolence. Many scientists seem to accept, a bit begrudgingly, the profit-orientation of their employers as an inevitable feature of modern life. Others were more critical, seeing the combination of market considerations with scientific research as giving rise to certain conflicts, whether with the scientific or intellectual merit of their work, or with its ability to address morally desirable ends. For example, the chief scientific officer of one Boston area firm expressed frustration in his dealing with venture capitalists, whom he saw as often impeding the very goals that he and his colleagues were working to accomplish:

> Sometimes when you deal with a bunch of capitalists . . . they have very little knowledge of science, very little understanding, extremely thin, like a film of knowledge. Sometimes it's a problem, especially when they believe they know more than they do. They just don't understand. [So,] sometimes you may not work on a specific disease even though you know that you have the technology, you know that you have the expertise, you know that there's a real possibility to cure patients. But you don't, because the market size is too small or there's not the interest of a business person of some kind, and it's sometimes frustrating.

Here, the concern for ensuring a high rate of return prevented medically valuable and scientifically feasible work from going forward (especially where the market was deemed too small to warrant an investment of the firm's capital). Other respondents were critical of market criteria, as in the case of a scientist in a large Bay Area firm, who was critical of his previous employers, who cared little about the scientific merit of their research and were often concerned with "just looking good on the stock market." These dissenting views, in which markets constrained the intellectual or moral benefits that science might provide, were decidedly in the minority.

The foregoing discussion of the rhetoric we found among scientists in industry prompts three important conclusions. First, and in sharp contrast to the academic scientists we interviewed, those working within the industrial domain spontaneously articulate a rich and cogent set of meanings that emphasize the social contributions their research provides to the wider public. Indeed, many of these scientists reportedly embarked on private sector or industrial careers precisely in order to conduct practical or morally benevolent research. Second, our industrial respondents seemed not only aware of but also quite capable of replying to the derisive view of 'applied' research that has traditionally obtained. Invoking a complex amalgam of rhetorical elements that drew on moral, intellectual and market-based themes, these respondents constructed compelling ideological ensembles that speak to the manifest needs of the wider society. Third, in developing the meanings they attached to their own work, many of these scientists drew on their own experiences in academia to identify what they see as institutional vulnerabilities in the latter realm: most notably, its vain and often self-absorbed character, its superficial commitment to social needs, and its individualistic or egotistical character. Such comparisons only draw further attention to the socially disconnected nature of academic research: a depiction to which academic scientists often provide only the weakest of retorts.

Conclusions: On Science, Markets and the Public Good

The analysis developed above provides the basis for a number of important observations concerning the ways in which academic and industrial scientists represent the meaning and the value of their work. As we have shown, the symbolic constructs that many academic scientists offer seem relatively weak in several senses. First, many scientists do feel little or no obligation to engage issues beyond their own intellectual concerns. In an example of what might be termed "ethical atrophy," the scientists in our study have come to take for granted their license to conduct research that is bereft of any wider societal benefit. Indeed, as shown, when moral claims *are* made, these are often little more than strategic gestures made to secure funding for research that only tangentially broaches real social needs. And although academic scientists often mobilize a derisive representation of industrial science, portraying the latter as subservient to commercial gain and thus lacking in intellectual merit, their efforts in this respect seem to ring hollow. As emerged at several points in our interviews, academic scientists are *themselves* vulnerable to the charge of seeking merely to expand their own "capital," engaging in a game of status accumulation that bears more than a family resemblance to the profit-seeking activities they themselves deride (Bourdieu 1984).

Academics' representations of science seem especially precarious drawn when compared to the symbolic constructs that their industrial counterparts articulate. As we have seen, our industrial respondents differ from the academics in several respects. To begin with, many report having been attracted to industrial positions precisely because the latter provide the opportunity to engage urgent medical and social needs. Eschewing what they see as superficial and vain abstractions, scientists in biotech firms prefer to pursue projects that have "real" societal implications. The precise ideological ensemble that we found varied in highly suggestive ways. Some scientists adopt a moral-pragmatic outlook, pure and simple. Others combine this problematic with either intellectual or market considerations, generating a more complex and often nuanced ideological ensemble. Whatever the precise form their rhetoric assumed, the industrial scientists we interviewed were usually able to mobilize a powerful set of symbolic constructs that seems likely to attract much more public support than academic orientations are likely to engage. *To the extent that such ideological accounts have an impact on the redrawing of institutional boundaries*—and we believe that impact is significant—*academic scientists seem ill-equipped to defend their position in an effective or compelling way.*

A key reason seems to be the conservative posture in which many of the academic scientists seem caught. Seeking mainly to shore up their traditional autonomy, the academics seem at times thrown onto the defensive, compelled to justify that which has been their entitlement for decades. Struggling to comprehend the changes swirling about their heads, yet only ever able to insist on their right to conduct science without any practical utility, the university scientists find themselves in a position that is analogous in certain respects to that held by 19th century aristocrats, whose culture of learned erudition was threatened by the rising tide of commercial interests and orientations. Armed only with the taken-for-granted cultural traditions of academia, these scientists seem poorly equipped to do battle, especially in a context that is marked by sharpening economic competition and growing fiscal pressures on public institutions, both in the USA and beyond.

Indeed, in responding to the commercialization of the university, scholars and scientists –including several of the respondents in our study— have often found it tempting to imbue their detached role with an aura of moral sanctity or purity (cf. Daniels 1967; Proctor 1991). This rhetorical strategy implicitly constructs what we hold to be an intellectually and politically indefensible opposition between the "sacred" (university science) on the one hand and the "profane" (commercial science) on the other. We have already suggested why we suspect this rhetorical strategy seems *politically* vulnerable. Our *intellec-*

tual rejection of this view rests on the wider critiques of positivism and scientific "innocence" that have been generated during the theoretical debates of the last quarter century, resting on Foucauldian critiques of power/knowledge (1979, 1980) and especially on Bourdieu's analysis of cultural capital (1977, 1984). This last assertion bears some explanation, given its connection to several points that emerged in our interviews. Rather than accepting science's traditional claims of purity and innocence, we take to heart the point made by several of our industrial respondents, for whom academic science constitutes a self-interested and self-absorbed game whose activities are largely oriented toward the accumulation of academic capital. Seen from this vantage point, the growing interaction between industry and the university portends not so much the danger of contamination of an "innocent" terrain as the erosion of deeply established myths about scientific purity.

Grounding our analysis historically and theoretically, we suggest that the post-WWII knowledge regime that developed in the United States largely relieved scientists of the need to justify their research on moral or societal grounds. While that regime provided a measure of stability and growth for both science and US capitalism, it has left a subtle legacy that is now taking its toll. Bereft of any vocabulary with which to engage issues that resonate within the public sphere, caught up in highly individualistic forms of status competition, and prone to rely on purely intellectualist measures of scientific value, academic scientists seem remarkably ill-equipped to influence the massive reconfiguration of institutional domains that is currently underway.

In developing these points, we do not mean add momentum to the surge of anti-intellectualism that has arisen in many quarters, nor to fuel anti-rationalist fears of scientific research. Rather, we suggest that in the face of the ongoing transformation of the knowledge economy and the university with it, academic scientists need to develop a distinct vision of the role of their work and its contribution to the public good. While many of the academic administrators we interviewed (and at least some of the faculty) seemed to have largely accepted the transformation of the university into a servant of industry, we suggest that academic scientists have grounds to argue for the distinctive social place of academic science in the emerging new economy. Toward this end we make five interrelated points.

First, we believe there is in fact an argument to be made for "knowledge for knowledge's sake," but this argument cannot be supported with mere assertions of entitlement. Instead, academic scientists need to argue for their contribution to the richness of human culture, much as artists do, and for their addition to our understanding of the universe and the place of human beings in it. Second, academic scientists need to make clear that, even if they are not always contributing to commodity production, they are adding to the knowledge commons. A knowledge commons argument (cf. Boyle 1996; Shulman

1999) avoids questionable claims of a linear path from basic to applied science (Stokes 1996) and making it requires more sophistication. However, this kind of position has plausibility and lacks self-indulgent overtones. Third, academic scientists can legitimately argue that they are contributing to the education of future citizens, not just future scientists. In collaboration with scholars in humanities and social sciences, scientists can develop programs that challenge scientific illiteracy in the broadest possible sense (cf. Wynne 1996). Fourth, in a context marked by increasing concern for licensing and revenues generated by intellectual property, especially among administrators, academic scientists might do well to mobilize an effort to dedicate significant portions of university licensing revenues to scholarships or community-oriented programs aimed at benefiting historically excluded or oppressed groups in the urban areas adjoining their own campuses. Doing so would serve the legitimation needs of many universities while also harnessing market mechanisms to social ends, thereby enabling scientists to re-engage questions of moral or social need. Finally, academic scientists are well-positioned to contribute to the development of science-based therapeutics which market structures cannot easily address. Examples (which occasionally arose in our own interviews) might include drugs for relatively rare or "orphaned" diseases or diseases prevalent in poor regions as well as research on organic agricultural methods that large biotech firms are loathe to pursue.

Contributing to the debate on the future of the university, academic scientists face an uphill struggle. The momentum behind the commercialization of the university is powerful, and the kinds of justifications of academic science that we outlined are not easily made into sound bites for politicians and the media. However, an argument for academic science based on individual interest and entitlement is not likely to endure in the current environment. Without the intervention of university scientists in new and more socially engaging ways that can challenge the claims of industry, the university is likely to become a subordinate arm of resource-rich corporations, or be reduced to increasing isolation and irrelevance.

Note

1. The first and second authors of this paper contributed equally to its conceptualization. The paper was originally presented at the conference on "Biotechnology, Commerce and Civil Society" at the Kulturwissenschaftliches Institut in Essen Germany on September 5, 2002. Data collection was supported by the Fund for the Advancement of the Discipline (American Sociological Association/ National Science Foundation), the Georgia Tech Foundation, and the Graduate School of the University of Wisconsin, Madison. We wish to thank the scientists and science managers who participated in the study, as well as Nico Stehr, Martin Schulte, Steve Fuller, Fred Buttel, Reiner Grundmann, Ann Kerr, Herbert Gottweis, and Karen Schaepe for their helpful comments and support along the way.

References

Bourdieu, Pierre (1977) *Outline of a Theory of Practice.* Cambridge: Cambridge University Press.
———— (1984) *Distinction: A Social Critique of the Judgement of Taste* Cambridge, MA: Harvard University Press.
Boyle, James (1996) *Shamans, Software, and Spleens: Law and the Construction of the Information Society.* Cambridge, MA: Harvard University Press.
Brint, Steven (2001) "Professionals and the 'Knowledge Economy': Rethinking the Theory of Postindustrial Society." *Current Sociology* 49, 4 (July): 101–132
Brooks, Harvey (1993) "Research universities and the social contract for science." In *Empowering Technology: Implementing a US Strategy.* Lewis M. Branscombe (ed.). Cambridge MA: MIT Press, 202–234
Bush, Vannevar (1945) *Science—The Endless Frontier.* Washington, DC: National Science Foundation.
Byerly Jr., Radford, Roger A. Pielke, Jr. (1995). "The Changing Ecology of United States Science." *Science* 269, 5230 (15 September):1531–3.
Daniels, G.H (1967) "The Pure-Science Ideal and Democratic Culture." *Science* 156: 1699–1705.
Dubinskas, Frank A. (1988) "Cultural Constructions: The Many Faces of Time". In *Making Time: Ethnographies of High-Technology Organizations.* Frank A. Dubinskas (ed.). Philadelphia: Temple University Press, 3–38.
Etzkowitz, Henry. and Andrew Webster (1998) "Entrepreneurial Science: The Second Academic Revolution," in *Capitalizing Knowledge: New Intersections of Industry and Academia.* H. Etzkowitz, Andrew Webster and P. Healey (eds). Albany, NY: SUNY Press, 21–46.
Foucault, Michel (1979) *Discipline and Punish: The Birth of the Prison.* New York: Vintage.
———— (1980) *Power/Knowledge: Selected Interviews and Other Writings,* 1972–1977. Colin Gordon ed. NY: Pantheon.
Gieryn, Thomas F. (1983) "Boundary-work and the Demarcation of Science from Non-Science: Strains and Interests in the Professional Ideologies of Scientists." *American Sociological Review* 48, 6: 781–95.
———— (1999) *Cultural Boundaries of Science: Credibility on the Line.* Chicago: University of Chicago Press.
Gross, Paul R. and Norman Levitt. (1994). *Higher Superstition: The Academic Left and its Quarrels with Science* (Baltimore, MD: Johns Hopkins University Press,).
Hackett, Edward J. (1990). "Science as a vocation in the 1990s: The Changing ORganizational Culture of Academic Science." *Journal of Higher Education* 61: 241–77.
———— (2001) "Organizational Perspectives on University-Industry Research Relations." In *Degrees of Compromise: Industrial Interests and Academic Values.* Jennifer Crossant and Sal Restivo (eds). Albany NY: SUNY Press, 1–22.
Hilgartner, Stephen (2000) *Science on Stage: Expert Advice as Public Drama.* Stanford: Stanford University Press.
Jin, Dengjian (2001) *The Dynamics of Knowledge Regimes: Technology, Culture and Competitiveness in the USA and Japan.* NY: Continuum.
Kleinman. Daniel Lee (1995) *Politics on the Endless Frontier: Postwar Research in the United States.* Durham NC: Duke University Press.
———— and M. Solvey (1995) "Hot Science/Cold War: The National Science Foundation After World War II." *Radical History Review* 63: 110–139.

—————— and Steven Vallas (2001) "Science, Capitalism, and the Rise of the 'Knowledge Worker': The Changing Structure of Knowledge Production in the United States." *Theory and Society* 30, 4 (August): 451–492.

Kornhauser, William (1962) *Scientists in Industry*. Berkeley: University of California Press.

Lamont, Michele (1992) *Money, Morals, and Manners: The Culture of the French and American Upper Middle Classes*. Chicago: University of Chicago Press.

Leicht, Kevin and Fennell, Mary (1998). "The Changing Context of Professional Work." *Annual Review of Sociology*, 215–232.

Marcson, Simon (1960) *The Scientist in American Industry*. N.Y.: Harper and Row.

Owen-Smith, Jason (2003) "From Separate Systems to a Hybrid Order: Accumulative Advantage across Public and Private Science at Research One Universities." *Research Policy* 1583: 1–24.

—————— and Walter W. Powell (2001) "Careers and Contradictions: Faculty Responses to the Transformation of Knowledge and its Uses in the Life Sciences." *Research in the Sociology of Work*, 10: 109–140.

Powell, Walter W. and Jason Owen-Smith (1998) "Universities and the Market for Intellectual Property in the Life Sciences." *Journal of Policy Analysis and Management* 41: 116–145

Proctor, Robert N. (1991) *Value Free Science? Purity and Power in Modern Knowledge* (Cambridge, MA: Harvard University Press).

Rabinow, Paul (1996) *Making PCR: A Story of Biotechnology*. Chicago: University of Chicago Press.

Shenk, D. (1999) "Money + Science = Ethics Problems on Campus." *The Nation*, March 22: 11–18.

Shulman, Seth (1999) *Owning the Future*. New York: Houghton Mifflin.

Slaughter, Sheila .and Lawrence Leslie (1997) *Academic Capitalism: Politics, Policies, and the Entrepreneurial University*. Baltimore, MD: Johns Hopkins University.

Stokes, Donald E. (1997) *Pasteur's Quadrant: Basic Science and Technological Innovation*. Washington, DC: The Brookings Institution Press.

Vallas, Steven Peter (2001) "Symbolic Boundaries and the New Division of Labor: Engineers, Workers and the Restructuring of Factory Life." *Research in Stratification and Social Mobility* 18: 3–37.

Wynne, Brian (1996) "Misunderstood misunderstandings: Social identities and public uptake of science." In *Misunderstanding Science? The Public Reconstruction of Science and Technology*. Alan Irwin and Brian Wynne (eds.). Cambridge: Cambridge University Press, 19–49.

9

Human Embryonic Stem Cells, Cloning, and the Transformation of Biopolitics

Herbert Gottweis

Understanding New Bio-political Strategies

On August 9, 2001 president George Bush Jr. gave his first nationally televised speech to the Nation from Crawford, Texas. He began with the following words:

> Good evening. I appreciate you giving me a few minutes of your time tonight so I can discuss with you a complex and difficult issue, an issue that is one of the most profound of our time. The issue of research involving stem cells derived from human embryos is increasingly the subject of a national debate and dinner table discussions. The issue is confronted every day in laboratories as scientists ponder the ethical ramifications of their work. It is agonized over by parents and many couples as they try to have children or to save children already born. The issue is debated within the church, with people of different faiths, even many of the same faith, coming to different conclusions. Many people are finding that the more they know about stem cell research, the less certain they are about the right ethical and moral conclusions. My administration must decide whether to allow federal funds, your tax dollars, to be used for scientific research on stem cells derived from human embryos. (CNN)

A few months earlier, in a much publicized speech held at the German Parliament, president Johannes Rau had addressed stem cell research. Rau pleaded that, in the light of German history, technical feasibility in medical research should never be an argument to relativize ethical concerns (Rau 2001).

There are not many "scientific breakthroughs" that raise so much interest and seem to pose such fundamental challenges to society to become central topics for presidential speeches and political debates in all of Europe, in the

239

United States and many other countries. Stem cell research, and related, cloning, are such topics.

The rise of stem cell research as a topic of public and political fantasy and interest began in November 1998. Two research teams, one headed by John Gearhart of Johns Hopkins University, the other lead by James Thomson at the University of Wisconsin, reported on a number of breakthroughs in the culturing of human embryonic stem cells. While Gearhart´s team had isolated embryonic germ cells from aborted fetuses (Gearhart 1998), Thomson and his collaborators obtained embryonic stem cells from embryos created by IVF and had grown them each for about five days until they had developed into a blastocyst (Thomson & al. 1998). Their research was widely interpreted as a crucial step in the development of new strategies to grow human tissues and even organs. (Cohen 1998) A few months later the new research about stem cells was named by "Science" among the top scientific advances of 1999 (Vogel 1999). It did not take long until the mass media hailed the work of Gearhart and Thomson as a "medical revolution" and the two scientists became media starts. This work in stem cell technology was reinforced by advances in animal cloning and somatic cell nuclear transfer technology that seemed to offer a way to bypass fertilization and, still to grow organs and tissues with the advantage that the ES cells from cloned human embryos would be matched to individual patients (Gurdon/Coleman 1999).

Much of the excitement about stem cells and cloning was caused by the fact that embryonic stem cells were seen as "pluripotent", which means they are capable of self-renewal and of differentiation into a wide variety of cell types. Hence, the ability to grow them in renewable tissue cultures could have broad applications in research and transplantations, in particular by offering new access to tissue and organs (NIH 2000). In other words, embryonic stem cell research potentially seemed to address what bio-medical discourse had defined as one of the central challenges in modern medicine: irreversible and terminal organ and tissue failure. The spectrum of such typically life threatening deficiencies reaches from scenarios affecting whole organs, such as heart or kidney diseases, to non-whole organ scenarios, such as diabetes and neurodegenerartive disorders, for example Parkinson's disease. In the past decades, modern transplantation medicine using allotransplantation—the grafting of organs from human donors—had been successful in replacing irreversibly damaged organs. But, so it is frequently pointed out, in many countries patients are still on long waiting lists for organ donations. (Bramstedt 2000). There were not enough organs available to meet the existing demand.

But in the late 1990s a number of experimental medical strategies seemed to offer an answer to what has been labeled by some representatives of the medical establishment as an "organ crisis". Among these strategies, the most important ones are tissue engineering; the creation of "bio-artificial" organs composed of live cells and artificial materials; xenotransplantation, the usage of non-human tissue and organs to treat organ and tissue failure; therapeutic cloning, the cloning of a person´s cells for its own medical use;—and human embryonic stem cell research, that focuses on the culturing of human embryonic stem cells with the hope they will lead to ways of growing tissue and organs.

However, these new experimental medical strategies did not only raise positive expectations with respect to the treatment of serious diseases and conditions. They also created a great deal of controversy and put pressure on policy making. While tissue engineering and "bio-artificial organs" have remained relatively uncontested, both, xenotransplantation and in particular cloning and embryonic stem cell research have given rise to heated debates in particular in Europe, in the United States and in Australia. What some interpreted as a "medical revolution", others saw as an attempt to engineer "superhumans", a revival of Nazi-eugenics in new clothes, or as a potential public health disaster. This controversy took on a number of interesting new features. It did not primarily materialize as a "clash" between different political groups, or between social movements and the state, but as a discussion, reflection, a process of public deliberation, involving presidents, prime ministers, and other policy makers, that raised their voice of cautioning, asking to wait and think carefully, inviting "the public" to take part in a conversation, and process of ethical reflection. Patient groups, activists, religious groups and many citizens actively partcipated in this dialogue, that took part in a number of different sites, such as local ethics committees, national bioethics commissions and parliaments.

In this paper I will argue that the current "public discussion" about stem cell research and cloning can help us to understand new strategies in contemporary biopolitics. Stem cell approaches and cloning are difficult to separate from one another, and related to other new medical technologies such as xenotransplantation, gene therapy, and tissue engineering. But their specificities make them especially interesting. I will discuss stem cell research and cloning as indicating the emergence of new strategies and constellations in the field of biopolitics. In a first step, I will show that these new biopolitical strategies are inseparably related to new biological technologies that have transformed representations of and interventions in life processes. I will emphasis that embryonic stem cell research and cloning are only the most prominent among a number of other strategies to "rebuild" and "reprogram" life on the cellular level. In the emerging biopolitical strategies, the focus has begun to shift from the emphasis on genetic factors to cellular mechanisms operating beyond the level of the gene. I will discuss how these new biological technologies connect to the construction of antagonistic narratives and positions in the struggle to give meaning to practices of "shaping life". New strategies that combine technologies of risk and of uncertainty are in the process of creating a space of governance in which practices of individual self-control connect in novel ways with imperatives of political-institutional decision-making.

Technologies and Realities of Stem Cell Research

The rise of stem cell research and cloning as new fields of cutting edge science reflects the confluence of a number of disciplinary developments in the life-sciences. On the one hand, contemporary biology is characterized by its strategy to study biological phenomenon on the level of macromolecules. Since the 1930s, the focus of modern biology has begun to shift from the cellular to the subcellular level of biological phenomena. In the practice of modern biology the locus of life phenomena was conceptualized at the sub-microscopic level (Kay 1993). Subsequently, with the shift from the protein paradigm to the DNA paradigm during the late 1950s, explaining the operation of DNA and understanding and handling its manipulation moved in the center of biological and medical interest. From the 1970s on, genetic engineering, then, during the 1980s genetic testing, gene therapy and the human genome project seemed to delineate a new future for bio-medicine where knowledge and mastery of DNA were the key to solve many of the important problems in medical research Nelkin/Lindee 1995).

However, during the 1990s it has become quite clear that there is a widening gap between the currently dominant genetic-technoscientific imaginary and the realities of medical practice and industrial application. The human genome project greatly helps the growth of the genetic testing industry, but offers little in the way of therapeutics. Despite all initial hype, gene therapy still has failed to prove its success in curing illnesses. However, supported by enthusiastic mass media, the geneticization of society continues and genetic information reconfigures our notions of self, health and disease (Kay 2000). In the meantime, the advocates of the "genetic revolution" have revised their medical future scenarios. At the same time, new lines of biological and medical reasoning and have gained ground.

The area of early post WW II molecular biology (about 1960–1980) was characterized by the notions of feedback, genetic programs, and thus genetic determinism. In what Evelyn Fox-Keller has called post-recombinant DNA developmental biology (1980-now), attention has begun to shift to cellular mechanisms operating beyond the level of the gene (Keller 2002: 200). This development is also reflected by a move in research away from the sequencing of genes to assigning some element of function to each of the genes in an organism.

The "post-genomic" era seems to be characterized by a broad effort to move beyond strictly genetic determinism, to acknowledge the problematic genomic complexity, and to focus on expressed genes (proteins). In this perspective, genes do play a restricted role within living organisms; they do not actively direct metabolic processes or the activities of cells. Rather, according to the "post-genomic" perspective the central players in the drama of molecular biology are in fact proteins. Thus, In the currently emerging (post-genomic) field of structural genomics, for example, interest focuses on the parts of the gene that are transcribed into messenger RNA, and so encode proteins. The idea behind what in the meantime is called the "structural genomics initiative" is to discover and analyze the three dimensional structures of protein, RNA and other biological macromolecules representing the entire range of structural diversity found in nature. (Abot 2000; Parekh 1999).

Today, cellular approches in biology and medicine are increasingly portrayed to offer a number of novel strategies to deal with central challenges in medical practice, from cancer to organ failure and neurodegenerative diseases. These new strategies view the conceptual framework of modern genetics as crucial, but in itself not sufficient to develop successful therapeutic approaches.

Cellular therapies are not altogether new and build on a longer history of research and experimentation. Cell theory, established in the middle of the nineteenth century, argued that all living organisms are composed of cells, and that cells can arise only from preexisting cells (Wolpert 2002). Among the the scientific fields interested in cell theory were developmental biology and embryology. Furthermore, evolutionary biology and reproductive sciences also took a strong interest in the complex nexus of problems in biology and in the life sciences During the early decades of the twentieth century, separate disciplines had emerged with distinct agendas, such as genetics, that studied the transmission of hereditary units; and embryology, that studied development. While this disciplinary "separation of labor" always seemed to arbitrary and was mainly motivated by the interest to create academic boundaries, nevertheless, it was effective for decades (Keller 2002: 124). Today, the boundaries between developmental biology, embryology and molecular biology and other fields are blurred and lines of work have begun to converge again (Clarke 2003). In the past decades many molecular biologist have turned to the study of development. With that turn has come an explosion of information such as between nucleotide sequences and protein regulatory of mRNA synthesis that make up the microdynamcis of developmental processes and, thus, redefine key concepts of developmental biology (Keller 2002: 194). One of these key concepts is the concept of the stem cell.

Stem cells are defined by their developmental potential. Stem cells are undifferentiated cells that can renew themselves and also give rise to one or more specialized cell types with specific functions in the body. Stem cells exist during development, but also occur in adult tissues. From the time of the discovery of radiation it has become increasingly clear that radiation damages rapidly dividing cells. These observations have led to the identification of the haematopoietic stem cell (HSC). Stem cells are also abundant in the developing brain and in two areas of the adult central nervous system (CNS): the hippocampus and the olfactory bulb. Mammals appear to contain some 20 major types of somatic stem cells that, for example, can generate muscle, blood, intestine, liver and heart (McKay 2000). Among stem cells, embryonic stem cells occupy a special place. As mentioned, early embryonic stem cells can differentiate into a huge variety of cell types. They are seen as „pluripotent", which means they are capable of self-renewal and of differentiation into a wide variety of cell types. Thus, embyonic stem cells can be used to investigate features that are specific to early human development. But they can also be used for therapeutic purposes, such as generating neurons for treating patients with Parkinson´s disease.

Embryonic stem cells were first isolated from the inner cell masses of mouse blastocytes in the early 1980s. Around the same time R.G. Edwards (one of the pioneers of IVF technology) and colleagues grew the fist human blastocyst in vitro 5 days after insemination. Both, Edwards work and the work on mouse embryos were closely related to the growth of reproductive medicine and the development of in-vitro fertilization (IVF) since 1962. (Edwards 2001). Not surprisingly, the breakthroughs in human embryonic stem cell research remained closely tied to the expansion of in-vitro fertilization technologies. But it was not before 1998, that a team of researchers under John Gearhart at Johns Hopkins University managed the first successful isolation and culturing of human embryonic germ cells (EG) cells. The pioneering Johns Hopkins University researchers obtained stem cells from aborted fetuses. The University of Wisconsin research team led by Thompson derived embryonic stem cells (ES) from spare embryos created in IVF clinics for the use of reproduction and donated by couples who no longer needed them. Researchers from U.S. company Advanced Cell Technology claimed that they had created an embryo from an enucleated cow egg and human nuclear DNA that gave rise to stem cells (Annas, Caplan, and Elias 1999).

James Thomson´s Wisconsin team´s work on the derivation of pluripotent human embryonic stem cells (ES cells) and the Dolly work in Britain by Ian Wilmut, Keith Campbell and colleagues in animal cloning created a new scenario for cellular therapies. Nuclear transfer subverts fertilization by replacing the female genetic material of an unfertilized egg with the nucleus from a different cell. This was first done successfully on frogs in the 1950s, in the United States and Britain. Mechanical disruption of donor cells was also tried in mammals. Until recently, however, it was an unsuccessful or unreproducible method of nuclear transfer. Consistent success in producing live, full-term animals was achieved in livestock by fusing a donor cell from an early embryo with either unfertilized or mock-fertilized eggs as recipients. The female genetic material is sucked out, then the recipient cell is fused with the donor nucleus using electrical or chemical methods. In most experiments, the donor nucleus comes from a dividing cell, and it should be able to divide in harmony with the recipient. Nuclear transfer in livestock, using somatic cells as donors and unfertilized eggs as recipients, has been successful (the most famous example being Dolly the sheep), but only in a small percentage of cases. Live mouse births were initially achieved only by using donor nuclei from very early embryos, although a piezo-electrically controlled microinjection device has facilitated success with the nuclei of adult cells (Gurdon/ Coleman 1999: 743–744). The combination of ES cell technology with cloning technology offered the theoretical possibility to derived ES cells from a patient and thus to avoid the problems of immune rejection (Lovell-Badge 2001).

While ES and cloning research expanded, the field of adult stem cell research also produced a host of much discussed advances. A number of recent papers seems to suggest that stem cells from various adult tissues can be reprogrammed. This would conflict with one of the "central dogmas"of developmental biology, namely that once a cell has become specialized, it can´t adopt a new identity. The most prominent of these studies was Catherine Verfaillie´s work on multipotent adult progeniitor cells (MAPCs), something like a "universal" stem cells that was never before identified. (Verfaillie 2002). These cells qualify as adult stem cells, but display characteristics close to ES cells. Another approach pursued is about finding a way to reprogramme any of the body's cells to create ES-like cells matched to the intended recipient without cloning an embryo. In particular the work by Azim Surani of the Wellcome/CRC Institute of Cancer and Developmental Biology in Cambridge seemed to making progress in this direction. Surani fused mouse white blood cells with embryonic germ cells—cells from the developing reproductive system that share many characteristics of ES cells. The white blood cell nuclei appeared to return to an embryonic state. Researchers at several of the leading companies interested in regenerative medicine are now rumoured to be stripping the nuclei from ES cells and embryonic germ cells, and fusing them with various types of cells in an attempt to wind back the developmental clocks of the latter. In the process, they hope to learn how to rewind cell development without using ES cells. One such company, PPL Therapeutics, claimed in January 2001 to have reprogrammed skin cells to form ES-like cells, some of which developed into heart muscle cells (Aldhous 2001). Against the background of these developments, influencial voices such as "Nature" have began to argue for a "Human Stem Cell Project." (Nature 2002, July 4).

First steps in this direction have been taken by the US National Institutes of Health (NIH).

New technologies of visualization and representation have played a crucial role in this rise of stem cell research. In the history of molecular biology the electron microscope has been the key instrument to visualize life phenomena on the submicroscopic level. But bringing molecules within view came at the price that these new technologies were of little help to study cellular and developmental dynamics. (Keller 2002: 217). In the last 20 years, a number of technological developments led to a "revitalization" of embryology and developmental biology. Techniques for introducing molecular markers, such as the microinjection of a purified protein that has bee coupled to a fluorescent dye served as visual probes of the cell´s internal dynamics. Furthermore, video and confocal microscopy were used to amplify the light intensity of images too weak to be seen with the human eye. Confocal laser scanning microscopy and computer reconstruction permitted the viewing of the structure and dynamics of a large range of intra—and intercellular activity. These new visualization technologies contributed to a shift in perspective away from structured and activity of genes to the importance of the activity of protein assemblies. It has become clear that gene products function in multiple pathways and that there are many more possible outcomes than there are genes. The new visualization technologies are also characterized by their "public dimension": photographs, video clips and CD-ROMs have brought the observation of intra—and intercellular dynamics to larger audiences of specialists and non-specialists. Crystal clear images of blastocysts and other cellular formations not only ornate the title pages of "Science" or "Nature" but become an integrative elements of public culture and art. "So lifelike can the animated spectacle be made to appear, that our perception of "real time" comes to be more and more closely assimilated with our perception of "reel time" .... Today, the term "visual reality" is used more or less indiscriminately to refer to computer-reconstructed images that the microscopist sees, to the display of these images the remote spectator sees, and to visual representations of molecular processes that no one has ever been able to see" (Keller 2002: 233).

The confluence of the technological and scientific developments in such different disciplines such as molecular biology, genetics, reproductive medicine, developmental biology, immunology, cell biology, and animal cloning indicates not only an epistemic shift in basic biology, but also a reorganization of the gaze of life-sciences. In the early history of molecular biology the locus of life phenomena was conceptualized at the submicroscopic level. Later on, techniques of recombinant DNA have made it possible to manipulate gene sequences. While even during the 1990s the discourse on life was characterized by "geneticization", attention has now shifted to the cellular and the protein level. In this process that involved the application of a broad array of new technologies representing life, the human body has become object of a new discourse of "rebuilding" and "reprogramming" with the cellular level moving into the center of interventionist practices.

Global Spaces and Local Narratives of Stem Cell Politics

The combination of advances in molecular biology, reproductive medicine and IVF-technology, genetics, development biology and animal cloning had a dramatic impact on the visibility and representation of life phenomena. Not only seemed the spectrum of possible interventions in the various stages of human development be broadly expanded. The new quality of visualizations of early human life also had a number of unintended political effects. A few decades ago, images of very early embryos were not broadly available. During the abortion debates of the 1970s and 1980s, ultrasound images of fetuses became an important device for abortion critics to convey an impression of early human life. Today, photographs of human blastocytes can not only be found in science journals or the general press, but also in publications and web-sites of the numerous critics of stem cell research and cloning. (Hartouni 1997). These pictures seem to convey the "life character" of very early human embryos that consist of only a few cells. They played an important role in the shaping of the debate on the ethics and acceptability of stem cell and cloning research.

Much of the debate on cloning and stem cell research that took shape from 1997 on seemed to be about human life, its beginnings, but also about acceptable strategies of controlling the creation and development of human life. To some extent, cloning and stem cell discourse recapitualtes abortion discourse. The various strategies to obtain embryonic stem cells, and their application in medical research and therapy have turned immediately into a site of political controversy in Europe, the U.S., Australia and other countries. There were many issues and topics raised in these debates ranging from the rights of embryos to the question of the potential risks for patients involved in these novel, experimental medical strategies, and the implications for women due to the possible increase in demand for "spare embryos". With the emergence of human embryonic stem cell and cloning research, old lines of argumentation from former controversies about fetal research and abortion were reactivated. At the same time new interpretations, facts, and styles of controversy affected the construction of the meaning of human stem cell research. Even today a cursory look at the stem cell/cloning debates in most industrialized countries might come to the conclusion that society and the state is faced with critical choices about the future of humankind. But only a few years after this debate has begun, it appears that the question of the social, ethical, and political acceptability of stem cell research and cell nuclear transfer technologies seems to be less a question "if" research should proceed than, rather, of "how", "when" and "under which conditions" it would continue.

A comparative perspective of stem cell and cloning regulations seems to support this interpretation. A number of countries have established very "liberal" regulatory regimes in this area. In Israel, the 1987 Extra Corporeal Fertilization Regulations 1987 prescribed terms and conditions for the authorization of retrieving, fertilizing, freezing and implanting fertilized ova for reproductive purposes. These regulations imply a ban on embryo research as far as deliberately fertilizing an ovum for research purposes is concerned. Since the law does not regulate surplus embryos initially created for IVF, and because there are no other laws affecting this kind of research, it is commonly regarded as being legal to use spare IVF embryos for stem cell research. In 1999, the Israeli Parliament, the Knesset, put into effect the Prohibition of Genetic Intervention Law. It prescribes a five-year period during which certain genetic interventions in humans are prohibited; "the creation of a whole human being who is absolutely identical, genetically-chromosomically, to another—a human being or an embryo, whether alive or dead" (human reproductive cloning); the creation of a human being through the use of reproductive cells, which have undergone a permanent intentional genetic modification (germ-line therapy).[1]

The Prohibition of Genetic Intervention Law is intended to put a hold on research in areas which are not yet regarded as safe. Although it pays lip service to potential moral concerns that Israel could be confronted with from abroad,[2] it regulates that "if the Minister (of Health, BP) finds that no harm will be caused to human dignity, he may permit, upon the recommendation of the Advisory Committee, and under conditions, which he shall determine by regulations, the performance of certain types of genetic intervention, which are prohibited according to section 3(2)."[3] There is a moratorium on human reproductive cloning, but somatic cell nuclear transfer (SCNT) is widely practised in Israel. There are no indications so far that the moratorium on human reproductive cloning will be renewed in 2003.

It would be inviting to explain the "liberal" regulatory regime in Israel with the impact of the Jewish religion. But, then, how do we account for the case of the UK? The United Kingdom has the most "liberal" regulatory regime for stem cell research in Europe. Already in 1990 legislation was passed (the Human Fertilization and Embryology Authority Act) that prohibited research on embryos older than 14 days. Research with earlier embryos was permitted when necessary for promoting advances in infertility treatment, about causes of miscarriages, for the development of more effective techniques of contraception, and for detecting chromosomal abnormalities (Mulkay 1997). In 2001, after a long discussion the new "Human Fertilization and Embryology Regulations" were passed that expanded the scope of research with early embryos. Whereas the 1990 regulations had focused on research in the context of infertility treatment and pregnancy, the new regulations included research with the purpose to increase knowledge about embryos, about serious disease, and the application of such knowledge. The newly added very broad categories effectively opened up widely the window for human embryonic stem cell research in the UK, also including what had been named "therapeutic cloning", the cloning of human stem cells for non-reproductive purposes.

On the other side of the regulatory continuum we find Germany. Germany has with the Embryo Protection Act a strict law which essentially outlaws most types of embryo research and, by implication, any private or public funding of such work. At the core of the 1990 Embryo Protection Law, which is part of the penal law, are a number of restrictions: prohibited is artificial fertilization that has any other goal than to result in a pregnancy, a measure precluding the creation of embryos for research purposes. Furthermore, the law prohibits any manipulation of embryos that served other purposes than their survival. The law defines an embryo as any fertilized egg cell beginning with nuclear fusion and, furthermore, any totipotent cell capable of division and development towards a human being (Iliadou 1999). With these provisions and definitions, German embryo regulations are quite similar to those regulating federally funded research in the US from the 1990s on,—with the important difference that the German regulations also encompassed privately funded embryo research and imposed a criminal penalty. In May 2001, the DFG, the German Research Association, began to lobby for the import of human embryonic stem cell lines from abroad as a "quick solution" for the needs of German medical research (TAZ, May 5, 2001). This lobbying effort culminated in a highly controversial decision of the German Parliament (Bundestag) on January 30, 2002. After a long and heated discussion a narrow majority of the representatives voted in support of a provision that allowed the import of human embryonic stem cell lines created before January 30, 2002 for research purposes. (Frankfurter Allgemeine Zeitung, January 31, 2002).

The United States represents something like a "middle of the road" position in the regulation of stem cell research. Under President Clinton guidelines regulating stem cell research were published on August 25, 2000 (NIH 2000b). At the core of the new guidelines was the decision to extend the scope of government support for embryonic stem cell research and to create a framework for regulatory oversight. While in the past the law permitted the use of federal funds for the derivation of embryonic stem cells from aborted fetuses, the situation was less clear with respect to the crucial issue of spare embryos donated by couples undergoing IVF. The August 25, 2000 guidelines, most importantly, permitted the usage of cells derived from IVF spare embryos for research purposes and constituted a forceful, unambiguous statement of support for embryonic stem cell research. George Bush´s much expected proclamation on August 9, 2001, that federal funds may be awarded for research using human embryonic cell lines that meet certain criteria, represented a continuation of Clinton´s approach, but imposed further restrictions. One year later, in July 2002, the President´s Council on Bioethics published policy recommendations in regard to human cloning, which also would have an impact on possible sources of stem cells. The majority recommendation was to issue a ban on reproductive cloning ("cloning-to-produce-children"), combined with a four-year moratorium on therapeutic cloning ("cloning-for-biomedical-research"). The minority recommendation was to ban reproductive cloning but to permit therapeutic cloning with strict regulation of the use of cloned embryos for biomedical research (PCB report).

Initiatives to regulate human embryonic stem cell research on a transnational level are only in their infancy. A number of committees have been set up and recommendations were given, such as by the UNESCO, the WHO and the Council of Europe and on the EU level. But these initiatives have not left their imprint on the level of national decision making.

This brief comparison of regulatory regimes in the field of stem cell and cloning research reveals the following picture. Indeed, there are significant differences between countries that are attributable to a broad range of discursive resources mobilized in political debate, ranging from religious narratives to history. However, as the example of Germany shows, even in a country known for its highly moralized political discourse human embyonic stem cell research is gradually introduced and legalized. In early 2000, there seems to be world-wide an agreement to reject and/or ban reproductive cloning, however, somatic cell nuclear transfer technology (often called therapeutic cloning) finds increasingly acceptance. Furthermore, a number of novel cellular technologies focused on redesigning or reprogramming cells, have not caught at all broader attention

A stunning feature of the current "public debate" about stem cell research and cloning is its intellectual and social style. Neither can the controversy be reduced to a "clash" between groups and institutions, nor do the arguments raised follow simple "Yes-No" patterns. The debate about stem cell and cloning research in the various countries has been sophisticated and on a high level. Connecting to earlier debates on abortion and embryo research, a massive body of theological, philosophical and bioethical literature has been mobilized since the late 19902. Christian views on how much dignity a fertilized ovum deserves ranges from radical Catholic positions (the early embryo is to be treated like a fully developed human being. See McCormick 1976; Walters 1976; Doerflinger 1999), to more liberal Protestant approaches, which are based on the conviction that moral questions are determined by individual conscience. Catholicism regards the human being and as a person as coming into existence at the time of conception, thus making it impossible to conduct any research on the embryo or fetus at any stage of development, if this research is not free of risk and notable pain and if it is not promising considerable benefit for the embryo itself (McCormick 1976). Nevertheless, some Catholic thinkers have been willing to recognize embryo research as potentially beneficial for humankind and Catholic approaches have become more diverse recently (Farley 2001).

The second body of religious literature relevant for our project is Judaism. Compared to other religions, Judaism has probably the most liberal attitude towards embryonic stem cell research. Since an embryo outside of the uterus is not regarded as an entity deserving human dignity, it can be used for research purposes.[4] Jewish Biblical and Talmudic Law holds that human status is acquired progressively during embryonic and fetal development. A fetus becomes a full human being only at the moment of birth. Creating embryos by cloning (through somatic cell nuclear transfer, SNCT), in order to harvest stem cells, can be justified and is in some cases even morally recommended. The technology itself is morally neutral; what counts is the rationale behind it, the motivation of the researchers, and what purpose the research is going to serve. If early-stage embryos are used for research aimed at finding cures for fatal diseases, it is regarded beneficial.

Both philosophical and bioethical writings can be found at both ends of the continuum of positions. The main cleavage can be found between philosophers and bioethicists[5] who perceive themselves as seeking for a secular ethics which is free from religious contents, and those who see their work shaped by their religious and cultural identities. Religious Christians and conservative thinkers are usually speaking of the "sanctity of human life" in its early stages, which deserves our respect and protection. Conservatives, who are sometimes reluctant to use explicitly religious terminology, replace the concept of "sanctity" and "God´s creation" with "dignity" and "nature", or simply "life" (Lauritzen, 2001).[6] In the United States, President Bush´s Council on Bioethics (PCB), which has only recently issued a report on embryonic stem cell research and human cloning (The President´s Council on Bioethics Report, 2002), formulating rather restrictive policy recommendations, consists of personalities that are commonly regarded as belonging to the conservative/religious camp (Caplan 2002). At the other end of the scale are philosophers and bioethicists who are putting their focus on individual autonomy and individual consent. Since most of them do not regard the very early embryo as a human being, they are lobbying for the (moral and legal) permissibility of research on the early embryo (Charo 1995; Davis 2002; Annas 1996).

Central elements of the philosophical/ethical discourse were taken up by the many political supporters and opponents of embryonic stem cell research. In the U.S., for example, the critics attacked stem cell research fiercly. The focus of their counter-narrative was on the representation of embryos as human beings (not a formation of of cells), their rights and the duty of law to protect them. Furthermore, adult stem cell research and other research strategies were portrayed as viable alternatives to human embryonic stem cell research. The decision of the U.S. government to go ahead with research in this area was criticized by many actors, there was even fundamental opposition demanding that the NIH withdrew its guidelines, a position in particular articulated by religious groups. The National Conference of Catholic Bishops wrote in one of its submissions: "The guidelines, for the first time on our national history, authorize the federal government to approve and regulate destruction of innocent human life for research purposes. They instruct researchers in how to harvest versatile 'stem cells' from living week-old human embryos, a procedure which kills embryos . . . " (Letter, January 31b, 2000). Or, as Orange County Right to Life stated: "You will be known as the cannibals of the 21st century if you use human pluripotent stem cells . . . for research and experimentation" (Letter, January 16, 2000).

By contrast, in Germany additional arguments played a very important role in the debate, semantically linking German history, in particular the experience of the Third Reich and of Nazi eugenics with current medical research on embryos. Central in this context was the argument that all had to be done to avoid the dreadful mistakes of the past, even if this may look exaggerated viewed from a perspective outside of Germany. Germany has a special responsibility in this respect, so the narrative went, even if living up to this responsibility means to sacrifice certain scientific or economic goals (Catenhusen 1998; Rau 2001; DIE ZEIT 2001). By connecting embryonic stem cells with Nazi eugenics and "special German responsibility", a core element of contemporary German political identity—the determination "not to repeat history,"—had been mobilized as a pivotal issue in the political struggle.

Equally important for the discursive construction of embryonic stem cell research in Germany was the mobilization of the metanarrative of human rights. Human rights instruments describe minimum conditions for humans to flourish and aspirational goals for a world in which all humans live in harmony. Many European countries, including Germany, have explicitly appealed to human rights in addressing issues of health care and biotechnology, and emphasized terms such as solidarity, human dignity, and the collective good. In contrast, the US legal discourse focused on the importance of negative rights without fully embracing the concept of positive rights or obligations between government and people. In American discourse, law and culture "rights" generally refer to individual rights based on non-interference rather than on the more expansive rights articulated in the human rights framework (Knowles 2000). In Germany, not only were references to a broadly understood notion of human rights compatible with the dominant law discourse , but, in addition, during the second half of the 1990s human rights had turned into a topic of broad social interest and concern. The passing of the "Bioethics Convention" of the Council of Europe in 1996 (Europarat, 1997) had caused an uproar in Germany, where a number of the proposed regulations were seen as undermining the high standards of the German human rights tradition. Eventually, a network of "Anti-bioethics" activists came into existence, which involved ten thousands of activists engaged in the question of human rights and bioethics. As one group active in this field, the "Arbeitskreis Bioethik Braunschweig wrote with respect to those paragraphs of the bioethics convention, which, in their view, seemed to introduce lower standards of human rights in Germany," . . . Developments in medicine and biology . . . question the dignity and the rights of many people. . . . what even a few years ago was seen as undemocratic, unsocial and inhuman, now is increasingly accepted . . . Should we really be condemned to repeat history, only because we don´t want to remember it?" (Arbeitskreis Bioethik 1999). Thus, opposition to stem cell research in Germany was not reduced to religious groups, but cut across the political spectrum from the Churches to the Green Party and various social movements.

The discursive context of ES research was not only created by critics. For many actors in medical, business and policy communities cell based medical approaches were a promise and description of a possible model of the future for medicine. As a NIH "Fact Sheet" stated: "Human pluripotent stem cells are a unique scientific and medical resource . . . (and) human pluripotent stem cell lines represent(s) a major step forward in the understanding of human biology . . . "(NIH 1999a: 1). Taking into account the huge potential for medical benefits of this type of research, funding under oversight was seen as the appropriate strategy for the NIH to pursue.

Under the Clinton administration, the U.S. government´s policy narrative connected stem cell research with more general themes of U.S. American political discourse. It connected to important political metanarratives. Political metanarratives describe general concepts and values of the political order and offer a conceptual framework that provides a polity and its subjects with an imagined, collective political identity. Hence, for a policy narrative to be powerful it needs to be framed as expressing deeper sets of values and social preferences (Gottweis 1998: 33). With American health and American leadership two core elements of contemporary U.S. political identity were mobilized and related to embryonic stem cell policy. Various statements in government reports and guidelines concerning stem cells left no doubt that the continuation of stem cell research in the U.S. would be critical to help Americans fight dreadful diseases for which there is currently no cure available (NIH 1999a; NBAC, 2000). In other words, the health and the lives of many Americans began to be connected to the practices of embryonic stem cell research. Furthermore, it was argued that federal funding for embryonic stem cell research would also help to sustain U.S. leadership in science and technology. "Federal funding is probably required in order for the United States to sustain a leadership in this increasingly important area of research (NBAC 2000: 60). There was no question, so the policy narrative went, that embryonic stem cell research raises all sorts of ethical and moral questions. But, one needs to consider that, according to the current consensus in the scientific community, embryonic stem cells are no embryos. Provided the adequate precautions were taken, research could continue in a manner which might lead to substantial benefits for the U.S. society and sustain scientific leadership of the U.S. in the world. Under President Bush Jr., however, this line of reasoning was modified, and arguments of balancing the promises of research against ethical concerns gained of importance.

While national discursive contexts took their impact on the emerging policies, simultaneously stem cell and cloning research operated in an increasingly globalized space. In 2001, the U.S. government had decided to allocate federal funds only to those stem cell researchers working with one or more of the 64 human embryonic stem-cell lines published by NIH. This list was not restricted to US institutions and included stem-cell lines from Sweden, India, and Israel. The German regulatory situation implies that German research in embryonic stem cells can only use already created stem cell lines from abroad. Some of the main companies in the field such as Geron and PPL Therapeutics have forged transnational alliances and cooperations. The Australian company Stem Cell Sciences Ltd that sees therapeutic cloning as integral to its plans to make patient-derived cell lines for screening has announced, that it will relocate to Edinburgh if the Australian government insists on a ban on therapeutic cloning (Finkel 2002: 48). And the Edinburgh bases former PPL therapeutics head of research, Alan Coleman, recently moved to Singapore to join ES Cell, a stem cell company started by researchers from Monash University, Australia (Birmingham 2002: 314). In China, the Peking University Stem Cell Research Center recently received a large grant from the University, the central government, and Chinese venture capitalists to set up a center to lead China's efforts in this area (Dennis, 2002).

Within a few years, stem cell research has advanced to one of the most attractive sub-fields of international biotechnology research and industry. Private companies have become important sites to shape the national and transnational space of stem cell research, and cooperate and/or compete with research efforts in the public realm, such as in universities. These developments in research and in industry have led to broadly based public debate with significant variations between countries. However, the rise of a global stem cell research and industry infrastructure seems to correspond with the gradual shaping of regulatory systems that put certain restrictions on research, but also enable research and industry to go ahead with most of their planned research.

Stem Cells, Biomedicalization, and Risk

On the social-epistemic level, the rise of stem cell research and cloning technologies resonated with a number of broader developments. Studies and experiments in ES research are not only scientific activities, they are also practices of social and political ordering. Human tissue created with ES technology are not only potentially life-saving, they also reflect images of the acceptable boundaries between humans and humans, understandings of the rights of embryos, and visions of what constitutes acceptable risks for citizens and for society at large. As Schaeffer and Shapin have shown so convincingly (1984), solutions to problems of knowledge are often solutions to problems of social and political order. In the medical field, one important expression of this phenomenon of multiple ordering has been subsumed under the term of "medicalization." Initially framed by Irving Zola (1972), the term medicalization theorizes the extension of medical jurisdiction, authority, and practices into increasingly broader areas of people's lives. By conceptually redefining particular phenomena such as alcoholism and drug abuse in medical terms, medicine became a new agent of social control for managing deviance.

Today medicalization understood as a co-production of science, technology and new social forms has become bio-medicalization (Clarke et al. 2002). Biomedicalization, located at the transition from the problems of modernity to the problems of post-modernity, is characterized by a shifting of the sites of control from external nature (i.e. the world around us) to the harnessing and transformative customizing of internal nature (i.e. biological and physiological processes of human and non-human life forms), often transforming life "itself." At the core of "biomedicalization" is the shift in medicine exerting clinical and social control over particular conditions to the capacities of an increasingly technoscientifically constituted biomedicine to effect the transformation of bodies and lives. Such transformations range from giving birth a decade or more after menopause to the capacity of genetically re-designing life. At the same time, biomedicalization refers to a deep-going institutional-organizational transformation of medicine, implying such diverse processes such as the production of new social forms by the usage of computer—and information technologies and the corporatization (HMOs) and commodification of research (Celera Genomics), products, and services in the medical system (Clarke et al. 2002).

We can view stem cell research, and cloning research as being indicative of the described process of biomedicalization. Previously, the central goal of medicine was to arrest abnormality and to re-establish the natural vital norm. But with the new cellular technologies and genetic, sub-cellular strategies the normativities themselves appear open to transformation. The line between correcting deviant genes that cause diseases and modifying genes to enhance athletic performance is a thin one. In a similar vein, stem cell approaches might help to cure Parkinson´s patients, but, in principle, they could also be used to improved brain functions Life now seems to be open to shaping and re-shaping and the distinctions between treatment and enhancement, between the natural and the prosthetic begin to blur. (Rose 2000: 15). The cellular therapies curently under development, such as therapeutic cloning or tissue engineering, seem to promise a vast expansion of the scope and depth of intervention in life processes. As the normativity of life begins to loose its contours, struggles about who we are, what we aspire and what we can hope for have become daily occurrence. Already now ethicists ponder about the implications of stem cell therapy in the human brain for personal identity.

The rising new strategies to "rebuild life" must also be seen in the discursive context of current shifts in health policy. From the last quarter of the 20th century onwards, a common set of challenges like demographic development, access to and quality of care, cost crisis, retrenchment of the welfare state or technoscientific innovations like modern biomedicine has concentrated to at least three phenomena that now have become the major driving forces for policy reform in the health care sector: Globalization, the crisis of the welfare state and the neoliberal narrative in health policy. They stand for increasing pressure for standardization, increasing significance of free market solutions and a managerial paradigm in most areas of social interaction, and for an acceleration of both technological and scientific innovation and its application in medicine. Since the 1970s, national health care systems increasingly have been applying similar tools and institutional designs have been developed to cope with similar policy problems and challenges. This led to a redefinition of hitherto stable policy patterns and fostered a global dynamics towards a technomanagerial paradigm in health policy that stresses the importance of increased scientification and efficacy in the provision and organization of medicine alike. the retrenchment of the welfare state, due to a global hegemony of a neoliberal narrative, did not entail less regulation, but led to micro-management and micro-regulation of patients´ and physicians´ behavior by means of the private market. Health care is increasingly perceived and treated as any commodity market (Scheil-Adlung 1998). The neoliberal health care discourse moved to a governmental style, where the social takes the form of markets. This reassertion of the role of the market in particular serves as a mechanism for constructing identities as targets for managed care action. The sick is regarded as a consumer, the physician as an entrepreneur on the health care market. The contrivance of markets became the technical mean for the reformation of all types or provision in the health care market (Dean 1999: 171–172).

Today, health is increasingly discussed in terms of self-control and framed within the language of an ethics of health, that requires the discipling of the individual conduct of life (Crawford 1984: 72–76) throughout the West. This managing of the self (Foucault 1994 [1975], 1983 [1976]) is also reflected in a multitude of technical and organizational novelties within health care, where managed care is the most important and most paradigmatic example. In the past, health policies were conducted based on the collection and tabulation of numerical information about populations and provided the rationale for hygienic strategies. Likewise, strategies to minimize risks of the environment, labor conditions or the maintainance of the body were central elements for public health strategies. While these strategies continue to be important, the focus of strategies has begun to shift from the group to the individual level. The ideal of the omnipresent state that would shape, coordinate and direct the affairs in all sectors of society has lost its grip on the public imagination. Accordingly, in the health field concentration has moved from "society as a whole" to "risky individuals", individual susceptibility (to genetic disease, for example), and, accordingly, to "risk groups" (Rose 2001). The proactive management of the human body has become a core element of collective and individual strategies of health maintenance.

Towards a New Politics of Uncertainty

Today support for stem cell technologies comes from a number of directions. Not only are governments and researchers prominent advocates of this line of research, also many patients, parents, bioethicists and other citizens seem to agree that stem cell research should proceed. Representatives of religious groups, various social movements, feminists and a variety of party denominations disagree with such positions. But all these groups and actors seem to share a new social and intellectual style to deal with the controversial topic of "rebuilding humans".

Foucault has pointed to the significant historical transition contemporaneous with the shaping of industrial capitalism, in which emphasis shifted from the primacy of sovereignty, law, and coercion or force "to take life" to the development of new forms of power constitutive of life. Such processes of subjectification can occur in the form of the subjection of individuals to techniques of domination, or through subtler techniques of the self. The then emerging biopolitics focused on the administration of life, in particular on the level of populations and was concerned with matters of life and death, with birth, health, illness and other processes sustaining the optimization of the life of a population (Foucault 1979; Dean 1999: 99). The activities of government and the state involved collecting, collating, and calculating data on the characteristics of the population (births, deaths, rates of disease, etc.) to be complemented by those of individuals who engage in practices of "self-government" exercise of power (Rose 2001).

A critical part of this newly emerging form of government was pastoral power. Pastoral power, in Foucault´s definition, no longer implied that individuals were led to salvation, but that they were assured of other, worldly god, such as health, well-being and security. Officials of pastoral power, who were previously members of religious institutions now spread into the whole social body finding support in a multitude of institutions such a family, medicine, psychiatry, and education (Foucault 1982). In the field of health and medical politics this meant that moved into the center of state action. But these strategies of bio-politics have lost ground towards the end of the 20th century (Rose 2001: 3). Certainly, programs of preventive medicine and public health still focus on a „nation´s health“. But these policies loose importance, are partially reconfigured in novel ways, and give way to new strategies to deal with issues of health. The state seems no longer be responsible to resolve a nation´s need for health. Instead, every individual citizens is now becoming an active partner in the drive for health. New organizations, communities, patient groups, self-help organizations and a multitude of newly emerged actors in the field of private insurance seem to have occupied spaces hithero filled by the state (Rose 2001: 3).

Today, pastoral power, in the sense of Foucault, takes on a new meaning. It now operates on a plural and contested field traversed by the empirical findings of researchers, the attitudes and standards generated by insurance companies and the codes and systems of meaning generated by bioethics committees and local medial ethics committees (Rose 2001: 10). The logic of this new bio-politics can be understood as being defined by a new rationality. The binary constellation of the normal and the pathological which was so essential in defining medical practices are now reorganized within strategies of the government of risk and uncertainty.

Risk is a way of ordering reality, of rendering it into a calculable form. Risks come into existence through complex and multiple processes of inscription, interpretation, and boundary work carried out by a variety of actors. Risk is a strategy of making events and situations governable and introduces a calculative rationality for governing the conduct of individuals, populations, and collectivities (Gottweis 1998: 77; Dean 1999).

Uncertainty refers to the phenomenon that certain problematizations and techniques of the self are sometimes not very precise and incalculable and thus less driven by "connaissance" and expert knowledge, but by other forms of knowledge. While, traditionally, uncertainty is seen as a "deficit", it can also be understood as a creative way to deal with the absence of agreement and to marginalize or subordinate statistical and expert models of risk management (O´Malley: 2000).

It is in this context that we need to locate the rise of bioethics and philosophical-ethical discourse as new system of cultural orientation. New biological strategies and technologies to "program and reprogram life" have opened up a new and global space of uncertainty for governance. While during the 1970s and 1980s political discourse on genetic engineering and its various applications focused on the risks associated with genetic engineering and the various strategies to control risk, today political-institutional strategies towards stem cell research and cloning are characterized by the extensive consideration of the ambivalences of theses lines of research and the exploration of their very meaning, applicability, impact and implications.

In this constellation, ethical reflection and ethics institutions that are less based on practices of calculative rationality but on deliberation and reflection gain of importance. The new modalities of government take on forms such as speaking about "bioethical problems", deliberating, confessing, and "telling truth." "*La règle explicite, accompagnée de sanctions, tend à laisser la place à une autorégulation, mais accompagnée d'argumentaires attendus. La police des corps tourne à une police des récits*" (Memmi 2000 : 15). Laws and regulations loose of importance in the shaping of medical and scientific developments. Instead, new institutionalizations of conversation, confession and negotiation rituals become increasingly central government technologies. Speaking and confessing "liberates". At the same time technologies of risk continue to be of relevance. Thus, in the newly emerging biopolitics risk and uncertainty operate as joint modalities of government. Bioethics committees, practices of risk individualization and self-steering, but also administrative agencies concerned, for example, with the surveillance of patients that have received engineered tissues are linked in novel ways in the emerging regime of biomedical regulation.

Not suprisingly, world-wide the rise of stem cell and cloning technologies has been accompanied by a vast mobilization of ethical expertise and an almost hectic movement of ethical institution building. In Germany, in 2001 the German parliament convened a parliamentary inquiry commission on "Law and Ethics in Modern Medicine" which, among other things was called to develop a position on the ethical and socio-political implications of embryonic stem cell research. Furthermore, the German Chancellor created a "National Bioethics Committee"—with embryo research as its first important agenda. In the US, Clinton had contacted the National Bioethics Advisory

Commission (NBAC) to prepare a review of the medical and ethical issues associated with human stem cell research. In September 1999, the National Bioethics Advisory Commission delivered its two volume report to President Clinton, in which the Commission offered a "political philosophy" of stem cell research (NBAC, 2000). The Commission considered it as its task to produce a statement in which a majority of the Americans should see their concerns and considerations reflected (Interview Hastings Center 2000). After a thorough discussion of the ethical, scientific, legal and social implications of stem cell research, the NBAC strongly endorsed the funding of human embryonic stem cell research. In 2002, President Bush had set up a new Council on Bioethics, a reaction to the many policy challenes connected with stem cell research and cloning. In one of its first actions the Council on Bioethics published Bioethics published policy recommendations in regard to human cloning. Countless local ethics committees such as those established at IVF-clinics dealing with the utilization of spare embryos complement this picture.

This newly emerging ethics-infrastructure has no mandate to make political decisions in the legal-regulatory field. But it sets in motion a process of deliberation, reflection and confession that connects people, science, culture, belief-systems, religion and other meta-narratives with the daily management of stem cell and cloning technologies. Surely, in the US as well as in Germany and the UK the question if human embyonic stem cell research should be conducted at all was a central issue in the political debate. Crucial about these debates were less the resulting decisions, but the very procedure of reflection set in motion. Institutions were created with much care and fanfare which made possible exactly this: ordered ways to problematize and define potentially controversial topics of medical research. The various ethics institutions and the mobilization of ethics arguments were not simply focused on "Yes-No" questions. Complex issues gained attention, such as the question of how to reach "parental consent" in the context of ES research; under which circumstances "embryo donations" should take place; and what the appropriate setting for "parental decisions" would be. In the US, in Germany or in the UK complicated legal constructions were created that ensure that no work with human embryonic stem cells would become possible without making the "parents" of the "research embryos" integral part of the decision-making structure.

At the first glance, the bioethical debate about the stem cell and cloning seems to be focused on a set of interrelated questions ranging from definitions of the emergence of human life and individuality, personality and the perils of the slippery slopes of contemporary medical technology. For example, objection to cloning surely is not only based on theological and/or philosophical definitions of human individuality, but also about on more general consideration of desirable social development. But, at a different level, this controversy is also about individualizing strategies in body politics. During the 1960s and 1970s the abortion debates were polarized between those who advocated the sanctity of life even at earlier stages of embryonic developments, and those who supported the rights of woman to decide about their bodies. In a way, the debate was about something "negative": should women have the right to terminate their pregnancy—or not? In the first decade of the 21th century the debate has taken a "positive" turn: do individuals have the right to use cells of their body to initiate processes of embryonic development with the goal to cure diseases? Should they be allowed to use embryo cells from other bodies to initiate treatments of illness? Is it acceptable to take somatic cells from humans be reprogrammed to create ES-like cells? While institutional politics has become deeply involved in the reflection of such issues, the debate has also clearly moved beyond the realm of legislatures and ethics institutions. Patient advocate groups such as those dealing with Parkinson and Alzheimer have turned into major political forces in the political struggles. Patients suffering from spinal injury or neurological diseases—some of them prominent—such as the British Member of the House of Commons, Anne Bagg, or the ex-superman Christopher Reed, have become vocal advocates for establishing a liberal regime for stem cell research and cloning.

As mentioned before, arguments in support of stem cell research and cloning are still advanced in the name of major social values, such as health, medical progress, modernity, or society. Risk regulation is expected to guarantee a certain level of safety of the new bio-medical technologies. At the same time, in resonance with the tendency of patients increasingly taking responsibility for their health and body, individuals and groups have started to claim their rights and position themselves accordingly in the political confrontation. In most countries arguments in favor of stem cell research have come under heavy criticism by a number of actors and groups ranging from churches to feminist activists. But these groups don´t face a monolithic state as their counter-part, but ethical positions, arguments and invitations to join bioethics boards. They don´t clash with police troops in front of abortion clinics or at demonstrations, but meet well-known theologians, patient representatives and philosophers in citizen´s conferences.

Currently, it seems that the idea of "Engineering Humans" has lost much of its threat. Against the background of processes of reorganization in the life sciences, biomedicalization and neo-liberal health discourse, individuals and groups have begun to contextualize their support for stem cell research and cloning, and, in a more general way, their endorsement of the idea of "re-building humans" as a new form of identity politics. Just as "knowing one´s genes" and adapting eating habits is an expression of a prudent life-style, the routine cloning of cell material or the storage of umbilical cord blood might become integral elements of the responsible management of one´s health and body. Multiple resistances against this trend will continue, but increasingly they seem to operate as functional elements of the emerging bioethical-dialogical apparatus. Thus, the new ethics discourse and its various forms of institutionalization appears to constitute an effort to link new strategies in the self-government of individuals with needs of post-modern governance under conditions of radical uncertainty.

Notes

1. The Prohibition of Genetic Intervention Law No. 5759 (cloning on Human Beings and Genetic Modifications for Reproductive Cells) (1998). The Knesset of Israel.
2. The purpose of this law is to provide for a limited period of five years, during which certain types of genetic intervention will not be performed on human beings, in order to examine the moral, legal, social and scientific aspects of such types of intervention and their implications on human dignity."
3. The Prohibition of Genetic Intervention Law No. 5759 (cloning on Human Beings and Genetic Modifications for Reproductive Cells) (1998). The Knesset of Israel.
4. Nevertheless, it should not be destroyed in vain, since it is human. See The Israeli Academy of Sciences and Humanities report 2001.
5. It is not useful, and not even possible, to draw a clear line between philosophers and bioethicists, since the location of bioethics as a discipline is not yet ultimately defined (For the emergence of bioethics as a discipline, see Caplan (1992); Carson/ Burns (1997); Charlesworth (1993); Clouser (1997); Dell´Oro/Viafora (1996); Elkeles (1996); Elliot (1999); Engelhardt (2000); Irrgang (1995); Jonsen (1998); Maclean (1993); Potter (1971); Rothman (1991); Sass (1988).

References

Abbot, Alison (2001) "Genetic Medicine gets real". *Nature,* 411, 410–412.
Aldhous, Peter (2001) "Can They Rebuild Us? *Nature,* 410: 622–625, 2001.
Annas, George J (2002) "Cloning and the U.S. Congress". *New England Journal of Medicine* 346(20), 1599–1602, May 16.
——— (1996) "The Politics of Human-Embryo Research – Avoiding Ethical Gridlock". *New England Journal of Medicine,* 334 (20): 1329–32.
Annas, George.J., Arthur Caplan, and Shermann Elias (1999) "Stem cell politics, ethics and medical progress". *Nature Medicine* 5(12), 1339–1341.
Arbeitskreis Bioethik Braunschweig (1999) Die Würde des Menschen ist unantastbar. Leaflet.
Birmingham, Karen (2002) "Stem Cell Scientists Moves to Singapore", *Nature Medicine,* 8: 314.
Bramstedt, Katrina A. (2000) "Arguments for the Ethical Permissibility of Transgenic Xenografting." *Gene Therapy,* 7, 633–634.
Caplan, Arthur L. (ed) (1992) *When medicine went mad. Bioethics and the Holocaust.* Totowa, NJ: Humana Press.
Caplan, Arthur (2002) "A council of clones. Bush´s bioethics panel will provide the advice he wants to hear". MSNBC online, http://www.msnbc.comnews689297asp. Last visited in August 2002.

Carson, Ronald A., and Chester R. Burns (eds) (1997) *Philosophy of medicine and bioethics. A twenty-year retrospective and critical appraisal.* Dodrecht: Kluwer Academic Publishers.

Catenhusen, Wolf. M. (1998) Rede auf Veranstaltung der Landesarbeitsgemeinschaft Selbsthilfe Behinderte July 17.

Charlesworth, Max (1993) *Bioethics in a Liberal Society.* Cambridge: Cambridge University Press.

Charo, Alta (1995) "The Hunting of the Snark: The Moral Status of Embryos, Right-to-Lifers, and Third World Women." *Stanford Law and Policy Review* 6(2).

Clarke Adele E. /Shim Jannet K/Mamo Laura/Fosket Jennifer R/Fishman Jennifer R (2002) Biomedicalization: Theorizing Technoscientific Transformations of Health, Illness, and U.S. Biomedicine, unpublished paper, San Francisco.

Clarke, Adele E. (2003/4) "Reproductive Science at the Carnegie Department of Embryology, 1913–1971." To appear in Jane Maienschein and Garland Allen (eds.) 100 Years of the Department of Embryology of the Carnegie Institution of Washington. New York: Cambridge University Press.

Clouser, K Donner (1997) "Humanities in the Service of Medicine: Three Models". In: Carson, Ronald A., and Chester Burns (eds), *Philosophy of medicine and bioethics. A twenty-year retrospective and critical appraisal.* Dodrecht: Kluwer Academic Publishers, 25–39.

Cohen, Cynthia B. (2001) "Leaps and Boundaries: Expanding Oversight of Human Stem Cell Research". In Holland, S., K. Lebacqz, and L. Zoloth (eds), *The Human Embryonic Stem Cell Debate.* Cambridge, Massachusetts: MIT Press, 209–222.

Cohen, Philip (1998) "Hold the Champagne". *New Scientists*, p. 8, November 14.

Davis, Dena (2002) "Stem Cells, Cloning, and Abortion: Making Careful Distinctions." *American Journal of Bioethics* 2(1): 47–9, Winter.

Dean, Mitchel (1999) *Governmentality. Power and rule in Modern Society*, London: Sage.

Dell´Oro, Roberto, and Corrado Viafora (eds) (1996) *History of Bioethics. International Perspectives.* San Francisco: International Scholars Publication.

Dennis, Carina (2002) "Stem Cells Rise in the East." *Nature* 419: 334–336.

Doerflinger, Richard (1999) "Destructive stem-cell research on human embryos". *Origins* 28: 769–73.

Edwards, Robert G. (2001) "IVF and the History of Stem Cells." *Nature* 413: 349–351.

Elkeles, Barbara (1996) *Der moralische Diskurs über das medizinische Menschenexperiment im 19. Jahrhundert.* Stuttgart: Gustav Fischer.

Elliot, Carl (1996) *A philosophical disease: bioethics, culture and identity.* New York: Routledge.

Engelhardt, H. Tristam Jr. (Hg) (2000) *The philosophy of medicine. Framing the field.* Dodrecht: Kluwer Academic Publishers.

——— (2000), *The Foundations of Christian Bioethics.* Lisse: Swets & Zeitlinger Publishers.

Europarat, (1997) Übereinkommen zum Schutz der Menschenrechte und der Menschenwürde im Hinblick auf die Anwendung von Biologie und Medizin. Übereinkommen über Menschenrechte und Biomedizin, April 4.

Farley, Margaret A. (2001) "Roman Catholic Views on Research Involving Human Embryonic Stem Cells". In Holland, S., K. Lebacqz, and L. Zoloth (eds), *The Human Ebryonic Stem Cell Debate. Science, Ethics, and Public Policy.* Cambridge, Massachusetts: MIT Press.

Finkel, Elizabeth (2002) "Australian Stem Cell Researrch." *Genetic Engineering News*, 22, May 1.

Fischer, Frank (1995), *Evaluating Public Policy*. Chicago: Nelson Hall.

Foucault, Michel (1979) *The History of Sexuality*, Vol 1: An Introduction, London : Allen Lane.

–––––– Michel (1982) "The Subject and Power" in Hubert Dreyfus and Paul Rabinow (eds.), *Michel Foucault : Beyond Stucturalism and Hermeneutics*, Brighton: Harvester, 208–226.

Gearhart, John. D (1998) "New Potential for Human Embryonic Stem Cells". *Science* 282: 1061–1062.

Gottweis, Herbert (1998) *Governing Molecules: the Discursive Politics of Genetic Engineering in Europe and in the United States*. Cambridge, Mass.: MIT Press.

Gurdon J.B. and Alan Coleman (1999) "The Future of Cloning." *Nature*, 402:743–746.

Hartouni, Valerie (1997) *Cultural Conceptions: On Reproductive Technologies and the Remaking of Life*. Minneapolis: University of Minnesota Press.

Iliadou, Ekaterini (1999) *Forschungsfreiheit und Embryonenschutz. Eine verfassungs— und europarechtliche Untersuchung der Forschung an Embryonen*. Berlin: Duncker & Humboldt.

Irrgang, Bernhard (1995) *Grundriss der medizinischen Ethik*. München: Ernst Reinhard Verlag.

Jonsen, Albert R (1998) *The Birth of Bioethics*. New York: Oxford University Press.

Kay, Lily(1993) *The Molecular Vision of Life: Caltech, the Rockefeller Foundation and the Rise of the New Biology*, Oxford: Oxford University Press.

–––––– (2000) *Who Wrote the Book of Life. A History of the Genetic Code*, Stanford: Stanford University Press.

Keller, F. Evelyn (2002) *Making Sense of Life: Explaining Biological Development with Models, Metaphors, and Machines*, Cambridge, Mass.: Harvard University Press.

Knowles, Laurie P. (2000). The Lingua Franca of Human Rights and the Rise of a Global Bioethic, Manuscript.

Lauritzen, Paul (2001) "Neither Person Nor Property: Embryo Research and the Status of the Early Embryo." *America* 184(10): 20, March 26.

Letter to NIH (2000) Comments on Stem Cell Guidelines, by Carolyn R. Aldige, President, NCCR, January 31.

–––––– (2000), Comments on Stem Cell Guidelines, by Stephanie Castro, AAMC, January 19.

–––––– (2000) Comments on Stem Cell Guidelines. By the National Conference of Catholic Bishops/United States Catholic Conference, January 31.

–––––– (2000) Comments on Stem Cell Guidelines. By Orange County Right to Life, January 16.

–––––– (2000) Comments on Stem Cell Guidelines, by Cyrus R. Kapadia, School of Medicine, Yale University, January 24, 2000.

Lovell-Badge, Robin (2001) "The Future for Stem Cell Research," *Nature*, 414: 88–91.

MacLean, Anne (1993) *The Elimination of Morality: Reflections on Utilitarianism and Bioethics*. London: Routledge.

McKay, Ron (2000) "Stem Cells – Hype and Hop,e, *Nature*, 406: 361–364.

Mc Lean, Margret R (2001) "Stem Cells: Shaping the Future in Public Policy." In Holland, Suzanne/ Kareb Lebacqz, and Laurie Zoloth (eds), *The Human Embryonic Stem Cell Debate*. Cambridge, Massachusetts: MIT Press, 2001.

Memmi, Dominique (2000) "Vers Une Confession Laique? La Nouvelle Administration Étatique des Corps." *Revue Francaise de Science Politique*, 50: 3–20.

Mulkay, Michael (1997) *The Embryo Research Debate. Science and Politics of Reproduction.* Cambridge University Press.

National Bioethics Advisory Commission (1999) *Ethical Issues in Human Stem Cell Research,* Volume I, p. 53. Bethesda, MD: Government Printing Office.

National Institutes of Health, Department of Health and Human Services, Public Health Service (2000) *Guidelines for Research Using Human Pluripotent Stem Cells.* Federal Register 51976 (August 25, 2000), Bethesda, Maryland: 2000b.

National Institutes of Health (1994) Report of The Human Embryo Research Panel. Bethesda (MD): NIH, September 27.

National Institutes of Health (2000a) *Stem Cells: A Primer.* Bethesda, Maryland.

Nelkin Dorothy., and M.Susan Lindee (1995) *The DNA Mystique. The Gene as a Cultural Icon,* Freeman: New York.

O´Malley, Peter (2000) "Uncertain Subjects: risks, Liberalism and Contract." *Economy and Society,* 29, 460–484.

Parekh Robert (1999) "Proteomics and Molecular Medicine." *Nature Biotechnology,* 17, 267–268.

Potter, Van Rensselaer (1971) *Bioethics: Bridge to the Future.* Englewood: Prentice Hall.

Rau, Johannes (2001) Rede bei der Sondersitzung des Deutschen Bundestages aus Anlass des Gedenktages für die Opfer des Nationalsozialismus, January 26.

Rose, Nikolas (2001) "The Politics of Life Itself" *Theory, Culture & Society,* 18, 1–30.

Rothman, David J (1991) *Strangers at the bedside. A history of how law and bioethics transformed medical decision making.* London: Basic Books.

Sass, Hans-Martin (ed) (1988) *Bioethik in den USA. Methoden, Themen, Positionen.* Berlin: Springer.

Shapin Steven/ Schaeffer Simon (1984) *Leviathan and the Air-Pump: Hobbes, Boyle, and the Experimental Life.* New York: Cambridge University Press.

Stiltner, Brian (2001) "Morality, Religion, and Public Bioethics: Shifting the Paradigm for the Public Discussion of Embryo Research and Human Cloning". In Lauritzen, Paul (ed), *Cloning and the Future of Human Embryo Research.* Oxford: Oxford University Press, 178–200.

Tauer, Carol (2001) "Responsibility and Regulation: Reproductive Technologies, Cloning, and Embryo Research." In Lauritzen, P. (ed), *Cloning and the Future of Human Embryo Research.* Oxford: Oxford University Press, 145–161.

The Israeli Academy of Sciences and Humanities (2001) Report on The Use of Embryonic Stem Cells for Therapeutic Research. August.

The President´s Council on Bioethics (2002) *Human Cloning and Human Dignity: An Ethical Inquiry. First Report of the Council.* Pre-publication version, July 10.

The Prohibition of Genetic Intervention Law No. 5759 (cloning on Human Beings and Genetic Modifications for Reproductive Cells) (1998) The Knesset of Israel.

Thomson, James A. (1998) et al., "Embryonic Stem Lines Derived from Human Blastocysts". *Science* 282 : 1145–1147.

Verfaillie, Catherine. M. et al. (2002) "Pluripotency of mesenchymal stem cells derived from adult marrow", *Nature* 418: 41–49.

Wolpert, Louis et al. (2002) Principles of Development. Second Edition, Oxford: Oxford University Press.

Vogel, Gretchen (1999) "Breakthrough of the Year: Capturing the Promise of Youth." *Science* 286: 2238–2239.

Zola, Irving (1972) "Medicine as an Institution of Social Control." *Sociological Review,* 20, 487–504, 1972.

Part IV

Biotechnology and Civil Society:
Case Studies

Introduction

J. Rogers Hollingsworth

Societies have long been troubled by how much to accept nature as it is, and how much to alter it to achieve some short-term goal. Over time, there have been increased efforts to change nature as societies have become more secular, and their technologies have become more complex and capable of having major effects. As a result of these efforts, there is now having a great deal of discourse about how safe it is to engage in genetic engineering of organisms, and what the social, economic, and political consequences are of genetically modifying organisms.

While the three papers in this section have strong implications for these issues, we should reflect on them within a larger comparative and historical context. We are living at a time when humans have more information about the world than ever before, and can transfer that information around the globe in only a matter of seconds. But information and knowledge are not the same thing. While we have much information about the world around us, our ability to understand this information is rather limited. Fortunately, these three papers provide an opportunity to assess how much knowledge our societies actually have about the substance and consequences of biotechnology.

The paper by Gísli Pálsson provides considerable insight about the biotechnology sector: the speed with which actors can acquire information (but their limited capacity to understand it), the eagerness of investors to profit from information about the health of a sizable population, and the gullibility of such investors. Pálsson's is an anthropological paper about an effort of a for-profit company (deCODE genetics) to develop a database containing the genealogies of Icelandic families, their medical records, and genotypes. One of the purposes of the data set was to identify and trace the genes which appear to occur with regularity within families and across generations. A former Harvard neurologist, Kári Stefánsson, in the late 1990s took the lead in forming deCODE genetics, which purchased medical records of Icelanders from the Icelandic Parliament. The company then obtained large sums of money from two large pharmaceutical companies—Hoffman-La Roche and Merck—and sold shares in the company to Icelanders as well as to investors around the world. The shares were listed on the NASDAQ Stock Exchange, and the price rose as high as $65.00 a share amidst great hype in what James D. Watson characterized as the "buy!—buy!—buy! days" (Watson, 2003: 319). Later, the price dropped to $1.55 and as of this writing, it is $2.20.

The development of the very complex, historical data set was based on several key assumptions. Iceland had a relatively homogeneous population on which there was rich demographic data extending back almost 500 years. With such a homogeneous population, it should be possible to obtain rich genetic insights about families for a number of common diseases. However, there is now increasing evidence that deCODE genetics was making questionable assumptions.

The Harvard population geneticist Richard Lewontin, as well as others, have reminded us that in most populations the gene pools are not only highly heterogeneous, but are constantly changing even when there is relatively little in-migration. We know from Pálsson's paper, as well as other studies, that there were visits over the centuries by "slaves, pirates, fishermen, and travellers" (also see Árnason et al, 2000). Moreover, populations are subject to continuous transfers of genes from unrelated species through viruses and other cellular particles. As Lewontin points out, all life forms—both plants and animals—are in potential genetic contact, and genetic exchanges among them are continuous. Thus, genetic transposition takes place not only among organisms within species but among distantly related organisms (Lewontin, 2001a, 2001c: Chapter 5).

Certain assumptions of the deCODE group seemed to challenge some of our best scientific understanding about the relationship between genes and diseases. For some years, there has been considerable hype in the biotech world about how first this and then that gene codes for a particular disease. However, fifty years after the discovery of the structure of DNA, the scientific community still does not know much about the function of most of the different nucleotides of genes. John Sulston, a recipient of last years Nobel Prize in Physiology or Medicine, and Georgina Ferry have made the sobering argument that the scientific community still has only a primitive understanding about the relationship between genes and disease (Sulston and Ferry, 2002: Chapter 7).

Scientists estimate that of the 3 billion nucleotides in the human genome, approximately 95 percent are junk DNA without a definable function. There are estimates that approximately 3 million nucleotides in the DNA of any single individual differ from those of any other individual. Not only is no individual free of nucleotides associated with common diseases but in any population the gene pool is very heterogeneous.

Now that the Human Genome project has been completed and the scientific community acknowledges that it has a poor understanding of the connection between genes and disease, scientists tell us that they knew all along that genes only specify the sequence of amino acids. Therefore, in order to understand the linkage between genes and most common diseases, we now must understand the sequence of proteins—a much larger project involving far more scientists and billions of dollars. As Sulston and Ferry observe, ". . . . we are right at the beginning, not at the end; we don't know what most of the genes look like, or when or where they are expressed. . . . Once we've found the genes, we need to work out what proteins they produce and to understand their time and place of expression. And until this is done, the linkage between genes and disease will be poorly understood" (Sulston and Ferry, 2002: 248, 256–257; also Lewontin, 2001c).

Meantime, an Icelandic scientist has now uncovered evidence that characterizing the Icelandic population as relatively homogeneous was basically incorrect. Einar Árnason of the Institute of Biology of the University of Iceland has recently published a study based on a systematic analysis of the primary data from 26 European populations and demonstrates surprisingly and rather conclusively that the Icelanders have been among the most genetically heterogeneous European populations. According to Árnason, those who had calculated the homogeneity of the Icelanders were using data involving mitochondrial DNA, databases now known to be filled with error (Árnason, 2003). Susan Lindee writing in *Science*—one of the world's leading scientific journals—observes that Icelanders "were conned into a corporate scheme that was the equivalent of selling swampland, entering into agreements that profoundly compromised their privacy. . . . the deCODE story is about speculative hype; rapid profits based on inaccurate information; and disadvantaged, ill-informed patient consumers" (Lindee, 2003: 433).

Of course the deCODE data set is not necessarily worthless, but it remains to be seen what the scientific community might do with it. It could prove useful for various types of epidemiological studies, and of course it has the potential for being a rich data source for social historians and anthropologists who want to study individuals and their families over long time periods—subjects very far from what most deCODE investors had in mind!

The next paper, by Elizabeth Ettorre (like the one by Pálsson) is a reminder that we are having a rather vigorous rebirth of eugenics, but eugenics with a style very different from that of the first half of the twentieth century. While scientists believe that our health is shaped by a combination of environmental and genetic factors, it is the genetic ones which received the greatest attention in recent years. We need to be mindful, however, that although there are diseases which appear to be triggered by a single genetic disorder, most genetic-based diseases are polygenic in nature. The disorders associated with a single gene are relatively rare, but with genetic screening and counseling it is possible to identify them. These are the ones which are of primary concern to Ettore.

One such example is thalássemia, a pernicious blood disorder more common in Asia Minor than in other regions. Thalássemia frequently results in death before age twenty-one. For some time, it has been possible not only to identify those who are carriers of this disorder but also to screen fetuses during the first trimester for the disorder. Ettore also points out that it has become possible to screen fetuses for other disorders associated with a single gene. When a fetus is diagnosed as having such a disorder, very painful and traumatic issues arise. She discusses in some detail how the practice of genetic screening of fetuses (and their termination) varies substantially from society to society. As her paper does not focus on within-society variation, it would be useful in future studies to have data on how screening within societies varies by income, education, and ethnicity.

Whereas the Ettorre paper has focused primarily on single-gene disorders, a number of scientists have made very strong claims in recent years about genes associated with a variety of diseases which are in fact polygenic in nature. Indeed, most of the common diseases in advanced industrial societies are polygenic: diabetes, cancer, heart disease, and hypertension, to mention but a few. For some years, there has been considerable competition among scientists as they have announced that they have found a gene for a particular disease. Having identified the gene, scientists and the research organizations in which they work—or some other firm, have then moved quickly to patent a test for determining whether an individual has that particular genetic disorder. Many in the scientific community and biotechnology industry have then engaged in a great deal of self promotion, though most of the tests have done little or nothing to advance the level of health of either an entire society or a single individual.

Most genes associated with a polygenic disorder tend to have only a small (or no) detectable effect in causing a disease. Whether an individual has a particular disease associated with a polygenic disorder depends on the other genes which interact with the so-called disordered gene, as well as with how these genes collectively are associated with a host of environmental factors. With a number of polygenic diseases, combinations of genetic factors tend to interact with *multiple* environmental factors before a disorder results. In short, scientists can identify certain environmental factors and particular genes as associated with a particular disease, but with the exception of a few relatively rare diseases (e.g., single genetic disorders), scientists cannot predict from genetic information that an individual will have a particular disease. True, if an individual knows she has a genetic component known to be associated with a particularly disease, she might modify her diet, engage in more exercise, etc.—doing most of the things it is prudent to do whether or not one has a particular genetic disorder.

The search for new genes reminds one of tulipomania in seventeenth century Holland (Lewontin, 2001c: 159). Biotechnology has become a major industrial sector in the US and part of Europe. Meantime there is an increasing blurring of the boundaries between biotech firms and university laboratories in the life sciences. Numerous university professors own significant amounts of stock in the firms which hold patents for tests to determine whether a patient has a gene associated with a disorder. The same kind of relationship exists between university professors and the firms which have developed equipment for sequencing DNA and proteins. This has created increasing concerns among some of our most distinguished scientists about the degree to which commercial activities are driving the research agendas of the scientific community (Kornberg, 1997) But will the promises of the fanfare and self-promotion be realized? Recently, John Bell, Regius Professor of Medicine at the University of Oxford, Aravinda Chakravarti of the Johns Hopkins University School of Medicine, and Peter Little of the University of South Wales suggested that it is likely to be many years before even our best clinicians have an understanding of the complex genetic and environmental factors causally associated with common human diseases—echoing the views of Sulston and Ferry (Bell, 2003; Chakravati and Little, 2003).

If the contents of the Pálsson and Ettorre papers are mild reminders that we should not be carried away by the hype and optimism of those who think that a genetic approach to improving the world is just around the corner, the Hindmarsh paper is a much stronger voice in expressing skepticism and pessimism about the consequences of using various biotechnological tools to transform nature.

The primary focus of the Hindmarsh paper is on networks of large agribusiness firms as well as other large-scale corporate actors who have, for some decades, been attempting to develop new strains of crops with high yields, many of which were expected to offer resistance to pests and/or weeds. Emphasizing many of the undesirable consequences of these activities, Hindmarsh's paper reflects a harsh indictment of large-scale actors who engage in efforts to alter nature in pursuit of corporate profits.

Because of its strong ideological framework, the Hindmarsh paper is very provocative, but serves the useful purpose of forcing us to think about a set of major problems not so commonly on scholarly agendas:

(1) Is genetic modification of plants and animals a recent practice or have humans been practicing genetic modification of organisms for thousands of year? And if some of the processes have long been around, what is it about the genetic modification of plants and animals in our our age which is so disturbing to many?

(2) For those who find the genetic modification of organisms objectionable, do they oppose all such practices or just certain ones, and if there are exceptions, on what basis do they rest?

(3) There are a host of interrelated questions about the governance of activities involving the genetic modification of organisms. If these technologies are to be tolerated under any circumstances, how should our societies determine who should be permitted to engage in these practices, and for what purpose? What should the decision making processing for such activities be? Should there be some kind of democratic process involving these activities? Since these practices can easily have global consequences, how does a world made up of nation states and independent actors develop some kind of broad public input to shape these decision making processes? What specific governance arrangements should be devised for coordinating these activities (Hollingsworth and Boyer, 1997; Hollingsworth, Schmitter, and Streeck, 1994)?

Most of these are not problems which the Hindmarsh paper directly confronts. But a deconstruction of his paper leads one to confront these issues more explicitly, as he is clearly—and in some cases very appropriately—quite concerned with the way these practices are being conducted. Even if we share Hindmarsh's concerns about the scale of genetic modification in our own day, it is important that we recognize that humans have been modifying organisms genetically for hundreds of centuries by crossing closely related species which do not normally interbreed in nature. But in recent years, scientists have been able to take the gene of most any specie and transfer it to another specie. In contrast to Hindmarsh, James D. Watson of DNA fame, applauds the recent advances in genetic engineering and draws a distinction between the historic and new practices as "the difference between agriculture's genetic sledgehammer and biotech's genetic tweezers (Watson, 2003: 157–158).

The Hindmarsh paper appropriately reminds us that engineering projects to alter the course of nature can have unintended consequences. Two questions frequently emerge in these debates, and these are embedded in the Hindmarsh paper. Does modifying organisms genetically pose a threat to our health or our environment. What are the effects of these practices on the political, social and economic environments of the affected areas. Of course, assessment of these consequences may be difficult to discern—possibly centuries after some intervention. In short, there are the tensions between short-term assessments and those of a long-term nature.

For those who are generally offended by laboratory techniques to modify organisms, are there conditions under which they would relax their hostility? If so, these need to be made explicit. Had the techniques of genetic engineering been available during the 19th century potato blight in Ireland which resulted in a large scale famine and the death of thousands of individuals, would modifying the potato by genetic engineering have been acceptable? We know in our own day that through genetic engineering techniques scientists have been able to reduce the probability of blight by various plant viruses.

At the present time, there are diseases such as malaria and schistosomiasis which lead to early deaths for millions of individuals. Scientists funded by many of the same organizations criticized in the Hindmarsh paper are attempting to minimize the incidence of these diseases by using genetic engineering practices. Moreover, the effort to develop vaccines against smallpox, polio, measles, diphtheria, typhoid fever AIDS and other diseases involve altering the immune system of individuals, though these activities are not as invasive as altering the genome of an organism. For those who take a purist stand against altering nature, do they also oppose this kind of biological engineering?

The three papers in this section turn our attention on a host of major problems for our age, and for this reason they collectively are highly useful for focusing our attention on several critical problems: What is our capacity to alter the course of nature to control disease and hunger? As we attempt to modify the course of nature with the technological tools at our disposal, can we assess the costs (social, economic, and political) of such interventions? The papers clearly demonstrate that we have enormous information at our disposal about rapidly developing technologies. But our societies are without the wisdom and knowledge to make the proper choices about the uses of the technologies that have been developed.

References

Árnason, Einar, H. Sigurgislason, and E. Benedikz. 2000. "Genetic Homogeneity of Icelanders: Fact or Fiction," *Nature Genetics*, 25: 373–374.

Árnason, Einar. 2003. "Genetic Heterogeneity of Icelanders," *Annals of Human Genetics*, January, 67: 5–16.

Bell, John I. 2003. "The Double Helix in Clinical Practice," *Nature*, January 23, 421: 414–416.

Chakravati, Aravinda, and Peter Little. 2003. "Nature, Nurture, and Human Disease," *Nature*, January 23, 421: 412–414.

Hollingsworth, J. Rogers, and Robert Boyer. 1997. *Contemporary Capitalism: The Embeddedness of Institutions*. New York: Cambridge University Press.

Hollingsworth, J. Rogers, Philippe Schmitter, and Wolfgang Streeck. 1994. *The Governance of Capitalist Economies*. New York: Oxford University Press.

Lewontin, Richard. 1992. "The Dream of the Human Genome," *New York Review of Books*, May 28. 39: 31–40.

Lewontin, Richard, 2001a. "After the Genome, What Then?" *New York Review of Books*, July 19. 48: 36–37.

Lewontin, Richard, 2001b. "Genes in the Food," *New York Review of Books*, June 21. 48: 81–84.

Lewontin, Richard. 2001c. *It Ain't Necessarily So*. New York: New York Review of Books.

Lindee, M. Susan. 2003. "Watson's World," *Science*, April 18, 300: 432–434.

Kornberg, Arthur. 1997. "Biochemistry at Stanford, Biotechnology at DNAX." Oral history interviews conducted by Sally Smith Hughes, Program in the History of the Biosciences and Biotechnology, Regional Oral History Office, Bancroft Library, University of California Berkeley.

Sulston, John, and Georgina Ferry. 2002. *The Common Thread: A Story of Science, Politics, Ethics and the Human Genome*. London: Bantam Press.

Watson, James D. 2003. *DNA: The Secret of Life*. New York: Alfred A. Knopf.

10

The Icelandic Biogenetic Project

Gísli Pálsson

In December 1998, the Icelandic Parliament passed a bill authorizing the construction of a national Health Sector Database. The central idea of that project is the assembly of medical records for the Icelandic population. The company deCode Genetics which outlined original plans for the Database received the license to construct it, in return for a fee. Founded in 1996, it operates in Iceland, although funded by venture capital funds co-ordinated in the United States. It has grown rapidly, employing about 600 people at the time of writing, a significant figure in a small economy traditionally focused on fishing. The Health Sector Database represents the core of a larger project, the Icelandic Biogenetic Project, that allows for the combination, under specific conditions and for specific purposes, of medical records, genetic information, and family histories. Similar projects are now under way in several other contexts, including Australia, Britain, Canada, Estonia, Norway, Singapore, South Africa, Sweden, and Tonga. One of the lessons of Iceland, deCode Genetics, and the Biogenetic Project lies in confronting the complexity of both the mapping procedures involved and the debates and conflicts that have surrounded the emergence of new modes of connection between cutting-edge research, cultural values, finance and politics (Pálsson and Rabinow 1999, 2003; Pálsson and Harðardóttir 2002). An important avenue to explore is that of the role of key metaphors. What do people mean when they speak of human genome research in terms of mapping—of charting genealogies and deciphering the "codes" of genetic material—and what are the implications of such a metaphor for human self-understanding? A series of recent publications address the importance of such a question from a variety of perspectives within anthropology, biology and history of science; see, for example, Rabinow 1999, Kay 2000, Keller 2000.

This article discusses the mapping concepts and strategies employed by deCode Genetics and the Biogenetic Project for the purpose of tracing the genetic background of a number of common diseases. I discuss two kinds of mapping involving, respectively, genealogical and genetic data. Each of the two mapping cultures of genealogists and human geneticists, I argue, has its own discourses and trajectories. Collectively, however, the cartographies of genomes and genealogies illustrate the intensification of the medical gaze (Foucault 1973) with the development of biotechnology and the "medicalization of kinship" (Finkler 2000).

Recent advances in the mapping of the human genome remind one of the 19th century "scramble" for colonies. Now that most of the habitat of the globe has been charted, documented and conquered, the West is increasingly turning its attention and interests to the "remotest corners" of living organism, in particular the human genome (Haraway 2000). Perhaps, though, the development of cosmic maps, beyond the Milky Way, represents a more appropriate parallel to genomic maps than projections of Earth and the entire solar system. Both projects have significantly altered the scale and meaning of the cartographic enterprise. Never has "anything," to paraphrase Wilford (2000: 463), encompassed so much and so little space; in the case of cosmic maps, the subject of mapmaking is infinitely larger than the maps themselves, while for genomic maps the reverse is the case. The cartography of the human genome, with the Columbuses of the New World of modern genetics charting the most minute contours of the human body armed with the perspective of the external observer, underlines the radical separation of nature and society characteristic of modernity. Such a separation was made possible thanks to the development of perspective and positivist science during the Renaissance and the Enlightenment that were to mould every kind of western scholarship. In a relatively brief period nature became a quantifiable, three-dimensional universe appropriated by humans. This "anthropocracy," to use Panofsky's term (1991), represented a radical departure from the enclosed universe of the Aristotelians constituted by the earth and its seven surrounding spheres. A related textual metaphor of the genomic era is that of the "Book of life." Nowadays, it is almost taken for granted that the organic phenomena of genes represent textual codes. This is, in essence, one of the central ideas of "mapping."[1] The mapping cultures of the twentieth century seem to have some basic ideas in common, including the metaphor of cartographies, a metaphor that echoes the modernist notion of discovery, expansion, and mastery.

The notion of "maps" is obviously used here in a fairly broad sense, for any kind of visual surrogates of spatial relations, including the social space of family histories (genealogies). To think of the tracing of family histories in terms of mapping is not as farfetched, however, as it may sound. Ingold points out that "the generation of persons within spheres of nurture, and of places in the land, are not separate processes but one and the same" and, therefore, "as Leach has put it, 'kinship is geography'" (Ingold 2000: 149). In fact, some representations of kinship have drawn upon spatial imagery. Medieval European representation of genealogies experimented with various means of visual imagery one of which was that of a flowing stream or a river. An interesting aspect of this experimentation, as we will see, was the theological tension between descending and ascending modes of representing family trees, between "going down" into the soil and "rising up" to the sky. This tension, Klapisch-Zuber points out, "obliges us to ask questions about the connections between language or text and the logic of graphic means of expression which are used to give a visual account of it" (1991: 112).

The deCode Project: Reykjavik versus Manhattan

Current work at deCode Genetics, independent of the planned Health Sector Database, typically begins with a contract with one or more physicians specializing in a particular disease with a potentially genetic basis. Through a contract with the pharmaceutical company Hoffman-La Roche, deCode Genetics focuses on research on twelve common diseases. In their practice over the years, the physicians have constructed a list of patients with the particular symptoms in question. This list is passed on in an encrypted form to a research team within the company, which, in turn, runs the information provided through its computers, juxtaposing or comparing patients' lists and genealogical records by means of specialized software developed by the company. The aim is to trace the genes responsible for the apparent fact that the disease in question occurs in families. Such an analysis may show, for example, that of an original list of about 1,000 patients, 500 or so cluster in a few families. In the next step, the physicians affiliated with the research team collect blood samples from patients and some of their close relatives for DNA analysis. In the final stage of the research, statisticians evaluate the results of the genetic analysis, attempting to narrow down in probabilistic terms the genes responsible for the disease. In the words of the leader of one of the research teams, "we track the recombination of DNA through each generation, using cross-overs to further localize the location." In practice, this is a highly complex interactive process combining different kinds of mapping, in particular genetic maps indicating genetic distances on a chromosome and more realistic physical mapping. Moreover, strategies of gene hunting are adopted and revised both intuitively in the laboratory or at the computer screen and in formal or informal meetings.

These procedures are not, of course, unique to deCode Genetics, not even in the Icelandic context. However, with the Biogenetic Project (see Fig. 1), with the inclusion of the Health Sector Database and family histories, the power of genetic and epidemiological analyses may grow exponentially, with far larger samples, more generations, and more families. The addition of the national medical records available since 1915 allows for the exploration of a set of new questions on the interaction among a number of variables apart from genetic makeup and genealogical connections, including variables pertaining to lifestyle, physical and social environments, the use of particular medicine, and degree and kind of hospitalization. The results may be useful, according to the designers of the project and the medical authorities, for pharmaceutical companies and for the medical service, yielding information about potential drugs, particular genes or proteins, and possible preventive measures in terms of consumption and lifestyle.

Among the many questions raised by Icelandic biotechnology and informatics and their articulation with local and global worlds of commerce is the following: What, if anything, makes the Icelandic gene pool a valuable commodity? Spokespersons for deCode Genetics emphasize that due to its demographic history the Icelandic population may have certain appeals to investors in genetic research. As a result of the successive reduction of the population during times of plagues and famine, they argue, the Icelandic gene pool is fairly homogeneous; branches of the family tree, so to speak, have repeatedly been cut off with a limited number of lineages (*ættir*; "clans" or "families") surviving to the present time. Moreover, geographic isolation has inhibited the replenishment of lost genetic diversity via immigration. Icelanders, however, are no genetic Robinson Crusoes. Throughout its written history, Iceland has regularly been visited by slaves, pirates, fishermen, and travellers. Recent research in biological anthropology (see Helgason *et al.* 2000, Helgason 2001), based on DNA analysis and demographic studies, indeed indicates that while Icelanders are more homogeneous than most other European populations they nevertheless contain a surprising amount of genetic diversity for a small island population.

Whatever the genetic and historical facts of the Icelandic gene pool, the Biogenetic Project has been the center of a controversy. Opposition to the Project seems motivated by several concerns, including potential infringements of personal autonomy and privacy, the ethics of consent, and the threat of biopiracy. Much of the heat of the opposition seems driven by an apparent sense among physicians of rather suddenly lacking authority in the biomedical domain, of losing dominion over public information largely constructed and controlled by them in the past. The Icelandic opposition, thus, above all reveals concerns about potentially dramatic changes in the practices and structures of Icelandic bioscience and medicine. Some academics have alleged that the restrictions of access to information and resources implied in the privileged contract of deCode Genetics with the Icelandic state will inevitably result in the stagnation of bioscience. Thus, the sub-text of some of the

Figure 10.1
The Icelandic Biogenetic Project

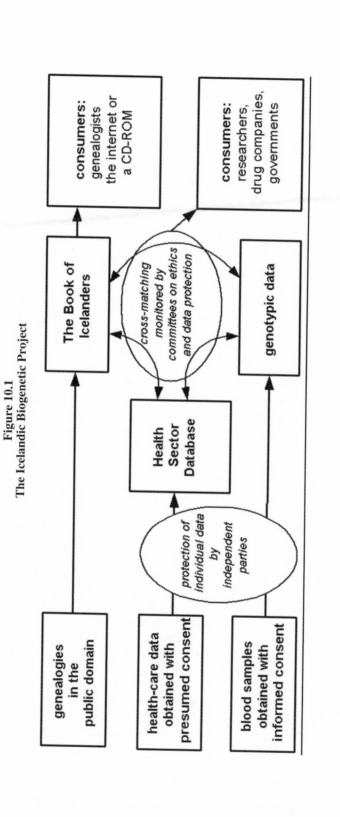

debates centers on where cutting-edge research on the Icelandic human genome occurs today and where it should be located in the future. Understandably, proponents of the project represent a more complex professional and social spectrum than the opponents, given the fact that they by far outnumber the critics. Those who have contributed op-ed pieces in support of the project emphasize concerns rather different from those of the opponents. deCode Genetics and the Biogenetic Project, they argue, will make possible much more biomedical research in Iceland, creating many new positions for scientists and laboratory assistants both within the company and at the University of Iceland. deCode Genetics, it is often pointed out, has attracted much investment from abroad and created numerous jobs for Icelandic scientists, many of whom in the absence of deCode Genetics would have been forced to seek employment abroad.

Apparently, the deCode Genetics project largely appeals to scientists, investors, shareholders and the public imagination on the grounds that the Icelandic population has been small (275,000 today), relatively homogenous, comparatively isolated, and passionate about keeping medical and genealogical records. An important asset for the Biogenetic Project is the availability of relatively detailed and complete family histories. Frisk Software in Reykjavík originally began the construction of a genealogical database on Icelanders early in the 1990s, starting with three censuses (1703, 1801, and 1910) that covered the whole country at sufficiently different points in time, to minimize overlap, as well as the up-to-date national records (*Þjóðskrá*). Later on, deCode Genetics signed an agreement with Frisk Software to speed up the construction of the database, now called the "Book of Icelanders", by adding information from a variety of available sources. The database now comprises twelve censuses taken from 1703 to 1930. In late 2002, the database was "published" on the internet (www.islendingabok.is) for restricted use by genealogical enthusiasts. Another version will be issued to deCode Genetics (Pálsson 2002). In the latter case, no names will be included, only numbers or IDs that allow for the combination of different datasets on a limited basis for particular purposes. A complex process of encryption, surveillance, and monitoring is designed to prevent illegitimate use of the data. Such a database, it is argued, combined with genetic and medical data, provides an invaluable historical dimension to the search for the presumed genetic causes of common diseases.

It has taken about four years for a team of researchers and computer programmers to compile all of the information contained in the Book of Icelanders and to design the necessary programs for displaying and analyzing it. Approximately 650 thousand people, less than a half of the total number of people born in Iceland since the Norse settlement, are recorded in the genealogical database. The whole point, of course, is not simply to record individuals but rather to be able to connect them to each other. The "connectivity index", the proportion of documented genealogical links between the individuals and their parents in the database, is close to 85%. Not only are there empty spaces in available records, there are lots of errors, too. Adoptions and wrong parenting pose a particular problem. Sometimes, families have "purified" their records, possibly to prevent disclosing information about teenage mothers or to avoid an image of inbreeding. Finally, at times the makers of the database are faced with evaluating conflicting pieces of information. Skúlason, the chief architect of the genealogical database, has likened the task to "working out a puzzle the size of a soccer field, with half of the pieces missing and the rest randomly scattered," a gigantic task indeed.

The founding premise of deCode Genetics is that the company is uniquely placed to achieve major breakthroughs in identifying the genes involved in the most common diseases of the advanced industrial world. deCode's vision, or program, of how to exploit available resources to the fullest is spelled out by Kári Stefánsson (Director) and Jeff Gulcher (Vice President, Research and Development). While the nuclear family has proved to be a useful unit in the study of monogenic disorders, they argue, for complex or "polygenic" disorders that are "sporadic," skipping generations, "isolated populations with strong founder effects" are essential (Gulcher and Stefánsson 1998: 523). For the decode team, the royal road to identifying the underlying cause of pathology is through linkage analysis, the aim of which is

> to determine whether there exist pieces of the genome that are passed down through each of several families with multiple patients in a pattern that is consistent with a particular inheritance model and that is unlikely to occur by chance alone. The most important asset of linkage analysis is its ability to screen the entire genome with a framework set of markers; this makes it a hypothesis-independent and cost-effective approach to finding disease genes (Gulcher et al. 2001: 264).

For the spokespersons of deCode's project, then, a relatively homogenous population with good genealogical as well as medical records (for precise phenotypic identification) is the ideal experimental site for linkage, linkage being, in their view, the ideal method of analysis.

Not only have critics of the Biogenetic Project raised concerns about its social implications, there are doubts as well about its scientific merits and rewards. Both the application of linkage analysis for the purpose of understanding complex diseases and the choice of relatively homogeneous and isolated populations remain contested. Thus, Risch suggests (2000) that while multiplex families and linkage studies will have a role to play on the future agenda, "instead of family-based controls, unrelated controls will emerge as a more powerful and efficient approach" and, moreover, sampling families "of varying ethnicity will . . . be advantageous from the perspective of enhancing evidence of causality as well as identifying genetic and/or environmental modifying factors" (Risch 2000: 855). Similar arguments were raised in a recent news feature in *Nature* (2000(406): 340–342) under the title "Manhattan versus Reykjavik." While modern biotechnology is shrouded in "genohype" (see Fleising 2001) and it is often difficult to disentangle the real, the virtual, and the rhetoric, theoretical and methodological issues such as these should, of course, be evaluated in terms of actual results. Some of the results of the deCode project may be impressive, including the mapping of Parkinson's disease (Gulcher *et al.* 2001: 266–7) and the demonstration of a strong familial component to longevity (Gudmundsson *et al.* 2000), but the significant breakthroughs repeatedly promised by the company and its main corporate financier, Hoffman-La Roche, have failed to appear. One possibility is that the linkage paradigm is in crisis. Another possibility is that success is just around the corner.

Mapping Relatedness

Given the centrality of familial relations in research projects such as those of deCode Genetics, it is pertinent to ask: What does relatedness involve and how is it understood and represented? With the works of Schneider (1984), Strathern (1992) and some others, the "classic" anthropological issue of kinship, of mapping relations through descent, was denaturalized and destabilized. Kinship, it was argued, is not necessarily "the same thing" in different contexts, to be routinely disentangled with the formal tools of the "genealogical method." Moreover, kinship, it seems, or rather *relatedness*, that is bonding deemed to be significant by the people involved (Carsten 2000), is best regarded as a complex *processual* thing, not a fixed, abstract geometry of social relationships. Relatedness, in sum, is continually "under construction." To some extent, recent developments in biotechnology have provoked such a conclusion. With artificial reproductive models, gene therapy, and genetic engineering, relatedness becomes not simply a matter of genealogical history but also a matter of consumer choice in a quite literal sense.

While, however, new reproductive technologies have challenged the structures of kinship, they should, perhaps, not be overrated. As Laqueur points out (2001: 79) in his survey and evaluation of the "strangeness" of connectedness in the age of sperm banks, ovum brokerages, surrogate motherhood, and similar reproductive techniques and practices:

> This strangeness . . . is not born of technology. It is at the root of kinship: heterodox ways of making families—high, low, or no technology—only expose it for what it is, as if our own, Western, structures were exposed to the scrutiny anthropologists more usually reserve for other people.

Laqueur concludes (p. 94) that "so far blood and flesh, mother and father, and sire and dam are as clear or as muddled as they have ever been." Somewhat paradoxically, while kinship analysis is in a state of flux, molecular biology has given genetic links a renewed, supreme status where there is little room for culture and social construction. And kinship diagrams are back on the scene, "deeper" and more elegant than before.

It may be tempting to think of genetic and genealogical models as being "pure" descriptions of relations and histories, untainted by the contexts that produce them. This is clearly not the case, however. The algebra of the kinship diagram, as Bouquet argues (2000: 187), has "its own historicity, making it an anything but neutral instrument." This historicity is manifested in a family resemblance of family trees, of "pedigree thinking," in a variety of disciplines. Darwin attempted to locate *homo sapiens* in the genealogy of life, a project, as Beer shows, that reflected the ideals of his society and literature: "He sought the restoration of familial ties, the discovery of a lost inheritance, the restitution of pious memory, a genealogical enterprise" (1986: 221). Just as genealogical diagrams were essential for tracking the paths of human nobility, Darwin reasoned, they were indispensable for naturalists interested in describing relations among other living things.[2]

Klapisch-Zuber (1991) provides an intriguing analysis of the genealogy and politics of lineage imagery in medieval European family histories. Medieval obsession with genealogical details and their visual representation, informed by the politics of inheritance and succession among European elites, is nicely demonstrated by some family diagrams drawn on rolls of parchment; avoiding the interruption of a new page, some of them were no less than 10 meters in length. Over time European lineage imagery was subject to much experimenting. One powerful image was that of the flowering tree which underlined the joyful proliferation of the lineage, drawing its vital energy from the earth and stretching into the divine light in the heavens. Such a horticultural metaphor appeared in various forms from at least the 11th century onward, but it was only in the 15th century that it acquired its canonical imagery, with a founding ancestor in the trunk of a tree and his descendants scattered above among its branches. An alternative imagery turned the tree upside-down, with the trunk in the sky. Such an image is reflected in Latin terminology of filiation (*descendentes, progenies*, etc.). A lower position in such a scheme not only indicated a chronologically later moment, it also suggested deterioration or demotion, a departure from the honored distant past. The descending imagery both documented the continuity of the lineage, the direct line between the present and the past, and the humble status of contemporary humans underlined in eschatological, Christian schemes.

Despite its joyfulness and its success in representing and reinforcing kinship, the ascending metaphor of the flowering tree was seen to be theologically problematic. Given the need to project the past in glorious terms, the image of the growing tree, with the ancestors (and the gods) in the soil and degenerated contemporaries in the heavens, was bound to be met with resistance if not disgust. The tree metaphor, in fact, was riddled with tensions. Not only was there tension between the competing images of ascending and descending, the ups and downs of kinship, there was also tension between the languages of roots and branches. One way of resolving the tension between the ascending image of the tree and the linguistic usage of "descent" was to place the roots of the family at the top of the image. And yet, such an image suggested multiple origins, not a single divine source, with the roots spreading outwards in different directions. Despite the theological complications and the botanical absurdity of the image of a tree that extends its roots into the sky, the metaphor not only survived but flowered into the present.

The medieval imagery of the tree was not exclusively focused on "blood" connections. Interestingly, 16th century genealogical trees showing the kings of Navarre in Portugal included their wives on discrete branches, mixing blood relationships and marital alliances in the same imageries. Nor should the tree imagery itself be taken for granted. In fact, as Klapisch-Zuber points out (1991: 110), it is "quite possible to adopt other graphic systems, simpler but equally effective, for visually presenting the obsessive repetition of genealogical descriptions." Rival metaphors, including those of the human body and the house, appeared from time to time in artistic representations of relatedness.

Medieval Iceland had its own projects of mapping relations and identities, embedded in church records and population registers (Grétarsdóttir Bender 2002). Frequently these documents offered in passing brief notes or commentaries about particular personalities, usually in the past tense:

> He was intelligent and knowledgeable about many things . . . . He had a tumor the size of a ptarmigan egg on one of his eyelids and became blind on that eye (a man born in 1802).

Often there are comments about a person's character and social history:

> He lost his priesthood due to premature intercourse (*offljóta samsængun*) with his wife (a man born in 1699).

Many of the comments indicate concerns with inbreeding, incest, and adultery:

> She had four children with her brother and killed them all, except the youngest one (a woman born in 1799).

Sometimes the records indicate a folk theory of the continuity of familial characteristics, the passing of individual traits from one generation to another:

Among his descendants, certain family characteristics have persisted, including tremendous energy, endurance and dexterity (a man born in 1755).

The idea that a person's character, capabilities and dispositions are partly determined by what one would now translate as "inheritance" appears early on in some of the Icelandic sagas. Thus *Njál's saga* (*Íslendinga sögur og þættir*, 1987, Ch. 42), one of the major Family Sagas, asserts that "nurture accounts for one quarter" of a person's dispositions (*fjórðungi bregður til fósturs*).[3]

Osteoarthritis: A Case Study

To illustrate the deCode approach to the exploration of the role of familial relations for explaining differential occurrence of common diseases, it is useful to focus on the team studying osteoarthritis (hereafter "OA"), one of the most common diseases of humans often affecting joints in fingers, knees and hips.[4] The methods used are also discussed in some of the publications derived from the deCode project (see, for example, Ingvarsson *et al.* 2000). The OA-team is one of the more established teams within the company, with about ten permanent members, mostly biologists and technical laboratory assistants, collaborating closely with several statisticians and two physicians specializing in OA. Their project started three years ago with the initiative of the physicians, then the pharmaceutical company Hoffman-La Roche arrived on the scene, and a contract was signed with the clinical collaborators, focusing on two particular phenotypes of the disease, OA of the fingers and hips. Later on, the study of OA of the knees was also incorporated.

Often, it has been assumed that OA "simply" comes with age and drudgery. Indeed, the Icelandic term for osteoarthritis, *slitgigt*, refers to the kind of arthritis that develops as people become "worn down" during the life course. When the deCode project started it was assumed that there was some underlying genetic factor, since siblings were known to have a higher risk than others of hip replacement. However, no one had successfully "cracked" a complex disease like OA or, in other words, identified the genetic factors involved in the phenotype. The identification of families with the right phenotypes, obviously the critical starting point in work of this kind, is somewhat problematic due to the nature of available sources. S.E. Stefánsson explains:

> It's not easy to find well-defined families. One of the problems with past records is that diagnoses often were poor. People didn't know the difference between rheumatoid arthritis and osteoarthritis.

"By using the 'Book of Icelanders,'" however, he suggests, his team is able "to show that OA is inherited, there is a founder effect. Simply by going back one generation after another. Patient groups have fewer founders than others. They are significantly different from control groups."

Having established a familial connection, the OA-team has set out to locate the genetic factors involved. S.E. Stefánsson elaborates on the relative advantage of the deCode Genetics team thanks to the "deep" genealogy of the Book of Icelanders:

> Most other groups are looking at sib pairs. They have less resolution than we have for linkage analysis as they don't have the genealogies. We only need to know how people are related. . . .

By running their encrypted patient lists (of people diagnosed with osteoarthritis) against the encrypted version of the Book of Icelanders, the OA-team explores "how people are related." Knowing the genealogical relationships, establishing meiotic distances (the number of links separating any two persons in a pedigree) among the patients, the researchers seek to confirm and narrow down candidate regions, i.e. regions with genes whose protein products are assumed to affect the disease.

Figure 10.2, which was drawn by the osteoarthritis team, explores genealogical relationships among a group of patients, in this case two pairs of sisters severely affected by osteoarthritis. The aim, of course, is to trace the genes responsible for the fact that osteoarthritis tends to occur in certain families. The numbers in Figure 10.3 show markers and alleles (alleles being the alternative forms of a gene or DNA sequence at a specific chromosomal location). Thus, the sister-pair on the left have allele 8 in common, possibly from one of the grandparents.

The "Allegro" software developed by deCode Genetics identifies common alleles and calculates lod-scores (z), the likelihood of genetic linkage between loci (unique chromosomal locations defining the position of individual genes or DNA sequences). The osteoarthritis team start by genotyping the DNA, using around 1000 markers, which are dispersed through out the genome. The alleles from the genotypes are then used to calculate the sharing of the genetic material between related patients. The results, displayed as lod-scores, guide them to the regions in the chromosome were they expect to find mutations. The findings from the gene hunt are passed on to the company's statisticians who evaluate every now and then how the search is going.

While S.E. Stefánsson is confident about his project, claiming that so far he has "the highest lod-score reported," he emphasizes that he is looking for more than a few genes:

> There are many mutations throughout the genome. And there are a number of mutations behind each joint [fingers, hips, and knees], causing the disease. We suspect there are 5 to 10 genes behind each joint.

When pressed about genetic determinism, interaction among genes, and the role of environmental factors, S.E. Stefánsson maintains that while OA is "clearly genetic" since it runs in families, it is a complex disease: "Osteoartritis is probably an interaction between genes. The environment probably doesn't matter much." Sometimes, the team has "genotyped hundreds and hundreds of samples without any lod-scores; everything is just flat." One of the problems is that of perceptual bias:

> The problem when you have a candidate gene is that you tend to shift your attention towards it. It's not unbiased. This might have been distracting me . . . . I spent months for nothing. I was absolutely convinced. We are getting more and more convinced now of a perceptual bias. Everyone in the business does this. You are literally stuck.

Occasionally the statistical results run counter to the expectations of team members who speak of statisticians "slaughtering" their lod-scores:

> In November, the statisticians slaughtered our lod-scores. We have a new search now, on slightly different grounds. We need a score of 3.7. I am still confident. I have dense markers.

The hunting for genes is a tiresome job with frustrations and disappointment as well as excitement and euphoria:

> We mapped the chromosome region by region, rebuilt it. Then we narrowed down even further, sequencing base-by-base. There are two candidate genes left on Chromosome A (a pseudonym). I think I have narrowed-down to a region.

> I keep on trying until something works, going by hunches. The first step is to use the lod-scores to guide us into the chromosome region. Then we add more markers to the region. If we are lucky, we can see the same markers in unrelated families with the same symptoms. Bingo!

To understand the work of the OA-team it is important to consider its social context. There is extensive competition between companies in the kind of work that the OA team does and, obviously, it affects the intensity of the work as well as the way in which results are presented:

> We could easily have published much more on various chromosomes . . . but we don't know how much lead we have. Other companies are working on this too.

Also, there is competition between teams within deCode Genetics. While project leaders internal to the company sometimes lean on each other, circumnavigating around common problems, there is competition between leaders and their teams for access to labs and machinery where one team slows others down. Moreover, there are interpersonal and organizational problems of coordination.

Figure 10.2
A Pedigree with Two Pairs of Sisters Affected
by Osteoarthritis of the Fingers

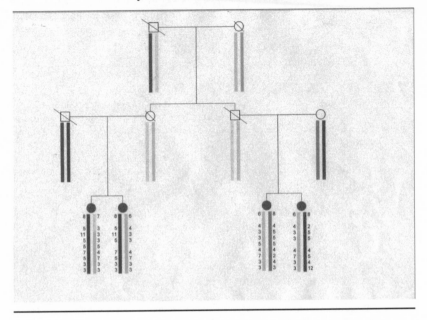

Figuring Kin

The fragmentary descriptions and glimpses from discussions with the osteoarthritis team presented above provide some indication about how they represent their reasoning about disease and relatedness. Maps and other forms of visual representation are not only useful tools for research purposes; they are worthy of attention in their own right, from the perspective of the "ethnography of viewing" (Orlove 1991), constituting and reflecting historical activities. And this applies to both genetic maps and the relational maps used to represent genealogies. deCode Genetics and its scientists and genealogists produce several kinds of genealogical trees. First, a common imagery projects genealogies as descending or going down; one example is the figure with the osteoarthritis patients presented above (Figure 10.2).

Another imagery shows genealogies as ascending into the past, or collapsing into the present, depending on the vantage point. Here, the main mission is to trace "ego's" roots as far as possible, focusing on direct lines between the present and the past rather than the flowering of the whole lineage. Figure 10.3 shows a family tree produced by the Book of Icelanders.

Figure 10.3
A Family Tree from the "Book of Icelanders"

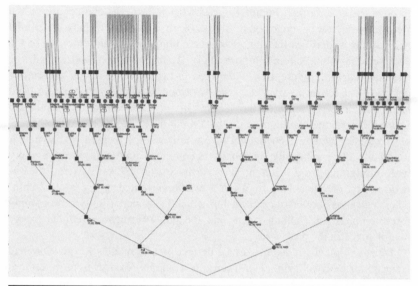

Finally, one kind of imagery presents pedigrees as neither ascending nor descending but as circular outward progressions; such an imagery is evident in the informal logo of deCode Genetics, the asthma-pedigree of Figure 10.4, reproduced on t-shirts and other publicity material (a similar image is also reproduced in some publications; see Gudmundsson *et al*. 2000: 746). Again, however, the tree imagery seems to be close by. In this case, the progression of time through the generations is represented by an image resembling a cross-section of a trunk of a tree. Just as natural history is engraved in the growth rings of the tree, genealogical history is encoded in the genealogical circle of the Icelandic family tree.

The history of the graphical representation of kinship in medieval Europe indicates that family trees are all but innocent. What could the figurative modes of Icelandic kinship possibly signify? Perhaps, given the variety of representation of genealogies in the deCode Genetics/Frisk Software project, one should not read too much into the differences between these figurative modes in terms of the graphics and layout of pedigrees. To some extent, the designers are "simply" motivated by straight-forward visual concerns and the practical constraints of their tools, programs and computer screens, much like medieval genealogists were motivated by the constraints of vellum, paper, and rolls of parchment. On the other hand, the different kinds of images obviously represent particular aspects of the deCode Genetics/Frisk Software genealogical project: one represents the search for mutant genes passed "down" through the generations (Figure 10.2), another reflects the ego-centric search for distant ancestors suggested by the Book of Icelanders (Figure 10.3), and still another underlines the rhetoric of the common roots and interests of the enclosed Icelandic "circle" (Figure 10.4). Apart from its visual appeal, the circular image of Figure 10.4 underlined in the public-relations material of deCode Genetics may serve, consciously or not, to foster a sense of unity and belonging. The reference to the "circle" of the community, the "Book" of Icelanders, and the continuity with the Viking past may, thus, indirectly suggest a rather narrow genetic notion of citizenship. Iceland, in particular Reykjavik the capital city, is rapidly becoming a multicultural community with immigrants from different parts of the world. To some extent, the genetic notion of citizenship implicated by the current database project competes with other notions of citizenship which have increasingly been gaining force, emphasizing human rights and the empowerment of ethnic groups marginalized in the past.

Trees and plants, it seems, "make perfect natural models for genealogical connections" (Rival 1998: 11). There are countless examples in the ethnographic literature of the metaphoric association of trees and kinship relationships in different times and places. The frequent metaphor of the tree, it may be argued, need not be surprising. Thus, Atran suggests (1990: 35) that as a life form trees may be "phenomenally compelling" to humans generally due to their ecological and historical role. Such a claim, however, seems to violate much ethnography. For Inuit groups in the barren Arctic; for instance, the idea of trees is probably radically different from, say, the trees experienced by inhabitants of South American rain forests (Fernandez 1998: 81). While the life-form of trees may not be evolutionarily significant for human cognition, trees may, as Rival suggests, "be potent symbols of vitality precisely because their status as living organisms is so uncertain" (1998: 23); trees die slowly, unlike animals they do not seem to have a "natural" life-span, and, finally, trees may be intensely alive and half-dead at the same time, composed of a mixture of dead and live tissue. Much like, perhaps, family trees.

How and why has the metaphor of the tree assumed the status it has in Western thinking as an organizing imagery? Klapisch-Zuber (1991) leads one to believe that the preoccupation with the tree metaphor has much to do with agrarian discourses on domination and succession. Deleuze and Guattari (1988) seem to agree, suggesting another metaphor, namely the one of the rhizome, a decentered cluster of interlaced threads where everything is potentially interconnected with everything else. Whereas the tree "always comes back 'to the same'", the rhizome has "multiple entryways" (1988: 12).[5] Should a model of relatedness, one may ask, only allow for a once-and-for-all transmission of

Figure 10.4
Neither Up nor Down: An Asthma-Pedigree with Eleven Generations

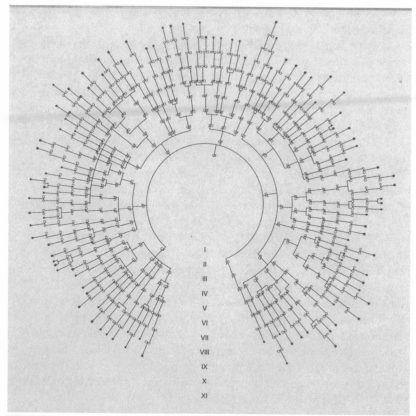

I
II
III
IV
V
VI
VII
VIII
IX
X
XI

"natural" substance from one generation to another? Much ethnography suggests different models (see Carsten 2000). In some societies, the transmission of substance is regarded as an ongoing process that includes breast-feeding, a process that may take several years after the moment of birth. More importantly, in some contexts kinship connections have little to do with shared substance. The Iñupiat of Alaska represent a particularly interesting case. Here, personhood is constantly being transformed through practice, through adoption, labor, and, above all, naming; personal essence is "largely influenced by names rather than inherited through shared substance" (Bodenhorn 2000: 140).

For biomedical and pharmaceutical companies, the Icelandic gene pool is obviously valuable capital precisely because of the presumed direct genealogical link of "real" Icelanders, through a few lineages, with the medieval past. I have discussed two kinds of mapping interrelated in the deCode Genetics project, involving genealogical and genetic data. While each of the two mapping cultures of genealogists and human geneticists has its own discourses and trajectories, they share, by definition, the notion that relatedness is both determined at the point of conception and a function of the number of "steps" separating any two persons, a notion captured by the "genealogical" image of the tree. The powerful discourse on the "book of life" established during the last century (Kay 2000) and the recent achievements of genetics and biotechnology have fostered a renewed interest in family histories and kinship diagrams. As we have seen, however, family trees are never innocent phenomena in the sense that they have a social life of their own, a biography informed by the contours of the cultural landscapes to which they belong. Genealogical models of trees embody the pragmatics and the social contexts of those who make them, but they also (and this follows from their cultural baggage) tend to inform the contexts where they are applied. As Haraway puts it (2000: 112), "map making is world making." Thus, the Biogenetic Project and the imagery and rhetoric associated with it may reinforce a rather narrow notion of "Icelandicness," a notion underlined in the nationalist discourse of the last century.[6] Not only is the notion of the blueprint of life surrounded by a growing uneasiness as it remains unclear what a "gene" is (Rheinberger 2000, Keller 2000), also the inclusion of genealogies in biogenetic projects is a contested issue, partly because their graphic representation invites controversial notions of identity and citizenship. Maps, whether genealogical or genetic, may look deceptively simple, but a critical engagement with them is an important element of the recent "spatial turn" (Cosgrove 1999: 7) in the sciences and the humanities.

Notes

Acknowledgements: Another version of this article appears in H.J. Rheinberger and J.-P. Gaudillére (eds) *The Mapping Cultures of the Twentieth-Century* (Routledge, 2003). The research on which it is based has been supported by several funds, including the Nordic Committee for Social Science Research (NOS-S), the Icelandic Science Fund, and the University of Iceland. I thank Kári Stefánsson, Director of deCode Genetics, and the osteoarthritis team at deCode Genetics, in particular Stefán Einar Stefánsson, the leader of the team, for their kind cooperation. Also, I am grateful to James Griesemer (University of California at Davis), Linda F. Hogle (Stanford University), Benjamin S. Orlove (University of California at Davis), Stacy Leigh Pigg (Simon Fraser University), Paul Rabinow (University of California at Berkeley), and the editors of this volume for useful comments and suggestions.

1. In contrast, during the eighteenth century some linguists seriously entertained the idea of *language* as being literally a natural organism. Thus, Franz Bobb argued

that languages must be regarded as "organic bodies, formed in accordance with definite laws; bearing within themselves *an internal principle of life . . .* " (cited in Newmeyer 1986: 23, emphasis added).

2. Pedigree thinking, in fact, is a common Western theme that reveals itself not only in the formal diagrams of kinship studies and evolutionary biology, but also in philology and the "Ethnologia" or *Völkerkunde* of museum collections. The genealogical view of the world outlined the common roots and relatedness of different groups and nations, providing the classificatory rationale for ethnographic collections and museum cabinets. Linguistics and biology presented a purified vision of languages and organisms as timeless artifacts with parallel roots and histories. In anthropology, the genealogical method had important implications for both theory and empirical approach: it "fixed birth as the defining moment of kinship, and fixed the instruments for its recording accordingly" (Bouquet 2000: 187).

3. The significance of genealogies during the saga age does not suggest that Icelanders were preoccupied with the structural relations of kinship. In fact, friendship was a powerful social relationship, judging from the accounts of the Family Sagas (see Durrenberger and Pálsson 1999).

4. I have been engaged in ethnographic research within deCode Genetics, focusing on a research team working on osteoarthritis. The decision to focus on the osteoarthritis team at deCoded Genetics was made after consultation with company staff. Fieldwork, conducted on and off during year 2000, focused on participating in team meetings and informal coffee-room discussions as well as interviewing all team members, some of them repeatedly. Also, several other people were interviewed, including statisticians, and those in charge of the "Book of Icelanders". Among the questions discussed during many of the interviews were: How does one become a skilful gene hunter? How do team members reason about genes, mapping, the discovery of genes, and the articulation of genes and environment for the explanation of differential occurrence of osteoarthritis.

5. The claim that tree metaphors are inherently Western and hierarchical is a bit overdrawn. The dualism of Deleuze and Guattari that radically separates the arborescent and patriarchal West, on the one hand, and the democratic and rhizomic South or East, on the other hand, indeed has its critics (Fernandez 1998). The persistent metaphor of the tree, which is at the core of the Western genealogical model, in fact can take several forms, depending, of course, on how one regards trees. After all, as Deleuze and Guattari admit (1988: 17), "trees may correspond to the rhizome, or they may burgeon into a rhizome."

6. In fact, the Biogenetic Project was foreshadowed by another grand plan in the 1960s to centralize a variety of information on Icelanders, a plan at the University of Iceland that drew upon concerns among local scholars since the 1930s with the purity of the "Nordic race" (Pálsson 1995).

References

Atran, Scott (1990) *Cognitive Foundations of Natural History.* Cambridge: Cambridge University Press.

Beer, G. (1986) "'The face of nature': Anthropometric elements in the language of *The Origin of Species*", in *The Languages of Nature: Critical Essays on Science and Literature.* L.J. Jordanova (ed.). London: Free Association Books.

Bodenhorn, Barbara (2000) "'He used to be my relative': Exploring the bases of relatedness among the Iñupiat of Northern Alaska", in *Cultures of Relatedness: New Approaches to the Study of Kinship*. J. Carsten (ed.). Cambridge: Cambridge University Press.

Bouquet, Mary (2000) "Figures of relations: Reconnecting kinship studies and museum collections", in *Cultures of Relatedness: New Approaches to the Study of Kinship*. J. Carsten (ed.). Cambridge: Cambridge University Press.

Carsten, Janet (ed.) (2000) *Cultures of Relatedness: New Approaches to the Study of Kinship*. Cambridge: Cambridge University Press.

Cosgrove, Dennis. (1999) "Introduction: Mapping meaning", in *Mappings*. D. Cosgrove (ed.). London: Reaction Books.

Deleuze, Giles and Felix Guattari (1988) *A Thousand Plateaus: Capitalism and Schizophrenia*. London: Athlone Press.

Durrenberger, E. Paul and Gísli Pálsson (1999) "The importance of friendship in the absence of states, according to the Icelandic sagas", in *The Anthropology of Friendship: Beyond the Community of Kinship*. S. Bell and S. Coleman (eds). Oxford: Berg Publishers.

Fernandez, James W. (1998) "Trees of knowledge of self and other in culture: On models for the moral imagination", in *The Social Life of Trees: Anthropological Perspectives on Tree Symbolism*. L. Rival (ed.). Oxford: Berg.

Finkler, Kaja (2000) *Experiencing the New Genetics: Family and Kinship on the New Medical Frontier*. Philadelphia: University of Pennsylvania Press.

Fleising, Usher (2001) "In search of genohype: A content analysis of biotechnology company documents". *New Genetics and Society* 20(3): 239–254.

Foucault, Michel (1973) *The Birth of the Clinic: An Archaeology of Medical Perception*. Transl. A.M. Sheridan. London: Tavistock.

Franklin, Sarah and Helen Ragoné, eds (1998) *Reproducing Reproduction: Kinship, Power, and Technological Innovation*. Philadelphia: University of Pennsylvania Press.

Grétarsdóttir Bender, Elín K. (2002) *Íslensk ættfræði* ("Icelandic Genealogy"). B.A. dissertation. Department of Anthropology. University of Iceland.

Gudmundsson, Hjalti *et al.* (2000) "Inheritance of human longevity in Iceland". *European Journal of Human Genetics* 8: 743–749.

Gulcher, Jeff *et al.* (2001) "The role of linkage studies for common diseases". *Current Opinion in Genetics & Development* 11: 264–267.

Gulcher, Jeff and Kári Stefánsson (1998) "Population genomics: Laying the groundwork for genetic disease modeling and targeting". *Clin Chem Lab Med* 36: 532–7.

Haraway, Donna (2000) "Deanimations: Maps and portraits of life itself", in *Hybridity and Its Discontents: Politics, Science, Culture*. A. Brah and A.E. Coombes (eds). Pp. 111–36. London: Routledge.

Helgason, Agnar (2001) *The Ancestry and Genetic History of the Icelanders: An Analysis of MTDNA Sequences, Y Chromosome Haplotypes and Genealogy*. Doctoral dissertation. Institute of Biological Anthropology, University of Oxford.

Helgason, Agnar *et al.* (2000) "mtDNA and the origin of the Icelanders: Deciphering signals of recent population history". *American Journal of Human Genetics* 66: 999–1016.

Ingold, Tim (2000) *The Perception of the Environment: Essays in Livelihood, Dwelling and Skill*. London: Routledge.

Ingvarsson, Thorvaldur *et al.* (2000) "The inheritance of hip osteoarthritis in Iceland". *Arthritis and Rheumatism* 43: 2785–92.

Íslendinga sögur og þættir, vols. I–III, (1987) Reykjavík: Svart á hvítu.

Kay, Lily E. (2000) *Who Wrote the Book of Life? A History of the Genetic Code.* Stanford: Stanford University Press.

Keller, Evelyn Fox (2000) *The Century of the Gene.* Cambridge, Mass.: Harvard University Press.

Klapisch-Zuber, Christiane (1991) "The genesis of the family tree". *I Tatti Studies: Essays in the Renaissance* 4(1): 105–129.

Laqueur, Thomas W. (2001) "'From generation to generation'": Imagining connectedness in the age of reproductive technologies", in *Biotechnology and Culture: Bodies, Anxieties, Ethics.* P.E. Brodwin (ed.). Bloomington: Indiana University Press.

Nature (2000) "Manhattan versus Reykjavik". News feature 406: 340–342.

Newmeyer, Frederic J. (1986) *The Politics of Linguistics.* Chicago: University of Chicago Press.

Orlove, Benjamin S. (1991) "Mapping reeds and reading maps: Representation in Lake Titicaca". *American Anthropologist* 18(1): 3–40.

Pálsson, Gísli (1995) *The Textual Life of Savants: Ethnography, Iceland, and the Linguistic Turn.* Chur: Harwood Academic Publishers.

—— (2002) "The life of family trees and the Book of Icelanders". *Medical Anthropology,* 21(3/4): 337–367.

—— (2003) "Decoding relatedness and disease: The Icelandic Biogenetic Project", in H.J. Rheinberger and J.-P. Gaudillére (eds). *The Mapping Cultures of the Twentieth-Century.* London: Routledge. (In press).

Pálsson, Gísli and Kristín Erla Harðardóttir (2002) "For whom the cell tolls: Debates about biomedicine". *Current Anthropology* 43(2): 271–301.

Pálsson, Gísli and Paul Rabinow (1999) "Iceland: The case of a national human genome project". *Anthropology Today* 15(5): 14–18.

—— (2003) "The Iceland controversy: Reflections on the trans-national market of civic virtue", in A. Ong and S.J. Collier (eds). *Global Anthropology: Technology, Governmentality, Ethics.* Oxford: Blackwell Publishers. (In press).

Panofsky, Erwin (1991) *Perspective as Symbolic Form,* trans. C.S. Wood. Cambridge, Mass.: Zone Books.

Rabinow, Paul (1999) *French DNA: Trouble in Purgatory.* Chicago: University of Chicago Press.

Rheinberger, Hans-Jörg (2000) "Gene concepts", in *The Concept of the Gene in Development and Evolution.* P. Beurton, R. Falk, and H.-J. Rheinberger (eds). Cambridge: Cambridge University Press.

Risch, Neil (2000) "Searching for genetic determinants in the new millennium". *Nature* 405: 847–856.

Rival, Laura (1998) "Trees, from symbols of life and regeneration to political artefacts", in *The Social Life of Trees: Anthropological Perspectives on Tree Symbolism.* L. Rival (ed.). Oxford: Berg.

Schneider, David M. (1984) *A Critique of the Study of Kinship.* Ann Arbor: University of Michigan Press.

Strathern, Marilyn (1992) *After Nature: English Kinship in the Late Twentieth Century.* Cambridge: Cambridge University Press.

Wilford, John N. (2000) *The Mapmakers.* New York: Vintage Books. Revised edition.

11

Comparing the Practice of Reproductive Genetics in Greece, UK, Finland, and The Netherlands: Constructing "Expert" Claims while Marking "Reproductive" Time

Elizabeth Ettorre

Introduction

This paper looks at key issues that become visible in a sociological analysis of the links between reproduction, genetics, expert knowledge building, space and time. Reproductive genetics is defined as the utilisation of DNA based technologies in the medical supervision of the reproductive processes. This is a sociological concept, suggesting that complex social and cultural processes are involved in the organisation and use of genetic tests for prenatal diagnosis (Ettorre 2002). In feminist contexts it exposes gendered processes in the medical management of reproduction: men and women are treated differently in this area of medicine.

The paper compares findings from a study of European experts in the UK, Finland, Greece and the Netherlands. The main assumption is that reproductive genetics relies on an individualistic, mechanistic view of a pregnant body marked by rigid definitions of gender as well as space and time. While this view is constructed by a variety of biomedical experts, it is shaped in spaces, distinguished by over-arching cultural themes. These themes are played out in 'national' spaces defined by racialised boundaries. In turn, these boundaries are marked out over time by nation states with geographical customs, and ethnic traditions. These European spaces actively constitute visible, so-

299

cial and cultural practices, while at the same time, these practices shape and re-shape space. National spaces are made 'locally' through social actions and power relations, making up the rules of particular societies and delineating state boundaries (McDowell 1999).

In these spaces, reproduction emerges as a social institution (Ettorre 2002) and matures into a regulatory system, focused on the making of bodies which should embody wholeness (*i.e.* limbs, torsos, crania filled with brains, etc.), health, well being and the future welfare of these societies. Reproduction appears as an organisation of activities and social relations, embodying notions of able-bodies, human survival and progress, while reproductive bodies become more valorised than ever before through medical technology. Thus, as a corporeal style, pregnancy is framed by this institution and combines with temporality and cultural spaces as a constituting and constituted context. Reproduction is a structured social practice that has a wide spatial and temporal expanse[1]. Pregnant bodies are synchronised and harmonised by the technologies of reproductive genetics. In this process, we can rightly ask, how and what reproductive space and time are available to women and how are these culturally constituted?

My paper is in three parts. Firstly, I will look generally at the mobilisation of reproductive genetics through surveillance medicine. Secondly, drawing on a study of European experts, I describe the specific cultural spaces of surveillance medicine in which experts shape their claims about reproductive genetics and how these claims mark reproductive time for pregnant women. Lastly, I will offer a brief discussion of the findings and some conclusions.

Methodology

The Sample

The source of empirical data presented in this paper is a qualitative study on experts' accounts of the use of pre-natal genetic screening in four European countries: UK, Finland, Netherlands and Greece. This is one study, which came from a European consortium of researchers carrying out a series of seven comparative studies in this area.

Given that the aim of the experts' study was to review the role of key players influential in public debates in each country, I wanted to find experts who were active in this area either clinically or academically. Initially, I hoped to interview at least ten experts in each country. The goal was to interview equal numbers of geneticists[2], clinicians, practitioners, lawyers and/ or ethicists, policy makers, public health officials and researchers. It was also decided that besides being known as an 'expert', a prerequisite for inclusion in the study would be fluency in English.

A potential sample of respondents was selected from a list of ten known experts drawn up by researchers (i.e. contract partners) in each of the four countries. Experts were known through their publications, work contacts and/ or national reputation within these researchers' networks. A final list for inclusion in the study was discussed and drawn up jointly by the author (who would carry out the interviews) and country researchers.

Data Collection and Analysis

After experts were selected, they were contacted by country researchers and asked whether or not they would be interested in providing their views. With two exceptions, all experts who were selected agreed to be interviewed. With the help of these local researchers, the author set dates when she would be visiting each country as well as arranged times and places for the interviews. Twenty-eight interviews were completed between October 1996 until December 1996. Before data collection began, the research group decided that in order to keep to the study timetable, an additional 14 interviews carried out during the Finnish pilot study in 1995 would be included in the main study. This meant that the final number of interviews was forty-five. These included: seventeen interviews for Finland, ten for Greece, nine for UK and nine for The Netherlands. The interviews were conducted in English, tape-recorded and lasted between thirty to ninety minutes: the average was an hour.

Here, it should be noted that although it was possible to reach the desired numbers of interviews in Finland and Greece, this was not possible in the Netherlands and the UK. Both countries were one short. This was due mainly to the study timetable and budget. All interviews needed to be completed by December 1996 and the researcher had one week's time to interview experts in each country. To account for this lack, seven 'unofficial' interviews (i.e. without the use of a tape recorder) were carried out: four in the Netherlands and three in the UK. These seven 'unofficial' interviews were mainly with medical students or biomedical researchers with expertise in the area. The data obtained from these 'unofficial' interviews were not used in the data analyses and were perceived by the author as providing background information in specific countries.

Experts were asked their views on genetic testing and screening in prenatal diagnosis. The interview questions revolved around their attitudes on the use of these techniques; their perceptions of the prevailing state of knowledge on legal, medical and ethical aspects; social effects; and policy priorities on local and national levels. All interview data were transcribed and key themes were identified by Word Perfect (Windows) Quick Finder Index. Subsequently, these themes were discussed and agreed amongst the research partners. Excerpts from the experts' interviews will be used in this paper. I should mention here that some variations of experts' attitudes occurred within specific disciplines (e.g. clinical geneticists disagreed with other clinical geneticists), amongst disciplines (e.g. differences between clinical geneticists, obstetricians, ethicists, policy makers) and between countries (e.g. differences between Dutch and UK experts). With regards the last issue, when cross cultural differences are emphasised in this area, we tend to see less clearly the sorts of inter-disciplinary disagreements (i.e. such as those between clinical geneticists and policy makers, etc.), which are taken for granted in single country studies (Kerr et al. 1997, Gilbert & Mulkay 1984). The focus is in this paper is mainly on cross-cultural variations.

Surveillance Medicine: Mobilising Genetics in the Community

As a cultural and social system, the medical establishment is a structure of meaning and behavioural norms, attached to particular social relationships and institutional settings (Kleinman 1991:31). It is worthwhile to look at how the social significance of experts and their professional norms are not only shaped by their authoritative claims and relations with those they treat but also practised within specific cultural settings that change over time. The assumption, here, is that the current biomedical discourse on 'reproductive genetics' upholds an observable method of working, facilitating the advancement of sophisticated genetic techniques. Thus, how 'reproductive genetics work' is organised within biomedicine and what is materialising within modern medicine to facilitate the growth of genomics are linked concerns.

Most if not all experts in reproductive genetics have been trained to look for illnesses or diseases in specific spaces—hospitals or clinical settings. Their work has been organised by the dominance of clinical medicine and informed by an 'old' bio-medical health care model (Bunton and Barrows 1995). At the same time, the emergence a newer or alternative form of medicine based on surveillance of healthy populations has developed (Armstrong 1995). The way in which traditional medical science has established 'the space' for illness (i.e. in hospital settings) is changing. Health is being redefined in terms that assess levels of functioning and well being in everyday living within social contexts (Tarlov 1996), while the policy challenge focuses a population's attention on preventing disease through public health messages (Blane, Brunner and Wilkinson 1996). In this context, Bunton and Barrows (1995:207) argue that a new public health has emerged. Proclaiming 'a new way of conceptualising the relationship between agent, environment and host' (Bunton 2002: 101), this new public health widens the relevant points of social contacts between professionals and patients into social interactions oriented toward the social body. As these points of social contacts are widened, health care interventions leave clinical settings and infiltrate into the wider population.

The new genetics is grounded in this new public health: it absolves the social structure of responsibility for disease (Wilkinson 1996:63). Atkin and Ahmad (1998:448) note that the public health message of genetics emphasises individual decision making over life styles. Genetics extends medicine's claims of competence to newer areas of personal and social life, including ideas about appropriate behaviour on the part of patients who are seeking or 'should be' seeking genetic services.

As the genetics message is circulated through the new public health, the traditional boundaries between health and illness are breaking down. For example, the paradigm of modern medicine, hospital medicine, has been based on separating those who are ill from those who are healthy. The hospital or the clinic has been the key site for the 'spatialisation of illness'. As an institutional setting, the hospital is traditionally the structured space where intervention takes place and where the medical professional observes, manages, treats and diagnoses disease. In this particular social space, illness and disease have a positive visibility with specific signs and symptoms. Medical professionals search for these indications as they focus their clinical gaze on the individual.

With the development of the new genetics, a newer paradigm, surveillance medicine (Armstrong 1995) appears. Here, the site of intervention is the community in contrast to the hospital. It is within this 'new' space of illness—"the community'—where healthy or unhealthy life styles as well as the combination of genes (i.e. faulty or not), a pregnant women's carrier status and risk factors are identified. In this movement from hospital to surveillance medicine, there is a shift in modern medical culture from looking at subjective signs and symptoms that sufferers, consumers, patients, pregnant women etc. experience when they feel sick to performing objective tests in the community. With regards reproductive medicine, the consequences of this shift has meant that surveillance medicine's tactics (Armstrong 1995), 'pathologisation' and 'vigilance', are played out on the bodies of pregnant women. These tactics accelerate the proliferation of genetic and other technologies into reproductive and foetal spaces. There is nothing new in the medical profession's surveillance of these spaces (Oakley 1984, Newman 1996). What is new are medical constructions of risk factors of pregnant women and both the technologies that allow detection of carriers and prenatal diagnosis of diseases and abnormalities. In the prenatal sphere, the genetic model, which sees abnormality as largely caused by genes (Scully 2002: 50) is privileged. As we shall see, through this model pregnant women are made to experience 'reproductive time' in a new way.

The over-medicalisation of pregnancy argument has been heard loudly and

Figure 11.1
The Shift from Hospital to Surveillance Medicine

Hospital Medicine   Surveillance Medicine

Symptom   Gene ('faulty' or not)

Sign   Disease   Patient   Risk Carrier

Individual   Community (life styles)

The 'Spatialisation' of Illness

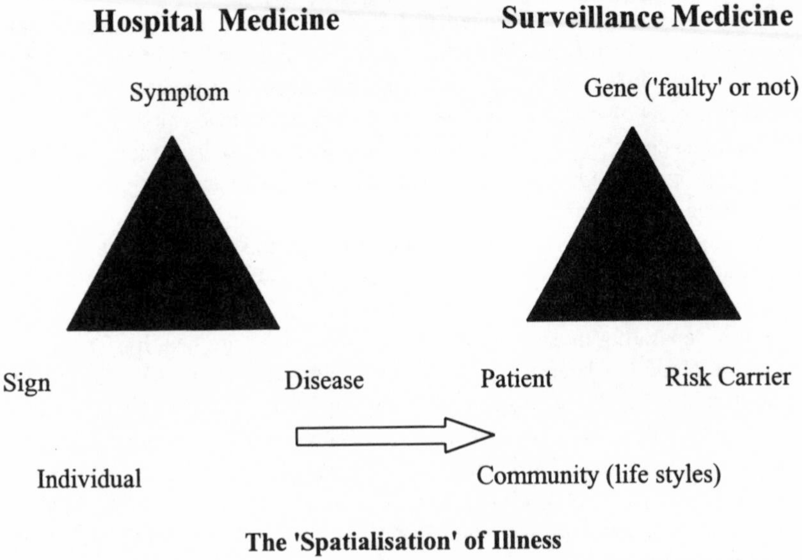

clearly in sociological circles for a number of years. However, that permeable boundaries exist between precarious normalities and future diseases and that this threat exists in the womb because these boundaries can be breached are relatively novel notions for pregnant women.

Tentative pregnancies (Rothman 1993) are temporal matters as well as temporally constituted. Physicians may ask questions about weeks of gestation and maternal age. However, for pregnant women, reproductive time takes on multiple dimensions beyond the nine-month timetable, when the consequences of their risks breach the boundaries between health and illness. Here, reproductive time can be seen to last a lifetime when they give birth to an abnormal baby.

Medical constructions of risk factors release 'reproductive' spaces for consideration of future illness potential. Thus, the results of a nine-month pregnancy can be extended into another vista—one of illness potential. Cultural, reproductive and temporal spaces intertwine as co-ordinates in which risk factors are identified and choices are made. In this surveillance process, pregnant women focus on illness as continuous possibility, rather than on the immediacy and/or practicalities of conception. The future is now. For them, the impact of reproductive genetics has meant a transition from a naturally based manner of time to a socially and more specifically medically, based one (Simonds 2002). While 'genetics is influenced by culture, shaping its priorities and ways of understanding disease and behaviour' (Kerr and Shakespeare 2002: 101), it has a profound influence upon the social and cultural contexts in which reproduction is organised and managed. In this context, Margaret Stacey (1992) has said:

> Technological advances in reproductive medicine affect people's lives, endorse certain values, run into stereotypes and have consequences for the management of relations that may well extend beyond their immediate application . . . To think of such technologies as having social dimensions provides a way of thinking about the multiple nature of their impact.

Here, thinking about the social and cultural dimensions of reproductive genetics allows us to consider the institution of reproduction both spatially and temporally. Reproductive genetics and the strategies of surveillance medicine are increasingly influencing reproduction. Reproduction embodies complex social, temporal and technological relationships and experts involved in these relationships are a structuring piece of surveillance medicine.

Reproductive Genetics within Different Cultures: Space and Time Reckoning

A complex interplay between biological, social and cultural processes and institutions such as medicine, science, gender and reproduction have standardised the way we currently reckon reproductive space and time. In the following discussion, I will draw upon the claims of a group of experts from four European countries. I will describe the specific cultural spaces in which they shape their claims about reproductive genetics and demonstrate how these claims mark reproductive time for pregnant women. My focus is on a comparison of experts' claims and identifying over-arching cultural themes country by country. These cultural themes include: thalassaemia in Greece, abortion in the Netherlands, ethics in the UK and care for pregnant women in Finland.

Greece's 'Thalassaemia Success Story'

Ten expert interviews were carried out with a paediatrician, an obstetrician, a clinical geneticist, two policy makers, three lawyers and two ethicists. The thalassaemia[3] success story emerged as the main cultural theme, as experts claimed that they were successful in dealing with thalassaemia. Their claims shaped the cultural space in which reproductive genetics was played out in Greece. In 1977, screening of thalassaemia began (Loukopoulos et al 1990) because it was seen as a 'Greek' disease, a public health problem. It was seen as 'living' in the Greek population. Greeks perceived it as a stigma which 'marked' carriers. For example:

The person has in his [sic] blood this defect. He [sic] has a stigma ... GR 4
Lawyer⁴

And

The stigma shows that this disease runs in your family. GR1 Policy Maker

As a stigma, Greeks saw thalassaemia as having a high level of concentration in the corporal volume of its people. It became 'nationalised' and enclosed culturally as Mediterranean anaemia. One expert stresses this 'cultural
boundedness':

We have . . . taken certain measures that . . . were positive in detecting Mediterranean anaemia because this is a problem in Greece. GR1 Policy Maker

While experts claimed that the national screening programme was a 'success story', success was possible only through a decrease in thalassaemia's
wide, corporeal sweep across the population.

We have had a great success . . . because we used to have approximately more than
200 new cases per year and now [there] are less than 10 cases . . . GR5 Medical
Geneticist

And

. . . We have a great problem with thalassaemia. There is an official
laboratory . . . for haemoglobin disorders . . . because the incidence is high. . . . The
result . . . is that we very rarely see now new cases . . . with thalassaemia. GR3
Obstetrician

Experts allege that the incidence in the total population is 'high' at 7% and
that 'there are special places that have higher incidences'. For example, one
expert says:

. . . There are special places that . . . have higher incidence (higher than 7%)
and . . . other places with lower incidence . . . 7% of the Greek population are carriers. That means that one in 14 couples are both carriers . . . GR3 Obstetrician

But, these exceptional places tend to be spatialised as 'rural areas':

We have big pockets of thalassaemia especially in [the rural areas]. GR1 Policy
Maker

Given these 'big pockets', it is not only important to take 'positive measures' but also to offer prenatal diagnosis and screening to couples before
they marry. One Medical Geneticist claims that while Greece has 'approxi-

mately 100,000 live births per year', there are '6,000 pre-natal diagnoses'. This means that '6% of the whole pregnant population are screened for chromosomal abnormalities'. In this expert's eyes, this is a very 'positive effect' of the national screening programme. Experts claimed that nowadays physicians rarely see a patient with an affected baby and this is the result of 'everybody' being part of the national screening programme or 'knowing before they get married':

> Now very rarely do you see a patient with an affected baby who becomes sick . . . All will have a prenatal diagnosis. Everybody is going for a test before having a baby and this is very important. GR3 Obstetrician

And

> The best thing is to take measures . . . and this can be done if [a couple] knows before they get married that they have both have this risk. This is being taken care of . . . before marriage. We have a blood test and that's the way to do it because if you know what is coming to you, then your choices are yours . . . GR1 Policy Maker

Another expert discusses the links between the national programme and prenatal diagnosis and how 'at risk' couples are 'detected':

> [Thalassaemia] is a single gene disease . . . In order to have an affected child, then two parents must have the trait . . . The couple is at risk and each pregnancy carries the 25% possibility of [having] an affected child. So . . . we screen and detect couples at risk. . . . When we find a couple at risk, we try to offer the option of having the child only if they (sic.) do antenatal diagnosis. . . . If there is an affected child, they have to go for termination of pregnancy . . . GR6 Paediatrician

This expert also notes the care and time that is needed in this process. He claims that one is lucky to proceed towards a first trimester termination:

> We've managed to reduce considerably . . . thalassaemia . . . There [are] certain centres all over . . . that do screening for detection of couples at risk. . . . We have had some [problems]. There were some false positives . . . [We] screened and later [found] the [fetuses] were normal . . . So you have to be very very careful . . . [We use] a blood test but you have to be experienced to do the diagnosis . . . In these centres, the diagnosis is quite efficient. If we have a couple at risk then there are organised units that we can refer this couple to [for] prenatal diagnosis. And when you go to prenatal diagnosis, we are dealing with haematological techniques. The DNA technique is more accurate . . . You can do it in the first trimester of the gestation. . . . With the modern techniques, we are capable [of doing] a diagnosis in 24 hours so you can know in week 10–12 of gestation that you can have termination of the pregnancy. So we proceed towards first trimester termination, we are quite lucky. GR6 Paediatrician

As seen from the above, the thalassaemia success story shaped experts claims about reproductive genetics. What is of interest is that no expert mentioned pregnant women when speaking of these matters. Pre-nuptial couples were their main concern and those with whom experts would press for a reproductive timetable.[5] This was probably because both parents must have the trait in order to have an affected child. On the other hand, it is the bodies of pregnant women that are temporally and technologically co-ordinated specifically during weeks 10–12 of gestation—not those of their partners. Thus, it could be said that reproductive time is employed to best advantage only when the space for gestation (*i.e.* women's wombs) is over looked. For Greek women, this implies that they while pregnant, there wombs become non-places (McDowell 1999). Non-places are invisible spaces in which transactions and interactions take place between already established customs (i.e. male privilege) and institutions (*i.e.* medicine, gender, science, and reproduction). Thus, at any given moment in time, the perceived wisdom about the spread of thalassaemia's corporeal volume in Greece will determine the sorts of technologies that are practised on 'their' pregnant women.

The Politics of Abortion:
Control and Liberation in The Netherlands

Nine expert interviews were carried out with a general practitioner, three obstetricians, a medical geneticist, a policy maker, a midwife, a researcher and an ethicist. The main over-arching cultural theme was the politics of abortion and experts claimed that the 'Christian Democratic Party' (CDP) featured centrally in political debates:

> Policy makers . . . are very much against large scale screening. . . . where the detection of an abnormality might lead to an abortion . . . that [the] government should support a screening programme [for] all women is a problem . . . It . . . even a problem to offer it to a specific age group . . . The reason for Parliament to pass this law against screening[6] [is] . . . . that [screening] was seen as inadmissible . . . because people (sic.) are already pregnant and [it is] inadmissible [as a] choice for abortion. . . . The total number of the population that refuses abortion on any ground, is some 10–15% . . . The right wing Christians . . . were . . . achieving influence [on] what was absolutely non-proportional to the number of the people in the population having the same views. . . . So it's very political . . . Sometimes genetic abortions are . . . taken as political . . . and handled irrespective of the needs of the people involved. NL 4 Clinical Geneticist

And

> We have a CDP . . . they were . . . in . . . government for 70–80 years . . . They had to talk about [legal] abortion which was forbidden . . . nobody wants to talk about it because you will get . . . problems within your coalition in . . . government. Now that they have gone away from . . . government . . . [the ruling party] are afraid that CDP will make a point of it opposition . . . We have a rather liberal abortion law, but if we talk about abortion because of genetic problems then there is a problem. NL6 Obstetrician

This expert continues:

Politicians ... have problems with screening because ... the result of screening, if something is found, is an abortion. That's their problem. That's why they don't want to talk about ... They always say, ".Oh, [screening is] no good because it will cost you a lot of abortions and there will be no advantages because handicapped people are no longer accepted in society.... They only see the problems.... They don't want to talk about it ... They don't see there's prenatal screening already, age screening ... family history ... what ever screening ... So the first thing I see ... are always the political problems.... NL6 Obstetrician

Another expert said quite simply:

The option of pregnancy termination is not a justifiable reason for a population screening programme. NL 4 Clinical Geneticist

In a similar context, another expert says:

[The government] doesn't like the abortion issue ... As long as we don't have any other treatment than termination of pregnancy; they don't like it as a political issue.... [Those] who have decided to legalise abortion to the 24th week actually don't ... have any problem with this because the decision lies with the woman ... Screening procedures now by the new law ... are okayed by the government. And you have to ask for a permit—a license by the government whether you can actually offer it to the public or not ... cervical screening, mammography, prenatal screenings by triple test ... NL 2 Obstetrician

This new requirement, 'asking for a permit' and 'needing a license' was viewed as problematic by some practitioners:

To do triple screening you will need a licence ... Now the situation is that the professionals don't want to ask for permission ... because they think the permission will be rejected, so they don't even ask.... I don't think that's [good]. I think you should ask permission because now it will stop the research in this field. Because if you don't [ask], you are not allowed to do serum screening. NL6 Obstetrician

This above expert noted that there were approximately 20,000 legal abortions per year that represented 10% of all pregnancies. He also said that there were 300 abortions for 'genetic reasons'. In his view, 'genetic abortions', although legal, were somehow 'traumatic' for the political parties:

... Legal abortions are only allowed in ... an emergency situation ... for the mother [if she] doesn't think [she] can continue the pregnancy ... for genetic abortions it's the same case. She says, "There is ... one reason or another I cannot continue the pregnancy". But politicians think it's something else. I don't know why, but they don't like talking about it ... they are afraid of it ... How long we have [had] legal abortion ... about 20 years and it has been a trauma for the political parties because they had a lot discussions about it ... NL6 Obstetrician

In discussing abortion within the context of prenatal screening, some experts spoke about how adopting this practice was seen by some politicians as going down 'the slippery slope':

> The government has decided that these . . . issues belong to the domain of individual responsibility because it belongs to the couple involved and in particular, the woman who is pregnant. . . . So the issue . . . is . . . [Is] Down's syndrome grave enough to terminate a pregnancy? It is not a matter of the medical profession. . . . It belongs to [the one] involved. And [there are] ethical implications. If you are . . . . against the termination of pregnancy for whatever reason, you must be against prenatal diagnosis. So our Catholic University (CU) hospital . . . [which is] under the pope's influence is the latest centre to do prenatal diagnosis . . . . Other arguments grew stronger and stronger and a couple of years ago they (CU) started doing it . . . It was down the slippery slope- . . . the eugenics [line] . . . We test for neural tube defects of chromosomal abnormalities . . . chromosomal abnormalities are something that mother nature always handles in the form of a spontaneous abortion—in almost all cases . . . We do not put any pressure on a couple to terminate their pregnancy. NL 2 Obstetrician

Another expert claimed that this 'slippery slope' was only in the minds of the politicians:

> Some [ethicists] . . . are focused on the undesirable effects of offering the option of pregnancy termination as a measure . . . and the problem of the . . . slippery slope . . . that people are going to accept fewer and fewer abnormalities in children which is a crazy argument . . . It simply doesn't exist for people who want to have children. [A] slippery slope around congenital and genetic diseases only exists in the minds of politicians . . . ethicists and church authorities who are far away from everyday reality of people who want to have children but faced with risk from the family history or previous affected children. NL 4 Medical Geneticist

A psychologist, who had carried out a study on pregnant women, found that there was a difference between abortion as a woman's right to choose (i.e. not wanting a child) and selective abortion as in prenatal diagnosis:

> Abortion in the context of prenatal diagnosis is a very different question than abortion if you don't want a child. I asked [women] if there was a difference between these two kinds of abortion and they all said that there was a difference. NL7 Research Psychologist

Echoing a similar point, an ethicist claimed:

> I think that [a woman's right to choose] is quietly accepted. People . . . realise that [there] are wanted pregnancies and that's very difficult for a woman to end a wanted pregnancy. You should never confront a normal abortion . . . [by] I want to get rid of the child (sic.) . . . I think that people do realise that the message is different in a way because we are talking about wanted pregnancies which will make the abortion different. NL 5 Ethicist

In the above, experts' claims are shaped by the politics of abortion which appear heated at times. While most accepted that pregnant women have a right to choose 'normal abortions' and this is protected in law up to 24 weeks, they perceive 'genetic abortions' as a different matter. 'Genetic abortions' are 'political' not normal. This is because in the context of prenatal screening, normal abortions appear as 'unwanted pregnancies', while genetic ones are perceived as 'wanted'. Here, time reckoning becomes intertwined with legal reckoning as divisions in the social production of reproductive space emerge. On the one hand, if experts press for a screening timetable with pregnant women, experts themselves are co-ordinated temporally and spatially by the law with whom they must reckon. On the other hand, whether women experience 'normal', legal abortions or 'genetic' political ones, their reproductive time is marked by their own desires to continue or not with their pregnancies. Contrary to their treaters, women's experience of pregnancy compresses reproductive space (i.e. their wombs) and reproductive time. Their pregnant bodies and the contents of their wombs are all that there are, as they are marked in a paradoxical space of legal control and personal liberation (i.e. a woman's right to choose).

Creating a Genetics Moral Order: Ethics and Reflexivity in the UK

Nine interviews were carried out with two medical geneticists, an epidemiologist, two policy makers, one public health official, two researchers and an ethicist. The main overarching cultural theme was the need for ethics in reproductive genetics. One expert, an ethicist herself, believed that the ethical issues are different than in other areas of biomedicine:

> Are . . . the ethical issues different in genetics from other areas? I think this might be the case . . . One is the attitude to information, because medical ethics [has] traditionally been about giving the patient all the information and more control, whereas genetics has lead to arguments . . . such as [the need] not to know . . . This is quite a new development. The second area relates to confidentiality and sharing of genetic information between family members . . . Genetic information can have such potentially far-reaching implications . . . Confidentiality must be strengthened rather than weakened . . . UK 9 Ethicist

Another believed that prenatal technologies bring a whole new 'cultural' relationship to ethics:

> The conundrum is . . . about ethics and the facts. We are assuming that it's mutual—technology and ethics . . . Technology brings with it a whole cultural relationship and it's one that science needs to be responsible about. UK 1 Researcher

Another expert linked ethics to a series of issues from choice to commercialisation:

[Ethics] are to make sure that there is adequate information provided ... to increase choice rather than to terminate ... pregnancies ... To allow choice ... is ... an ethical issue ... Commercialisation raises the ethical problem ... This captive situation ... raises a big ethical problem ... whether [or not] you call pregnancy a captive situation ... [You] introduce the idea of the test to somebody during the pregnancy ... The idea is to introduce it before there is a pregnancy, if you can. Once the person is there and you say would you like this, they are likely to say yes more ... than if they weren't pregnant at the time. UK 3 Clinical Geneticist

Linked to the issue of choice is the issue of informed consent that some believed was crucial. One expert noted that in the past women had prenatal screening without proper informed consent:

[From early research] ... women were not being asked for informed consent ... They were undergoing prenatal tests without [it]. So informed consent is a crucial issue that has to be addressed right now. UK 1 Researcher

In this context, another expert claimed that:

... Women should be better informed ... UK 5 Public Health Official

Another expert echoed:

... There are women ... that don't know enough about what is actually happening. It is important ... that it is a conscious decision to have the test, [that] they have chance to think about it ... At each stage of the process, they have a chance to reflect and consider so at the end of it they can say, yes I did considered it ... And if the outcome is not exactly what they wanted, ... they could say everything was explained to me properly and I had a reasonable chance to make ... the right decision ... What's important is, that people have a choice as to whether [or not] to get into that situation in the first place. UK 6 Epidemiologist

Nevertheless, another expert thought that informed consent is a very difficult concept:

We have to deal with ... the concept [of] informed consent, because ... we have to be very open to patients ... informed consent is a very difficult one for most people. UK 7 Ethicist

Linked with this discussion is the idea of how information is communicated in the process of gaining informed consent:

There is a notion that the problem starts with the question, Is the information any good? ... Are the results communicated appropriately? and How much counselling and by whom? and [How much] supervision is required? There are then issues about confidentiality. There is the basic fact that genetic information is familial information and what are the implications of that? UK 8 Ethicist

Also, another question arose: How is informed consent linked to responsibility towards one's patients?:

When . . . we introduce new things which [were] not possible before.., it creates responsibility . . . From the time that that's preventable within the medical and scientific systems, . . . there is a responsibility for every movement . . . This responsibility should be constant to the patients because if it's not, if they have not been informed that they are at risk and what their options are [then] they have an affected child without being informed that is absolutely catastrophic and . . . they . . . tend to sue the . . . doctor. UK 4 Clinical Geneticist

Other experts link ethics with the public understanding of science. Here, one believed that 'scientific facts' should not be separated from ethics:

When the public becomes well informed about scientific facts, then we will be in a better position to make ethical and moral judgements about many problems. . . . There are certainly a lot of people writing and questioning, . . . but [ethics) is not the dominant issue in the public arena. We are not an informed public. UK 1 Researcher

Other experts echoed their concern about an uninformed public:

The public is largely informed by what they read in the papers . . . [which] is misleading. UK 9 Ethicist

And

[We need] to increase the level of public . . . knowledge . . . to have . . . genetics ventilated in the widest possible way . . . making knowledge freely available. UK 3 Clinical Geneticist

Another ethical issue was the failure to deliver equitable services:

We have failed to be interested in the real ethical problem, which is our failure to deliver the service. It is delivered inadequately and inequitably. That's my ethical perception. UK 4 Clinical Geneticist

In the UK, concerns for ethics shape experts' claims about reproductive genetics. However, some say 'genetic ethics' are different from 'bioethics'. This is because conventional bioethics enforces the need to know while 'genetic ethics' may uphold the need not to know. Bioethics defends sharing of information; 'genetic ethics' doesn't because it considers the far-reaching temporal and spatial implications of genetic knowledge. Experts perceive 'genetics ethics' as facilitating the acceptance of technologies in the public domain as well as establishing a normative framework for the institution of reproduction. These ethics assist the construction of a genetics moral order in which pregnant women's bodies become viewed as reproductive, albeit captive resources. Reproductive genetics thrives on the moral mediation as well as scientific intervention of biomedics. British experts claim that they need to exert 'responsibility'. But, more importantly, public accountability and informed consent are needed to ensure the circulation of a genetic moral order.

In this moral order, reproductive genetics may inevitably cause disruptions and transformations in the temporal links between pregnant women. Some may go to term, other may not. Nevertheless, experts implied that pregnant women need time to make the 'right' (*i.e.* ethical) decision before these temporal links are broken. Thus, for pregnant women, 'reflexivity' or 'making space to make *ethical* decisions' emerges as an important piece of reproductive time.

Setting Reproductive Clocks for Maternity Care in Finland

Seventeen interviews (including pilot interviews) were carried out with one gynaecologist, seven medical geneticists, four policy makers, two public health officials, one researcher and two lawyers. The overarching cultural theme was care for pregnant women. In Finland, a maternity care system has been in existence since the 1940s and experts claim that this system provides an appropriate infrastructure for prenatal screening and diagnosis, offered to a captive 'treatment' population—pregnant women. Experts are unanimous that this system is very 'well-received' and 'appreciated'. One expert said that this system has been the 'backbone of developments in primary health care', while another expert spoke of the 'trust' that pregnant women had and the high uptake amongst this group:

> . . . When people [sic.] get pregnant, they get their first visit at maternity health [centres]. 99% of women go there before 15 weeks . . . because . . . they get money and . . . all the care that they [need] . . . They rely very much on these centres; they trust them. . . . those who are pregnant for the first time . . . [go] at once . . . They will [go] when [they] are . . . 10 or 12 weeks . . . For the first visit . . . they will get to know about these things [i.e. prenatal diagnosis]. If the [woman] is over . . . 40 years, the health care nurse will tell them that there is a possibility of having amniocentesis because of [the] chromosome risk . . . If there is serum screening, they will tell [them] about it. . . . They pass [on] the knowledge because it's their job. F16 Medical Geneticist

Another expert implied that 'trust' meant that the system should be cautious:

> If something is offered . . . for pregnant mothers . . . in the [maternity] . . . care system, the . . . majority will accept it . . . [The] Finnish health care system should be very cautious in what it offers because if it offers something, everyone takes it . . . Trust in the . . . system is extremely strong . . . .If this system offers something, it means that it is . . . good . . . [Generally] our health care has not had any . . . big catastrophes . . . people really do trust [it]. F5 Medical Geneticist

This view is consistent with the claim that Finns generally trust health professionals:

. . . There has never been a big public outcry on any of these [screening] issues. Usually Finns . . . trust the health professionals . . . For instance, immunization—there is nothing statutory . . . it is all voluntary, but people follow [it] 100%. . . . There is tremendous trust in the work of public health nurses who carry out these practical things. F13 Policy Maker

One expert claimed that when women come forward for maternity care, they are urged on by their 'need' to have healthy babies:

. . . [Pregnant] women . . . want to have healthy children. . . . They want to have any test that will tell them that their baby is OK. This is a basic, endless need. They will have as many tests as possible, if they can . . . if somebody else pays. I'm sure . . . F4 Medical Geneticist

This 'free' maternity system has provided an infrastructure for prenatal diagnosis and screening:

Women know the medical [system] . . . Because of the system which started in the 1940s . . . , they . . . unite the screening system to that [system] . . . [For them] this is a natural system . . . They don't know that [this system] is put into the law [or] think [of] . . . it as a political matter. They have been served before without screening and when the screening started, they noticed only that it is extra to the old system. I think that is the way . . . they . . . see it. F6 Policy Maker

And

100 % [of pregnant women] will get the information [about screening] when they go to the maternity health care centre . . . " F16 Medical Geneticist

And

. . . There is . . . [a] kind of consumerism here . . . the network is there . . . You . . . have a basic program . . . It is very difficult to say . . . "Oh thank you, I don't want [the screening]" or . . . .I [won't] take this" . . . The more you offer things, the more people consume them. So if you are screening . . . or if you offer these services, people will use them. F15 Ethicist

But one expert said the 'carefree days' (*i.e.* early days of the maternity system) are gone. While women are inducted in a system in which prenatal screening 'has really made it'; they are not prepared if problems arise:

. . . The care [free] days are gone . . . It's not only chromosome analysis but ultrasound that really has made it . . . Almost everyone (sic.) will have ultrasound and it will reveal quite a lot of things . . . and [sometimes] very unexpected [things] . . . Very often people (sic) when they . . . [hear about] ultrasound, . . . will go [to] see the baby. They [are not] really . . . prepared . . . that . . . problems might be found. F16 Medical Geneticist

In a similar context, another expert says:

> Traditionally we have had . . . rhesus screening. For over 10 years, we have had Down's screening offered to mothers over 35 or 37 . . . One thing . . . offered to all pregnant women [is] ultrasound screening . . . Sometimes . . . one finds . . . genetic malformations . . . A rather new thing is [Maternal Serum Screening] for Down's syndrome. F5 Medical Geneticist

Another expert claims that more thought needs to be given to the issue of population screening:

> We need to think very carefully about whether we want population based screening . . . We . . . have certain units mainly for genetics. Should we keep population screening . . . for families with a defined genetic problem? F16 Medical Geneticist

As seen from the above, the existence of the Finnish maternity care system since the 1940s shaped experts' claims about reproductive genetics. In the eyes of experts, pregnant woman are marked as much by their need to consume as their need to reproduce. These consumption needs emerge from their trust in the long established, well-serviced maternity care system, while their reproductive needs revolve around reproducing healthy children. What is of interest is that few experts mentioned problems and when these arose, they were contextualised in the context of maternal age. Thus, it could be said that for Finnish women, reproductive time is employed to best advantage when young rather than old bodies reproduce. Temporal formulations for normal reproduction are organised at a collective level. Pregnant bodies are synchronised and harmonised into a state wide, servicing system in which age becomes an anchor. Rather than a source of energy, time becomes somewhat of a burden for those whose biological clocks are perceived as not synchronised with their reproductive ones.

Constructing Expert Claims, while Marking Reproductive Time

As we have seen, the findings revealed overarching cultural themes, existing in each country. In Greece, the thalassaemia success story brought into focus the medical profession's achievements with prenatal technologies whether in urban or rural contexts. Reproductive time was employed to best advantage when the genes of pre-nuptial couples rather than the bodies of pregnant women were the spotlight of concerns. Central to reproduction, women's bodies became non-places in reproductive genetics. In the Netherlands, the politics of abortion shaped experts' concerns, as they made a distinction between 'normal' and 'genetic abortions'. There was a division in the social production of reproductive time. Time reckoning for experts became linked with legal reckoning, while time reckoning for pregnant women was linked with their own desires. Caught between the law and their right to choose, women found that reproductive space and time became compressed. For UK experts, 'genetic ethics', differed from 'bioethics'. 'Genetic ethics' helped to facilitate the advancement of new technologies and a genetics moral order. In this social space, experts needed to exert 'responsibility', while pregnant women needed reflexive time to make the 'right' ethical decision. Finnish maternity care shaped experts claims about reproductive genetics. As consumers and reproducers, pregnant women's needs were marked by their trust in the maternity care system and their desire to reproduce healthy children. Reproductive time was employed to best advantage when young rather than old bodies reproduced. This was because in Finland temporal formulations for normal reproduction were organised at a collective level.

In conclusion, culture plays an important role in establishing the visibility of specific illnesses and in shaping the time and spaces for reproduction in particular societies. Within the context of surveillance medicine in four European societies, marking reproductive time constructs social relations within the institution of reproduction,[7] albeit how reproductive time is marked or standardised varied between countries. Nevertheless in all countries, it is clear that reproductive time is becoming increasingly commodified[8] and marking reproductive time involves complex gendered practices. Simply, reproductive time is becoming 'product' oriented. It is progressively being linked to outcome (*i.e.* the production of 'normal' babies), while the bodies of women, not men, are temporally and spatially co-ordinated in this process. Here, I ask, 'What else is new?' I have no new answer, except that commercialisation as well as 'medicalization, routinization and informed choice' (Pilnick 2002: 65) characterise this process more now than ever before. Nevertheless, I contend that an understanding of how key players construct reproductive bodies and the sorts of strategies they use to mark 'reproductive time' is important. This understanding helps us to further understand current cultural and clinical practices being developed in this area. The more we, as sociologists, uncover the somewhat invisible practices of surveillance medicine, the more we challenge the inequalities that become embedded in the institution of reproduction. Let us use time as a resource, as we begin to challenge expert's marking of reproductive time.

Notes

Acknowledgements: This work emerges from a research project, 'The development of prenatal screening in Europe: the past, the present and the future', funded by the European Commission DGXII BIOMED2 (Contract Number BMH4-CT96–0740) from June 1996-June 1999. This project was co-ordinated from University of Helsinki by the author. The author would like to thank all experts who were interviewed for this study as well as European partners who participated in the project.

1. In discussing institutions within the context of time-space analysis, Giddens (1981) defines institutions as 'structured social practices that have broad spatial and temporal extensions'.
2. In some countries, clinical geneticists were those physicians who counselled individuals about the possibilities of genetic diseases; in other countries, physicians who did the same work were referred to as medical geneticists.
3. Thalassaemia is a characteristic of the blood and carriers have smaller as well as an excess of red blood cells in comparison to non-carriers. Thalassaemia can cause severe anaemia because red blood cells cannot make enough haemoglobin. Treatment is periodic blood transfusions, but this causes high concentrations of iron in the carriers's organs. Dangerous concentrations of iron will be removed by Desferal infusions on an almost daily basis. For carriers, this treatment scenario can go on for the whole of their life span (i.e. up to 40–45 years of age).
4. In order to maintain the anonymity of respondents, interviews are coded by country codes and specific numbers. GR is the code for Greece, NL for the Netherlands, UK for the United Kingdom and FI for Finland. For example, GR1 indicates number one interview for Greece.
5. For a general discussion of the importance of timetables in clinical settings, see Roth (1963).
6. In July 1996, *The Population Screening Act* was enacted. This meant that in order to offer serum screening for pregnant women, one would have to apply for a permit.
7. For a general discussion of the importance of time in the social construction of subjectivity, see Zerubavel (1982, 1997).
8. For an interesting discussion on how time itself is commodified, see Adam (1998).

References

Adam, Barbara (1998) *Timescapes of Modernity:the environment and invisible hazards*. London: Routledge.

Armstrong, David (1995) The rise of surveillance medicine", *Sociology of Health and Illness*, 17(3):393–404.

Atkin, Karl and Ahmad, Waqar (1998) Genetic screening and haemoglobinopathies: ethics, politics and practice", *Social Science and Medicine*, 46(3):445–58.

Blane, David, Brunner, Eric and Wilkinson, Richard (1996) The evolution of public health policy: an Anglocentric view of the last fifty years", in *Health and Social Organization: Towards a health policy for the twenty-first century*. David Blane, Eric Brunner, and Richard Wilkinson (eds.). New York: Routledge. 1–17.

Bunton, Robin (2002) Genes, technology and public health", in *The New Genetics and Public Health*. Alan Petersen and Robin Bunton. London: Routledge, 67–102.

Bunton, Robin and Barrows, R. (1995) Consumption and health in the 'epidemiological' clinic of late modern medicine", in *The Sociology of Health Promotion*. Robin Bunton, Sarah Nettleton and Roger Burrows (eds.) London: Routledge. 206–22.

Ettorre, Elizabeth (2002) *Reproductive genetics, gender and the body*, London: Routledge.

Giddens, Anthony (1981) Agency, institution, and time-space analysis", in *Advances in social theory and methodology: Toward an integration of micro-and macro-sociologies*. Karin Knorr-Cetina and Aaron V. Cicourel (eds.) London: Routledge and Kegan Paul. 161–174.

Kerr, Anne and Tom Shakespeare (2002) *genetic politics: from eugenics to genome.* Cheltenham: New Clarion Press.

Kleinman, Arthur (1991) Concepts and a model for the comparison of medical systems as cultural systems", In *Concepts of health, illness and disease.* (second edition) C. Currer and M. Stacey (eds.) New York and Oxford: Berg. 29–47.

Loukopoulos, D., A. Hadjis, M. Papadakis, P. Karababa, K. Sinopoulous, M. Boussious, P. Kollia, M. Xenakis, A. Antsaklis, M. Spyridon, A. Loutradis and P. Fessas (1990) Prenatal diagnosis of Thalassemia and of sickle cell syndromes in Greece", *Annuals of the New York Academy of Science,* 612: 226–36.

McDowell, Linda (1999) *Gender, Identity and Place: Using Feminist Geographies.* Cambridge: Polity Press.

Newman, Karen (1996) *Fetal Positions: Individualism, Science and Visuality.* California: Stanford University Press,

Oakley, Anne (1984) *The Captured Womb, A history of the Medical Care of Pregnant women.* Oxford: Blackwell.

Pilnick, Alison (2002) *Genetics and society: an introduction.* Buckingham: Open University Press.

Roth, Julius A. (1963) *Timetables: Structuring the Passage of Time in Hospital Treatment and Other Careers.* New York: The Bobbs Merrill Company.

Rothman, Barbara Katz (1993) *The tentative pregnancy: How amniocentesis changes the experience of motherhood.* (new edition) New York: Norton.

Scully, Jackie Leach (2002) A Postmodern disorder: Moral Encounters with Molecular Models of Disability", In *disability/postmodernity.* Marian Corker and Tom Shakespeare (eds.) London: Continuum. 48–61.

Simonds, Wendy (2002) Watching the Clock: Keeping time during pregnancy, birth and post partum experiences", *Social Science and Medicine* 55: 559–70.

Stacey, Margaret (1992) Introduction: what is the social science perspective?", In *Changing Human Reproduction: Social Science Perspectives.* Margaret Stacey (ed.). London: Sage. 1–8.

Tarlov, Alvin R. (1996) Social determinants of health: the sociobiological translation". In *Health and Social Organization: Towards a health policy for the twenty-first century.* D. Blane, E. Brunner, and R. Wilkinson (eds.) London and New York: Routledge. 71–93.

Wilkinson, Richard G. (1996) *Unhealthy Societies: The Afflictions of Inequality.* London and New York: Routledge.

Zerubavel, Eviatar (1997) *Social Mindscapes: an invitation to Cognitive Sociology.* Cambridge, Massachusetts: Harvard University Press.

———— (1982) The Standardization of Time: A Sociohistorical Perspective", *American Journal of Sociology* 88:1–23.

12

GM Policy Networks in Asia: A Discursive Political History of the "Doubly Green Revolution"

Richard Hindmarsh

In his keynote address to Bio-Malaysia 2002 participants, [Malaysia's Prime Minister] Dr Mahathir said: "We need to establish biotechnology as another pillar in the development of our knowledge-based economy." . . . In 1999, Biotek struck a partnership with the Massachusetts Institute of Technology (MIT) to develop and train scientists in areas like genomics, bioinformatics and bioprocessing . . . to nurture a group of professionals capable of spearheading the development of [the] biotechnology industry in Malaysia . . . (Sharif 2002).

With much focus on modern biotechnology in industrialised countries over the last three decades, Asian biodevelopment, now gaining momentum, has largely gone unnoticed, yet it began in the early 1980s. Despite many failures of science and technology for development, third world countries of late are increasingly turning to the alluring promise of biotechnology for development, especially to either attain "food security" or decrease food dependency on the North. That promise though rests on the vision of a "doubly green revolution" first cast by the US Rockefeller Foundation. The Foundation was a central developer of the earlier "green revolution"; the transfer of industrial agriculture from North to South which, however, after initially attaining some success in raising agricultural productivity, failed in its grand promise to "feed the hungry".

The new promise of the "doubly green revolution" is to make good that promise but this time using genetic engineering, popularly situated as genetic modification (GM). The promise is "doubled" as it will also address the food problems of population growth now rising at an estimated 85 million people a year, mainly in the South (Population Reference Bureau 2002). In addition, it will do all this in a "cleaner and greener" manner than before. The UN Food and Agriculture Organisation (FAO) (2000: 2) offered a conservative version of the new promise:

> The "green revolution" was responsible for accelerating food and agricultural, in particular, cereal production. However, the impact of the "green revolution" is now on the wane. Biotechnology, if properly integrated with other technologies for food production, may offer a means of triggering the next "green revolution". It offers great opportunities for enhancing food and agricultural production, quality and nutritional improvement, prevention of pre—and post-harvest losses and bioremediation and environmental improvement.

Other reasons, however, are more political economic as signalled by *The Business Times* (2001: 3): "Asia's burgeoning biotechnology sector is an oasis of rich pickings for investors as governments in the region lead the drive to develop the industry." And with GM crops an apparent disaster in the US and Canada, where GM soybeans, corn and canola are estimated to have cost the US economy at least $12 billion since 1999 in farm subsidies, lower crop prices, loss of major export orders and product recalls (Meziani and Warwick 2002), Asia thus offers potentially an extremely lucrative site for GM development. First, there is Asia's AUD$685 billion food market with 12 percent of the market met with imports (Whitfield 2001); second, Asia was the world's largest seed consumer in the 1990s; and third, in 2000, Asia accounted for 25 percent of worldwide agrichemical sales.

More politically, biodevelopment in Asia has appeal for legitimation strategies. For example, if the GM agri-food industry can become established in Asia, then that would undoubtedly pressure Northern governments to absorb more earnestly the intense and influential GM protest occurring in their own backyards. Moreover, Asia offers a facilitative site for GM experimentation to overcome its increasingly difficult technical problems (for example, see Traavik 1999; Clark 2001; Davies 2003). This resonates with the experience of the South as a dumping ground for some of the North's most toxic and harmful products banned in Northern countries, especially pesticides and pharmaceuticals. With non-existent or minimalist regulatory regimes, with complicit governments seeking modern development but burdened by debt and under-development, with poorly informed populations, and with civil society organisations (CSOs) thin on the ground and poorly resourced, Asia is further seen to offer a promising potential for establishing GM. Perhaps most significantly, the South offers a conduit for enhanced consolidation of industrial agriculture through current GM development. This is because even if GM cannot overcome its complex technical problems, it currently has the momentum and developing infrastructure to provide a persuasive avenue for the expansion of monoculture systems, especially through corporate seed takeovers, public-private sector plant breeding convergences (for example, Kloppenburg 1988; Hindmarsh 1999; Hindmarsh and Hindmarsh 2002), and through the adoption of western intellectual property (IP) regimes.

Yet, as in the North, a growing contestational movement to a GM Asia has also emerged. It engages peasant farmers' movements, women's groups, farm workers, fisherfolk, indigenous peoples, dissenting scientists, religious leaders, and consumer and environmental CSOs. All have indicated how they, or their constituencies, will be disadvantaged by GM applications. While the Asian movement shares the same environmental and social concerns about genetic engineering as the broader global movement, it also presents unique cultural differences concerning food and agricultural perceptions and practices. Yet, as elsewhere, those concerns are being largely glossed over or ignored by powerful bioindustrial interests.

A major critique of the contestational movement is that GM development in the South represents a new form of colonisation—"biocolonisation"—that builds on neocolonialism and the induced technological dependency of the green revolution, with its many adverse environmental and social impacts (as discussed below). A key concern is that GM research in third world countries is primarily focused on herbicide resistant crops (Huang et al. 2002). Globally, this area accounts for some 80 percent of GM crop research and development (R&D) (Shiva 2000). Not only are the adverse environmental impacts of chemical agriculture well documented, as are its high input costs, but the World Health Organisation estimates that 25 million cases of acute occupational chemical pesticide poisonings occur each year in developing countries (CABI 2000: 1), due to lack of protection while spraying, product labels not translated into local languages, or poor education about pesticide use and misuse.

The meaning of food is another key area of concern. As well as sustaining bodies, food strongly sustains national, ethnic, and social identities. With food playing a central part in religious and cultural festivals, some foods are almost sacred. For example, the "sacred cow" has been a part of India's cultural ethos since time immemorial. This stems from the many benefits rendered from the cow to provide sustenance: food (milk), labour (ploughing), and fuel and manure (dung). Hindus regard all living creatures as sacred-mammals, fishes, birds, and more. The cow, seen as a "complete ecology"—as a symbol of abundance—in providing so much, symbolically represents all other creatures. And to Muslims, scavengers (like pigs) are forbidden as food because they might carry disease or something harmful, and in the religious sense something impure. To be "good" behaviourally and healthy physically, and attain pure spirituality, Muslims must eat food free of harmful substances. Thus, GM foods with genes inserted from foods considered "unclean", afforded religious attributes, from non-food sources not readily identifiable, or of human-origin DNA, represent profound implications for Asian cultures where religion is central to value and identity.

Growing concerns are thus held in Asia about many issues concerning biodevelopment, including, inadequate regulatory procedures, "altered goods", lack of GM food labelling, the continued appropriation of genetic resources from centres of biodiversity by the North (Christie 2001), increasing control of agrifood production by multinational conglomerates, cultural breakdown, or inappropriate technology transfer and technological dependency. Moreover, feeding the hungry and growing populations, it is argued, cannot be accomplished just by technical approaches aimed at increasing yields. This is because food shortage and distribution problems are intricately interconnected to a variety of complex social and geopolitical aspects where the technical is but one, albeit an important one. Instead, grassroots movements have demonstrated their preference for sustainable, community or peasant agriculture, organic farming, food redistribution, land reform, and "food sovereignty" in such events as the "People's Caravan", which saw a mobilisation of people's movements in 2000 that marched from India to the Philippines protesting against genetic engineering, pesticides, and globabisation (Hindmarsh 2001, 2003).

The contestational-GM movement in the South has especially voiced its opposition to multinational "life science" conglomerates like Monsanto, Aventis and Syngenta. Yet, while these companies represent the increasingly "visible" face of the bioindustrial complex in the South, they are only part of that complex. Another important part, "not so visible", is GM interests (or "agents") who operate at the "hidden" infrastructure level and target public sector organisations, especially national agricultural research systems (NARS).

Key GM infrastructure agents operating in this terrain include the Rockefeller Foundation, the Association for South-East Asian Nations (ASEAN), the Asia-Pacific International Molecular Biology Network (A-IMBN), the US Agency for International Development (USAID), and the Asia-Pacific Association of Agricultural Research Institutions (APAARI). Other bilateral and multilateral biotechnology networks include the Food and Agriculture Organisation/United Nations Development Program (FAO/UNDP) Biotechnology Development Network for Animal Production and Health Project, and the Cassava Biotechnology Network, but they are minor compared to those others (FAO 2002), which are central to laying the foundations for biodevelopment according to western discourses of economic growth and science and technology for progress.

Given the high focus of much of the literature in third world biotechnology studies on the GM multinationals, or conversely the dearth of focus on the GM infrastructure agents, this chapter is interested to explore the nature and activities of those agents. This can yield insights by which to better understand the full scope of biodevelopment in Asia, and, in turn, the marginalisation of civil society concerns and the social and environmental implications of that marginalisation. To investigate them as political economy phenomemon, they are first conceptually situated as interorganisational networks that configure a discursive GM policy field of biodevelopment.

The GM Policy Field of Biodevelopment

The contention that GM infrastructure agents are laying the groundwork for corporate biotechnology in the South, and elsewhere, is not new. Indeed, these developments are simply an extension of the green revolution technology platform and in the North reflect what has been occurring with biotechnology since the early 1970s, and therefore with ongoing intensive agriculture developments.

Thus, when we explore the emergence of modern agro-biotechnology we find it already embedded within pre-established dominant political-economic and technocratic systems of governance, and of R&D sites. Governance here refers to the state as "one important site of government among others", including: "Markets, research institutes, biotechnology companies, and financial institutions . . . [which] contribute to making things governable, and are parts of a larger structure" (Gottweis 1998: 29). GM infrastructure agents are added to the cast here.

Underpinning structure or governability is relational power. As Herbert Gottweis elaborated, relational power goes beyond the repressive side of power to the productive side of power where neither "A nor B nor institutions with their biases and political ideologies . . . 'simply exist' as power phenomena. They come into existence through discursive processes that transcend the traditional boundaries of the political . . . In this way regimes of governability can be understood as sites where individuals are shaped and constructed" (p. 20). With regard to regimes of governability concerning contemporary technological change, Stephen Hill's notion of the technological frame as a shaping medium is instructive,

> behind the artefact stands the whole *background* frame of factory, transport, energy, communications, market and knowledge systems—a contextual grammar . . . Sedimented into this background text are the *developed* cultural assumptions of order that the system implies—concerning capital, power, ideology, knowledge and morality—all smoothly integrated into an aesthetic that puts active human constitution of meaning (and therefore control) at service of the technological frame itself. And the trajectory of the technological frame . . . is controlled by capital interests with a rich international power base . . . (Hill 1988: 24).

Through technology transfer and globalisation, the technological frame thus represents the creation of a particular spatio-temporal and geopolitical *shape of demand*, that is, it creates a "technological context for daily life . . . [that] limits and focuses the future social developments that are likely to follow . . . " (p. 26). In the globalisation context, technological innovation is then expressed spatially as a "[m]utual reciprocity between regional innovation systems and global networks" (Castells 1989: 25), featuring collaborative R&D networks, technological convergence, strategic alliances in advanced technology sectors, and inter-firm processes of permanent innovation and cooperation. Concerning the influence and outcomes of such networking *The Ecologist* found that:

> Today, economic and political power is entrenched in a network of interest groups whose influence on policy lies in the scope and intricacy of the mutually beneficial, though often uneasy, alliances that hold them together. Such alliances now bind industrialists to government officials, companies to the military, the military to the state, the state to aid agencies, aid agencies to corporations, corporations to academia, academia to regulatory agencies, and regulatory agencies to industry. Although the alliances may be unequal, all the partners have something to gain from joining forces. The result is a web of interlocking interests that effectively ensures that what is deemed "good" for those interests is deemed "good" for society at large (*The Ecologist* 1992: 157).

Transposing such phenomemon to biotechnology, Richard Hindmarsh found with regard to the global and local GM policy terrains:

> The orientation of agenda control over the international biodevelopment and regulatory agendas is quite clear. It involves three central bioscientific interest groupings found in the science community, government and industry. Together these groupings are defined as bioscientific-industrial interests, where each has its own elite . . . The overall orientation of agenda control has been to develop biotechnology unhampered by external interests that object to, or that are in opposition to, either genetics experimentation or bioindustrialisation, even where such interests represent valid and intense community concerns (Hindmarsh 1994: 421).

With the development and rapid expansion of a certain technological frame, supported by such powerful interest networks, other technological choices thus become constrained (see also Senker 1992: 354). Arguably, this was the intent behind the green revolution and is now the intent behind the GM doubly green revolution, where, for our purposes here, GM is the artefact that Hill refers to above. But how is the biotechnological frame transferred and "encoded" onto the policy landscape of the South?

Many avenues for technology transfer exist, not least through the technology management strategies of multinational corporations (Hindmarsh 1998), or through their marketing and distribution networks, or through bilateral tied aid programmes. Yet, with regard to the background texture of the technological frame—to the agency of the not so visible infrastructure agents and the dynamics of agenda control, which proactively seek to disempower community concerns about mega-technological change—we need to go to a deeper or "substructural" level of explanation. As Ernst (1983) pointed out, "in order to capture the impact of new technologies . . . it is necessary to analyse explicitly the forces *behind* the development and application of these technologies".

A useful theory to understand such dynamics is interorganisational network theory (Benson 1978), which focuses on interorganisational networks as centrally important features of advanced industrial societies (Benson 1983: 137). Here, organisations interact in strategic power networks to attain and defend resources, and strive for centrality in networks of inequality based upon an exchange formulation (Cook 1977). In the task environment, for example, of the agricultural development domain of the South, resource poor or sub-dominant organisations, such as agricultural research systems, "cluster" around a few resource rich mediating or controlling organisations, such as development and aid agencies and corporate philanthropic foundations of the North.

A policy sector or "organisational field" is thus formed, where interorganisational relationships combine in a network effect (Freeman and Barley 1990). An interorganisational network can thus be likened to the notion of core and periphery, similar to Immanuel Wallerstein's (1974) concept of economic domains. Positional power in the network is gained through the provision of services or resources "vital to all or a large number of organisations in the network" (Benson 1978: 77), for example, funding, authority, information, organisation. Power becomes manifested as centrality in the network, where authority is achieved over "strategic contingencies confronted by the peripheral organisations", for example, agricultural productivity, food security, or progress. Central to the exercise of authority is the external application of an ideological-technological commitment or discourse (the mediation of ideology, ideas and practice which assign particular meanings to reality).

How then is any particular discourse applied? Actor-network theory—as expounded by, for example, Michel Callon (1986)—provides a useful explanation that can complement interorganisational network theory. Here, actors, engaged in "networks of meaning", "articulate conceptions of the world and the roles of the actors that are in it, and impose these conceptions on one another: in short they . . . *translate*" (Law 1986: 32). The translation process involves problematising an issue (defining it through "claims" about reality and then providing the solution, in this case, GM); enrolling allies and building social coalitions; blocking other knowledges and/or alternatives (such as those of grass roots movements, and organics); and mobilising allies to support the claims (of GM). Networks of knowledge-power are thus constituted, to mediate and determine technological agendas of change (Clegg 1989: 204), through the construction of "policy narratives" that "serve to integrate the various sites that constitute a regime of governability" (Gottweis 1998: 31), and to define its fields of action for policymaking (ibid.).

Such sites in interorganisational network theory include not only those in the policy field constituted, but also groups and "structured interests" in the wider society. This involves the action of policy networks (Keller 1984), which coalesce legislative, administrative and other elites and external support groups across society, and which act to control policy making as brokers and policy coordinators (Benson 1983: 159). Notions of westernised elites, compradors, the international capitalist class, the "political-scientific elite" (Martin 1992: 88), and the "technological élite" (Dickson 1988), have currency here.

Extending the concepts of translation theory, challenges to the dominant regime of governability are acted upon by the established interests of a policy field through an array of strategic options or mechanisms of power. One example is where, through the mobilisation of the GM policy narrative, a technical approach for bioindustrial development is translated as optimal—formulated and implemented by experts. As part of that mobilisation, it has been the experience that genuine public participation and consideration of the broader social, ecological and ethical issues have most often been organised off the policy agenda (Hindmarsh 2001). Shaping the policy agenda in this way is known as the "mobilisation of bias" (Schattschneider 1960: 71). In other words, as the dominant policy narrative is mobilised, legitimised and popularised, civil society policy narratives are inhibited unless forceful counter strategies can be employed by civil society or its representatives.

In sum, the configuration of a powerful policy field using interorganisational process and an ensemble of strategies significantly influences policy making. In this context, how then are we to go about exploring the policy field of GM infrastructure agents in Asia? Adopting a chronological method I investigate the "agents" as they (apparently) emerge in the policy landscape. First, I look at the Rockefeller Foundation, and do so in substantially more detail than other key agents. This is because the Foundation was a core broker and policy field coordinator of the molecular biology endeavour—the underpinning science of genetic engineering and modern biotechnology, at the same time as it was a core developer of agricultural genetics and monoculture high yielding plant varieties and their transfer to the South as the green revolution, where simultaneously the Foundation was a core policy coordinator for its expansion. More recently, the green revolution has served as a platform for the biorevolution, or the so-called doubly green revolution of which the Rockefeller Foundation is also a key framing infrastructure agent, and broker, in Asia and now in Africa. It is also notable that the green revolution marked USAID as an early ally of the Foundation in these endeavours. Following on from the account of the Rockefeller Foundation, I then look at other key infrastructure GM agents emergent in Asia. Finally, I finish with some reflections and conclusions about the emergent GM policy field, and the associated social and environmental implications of GM agriculture.

The Rockefeller Foundation

The Rockefeller Foundation emerged in the early 20th century amidst social upheaval in the US that marked the transition from mid–19th century US as primarily rural and agricultural to the new corporate and urban technoindustrial order. One manifestation of the unrest was the progressive era (c.1895–1920), which saw the American political system grow less democratic (Burson nd). To overcome widespread disaffection with the new order's gross inequalities and labour relations, and to strengthen the institutions of capitalism (Brown 1979), elite managerial ideals combined with corporate philanthropy.

In that climate, the Rockefeller Foundation emerged in 1913, the research policy of which supported scientific progress to both advance science, and to maximise the total "social returns" from science. Foundation trustees were leading administrators, capitalists and scientists, interested in preserving the contemporary social order. In retrospective analysis of the cultural meaning and social practice of science, scholars concur that the Rockefeller Foundation program has had a profound impact on science as well as on the life sciences (for example, Fisher 1983). Pnina Abir-Am (1982: 343) emphasised the Foundation's role in preparing the stage for the emergence of "Big Science" through its cultivation of entrepreneurial scientists, where inherent was "objective knowledge" that omitted evaluation of the sociopolitical context of science (Weindling 1988: 137). In turn, Paul Weindling posited that Rockefeller patronage marked a shift "from the wealthy individual patron to bureaucratic and corporate management of science policy by scientifically trained experts" (p. 119). And Edward Yoxen (1981) concluded that the Foundation played a major role in shaping medical and university education, political reform, public health, social welfare, scientific research and agriculture worldwide. Inderjeet Parmar (2002: 235) agreed, "the Foundation directly participated in US foreign relations through numerous initiatives—notably in the fields of education and healthcare. These have been interpreted as forms of 'cultural imperialism'". In the broader realm of biodevelopment, Timothy Evans (nd) found that the Foundation's

> niche is as a catalyst or incubator of public-private partnerships for specific global product development priorities . . . These partnerships are virtual, not-for-profit organizations that use private sector know-how to exploit the best opportunities globally for accelerating product development. The new entities help fill the voids in financial, technical, and human resources . . . The partnerships are critical, be-

cause no single partner, be it researchers, biotechnology or pharmaceutical companies, bilaterals, or multilaterals, could take on these challenges alone. (pp. 2–3)

A central part of the Foundation's early biology policy narrative was to embrace "engineering biology"—which had emerged by 1900 with a view to *transform* nature as "raw material"—to "reconstruct" the natural order to make it "rational and efficient", to create a "technology of living substance" (see Pauly 1987: 51). In 1901, the term *Biontotechnik* surfaced (in Europe) to define the modification of living organisms through technology (Bud 1993: 53). Soon thereafter, (mechanistic) genetics emerged to provide the technical avenue for engineering biology, with control of heredity, and ultimate power over nature, in the offering (see Hindmarsh and Lawrence 2003).

Enrolled to such grand visions, in the late 1920s, the Foundation began its eugenics inspired "Science of Man" behavioural genetics project aimed at social control, which also appealed to the technocratic elite then dominating US culture. Lily Kay (1993: 8) has situated the beginnings of molecular biology within that project, and Philip Regal argued the influence on the project of "the general spirit of Bacon's *New Atlantis* and Enlightenment visions of a trouble-free society based on mastery of nature's laws and scientific/technological progress" (Regal 1996: 18). By the 1930s, however, those projects had become a liability because of new knowledge and their stigma of racial, class, gender and ethnocentric prejudice and political propaganda. Despite this setback: "For the architects and champions of a science-based technological utopianism" (Kay 1993: 9), eugenic goals remained to play a significant role in the molecular biology program, as Kay noted: "The molecular biology program, through the study of simple biological systems and the analyses of protein structure, promised a surer, albeit much slower, way toward social planning based on sounder principles of eugenic selection" (ibid.).

The origins of molecular biology are traced to the Rockefeller Foundation's *Annual Report* for 1938 authored by physicist Warren Weaver, director of its Division of Natural Sciences. Weaver's approach—along with mathematician and then president of the Foundation Max Mason—was to "modernise" biology by recasting research in biology to the disciplined methodological and technological rigour of the physical sciences (Yoxen 1983: 22), from classical physics, mathematics and chemistry to the biological sciences of genetics, embryology, physiology, immunology, and microbiology. Like physics, molecular biology became devoted to finding the "ultimate littleness of things" (Yoxen 1981: 345), and became defined interchangeably as the "biology of molecules" or as "sub-cellular biology" (Abir-Am 1982).

Molecular biology was subsequently and significantly incubated by the Foundation, along with others including the UK's Medical Research Council, which the Foundation also used as a conduit to disburse molecular biology funding in Britain (Paul 1998: 61). The Foundation's program dwarfed others with a disbursement of US$90 million to support molecular biology between 1932 and 1957 through an extensive system of grants and fellowships, and institution building. Though by no means wholly responsible for building the new approach to studying (and "engineering") life, Gottweis argued that "by privileging the molecular biology approach over the evolutionary, ecological, and organismic traditions, the Rockefeller Foundation emerged as a critical coordinating agency" (Gottweis 1998: 43–44). As Gottweis further elaborated:

> Its financial muscle reinforced the ongoing disciplinary tendencies, and the foundation became an integral part of a system of power relations. The foundation's importance was the result of a multifaceted process of enrolment and boundary work that defined particular individuals, structures, representations and institutions as elements in a new configuration and linked them together through processes of legitimization and distribution of cognitive authority. (p. 44)

With a resulting strong research network and policy field configured around molecular biology discourse, scientific discoveries followed. Two became turning points for its success. First, in 1944, Avery, McCarty and MacLeod of the Rockefeller Institute for Medical Research discovered that DNA transmitted hereditary "information" (Fuerst 1982: 269). It was this finding, later acclaimed the Rockefeller University that "set the course for biological research for the rest of the century" (The Rockefeller University 2001: 2). Subsequently, after 1945, an international research community formed and primarily consisted of a network of laboratory directors channelling funds into universities and medical schools (Yoxen 1982), to conceptually redefine biology along molecular lines. The second major turning point occurred with the discovery of the double helical structure of DNA in 1953 by Francis Crick and James Watson. Following that success, in 1958, Crick and Watson formulated the initial key principle of molecular biology, the Central Dogma: "DNA makes RNA makes protein". The dominant notion of genetic determinism thus held, and became characterised in neo-Darwinian terms through natural selection "in terms of gene 'encoding' characteristics of individual organisms" (Wills 2002: 3).

Other discoveries followed: by 1966, the genetic "code" had been fully "deciphered" (see Hindmarsh and Lawrence 2003); in 1967 an enzyme (DNA ligase) that causes DNA chains to join together was isolated; and, in 1970, restriction endonucleases, which cleave DNA at specific sites, were isolated. These formed the central techniques for recombining DNA, discovered in 1973. Accompanying the discoveries were rewarding devices in the form of many Nobel prizes for molecular biologists in physiology or medicine, where the Rockefeller Foundation had sponsored many of the scientists. The prizes served to confer additional status upon, and legitimation of, the molecular biology approach. It acquired a reputation in biology for where the real excitement lay, and funding increased dramatically for the field.

Parallel to such developments though were other important ones—central to this story—in another central arena of genetics that the Rockefeller Foundation engaged with. During the 1920–40s, the Foundation became enrolled to agricultural genetics with hybridisation developments in the US producing an "improved" corn crop for industrial agriculture (Berlan and Lewontin 1986: 45). (This would align the Rockefeller Foundation's eugenic notions of improving humans to the broader one of improving Nature, in the tradition of the Baconian project.) Dramatic commercial returns subsequently resulted in the mid–1930s from hybrid seed-corn sales, with farmers enrolled to the new hybrids needing to purchase them each growing season. A stagnant commercial seed trade became revitalised (Kloppenburg 1988), and from then onwards, congressional agriculture funding committees also became supportive of genetics R&D. Concomitantly, linking to other (economic, political and legal) sites of governability, the US and the UK began to institutionalise private ownership of biological R&D with patent acts. That further defined the discourse and future of biotechnics as commercial and entrepreneurial.

The Green Revolution

Such developments led also to the idea of a "green revolution" being explored in a meeting between Rockefeller Foundation president Raymond Fosdick and US Vice President Henry A. Wallace, the underlying *private* vision being political and economic (Kloppenburg 1988: 158). The political benefits projected were to achieve social stability through increased food production and a strengthened middle-class peasantry to counter communism, and to make the world safe for profits (Cleaver 1972: 82). By association, the alignment of agricultural production globally to modern industrial capitalism would accrue commercial benefits for Wallace as the founder of the forerunner of Pioneer Hi-Bred (hybrid seed), and for the Rockefellers through the sale of Standard Oil petrochemical energy and products.

Alongside that covert private vision, the overt *public* vision and policy narrative to enroll others was that of "feeding the hungry through intensive agriculture". The Rockefeller Foundation initiated its Mexican Agricultural Program in 1943. Described as a "volatile mix of business, philanthropy, science, and politics" (Kloppenburg 1988: 158), its implicit goal—to diffuse hybrid high yielding varieties (HYVs) with high response to agrichemicals—appeared confirmed when the Rockefeller's International Basic Economy Corporation heavily invested in 1946 in the only Brazilian hybrid-seed-producing firm. Other Western interests followed suit, for example, grain merchant

Cargill initiated hybrid seed-corn production in Argentina in 1947. Diffusing this programme into Kenya in 1956, USAID and the Rockefeller Foundation funded a hybrid corn-breeding programme under which purchasers of seed were required to buy fertilisers (Barkin and Suarez 1986: 29; Kloppenburg 1988: 158).

By the 1960s, a whole series of green revolution programmes had been implemented in other third world countries including India, the Philippines, and Indonesia. Subsequently, in India, the consumption of fertilisers rose from 5.5 million tonnes in 1980–81 to 13.5 million tonnes in 1992 (Shiva 1993: 25,27). In the Philippines, the Rockefeller and Ford Foundations founded the International Rice Research Institute (IRRI) in 1960; the establishment of which Alvares (1986) commented was "part of America's efforts to control and direct rice research in Asia". Rice is by far the world's most important food crop with approximately 90 percent of the crop grown in Asia. To date, IRRI has produced more than 300 monoculture HYVs (see Hindmarsh and Hindmarsh 2002: 3).

The adoption of HYVs also created lucrative profits for agrichemicals and biocides because of the high vulnerability of genetically uniform monocultures to insect and pest attacks, as well as to weed proliferation due to the intensive fertiliser use. In the Philippines, to profit from the green revolution, Rockefeller's Standard Oil set up 400 agro-service centres for ESSO fertiliser, seeds, pesticides, implements, and extension advice (George 1976: 118–19). IRRI's annual reports from 1963–82 show the institution receiving grants from many US and European chemical corporations among them Monsanto, Shell Chemical, Union Carbide Asia, Bayer Philippines, Eli Lily, Occidental Chemical, Ciba Geigy, Chevron Chemical, Upjohn, Hoechst, and Cyanamid Far East (see Hindmarsh and Hindmarsh 2002: 3).

To entrench the green revolution's intensive, industrialised methods of production, the Rockefeller and Ford Foundations, along with other western agencies, created the Consultative Group on International Agricultural Research (CGIAR) in 1971 to coordinate the interorganisational network of international agricultural research centres (IARCs, now renamed "Future Harvest Centers"), established with the diffusion of the green revolution. The CGIAR now employs more than 8500 scientists and support staff in more than 100 countries, and in 1998, represented about four percent of total global expenditure on agricultural research. Sponsors, and policy actors, of the CGIAR include about 28 countries in the North and key agricultural ones in the South (although in 1993, only one percent of funding derived from Southern governments (Rangnekar 1996)), the Ford, Rockefeller and Kellogg Foundations, and international and regional aid and development organisations, including the World Bank.

Yet, challenging the promise of the green revolution to feed the hungry was that only third world farmers with the necessary resources to adopt the technology such as well-irrigated and fertile land or the financial capability to invest were able to successfully adopt its technology. Consequently, while the adoption of the technology created new avenues of profit for large farmers, that, in turn, led to land consolidation and a trend towards the use of labour saving inputs such as tractors and agrichemicals. In that process, small or tenant farmers and landless labourers were severely disadvantaged. Although a significant increase in agricultural productivity initially occurred there were many adverse social impacts as well, including a widening income gap between rich and poor, increasing tenure displacement, landlessness, unemployment, indebtedness, poverty, cultural breakdown, social conflict, increased hunger and malnutrition, and deepening technological dependency (for example, George 1976; Hindmarsh 1990).

Ecological imbalance also resulted from increasing dosages of pesticides, and noticeable genetic erosion also emerged to play havoc with traditional polyculture farming systems. For example: "Prior to the diffusion of HYVs, over 100,000 rice varieties thrived in farmer's fields. By the mid–1980s, just two HYVs occupied 98 percent of the entire rice growing area of the Philippines" (Hindmarsh and Hindmarsh 2002: 3). One of those was rice variety IR8. It launched the green revolution because of its high yield potential but it also featured poor quality and a lack of resistance to common rice diseases and pests (Rangnekar 1996). Following the plight of diminishing biodiversity were other severe environmental impacts. They included salinity, soil erosion, and depletion of micronutirents, such as zinc, due to constant application of chemical fertilisers. These problems would eventually contribute to reduced yields and on many green revolution lands, yields are now in wide decline or are stagnating. In addition, land consolidation led to marginal lands being cultivated, which further increased environmental degradation.

Paradoxically, the stated mission of the CGIAR—now the most influential third world agricultural R&D body—was to promote "policies to reduce poverty, improve food security and nutrition, and alleviate pressures on fragile natural resources" (CGIAR nd). It was to undertake this through R&D, capacity building and policy support. Following on from the green revolution the CGIAR is now situated as a primary "public sector" conduit for the "bio-revolution" or as the incumbent Rockefeller Foundation's president Gordon Conway penned, the "doubly green revolution" (Conway 1998).

The Doubly Green Revolution

Over the past decade, private sector collaboration has strengthened with the CGIAR. The rationale for this was revealed at a World Bank forum— *Agricultural Biotechnology: Opportunities for International Development*, held in Canberra, Australia, in 1989. Participants included many western development and aid agencies, the Rockefeller Foundation, biotechnology and seed TNCs, and representatives of Southern countries especially from those that house centres of biodiversity (or genetic resources), that is, CGIAR sites.

The primary points of the World Bank's policy narrative were that developing countries should only concentrate on "orphan" crop research, the North, with its cutting-edge resources, would concentrate on the commercially important ones; that transfer of biotechnology was conditional on western patent systems and voluntary regulatory systems; that capacity building for biotechnology was necessary; and, that the CGIAR needed to collaborate with the private sector. The overall thrust was for western patent protection regimes to be put in place for any large-scale diffusion of biotechnology products aimed at raising food productivity. The latter claim again reflected the "feeding the hungry" discourse and amended it such that biotechnology would help overcome both past and existing problems of green revolution food production, especially declining yields. Yet, the focus on intellectual property rights contradicted the traditional role of the CGIAR to process information, inventions, processes, biological material and other research products, funded or developed by the CGIAR, as public goods. This further defined that the application of genetic engineering was to be embedded in a commercial and entrepreneurial frame.

Nearly a decade before, the Rockefeller Foundation had significantly helped to lay the groundwork for such policy directives to emerge, especially concerning rice. In the early 1980s, chemical, agribusiness and pharmaceutical corporations were earnestly developing GM in the North, building on a platform of many small biotechnology companies established earlier by a wave of entrepreneurial academic scientists, especially in the US. Concurrently, the Rockefeller Foundation investigated biotechnology prospects for the world's major food crops. In 1984, it began a 15-year funding program for rice biotechnology in the South called the International Program on Rice Biotechnology (IPRB). Similar to the earlier European and US molecular biology network the Foundation had established, it brokered a policy and R&D network to translate and establish the new molecular rice technological frame. The IPRB dispensed almost US$105 million—an average of US$6.2 million annually—for its technology generation and application phases (Hindmarsh and Hindmarsh 2002: 7).

The first phase lasted seven years and funded research in 46 enrolled advanced research institutions, primarily in the US, Europe, Japan and Australia—all centres of commercial biotechnology. A scientists' network was also enrolled of approximately 700 scientists from over 30 countries, with more than 400 Asian scientists participating. In addition, all relevant CGIAR centres' biotechnology capacity was upgraded, those being IRRI, the International Centre for Tropical Agriculture (CIAT) and the West Africa Rice Development Association (WARDA). Promising Asian scientists were sent to laboratories in the North, and funding was provided to Asian facilities that supported those scientists' work on their return. The network focussed on incorporating specialised traits into rice varieties, including yield-enhancement, disease-resistance, insect-resistance, grain-quality, abiotic stress tolerance, including drought and salinity, and improved micronutient content, an endeavour the Foundation heralded as the "invention of rice biotechnology".

Scientific breakthroughs again resulted: rice was the first cereal to be regenerated from a protoplast in 1986–88; a DNA molecular marker map was achieved by 1988, and the first experimental transformation was accomplished in 1988–90. Rapid progress occurred with host-plant resistance. The discoveries also revealed the importance of rice to understanding the biological functions of cereals. Here—it was posited—lay the key to "decoding" six of the world's major cereal food crops (ibid., p. 8). In 1991, a detailed genetic map of rice—developed at Cornell University also with Rockefeller funding—was disseminated to rice breeders worldwide to facilitate the creation of improved rice varieties (Rockefeller Foundation nd).

Meanwhile, in far off Mexico, the Foundation was revealing its more entrepreneurial side in funding a collaborative partnership between life sciences conglomerate Monsanto and the Center for Advanced Studies (CINVESTAV)—a government research laboratory—to develop, through biotechnology, virus resistance potato varieties for resource-poor Mexican farmers. The partnership involved two CINVESTAV scientists working with Monsanto scientists to learn how to conduct potato transformation. In return, Monsanto was granted the rights to use its virus-protection technology in certain varieties of potatoes, following approval and commercialisation (Monsanto 2001).

Back in Asia, the Asian Rice Biotechnology Network (ARBN)—coordinated by IRRI—was established (in 1993) to enhance the biotechnology capacity of its NARS partners. The final group of Biotechnology Career Fellows was also selected. Launched in 1984, alongside the IPRB, the program established an R&D network of 183 fellows—many of whom had risen to prominent research positions in their home countries—to update their biotechnology skills and the development of collaborative research projects (Hindmarsh and Hindmarsh 2002: 8). In 1995, a Foundation funded team of US and Asian scientists cloned a gene for resistance against bacterial blight in rice. In 1997, IPRB scientists confirmed that all cereals had essentially the same basic genes as rice, and by 1998, comparative mapping across grass species became possible.

Turning to the second phase of the program, it focused on research for bioproduct development through technology transfer to research institutions and rice breeders. Again, research grantees and fellows were enrolled from both North and South. By 1994, the program had supported 130 projects in 26 countries with 69 located in developing countries. Approximately 62 percent of grant funds and about the same proportion of total research funds went to China and India with 56 percent of world rice production cultivated on 50 percent of the world's rice area (ibid., p. 9). Scientific breakthroughs continued to emerge.

Continuing also was the translation of the promise of feeding the hungry through biotechnology, even though the Foundation emphasised a technical approach and did not address the real causes of underdevelopment such as structural adjustment policies, debt, or inappropriate technology transfer (George and Sabelli 1994). Also ignored were "genuine" participatory approaches, for example, as called for by the World Commission for Environment and Development in 1987. Even though the Foundation admitted that farmers had a deep personal knowledge of farming conditions, a comprehensive assessment of their opinions was dismissed, paradoxically, as being too expensive and thus unwarranted (Evenson et al., 1996: 395–96). Also dismissed were low input systems, the prefernce of the majority of farmers in Asia. They were portrayed as being unsustainable and incapable of feeding increasing populations despite that preference and despite convincing counter-evidence being availbale over some time (for example, Parrott and Marsden 2002). Contesting alternatives were thus organised off the policy agenda.

In 1999, with the biotechnology rice program well under way, with rice genomics programs fostering, with GM rice capacity building occurring across Asia, and with a strong GM policy field developed, the Foundation concluded that its infrastructure-building role was over and that it was time to turn to Africa.

Fruitful legacies for biodevelopment included China, India and Korea firmly integrating biotech into national rice research programmes, with the Philippines, Thailand and Vietnam all moving in that direction; and, IRRI setting up the Asian Rice Biotechnology Network to engage with much infrastructure building with NARS partners. Additionally, IRRI's 2002–04 Plan was strongly committed to bioproduct development—including herbicide-tolerant rice—in a "partnership" network with development CSOs, extension agencies, and private companies including the Asia Pacific Seeds Association (APSA), which boasted a membership of major seed and biotechnology companies including Monsanto, Novartis, Syngenta, DuPont, Aventis, and RiceTec.

We now turn to other key GM infrastructure agents that emerged in the wake of the Rockefeller Foundation.

Other Key GM Infrastructure Agents in Asia

The Association for South-East Asian Nations

A central ASEAN agency for biotechnology is the ASEAN Committee on Science and Technology (COST) (established in 1978). In 1989, its Sub-Committee on Biotechnology was formed to implement regional biotechnology projects. Its priority areas included disease treatment and prevention, crop productivity and product quality, and better environmental resource management. Its main objectives were to establish the ASEAN biotechnology information network, as well as collaborative joint ventures with the private sector. Its dialogue partners and main funders are Australia, Canada, the European Union, Japan, India, New Zealand, and the Republic of Korea. Some eight research projects are in the pipeline. Other ASEAN bodies are also implementing biotechnology-related activities, for example, the Senior Officials Meeting of the ASEAN Ministers for Agriculture and Fisheries (SOM-AMAF). Since 1998, this body has been exploring the possibility of harmonisation of national guidelines and regulations for biotechnology. There has also been the publication of two books: *Biotechnology for Development*, and *The ASEAN-Australia Biotechnology Directorate*. An Asian "Biotechnology Atlas" is also under development (Tambunan 1999).

Areas of development include plant biotechnology, animal biotechnology, an ASEAN-Canada Biotechnology Information Network; utilisation of tropical rainforest plants from Indonesia, Malaysia, Philippines, Thailand and Vietnam for chemical and biological prospecting of the plants; development of biological agents for pest and insect control, and the development of transgenic or genetically engineered plants.

The US Agency for International Development

In designing an agricultural biotechnology program in 1990, USAID drew on its experience of supporting the Monsanto-Kenyan Agricultural Research Institute (KARI) program on disease-resistant sweet potato (Lewis 1999). With the help of the US National Research Council, priorities included institutional management issues, especially capacity to address IPR and biosafety, and other technology transfer issues through private-public sector partnerships. During the 1990s, collaborations were supported largely through the Agricultural Biotechnology Support Program (ABSP) of the Michigan State University. The ABSP enrolled a number of US universities, US and Southern companies, CGIAR centres, and NARS. Some examples included: ICI Seeds (Zeneca) and the Central Research Institute for Food Crops Indonesia to develop Bt tropical corn; and, Pioneer Hi-Bred and the Egyptian Agricultural Genetic Engineering Research Institute to develop Bt corn. The ABSP's efforts in IPR have covered both plant variety protection and patent forms of IPR. Michigan State University has so far served as the contractual intermediate on most research agreements between companies and public research institutions in the South.

The Asia-Pacific International Molecular Biology Network

The A-IMBN was established in 1997 to implement biotechnology across Asia. It also represents an interorganisational network of scientists, scientific institutions, national and international agencies, and industry, many of which overlap other GM policy networks. The A-IMBN was conceived by researchers at the Institute for Molecular Biology and Genetics at Seoul National University, and the Institute of Medical Science of Tokyo University. It succeeds the failed Asian Molecular Biology Organisation (AMBO) established in 1980 by US scientists and Kenichi Arai, the current A-IMBN president (and also Director of the Institute of Medical Science of Tokyo University) (A-IMBN nd).

The model for AMBO, and now for the A-IMBN, was the influential European Molecular Biology Organisation (EMBO)—a private scientific organisation supporting molecular research biology and in conjunction, its minimalist regulation (Wright 1986: 599). Participants in the A-IMBN include 243 scientists from Australia, China, Chinese Taipei, Hong Kong SAR, India, Indonesia, Israel, Japan, Korea, Malaysia, New Zealand, the Philippines, and Singapore. Nominations to join have been received from Thailand, Canada, the US, Pakistan, and Vietnam. International linkages include many genetic engineering and biotechnology research organisations, development agencies, including the FAO and biotechnology companies.

In 2000, the A-IMBN formulated a five-pronged vision involving: (1) infrastructure development across Asia; (2) a regulatory/cultural environment: to encourage biodevelopment, for example, with regard to IP regulations, attitudes accepting of biotechnology, and entrepreneurship; (3) legislation and policies: to promote biotechnology, and to encourage careers and entrepreneurship; (4) human resources development: to promote school and academic education; and, (5) finance and resources mobilisation: to facilitate national, international and private funding, to encourage investment, and to nurture academia and industry links (Tambunan 1999).

By 2001, it had begun to develop the following initiatives: a media program that involved training promising young journalists to present pro-biotechnology perspectives; a public education program aimed at public acceptance of GM; the preparation of information resources and materials for elementary and high school students; encouragement of bioindustry-academia collaborations; and the setting up of A-IMBN laboratories, the first one being established in 2001 in biomedicine at Singapore's Institute of Molecular and Cell Biology.

The Asia-Pacific Association of Agricultural Research Institutions

The APAARI represents yet another biotechnology interorganisational policy network involving the development of NARS in the Asia-Pacific region through inter-regional and inter-institutional cooperation. Its constitution was adopted in December 1990 by the General Assembly in its second meeting held at the UN Food and Agriculture's Regional Office for Asia and the Pacific (FAO-RAP), Bangkok. Members include Australia, India, Japan, the Republic of Korea, Taiwan, and Thailand, Bangladesh, Iran, Pakistan, Malaysia, the Philippines, Fiji, Nepal, Papua New Guinea, Sri Lanka, Vietnam, and Western Samoa (APAARI 2001).

During 2000–01, APAARI signed a letter of agreement with FAO-RAP wherein the FAO would provide financial support for studies and a regional biotechnology consultation with selected Asian countries. The studies would assess biotechnology needs and capacity regarding areas of potential concern; policy advice, training and human resources development; identification of institutions and individuals involved in biotechnology. An expert consultation was to be organised.

In March 2002, the FAO-APAARI Expert Consultation on the Status of Biotechnology in Agriculture in Asia and the Pacific March was held in Bangkok, with the participation of NARS, CGIAR centres, CG Institutions, CSOs, and the private sector, including Aventis, Monsanto and Syngenta. The large biotech conglomerates portrayed 'that their businesses were trying to be socially responsible and spoke of the need for promoting greater public awareness of the issues linked to biotechnology use in agriculture' (ibid.). By way of contrast, the CSOs 'questioned the use of biotechnology to merely increase food production if this could not reach the hungry. They underlined the right to adequate, safe and culturally acceptable food, right to informed choice and right to democratic participation' (ibid.). The meeting's key recommendations—which favoured the private sector—were to evaluate the broader impact of biotechnology on society and establish biosafety and regulatory frameworks, private and public sector partnerships, and regional/international collaboration and capacity building.

Later, in September 2002, a conference was held in Kuala Lumpur called "Capitalise on Genetic Modification in the Food Industry: Profit from innovations and strategies to comply with upcoming government directives". Sponsored by the Malaysian Biotechnology Information Centre, Ram Badam Singh, former Assistant Director-General & Regional Representative: Asia & the

Pacific, FAO, delivered a talk called "Biotechnology and biosecurity: Towards an evergreen revolution" (Singh 2002). In recognition of both the promise and risks of biotechnology, Singh emvisaged a "National Commission on Biotechnology-Biosafety-Biodiversity-Biosecurity" in each country. Regional databases would monitor crop productivity, production and ecological attributes (gene-pollution, ecological effect, use of pesticides and herbicides, emergence of pest resistance, and impacts on biodiversity).

Reflections and Conclusions

Clearly, GM infrastructure agents (including the Rockefeller Foundation), building on the Rockefeller Foundation's early green revolution initiatives and policy narratives, are incubators for GM agrifood development, just as Evans found the Rockefeller Foundation was for biomedical product development. Here, as brokers and coordinators, they enrol public sector organisations to the GM policy narratives and private sector networks of the North, laying and consolidating the foundations for commercial biotechnology.

As discussed, central infrastructure agents include the Rockefeller Foundation, the CGIAR and its Future Harvest Centres, ASEAN, the A-IMBN, the FAO-RAP and APAARI, and USAID. Building upon the green revolution technological frame and platform, and having vital network resources these organisations have been able to position themselves at the centre of the policy field of agriculture for development.

Attaining centrality in this network of inequality has empowered those agents to increasingly define and legitimise progress and development as GM, even though many significant problems of GM exist and have been recoginsed. Biodevelopment is further facilitated where central actors in technology transfer network organisations, like the CGIAR, are interlinked to other powerful GM policy brokers in the global domain, like the World Bank, and multinational biotechnology companies. The increasing linkage of the CGIAR to the private sector was further signalled at the Annual General Meeting of the CGIAR in late October 2002. There, the Syngenta Foundation for Sustainable Agriculture was acclaimed as a new member of the CGIAR (2002). Syngenta, at that time, was the world's largest agrichemical and life sciences corporation. In response, grassroots critics in the South branded the CGIAR as CG(I)AR, the "Consultative Group of (Industrial) Agricultural Research" (Sharma 2002).

Emphasising the cohesion of the GM policy field is the concurrent membership of many participating organisations in the many interorganisational nodes forming the field, with similar strategies and discourses deployed. This is well illustrated where IRRI networked with APAARI, the Global Forum on Agricultural Research (GFAR), the CGIAR, USAID, the Rockefeller Foundation, and the Ministry of Foreign Affairs of The Netherlands to organise a Council for Partnership on Rice Research in Asia (CORRA) workshop, aimed at reinforcing the need for the South to adopt western IP regimes. CORRA is an informal organisation of the world's main rice producing nations, and was set up by the leaders of the NARS in Bangladesh, China, India, Indonesia, Korea, Malaysia, Myanmar, Thailand, the Philippines, and Vietnam. An IRRI press release after the workshop announced:

> While the idea of one company owning a popular variety is well established in crops such as wheat and maize, this is still unheard of in the Asian rice sector, where even newly developed varieties are always made freely available to all farmers. But with the advent of biotechnology and with World Trade Organization (WTO) rules and regulations looming on the horizon, such traditions are changing fast. The Chairman of the Council for Partnership on Rice Research in Asia (CORRA), Dr. Joko Budianto from Indonesia, said that it is very important for rice-producing nations to master the complexities of PVP [Plant Variety Protection] and IP laws as quickly as possible, otherwise their research efforts may suffer. "These PVP and IP legal requirements are new for many of us in rice research and production, but we have to study and introduce the necessary legislation as quickly as possible," he said. (IRRI 2000: 1)

Such developments align with trends of emerging monopoly control over key biotechnology patents by corporations and institutions in the North. Already over 600 biotechnology patents have been secured for rice with the top 17 patent holders controlling 56 percent (Hindmarsh and Hindmarsh 2002: 4).

Another illustrative example of the enmeshment of GM interorganisational networks is where senior members of the Australian biotech community are part of the A-IMBN, including Biotechnology Australia—the federal agency charged with developing biotechnology in Australia and the implementer of Australia's "National Biotechnology Strategy". The strategies of the A-IMBN clearly mimic some of Biotechnology Australia's, which, in turn, draw upon US policy initiatives (for example, House Committee on Science 1998), and upon TNC-state-bioscientist policy alliances in Australia and earlier OECD policy recommendations (for example, see ASTEC 1993).

Such enmeshment and outcomes well support the notion of "bio-colonisation" that GM critics in the South have portrayed the transfer of biotechnology from the North to be. Strengthening that notion is that while much of the language of policy texts of the infrastructure agents pertains to notions of environmental and social responsibility, no reference is given to existing and local practises of producing food and environmental well-being such as community, organic or peasant sustainable agriculture, nor is reference in decision-making processes to peasant movements, small farmers, or genuine community participation, apparent.

Yet, signalling an urgent need for genuine community participation with regard to GM agriculture is the case of Argentina. Six years ago, in 1996, some 90 percent of Argentine farmers adopted Monsanto's Round-Up Ready (RR) soya beans on the promise that it would make it cheaper to farm because of increased yields and of having to apply only one herbicide instead of many. Although exports have increased rapidly:

> the growth in output is exclusively the result of an increase in the area of land under soya bean cultivation. Despite the early promises, RR soya beans have had five-six percent lower yields than conventional soya . . . Because of the evolution of vicious new weeds, farmers have had to use two or three times more pesticides than previously. Overall, total costs have risen by 14 percent. Soya prices have dropped as a result of increased global production . . . No longer able to compete, small-scale Argentine farmers are going bankrupt . . . Even more alarming is the ecological damage . . . Soya is not bringing wealth to Argentina. "We are being occupied by the seed multinationals that have patented life and are forcing us to pay tribute to them," says [Eduardo] Rulli [a leading Argentine agronomist]. "The more we produce the poorer we become." . . . Economic output is predicted to fall by at least 15 percent this year. (Branford 2002: 23)

Thus, in reflecting upon the experience of the green revolution, upon monopoly corporate biotechnology trends now clearly emerging, upon the technical difficulties of GM crops such as gene flow, and upon the dismal experiences of GM crops in Argentina, it is increasingly obvious that promotion of the GM doubly green revolution is more about economic and political imperatives, than of satisfying any public vision of benevolence portrayed. It is in this context that its impacts will be more considered "doubly", on one hand demonstrating a likely escalation of the adverse impacts of industrial agriculture, and on the other hand, expanding the power and profits of the enmeshed GM policy field—comprised of the "not so visible" infrastructure agents and the "more visible" corporate giants—operating together under the banner of the "doubly green revolution": a metaphor that can now be portrayed as not only offering, but also as challenging, that alluring promise of biotechnology for development.

Note

*Acknowledgements:*The inspiration for this chapter came from my participation in a consultancy report, at the bequest of Sarah Hindmarsh, on GM rice in Asia for the Pesticide Action Network Asia Pacific, Malaysia. That report—*Laying the Molecular Foundations of GM Rice Across Asia*—has oft been cited here. In addition, the chapter is an outgrowth of papers presented at the Biotechnology, Commerce, and Civil Society Conference, Institute for Advanced Cultural Studies (Kulturwissenschaftliche Institut) Essen, Germany (5–7 September 2002), and the Peasant Scientist Conference, Kuala Lumpur, Malaysia (28–30 September 2002).

References

Abir-Am, Pnina (1982) "The discourse of physical power and biological knowledge in the 1930s: A reappraisal of the Rockefeller Foundation's "Policy" in molecular biology," *Social Studies of Science* 12: 341–82.

A-IMBN (Asia-Pacific International Molecular Biology Network) (nd) (http://www.a-imbn.org).

Alvares, C. (1986) "The great gene robbery," *The Illustrated Weekly of India* 23 March: 6–17.

APARRI (2001) Proceedings, The Sixth Executive Committee Meeting of APAARI and Expert Consultation on Regional Priority Setting for Agricultural Research for Development in the Asia-Pacific Region, 12–14 November 2001, Bangkok, Thailand.

ASTEC (Australian Science and Technology Council) (1993) *Gene Technology: Issues for Australia*, Occasional Paper No. 27, Australian Government Publishing Service, Canberra.

Barkin, D. and B. Suarez (1986) "The transnational role in Mexico's seed industry," *Ceres* 114: 27–31.

Benson, J. Kenneth (1978) "The Interorganizational Network as a Political Economy," in *Organization and Environment* L. Karpik, (ed). London: Sage.

Benson, J. Kenneth (1983) "A Framework for Policy Analysis," in *Interorganizational Coordination* D. Rogers and D. Whettan (eds). Iowa: State University Press.

Berlan, J-P. and R. Lewontin (1986) "The political economy of corn", *Monthly Review* 38: 35–47.

Branford, Susan. (2002) "Why Argentina can't feed itself—how GM soya is destroying livelihoods and the environment in Argentina," *The Ecologist* 32(8): 23.

Brown, Richard (1979) *Rockefeller Medicine Men: Medicine and Capitalism in America.* USA: University of California Press.

Bud, Robert (1993) *The Uses of Life: A History of Biotechnology.* New York: Cambridge University Press.

Burson, George (nd) *Progressive Movement & the 1920s*, U.S. History Curriculum, Aspen School District, Aspen, Colorado (http://www.jmu.edu/madison/teach/burson/prog.htm).

CABI Bioscience (2000) "Pesticides: is there an alternative?" CABI press release, 29 February.

Callon, Michel (1986) "Some Elements of a Sociology of Translation: Domestification of the Scallops and the Fishermen of St Brieuc Bay," in *Power, Action and Belief: A New Sociology of Knowledge?* J. Law (ed). London: Routledge & Kegan Paul.

Castells, Manuel (1989) *The Informational City: Information Technology, Economic Restructuring, and the Urban-Regional Process.* Cambridge: Basil Blackwell.

CGIAR (nd) http://www.cgiar.org/research/res_global.html.

CGIAR Online (2002) "From strength to strength: New members expand CGIAR alliance," 30 October 2002 (http://www.cgiar.org/publications/news021030 members.html).

Christie, Jean (2001) "Enclosing the Biodiversity Commons: Bioprospecting or Biopiracy?" in *Altered Genes II: the future?* Richard Hindmarsh and Geoffrey Lawrence (eds). Melbourne: Scribe.

Clark, Ann. (2001) Ten reasons why farmers should think twice before growing GE crops (http://www.plant.uoguelph.ca/faculty/eclark/10reasons.htm).

Cleaver, H. (1972) "The contradiction of the Green Revolution," *Monthly Review* 24: 80–111.

Clegg, Stewart (1989) *Frameworks of Power*. London: Sage.

Conway, Gordon (1998) *The Doubly Green Revolution: Food for All in the Twenty-first Century*. New York: Comstock.

Cook, Karen (1977) "Exchange and power in networks of interorganizational networks," *The Sociological Quarterly* 18: 62–82.

Davies, Philip (2003) "Gene Flow & Genetically Engineered Crops," in *Recoding Nature: Critical Perspectives on Genetic Engineering*, Richard Hindmarsh and Geoffrey Lawrence, (eds). Sydney, UNSW Press, in press.

Dickson, David (1988) *The New Politics of Science*. USA: University of Chicago Press.

Ernst, D. (1983) *The Global Race in Microelectronics: Innovation and Corporate Strategies in a Period of Crisis*. Germany: Frankfurt University.

Evans, Timothy G. (nd) Health-related global public goods: Initiatives of the Rockefeller Foundation, unpublished paper (http://www.undp.org/ods/monterrey-papers/evans.pdf.

Evenson, Robert, Robert Herdt, and Moazzem Hossain (eds). (1996) *Rice Research in Asia: Progress and Priorities*. Cambridge: CAB International in association with IRRI.

FAO (2000) Twenty-Fifth FAO Regional Conference for Asia and the Pacific: Implications and Development of Biotechnology, FAO, APRC/00/5.

Fuerst, J. (1982) "The role of reductionism in the development of molecular biology: Peripheral or central?" *Social Studies of Science* 12: 241–78.

Fisher, Donald (1983) "The role of philanthropic foundations in the reproduction and production of hegemony: Rockefeller Foundations and the social sciences," *Sociology* 17(2): 206–231.

Freeman, J. and S. Barley (1990) "The Strategic Analysis of Inter-organizational Relations in Biotechnology," in *The Strategic Management of Technological Innovation* R. Loveridge and M. Pitt (eds). John Wiley and Sons.

George, Susan (1976) *How the Other Half Dies*. Penguin.

George, Susan and Fabrizio Sabelli (1994) *Faith and Credit: The World Bank's Secular Empire*. Penguin.

Gottweis, Herbert (1998) *Governing Molecules: The Discursive Politics of Genetic Engineering in Europe and the United States*. London: MIT Press.

Hill, Stephen (1988) *The Tragedy of Technology: Human Liberation Versus Domination in the Late Twentieth Century*. UK: Pluto Press.

Hindmarsh, Richard (1990) "The need for effective assessment: sustainable development and the social impacts of biotechnology in the third world," *Environmental Impact Assessment Review* 10(1–2): 195–208.

Hindmarsh, Richard (1994) Power relations, social-Ecocentrism & genetic engineering: Agro-Biotechnology in the Australian context (unpublished PhD thesis, Griffith University).

Hindmarsh, Richard (1998) "Globalisation and Gene-Biotechnology: From the Centre to the Semi-Periphery," in *Australasian Food and Farming in a Globalised Economy: Recent Developments and Future Prospects* David Burch, Geoffrey Lawrence, Roy Rickson and Jasper Goss, (eds). Melbourne: Monash University Publications in Geography.

Hindmarsh, Richard (1999) "Consolidating control: Plant variety rights, genes and seeds," *Australian Journal of Political Economy* 44: 58–78.

Hindmarsh, Richard (2001) "Constructing Bio-utopia: Laying Foundations Amidst Dissent," in *Altered Genes II: the future?* Richard Hindmarsh and Geoffrey Lawrence, (eds). Melbourne: Scribe.

Hindmarsh, Richard and Geoffrey Lawrence (2003) "Recoding Nature: Deciphering the Script," in *Recoding Nature: Critical Perspectives on Genetic Engineering*, Richard Hindmarsh and Geoffrey Lawrence, (eds). Sydney: UNSW Press, in press.

Hindmarsh, Sarah (2001) *The People's Caravan 2000: Land and Food Without Poisons Proceedings*, PANAP, Malaysia.

Hindmarsh, Sarah (2003) "Resistance in Asia: Voices of the People's Caravan," in *Recoding Nature: Critical Perspectives on Genetic Engineering*, Richard Hindmarsh and Geoffrey Lawrence, (eds). Sydney, UNSW Press, in press.

Hindmarsh, Sarah and Richard Hindmarsh (2002) *Laying the Molecular Foundations for GM Rice Across Asia*, PAN Policy Research & Analysis, 1(May), Malaysia: Pesticide Action Network Asia Pacific (PANAP).

House Committee on Science (1998) *Unlocking Our Future Toward a New National Science Policy*. A Report to Congress by the House Committee on Science, September 24.

Huang, Jikun., Carl Pray and Scott Rozell (2002) "Enhancing crops to feed the poor," *Nature* 418: 675–84.

IRRI (2000) "Rice nations urged to prepare for PVP and IP," IRRI press release, March 29 (http://www.biotech-info.net/rice_nations.html).

Kay, Lily (1993) *The Molecular Vision of Life: Caltech, The Rockefeller Foundation, and the Rise of the New Biology*. New York: Oxford University Press.

Keller, L. (1984) "The political economy of public management," *Administration and Society* 15(4): 445–74.

Kloppenburg, Jack R. Jnr. (1988) *First the Seed: The Political Economy of Plant Biotechnology, 1492–2000*. Cambridge: Cambridge University Press.

Law, John (ed). 1986. *Power, Action and Belief: A New Sociology of Knowledge?* London: Routledge & Kegan Paul.

Lewis, J. (1999) "Leveraging Partnerships Between the Public and private Sector—Experience of USAID's Agricultural Biotechnology Program," in *Agricultural Biotechnology and the Poor: An International Conference on Biotechnology* G.J. Persley and M.M. Lantin (eds). Convened by the CGIAR and the US National Academy of Sciences, 21–22 October 1999, World Bank, Washington DC (http://www.cgiar.org/biotech/rep0100/contents.htm).

Martin, Brian (1992) "Scientific fraud and the power structure of science," *Prometheus* 10(1): 83–98.

Meziani, Gundula and Hugh Warwick 2002. *Seeds of Doubt: North American Farmers' Experiences of GM Crops*. UK: Soil Association (http://www.soilassociation.org/web/sa/saweb.nsf/librarytitles/seedsofdoubt_summary.html).

Monsanto (2001) Monsanto welcomes UN report on biotech's benefits for developing world, 9 July (http://www.monsanto.com/monsanto/media/01/01jul09_un_biotech.htm).

Parmar, Inderjeet (2002) "To relate knowledge and action: The impact of the Rockefeller Foundation on foreign policy thinking during America's rise to globalism 1939–1945," *Minerva* 40: 235–263.

Parrot, Nicholas and Terry Marsden (2002) *Real Green Revolution, Organic and Agroecological Farming in the South*. UK: Greenpeace Environmnetal Trust.

Paul, Diane B. (1998) *The Politics of Heredity: Essays on the Eugenics, Biomedicine and the Nature-Nurture Debate*. Albany: State University of New York Press.

Pauly, Philip (1987) *Controlling Life: Jacques Loeb and the Engineering Ideal in Biology.* New York: Oxford University Press.

Population Reference Bureau (2002) *Human Population: Fundamentals of Growth Population Growth and Distribution* (http://www.prb.org/Content/NavigationMenu/ PRB/Educators/Human_Population/Population_Growth/Population_Growth.htm).

Rangnekar, D. (1996) "CGIAR: Agricultural research for whom?" *The Ecologist* 26(6): 259–71.

Regal, Philip (1996) "Metaphysics in Genetic Engineering: Cryptic Philosophy and Ideology in the 'Science' of Risk assessment," in *Coping with Deliberate Release: The Limits of Risk Assessment* Ad van Dommelen (ed). Tilburg: International Centre for Human and Public Affairs. ????

Rockefeller Foundation (nd) *A History* (http://208.240.92.21/rocktext/t_1990.html).

Schattschneider, Elmer E. (1960) *The Semisovereign People.* New York: Holt, Rinehart and Winston.

Senker, P. (1992) "Technological change and the future of work," *Futures* May: 351–63.

Sharif, Raslan (2002) "Building a biotech future," *The Star* (Malaysia), Thursday, 10 October.

Sharma, Devinder (2002) "CGIAR openly adopts corporate agenda," AgBioIndia Mailing List, 5 November.

Shiva, Vandana (2000) *Stolen Harvest: The Hijacking of the Global Food Supply.* London: Zed.

Singh, Ram Badam (2002) "Biotechnology and biosecurity: Towards an evergreen revolution," paper presented at the Conference 'Capitalise on Genetic Modification' Kuala Lumpur, Malaysia, 24–25 September 2002.

Tambunan, D. (1999) "Priorities in biotechnology cooperation in ASEAN," paper presented at the ASEAN-Korea Workshop on the Formulation of a Biotechnology Atlas, Taejon, Korea, 30 August–4 September.

The Business Times (2001) "Asia's biotechnology sector offers investment opportunities: report," *The Business Times*, 20 November (http://www.asia1careers.com/ promo/lifesciences/ls-news1.htm).

The Ecologist (1992) "Whose Common Future?" Special edition, *The Ecologist*, 22(4): 157.

The Rockefeller University (2001) "A century of science for the benefit of humankind: The Rockefeller University celebrates 100 years of discovery in 2001" ("http://www.rockefeller.edu/history.php" http://www.rockefeller.edu/history.php).

Traavik, Terje (1999) *Too Early May Be Too Late: Ecological Risks Associated with the use of Naked DNA as a Biological Tool for Research, Production and Therapy,* Research Report for DN 1999–1, Directorate for Nature Management, Tröndheim, Norway.

Wallerstein, Immanuel (1974) *The Modern World System: Capitalist Agriculture and the Origins of the European World Economy in the Sixteenth Century.* London: Academic Press.

Weindling, Paul (1988) "The Rockefeller Foundation and German Biomedical Sciences, 1920–40: From Educational Philanthropy to International Science Policy," in *Science, Politics and Public Good,* Nicholaas Rupke (ed). UK: MacMillan.

Whitfield, K. (2001) "Digesting the GM debate," *Supermarket to Asia* 5(1): 36–37/39.

Wills, Peter R. (2002) "Biological complexity and genetic engineering," paper presented at the Environment, Culture & Community Conference, 2–5 July 2002, University of Queensland Ipswich, Australia.

Wright, Susan (1986) "Molecular biology or molecular politics? The production of scientific consensus on the hazards of recombinant DNA technology," *Social Studies of Science* 16: 593–620.

Yoxen, Edward (1981) "Life as a Productive Force: Capitalising upon Research in Molecular Biology," in *Science, Technology and the Labour Process: Marxist Studies (1)* L. Levidow and R. Young (eds). London: CSE Books.

Yoxen, Edward (1982) "Giving Life a New Meaning: The Rise of the Molecular Biology Establishment," in *Scientific Establishments and Hierarchies* N. Elias, H. Martins, and R. Whitley (eds). Holland: D. Reidel Publishing.

Yoxen, Edward (1983) *The Gene Business: Who Should Control Biotechnology?* New York: Harper and Row.

Conclusions

Shape the Body, Watch the Mind—
The Brave New World of Individualism
in the Age of Biotechnology

Reiner Grundmann

Nico Stehr has, for a second time, provided me with the opportunity to write some concluding remarks to a collection of conference papers. This places me in a position of double privilege, firstly as the only person other than the editor who has, so far, read all of these very fine papers, and secondly as a privileged reader who can comment on these papers without having to face the authors' reactions and responses—at least for now! However tempting, my intention here is not to deconstruct these contributions. Rather, I would like to condense what I see as major points into a synopsis, marking the issues that in my view have emerged during the conference, the discussions and feedback, and the process of rewriting.

Fuller starts the first section with the development of an analogy between socialism and ecology. Both are the heirs of Christianity, one is on the decline, the other on the rise. Socialism essentially completed the secularization of Christianity promised by the Enlightenment. According to Fuller, it combined a broadly utilitarian, pro-science and pro-industry policy perspective with an overarching sense of responsibility for all of humanity, especially its most vulnerable members. The early 19th century debate between conservatives and socialists "was even couched as an anti—vs. pro-growth argument, as it is today—only with the factory, not the laboratory, functioning as the lightning rod for people's hopes and fears . . . Nowadays the two groups are defined as Ecologists and Neo-Liberals, respectively, and their spheres of concern have somewhat expanded. Ecologists extend their paternalism across species, while Neo-Liberals believe that the state inhibits everyone's—not merely the poor's—enterprising spirit . . . " While this is certainly a simplifi-

349

cation[1] it provides us with a useful starting point to think about two basic values affected by biotechnology: equality and perfection. Like the old question of inheritance of wealth, the potential of biotechnology raises the question of accumulation of advantage over generations. Whereas we can imagine confronting this issue on the basis of our experience gained in dealing with unequal economic resources and opportunities, the question of a "perfection" of humanity poses far deeper problems. While the equality issue makes (welfare) state intervention acceptable, human perfection has stopped being seen as part of a common issue of humankind. Instead, it is increasingly seen as a private issue that should be dealt with in terms of personal (even legal) responsibility. This is the deeper message of Fuller's paper: whilst sociology was linked to the socialist project and the collective betterment of humankind, and humankind[2] was the active motor of change, ecology does not have such a collective reference point which could transform itself. It is therefore essentially paternalistic and gives nonhumans rather benignly the benefit of the doubt "simply because less is known about them". In Fuller's view it is therefore helpless against pushes towards the individualization of genetic perfection:

> A sign that both the ecologists and the neo-liberals have evacuated the ground previously held by the red parties is that the welfare of the most vulnerable members of human society is largely abandoned as an explicit policymaking goal . . . Indeed, there is a tendency for both ecologists and neo-liberals to speak as if the fundamental problems of poverty and immiseration that gave rise to the labor movement and socialist parties have been already more-or-less solved . . . But both sides of the analogy turn out to be empirically flawed and maybe even conceptually confused, if they assume that social progress, once made, is irreversible and hence worthy of benign neglect.

This certainly applies to several modern (or postmodern) theories of contemporary societies.

Nikolas Rose traces the emergence of what he calls the neurochemical self through the "fundamental transformation of the locus of psychiatric care from the closed world of the asylum to an open psychiatric system" in which the use of pharmaceutical drugs have played a key role. In the USA, this had led to an increased use of these drugs such that by 1970 one woman in five and one man in thirteen was using minor tranquillizers and sedatives. Again, since the 1970s this has gone up as the proportion of psychiatric patients receiving prescriptions increased from twenty five percent of all office visits in 1975 to fifty percent by 1990. Data for other countries suggest similar developments.

What are the reasons for the phenomenal rise in availability and prescription of psychiatric drugs? Rose sees social norms celebrating individual responsibility and personal initiative as a potent force; the opposite of that norm of "active self-fulfillment is depression, now largely defined as a pathology involving the lack of energy, an inability to perform the tasks required for work or relations with others." Thinking of the 1980s and 1990s with the rise of the "yuppie" (and its opposite, the "loser") there is certainly something to this explanation based on a general cultural condition. However, Rose examines the mechanics for this rise in the uptake of psychiatric drugs in closer detail and identifies "disease mongering" as a key marketing tactic. This involves alliances formed between "drug companies anxious to market a product for a particular condition, biosocial groups organized by and for those who suffer from a condition thought to be of that type, and doctors eager to diagnose under-diagnosed problems." Close alliances emerge between actors from medical professions, science, drug companies and licensing authorities. Indeed, many of these have financial interests in relevant drug companies. Shareholder value, trial results, and licensing are closely interlinked which makes independent regulation based on impartial science (remember the old ideal of science based policy?) unlikely (see Grundmann and Stehr 2003).

Rose interprets these changes with Deleuze's notion of social control. This means that regarding health, "the active and responsible citizen must engage in a constant monitoring of health, a constant work of modulation, adjustment, improvement in response to the changing requirements of the practices of his or her mode of everyday life." In contrast to Foucault's notion of discipline, "these new self-technologies do not seek to return a pathological or problematic individual to a fixed norm of civilized conduct through a once-off program of normalization. Rather, they oblige the individual to engage in constant risk management, and to act continually on him or herself to minimize risks by reshaping diet, lifestyle and now, by means of pharmaceuticals, the body itself. The new neurochemical self is flexible and can be reconfigured in a way that blurs the boundaries between cure, normalization, and the enhancement of capacities. And these pharmaceuticals offer the promise of the calculated modification and augmentation of specific aspects of selfhood through acts of choice." Like Fuller's analysis regarding genetics, Rose also highlights the individualization of risk with regard to psychic well-being.

Best and Kellner in their contribution address the issue of cloning. They argue that current problems with the cloning of animals make the cloning of humans unacceptable. Reproductive cloning would catapult us into a new stage of history, "with significant and potentially disturbing consequences." However, the authors are pointing to the positive potential of stem cell research that should "not be blocked by problematic conservative positions." Nonetheless, they call for public scrutiny and democratic mechanisms that ensure that the emerging genomic sciences are undertaken by "scientists with a keen sense of responsibility and accountability." Here, then, we have an example of a position that is not ready to give up collective goals of human betterment, albeit, ironically, arguing from an animal rights perspective. In line with much writing on animal rights, their position seems to rest on a utilitarian logic, which finds fault in the conservatives' defense of the sanctity of embryonic cells while "thousands of people continue to suffer and die from Alzheimer's, Parkinson's disease, diabetes, paralysis, and other afflictions." The authors' political background (critical theory and radical democratic politics) explains this position, rejecting conservative theologies, questioning the neo-liberal acceptance of corporate capitalism and emphasizing the "implications of the privatization of research and the monopolization of knowledge and patents by huge biotech corporations." Old shades of red have mingled with new shades of green. What solutions are offered here? Best and Kellner seem somewhat at a loss. They realize that in the field of biotechnology, scientists collude with corporations. Yet all they can say is that it is "time for scientists to awaken to this fact and make public accountability integral to their ethos and research." More generally, they call for a "postmodern metascience" that engages in dialogue and communication with citizens. This is a recognized problem germane to the public understanding of science debate. It is doubtful that ethical imperatives will suffice unless we are able to develop institutions which can check the otherwise unfettered development of knowledge and capital (see Grundmann and Stehr 2003).

How new is the new genetics? Anne Kerr challenges pronouncements that the new genetics represents a transformation, a fundamental shift away from the old eugenics, a position taken by Nikolas Rose and Paul Rabinow. As I have noted, Rose argues that contemporary societies operate a "logic of control." They rest on individual responsibility and choice, not on state orders. As Kerr points out, "genetic counseling is repeatedly cast as non-directive in these accounts and explicitly contrasted with eugenics. According to this view, patients' autonomy and their rights to information are privileged above professional's role in advising and guiding their clients. Another reason why this is different from old eugenics is that patients' entitlements to access to genetic services are emphasized, in contrast to their obligations to use them."

However, there is unequal access to power and hence to patients influencing decisions in this area. Through this line of reasoning Kerr tries to show the continuity between old eugenics and new genetics, focusing on examples from the UK: "Decision-making about the allocation of resources to fund research and services, and about the appropriate regulatory mechanisms to oversee them, is still dominated by professional scientists, and allied professionals with a similarly technocratic outlook, alongside government and industry representatives. All of these groups share an interest in economic gain, as well as intellectual kudos, values that mediate their definition of the 'public good' that genetics is supposed to serve. The obligations of professionals and funding-bodies tend to be constructed in such a way that they compliment rather than undermine this corral of entitlements." On the other hand, "the entitlements of clients and publics are often cast in terms of quality services, information, and choice, rather than active involvement in decisions about *limiting* service provision. It seems that patients' and the public's entitlements are often narrowly expressed in relation to their role as citizen-consumers of already existing services. . . . The balance between entitlements and obligations remains weighted in terms of professional entitlement and patient or public obligations and the slippage around patient and professional entitlements, obligations and immunities supports this weighting." She concludes by alerting us to "demands for individuals' rights to genetic choices and citizens' rights to involvement in policy making about genetics, given the obligations that the language of entitlement can mask. This is particularly important when socially excluded groups are concerned. Their rights not to make genetic choices, and not to participate in "public debates" that are of little interest or importance in the context of their everyday lives, are being overlooked." In a way, this makes the point that there is growing social pressure on individuals to accept the offerings of the new genetics—a point Rose would probably agree with.

Susanna Hornig Priest and Toby Ten Eyck present data and analysis of the media discourse on biotechnology from 14 European countries, Canada, and the US. They develop the thesis that the media has the power to frame the debate by defining issues in certain ways. In representing particular points of view as legitimate whilst marginalizing others the media contributes "to the formation of an opinion climate in which public debate on certain issues can be discouraged or even suppressed while attention is focused on others, and some actors and positions are taken more seriously than others." Looking at differences between the US and Europe, Priest and Eyck point out that "some European populations have available a broader range of legitimized opinion from which to construct an imagined opinion scale." This is to say that voices concerned about the environment and public health are perceived as more mainstream in Europe compared to the US. Whereas in most countries there is a higher acceptance of biotechnology for medical applications (compared to a lower acceptance for agriculture and food), it has been shown that the US has a higher level of acceptance of agricultural or food applications. In addition, the mainstream elite papers in the US are "dominated by the Associated Press agenda (and heavily influenced on technical issues by information subsidies from mainstream institutions such as large corporations and research universities). While the most elite papers in much of Europe reflect similar dynamics, the likely generally greater prominence and legitimacy of dissenting views may well have contributed to more vigorous and open public debate on questions related to biotechnology." In other words, both the structure of the media and the range of legitimate opinions are more diversified in Europe compared to the US. This is a reversal of the situation from the 1960s up until the 1980s when then US was leading in terms of both environmental awareness and regulations.

Mary Douglas once famously remarked, "pollution is matter out of place". Genetic pollution in agriculture refers to the movement of genetically modified genes between plants. In conventional terms one would see this is a problem for the owners of fields and plants that become polluted. But not so in the age of biotechnology and intellectual property rights: now, the polluting party makes claims about the presumed benefits that accrue to the "passive" recipient of the patented plants. Javier Lezaun traces a landmark case involving Canadian farmer Percy Schmeiser and the biotech giant Monsanto. Monsanto had found traces of its proprietary herbicide resistant canola on Schmeiser's fields and sued the farmer for patent infringement. Taking Jasanoff's clue that "the law is called upon to fix the leaky walls between the worlds we construe as social and natural, to recreate normative order when previous understandings have been stretched to the fraying point", he reconstructs the arguments advanced in the court case. Whereas the defense argued that Monsanto's invention of herbicide resistant canola produced a noxious plant that can spread easily without human intervention (hence Monsanto should not have the right of a patent in the first place) and that Schmeiser had no intention of using it (i.e. applying Monsanto's Roundup herbicide), the judge ruled that the farmer's intentions were not relevant here. Important was the use of the patented plants, no matter if this use involved Monsanto's herbicide or not.

With respect to the defense's argument that the GM gene spread replicated without control of the patent holder, the judge argued that Monsanto "did in fact endeavor to control the dissemination of its proprietary genes and the plants in which it is contained." This was achieved through a contract (Technology Use Agreement that farmers have to sign when purchasing such seeds) the purpose of which is "precisely to limit the number of users and the kinds of uses of the technology, and therefore to control the spread of the patented object." As Monsanto also carries out continuous inspections and audits of farmers thought to be growing the genetically modified canola without authorization, and assists in the removal of unwanted Roundup Ready canola plants, the judge reasoned that "the plaintiffs undertook a variety of measures designed to control the unwanted spread of canola containing their patented gene and cell" and concluded that Monsanto's patent had been infringed, and that the farmer should pay damages to Monsanto. Welcome to the brave new world of biotechnology!

Is genetic discrimination good? The very question seems to be frivolous, but in the light of the previous example we should perhaps pause and ponder its merits. Alexander Somek shows how in legal theory there are proponents of exactly such a position. While the overwhelming majority of the population and of legal scholars rejects genetic discrimination, it is not without its defenders. The major argument is that genetic testing provides a reliable means of "enhancing efficiency in the underwriting and rating of insurance contracts on the one hand and in the allocation of jobs on the other." Somek sees a wellspring of arguments in favor of genetic discrimination. Health insurers could face huge economic problems through adverse selection and "moral hazard". Insurers with disproportionate numbers of "bad risks" will have to cross-subsidize and even face economic collapse, leaving everyone else without proper cover. But as Somek points out there are three major reasons against genetic discrimination. Firstly, the availability of genetic information could lead to stigmatization and irrational behavior towards persons presumed to posses certain genes: "Genetic knowledge should not be relevant when it comes to granting access to work and work-dependent social benefits, such as health insurance. In other words, the claim is that having a fair share of social primary goods should not be made dependent on what nature has written into our genes." The second reason refers to the lack of control of, and hence responsibility for, our genes: "Genetic discrimination would be tantamount to holding persons *responsible* for conditions that are, by definition, beyond their control." Some would even say that society has a "responsibility to indemnify people against the ill luck that they suffer in the lottery of nature." The third argument says that markets cannot work properly without market correcting mechanisms; there is no free market of competing atomistic individuals without the antidote of cooperation, solidarity and social trust. All of this is important but could be challenged through the new genetics and screening programmes. In other words, the shift of responsibility onto the individual could undermine much of Somek's solidaristic perspective and open up individualistic approaches. Fortunately, so far it does not seem to make economic sense for health insurers. As he points out, in the US most health insurance is sold on a group basis through large employers without individual underwriting.

Investigating several main biotech research sites in contemporary USA, Steven Vallas et al. see an institutional reconfiguration in which a process of asymmetrical convergence is underway

in which the boundaries between previously distinct organizational fields are beginning to collapse . . . as universities and corporations interact with increasing frequency, their internal structures and practices grow increasingly isomorphic. Organizational logics previously unique to industry have increasingly been imported into academia, *and vice versa*. In their effort to attract scientific talent and to establish their reputations, biotechnology firms have found it useful to adopt academic conventions that have not traditionally been found within industry (e.g., support for journal publication, intellectual exchanges, and provision for basic or "curiosity-driven" research). At the same time, academic institutions increasingly foster entrepreneurial management practices (e.g. stressing success in acquiring external funding in faculty evaluation, quantitative performance metrics), suitably redefined to make them more palatable to the professoriate.

The authors rightly point out that "these reconfigurations . . . have generated new structures of knowledge production that defy inherited normative traditions and give rise to anomalies, contradictions, and ironies." One of the ironies seems to be that industry research labs are now seen as providing possibilities for blue-sky research whereas university research has constantly to prove its usefulness in practical applications. What is more, while in industry a sense of collective spirit is present, academics were seen as obsessed with their own individual career enhancement through the accumulation of publications. This adds further interesting facets to the picture of biotechnology companies.

Biotechnology in its various guises has been embraced in different ways across the world. Herbert Gottweis undertakes a comparative study of the United Kingdom, Germany and the United States. The UK has the most liberal regulatory regime for stem cell research in Europe allowing human embryonic stem cell research, including therapeutic cloning, the cloning of human stem cells for non-reproductive purposes. In contrast, Germany has stricter legislation, essentially outlawing most types of embryo research. Germany's history explains much of this rigorous stance. The United States represents something like a half way house between the UK and Germany in the regulation of stem cell research. President Bush's Council on Bioethics recommended ban being issued on reproductive cloning combined with a four-year moratorium on therapeutic cloning.

Gottweis also observes two features of the intellectual and social style of current debates; that there is not a clash between groups and institutions, and that the arguments raised do not follow simple "Yes-No" patterns. "The debate about stem cell and cloning research in the various countries has been sophisticated and on a high level." Connecting to earlier debates on abortion and embryo research, a massive body of theological, philosophical and bioethical literature has been generated since the late 1990s. Much like Nikolas Rose in his case study of pharmaceutical drugs, Gottweis sees the new genetic technologies as an instance of "individualizing strategies in body politics." Whereas previously "the central goal of medicine was to arrest abnormality and to re-establish the natural vital norm . . . with the new cellular technologies and genetic, sub-cellular strategies the normativities themselves appear open to transformation."

Gísli Pálsson presents the case of the Icelandic Biogenetic Project where medical records for the Icelandic population are collected. The Icelandic gene pool seems especially interesting as it is fairly homogeneous as a result of the successive reduction of the population during times of plagues and famine. Moreover, geographic isolation has restricted genetic diversity. The Health Sector Database at its core allows storing and analyzing of medical records, genetic information, and family histories. Pálsson explores the important role of metaphors in this process, especially those applied to genetic and genealogical data, such as gene "mapping" or "hunting" and "flowing streams" or "family trees". Such different kinds of images underscore particular aspects of the software used in the genealogical project, such as representing mutant genes passed down through the generations, the self-obsessed search for distant ancestors, or the rhetoric of the common roots and interests of the enclosed Icelandic "circle". All of those metaphors are fraught with meaning and controversy, as the long and contested history of the tree metaphor shows. As Pálsson points out with regard to the circular image (which is also the logo of deCode Genetics, the company centrally involved in the Health Sector Database) "apart from its visual appeal, the circular image may serve to foster a sense of unity and belonging." It can be seen as a symbol for a rather narrow genetic notion of citizenship, competing with images of a multicultural community with immigrants from different parts of the world and thus other notions of citizenship, emphasizing human rights and the empowerment of ethnic groups marginalized in the past.

Elizabeth Ettorre presents data from four European countries on pre-natal genetic screening based on interviews with experts and practitioners in the field. Her main finding is that culture plays an important role in establishing the visibility of specific illnesses and in shaping the time and spaces for reproduction in particular societies. This is to say that related to prenatal screening different issues were given priority in different countries. In Greece it was thalassaemia (a blood related disease) where the "genes of pre-nuptial couples rather than the bodies of pregnant women were the spotlight of concerns." As thalassaemia is a single gene disease (both parents need to have the trait in order to affect the child) "knowing before they get married" (and thus avoiding pregnancy) is therefore essential. In the Netherlands genetic screening was very much seen in the political context of abortions being problematic. As pregnancy termination was not a justifiable reason for a population-screening program, experts made a crucial distinction between "normal" and "genetic abortions" where only the former are protected by law. In the UK the main issue was the development of ethical guidelines such as informed consent and choice, hence high priority was given to informing the public and especially women before pregnancy. In Finland trust in the health system is so high that pregnant women usually accept screening programs and the recommendations made on their basis: "As consumers and reproducers, pregnant women's needs were marked by their trust in the maternity care system and their desire to reproduce healthy children."

Richard Hindmarsh delineates the emergence of the "doubly green revolution" in Asia. Doubly because according to the propagators of the term, new GM plants will not only enhance food and agricultural production but also prevent pre—and post-harvest losses and improve the environment. Hindmarsh points out that "GM infrastructure agents" have built upon the green revolution technology platform that had been developed in earlier decades. Key agents were the Rockefeller Foundation, the US Agency for International Development (USAID) and the Consultative Group on International Agricultural Research (CGIAR, founded, inter alia, by the Rockefeller and Ford Foundations). Drawing upon network and discourse theory, Hindmarsh shows how such central nodes in interorganisational networks have shaped a policy agenda and public discourse, mobilizing values like hunger, progress and productivity. While key actors had a private vision of achieving political stability in Asia, viz. increased food production and a strengthened middle-class peasantry to resist communism, publicly they promulgated the vision of feeding the hungry through intensive agriculture.

The new promise of the "doubly green revolution" is to repeat that promise but this time using genetic engineering, of which the Rockefeller Foundation is also a key framing infrastructure agent and broker, in Asia and beyond. Western patent protection regimes are put in place before the large-scale diffusion of biotechnology products aimed at raising food productivity. Again, the dominant public discourse was to raise food productivity and feed the hungry, this time wedded to the potential of biotechnology which "would help overcome both past and existing problems of green revolution food production, especially declining yields. Yet, the focus on intellectual property rights contradicted the traditional role of the CGIAR to process information, inventions, processes, biological material and other research products, funded or developed by the CGIAR, as public goods. This further defined that the application of genetic engineering was embedded in a commercial and entrepreneurial frame." Hindmarsh concludes that this shows the power of such interorganisational networks, spanning and forming the background texture of the GM policy field, leading to a monopoly control over key biotechnology patents by corporations and institutions in the North, vindicating the GM critics' charge of bio-colonization.

Biotechnology is a vast field and the issues raised by it are staggering. The papers collected in this volume contain studies on biotechnology applications in food and medicine (with human applications receiving most attention). They show the cultural and political diversity in the promotion and reception of these applications around the world. Nearly all express concern about the radical changes that are upon us. We seem to have lost some of the central institutions that could deal with these issues and give reassurance, above all the welfare state as a promoter and protector of the public good. With the proliferation of private property regimes and the opening up of new spaces for individual choice, a strong push towards individualization occurs. As Nico Stehr notes in his introduction, "one thing is evident, future conflicts, tensions and opportunities generated by knowledge and by artifacts emerging from biotechnology will be enormous." These battles will be fought between special interest groups such as pharmaceutical companies, medical researchers, doctors, public health practitioners, patient groups, church representatives, public intellectuals, and others. All of them will make the case that they are defending the public good. Policy-makers will form alliances to suit their purposes; allies could change from case to case and over time. Fuller's stance that a democratic framework is the most crucial thing, as it will allow us to regularly examine and possibly reverse some of these developments is only half of the story. Important as it is, democratic institutions may offer too little since irreversible features inherent in biotechnology applications may thwart such revisions. The awareness on all sides that we are taking such huge risks gives these debates a fundamental and at times fundamentalist character.

Notes

1. It misses the point that Marx wavered between support and condemnation of science and technology as embodied in large-scale industry (Grundmann 1991). Contemporary Marxists are also split over this issue.
2. Actually humankind and the working class were linked in Marx's theory in that the special interests of the working class were identical to the interests of humankind.

References

Grundmann, Reiner (1991) *Marxism and Ecology*. Oxford: Oxford University Press.
Grundmann, Reiner and Nico Stehr (2003) 'Social Control and Knowledge in Democratic Societies," *Science and Public Policy*, Special Issue (June).

About the Authors

Steven Best is Associate Professor and Chair of Philosophy at the University of Texas, El Paso. He has published numerous books and dozens of articles and reviews in the areas of philosophy, cultural criticism, mass media, social theory, postmodern theory, and animal rights. His last two books with Douglas Kellner, *The Postmodern Turn* and *The Postmodern Adventure*, won awards for best social theory and philosophy books of the year. Best is active with animal rights causes and has his own radio show, Animal Concerns of Texas. His forthcoming books are *Terrorists or Freedom Fighters? Reflections on the Liberation of Animals* (Lantern Books 2003) and *Animal Rights and Moral Progress: The Struggle For Human Evolution* (Roman and Littlefield, 2004). Many of his writings can be found at: http://utminers.utep.edu/best/

Frederick H. Buttel is William H. Sewell Professor of Rural Sociology and Professor of Environmental Studies at the University of Wisconsin, Madison. He is also Co-Director of the Program on Agricultural Technology Studies at UW-Madison and a Senior Fellow at the Center on World Affairs and the Global Economy (WAGE). His main research interests are in environmental sociology (particularly theories of environment-society relationships and environmental reform) and the sociology of the environmental and agricultural sciences (particularly the global struggle over GM foods/crops, the "molecularization" and "geneticization" of agricultural research, and the social implications of technological change). He was elected a Fellow of the American Association for the Advancement of Science (AAAS) in 1987 and is Past President of the Rural Sociological Society, of the Agriculture, Food, and Human Values Society, and of the Environment and Society Research Committee (RC 24) of the International Sociological Association. Buttel is Co-Editor of *Society and Natural Resources*, Editor of *Research in Rural Sociology and Development*, and is the author or editor of 15 books, and author of over 220 refereed journal articles and book chapters and 150 reviews and nonrefereed publications.

Elizabeth Ettorre is currently Professor of Sociology at University of Plymouth. Born in 'New England', she came to the UK in 1972 upon completion of her BA in Sociology at Fordham University, New York. After finishing her Ph.D. in Sociology (1978) at the London School of Economics and Political Science, she became a Research Sociologist at the University of London for a number of years. In the early 90s, she went to work in Finland. She holds honorary academics posts as a Docent in Sociology at Abo Academy University and University of Helsinki and is an honorary fellow at EGenis, Genetics and Society Research Centre, Exeter University. Her research interests include: sociology of substance use; gender; bioethics; sociology of the new genetics; occupational health and mental health. She has published widely in gender studies and the sociology of health. Her books include: *Lesbians, Women and Society* (1980); *Women and Substance Use* (1992); *Gendered Moods* (1995) with Elianne Riska; *Women and alcohol: a private pleasure or a public problem?* (1997); *Reproductive genetics, gender and the body* (2002); *Before Birth* (2001) and *Revisioning Women and Drug Use* (forthcoming).

Steve Fuller (born 1959, New York City) is Professor of Sociology at the University of Warwick, UK. Originally trained in the history and philosophy of science (Ph.D., 1985, University of Pittsburgh), he is the founder of the research program of social epistemology. It is the name of a quarterly journal he founded with Taylor & Francis in 1987, as well as the first of his eight books: *Social Epistemology* (Indiana University Press, 1988 [2nd edn. 2002]), *Philosophy of Science and Its Discontents*, Guilford Press, 1989 [2nd edn. 1993]), *Philosophy, Rhetoric and the End of Knowledge* (Lawrence Erlbaum Associates, 1993 [2nd edn. 2003]), *Science* (Open University Press and University of Minnesota Press, 1997; translated into Japanese, 2000), *The Governance of Science: Ideology and the Future of the Open Society* (Open University Press, 2000), *Thomas Kuhn: A Philosophical History for Our Times* (University of Chicago Press, 2000), *Knowledge Management Foundations* (Butterworth-Heinemann, 2002), *Kuhn versus Popper: The Struggle for the Soul of Science* (Iconbooks, 2003). He is currently work on two books – one on the philosophical foundations of science and technology studies and the other on the future of sociology. The paper in this volume is part of the latter project.

Herbert Gottweis, studied political science and history in Vienna and Rochester, New York. He has taught political science and science studies at the universities of Salzburg, Cornell, and Hong Kong University of Science and Technology. He is currently professor of political science at the University of Vienna. He is author of *Governing Molecules: The Discursive Politics of Genetic Engineering in Europe and the United States* (MIT Press, 1998), and of *Administrated Bodies. Strategies of Health Policy in Germany and in the United States* (forthcoming in German at Boehlau Verlag, Vienna/Leipzig 2003). Gottweis currently works on a book about stem cell research and cloning in a comparative perspective.

Reiner Grundmann is a sociologist and political scientist by training. He studied sociology at the Free University in Berlin and obtained his PhD in Political and Social Sciences from the European University Institute, Florence. He was with the Wissenschaftszentrum in Berlin (Germany) and the Max Planck Institute for the Study of Societies (Cologne, Germany). Currently he is Senior Lecturer at Aston University, Birmingham, UK, where he teaches sociology within the Business School. His main research interests are in social and political theory, and the sociology of science, technology, risk and the environment. His book publications include *Marxism and Ecology* (1991), and *Transnational Environmental Policy: Reconstructing Ozone* (2001). Together with Nico Stehr he co-edited *Werner Sombart: Economic Life in the Modern Age* (2001).

Richard Hindmarsh lectures in environmental policy, regulation and politics at the Australian School of Environmental Studies, Griffith University, Brisbane. He previously lectured in Nature & Technoscience Studies at Contemporary Studies, The University of Queensland. He has a first class honours degree in Environmental Studies and a PhD in Science, Technology & Society Studies, and has held an Australian Research Council Postdoctoral Research Fellowship. Richard's research interests include social and environmental aspects of biotechnology, environmental policy, third world development, and the political ecology of toxic algae blooms. His recent co-authored/ co-edited books include *Altered Genes* (1998; revised edition 2001, Scribe), and *Recoding Nature: Critical Perspectives on Genetic Engineering* (UNSW Press 2003, in press). Richard recently co-authored a report called "Laying the Molecular Foundations of GM Rice Across Asia" (2002), and is currently writing a social history of biotechnology development and regulation in Australia.

J. Rogers Hollingsworth is Professor of Sociology and History at the University of Wisconsin. Awarded honorary degrees by the University of Uppsala (Sweden) and by Emory University, he is the author or editor of numerous books and articles on comparative political economy. One of his major research interests is the study of how organizational and institutional factors influence different types of innovations. His recent publications include *Advancing Socio-Economics* (with Karl Müller and Ellen Jane Hollingsworth, 2002); *Contemporary Capitalism: The Embeddedness of Institutions* (with

Robert Boyer, 1997); *Governing Capitalist Economies* (with Philippe Schmitter and Wolfgang Streeck, 1994); and *The Search for Excellence: Organizations, Institutions, and Major Discoveries in Biomedical Science* (with Ellen Jane Hollingsworth and Jerald Hage, forthcoming 2004). He is past President and also Honorary Fellow of the Society for the Advancement of Socio-Economics. His email address is Hollingsjr@aol.com.

Douglas Kellner is George Kneller Chair in the Philosophy of Education at UCLA and is author of many books on social theory, politics, history, and culture, including *Camera Politica: The Politics and Ideology of Contemporary Hollywood Film*, co-authored with Michael Ryan; *Critical Theory, Marxism, and Modernity*; *Jean Baudrillard: From Marxism to Postmodernism and Beyond*; *Postmodern Theory: Critical Interrogations* (with Steven Best); *Television and the Crisis of Democracy; The Persian Gulf TV War; Media Culture*; and *The Postmodern Turn* (with Steven Best). He has recently published a book on the 2000 presidential Election, *Grand Theft 2000: Media Spectacle and the Theft of an Election*, and *The Postmodern Adventure. Science, Technology, and Cultural Studies at the Third Millennium* (co-authored with Steve Best). He has just published two books on *Media Spectacle* and on *September 11, Terror War, and the Bush Presidency*.

Anne Kerr is a lecturer in the Department of Sociology, University of York, with specialist interests in genetics and gender. She has authored and co-authored a range of articles on professional and public accounts of genetics. Her most recent publication, *Genetic Politics: From Eugenics to Genome* was written with Tom Shakespeare (2002, New Clarion Press). She is currently working on an ESRC-funded project entitled Transformations in Genetic Subjecthood (http://www.york.ac.uk/res/tigs).

Abby Kinchy is a graduate student in Sociology and Rural Sociology at the University of Wisconsin-Madison. Her research is in the sociology of science, knowledge and technology, with particular emphasis on agriculture, international trade and development, and the role of experts in political struggles. She recently completed a study of the Ecological Society of America, examining how and why the organization constructs boundaries between science and environmental politics. Abby is currently looking at the ways that science and technology have been incorporated into Hindu nationalist discourses in India today, and she continues to work with Daniel Kleinman on questions about the international regulation of biotechnology. She is also active in the anti-war movement. In 2003, she received the Department of Rural Sociology's John H. Kolb Award for academic achievement.

Daniel Kleinman is an associate professor in the Department of Rural Sociology at the University of Wisconsin, Madison, where he is also affiliated with the Science and Technology Studies Program. He is the author most recently of *Impure Cultures: University Biology and the World of Commerce* (2003, University of Wisconsin Press). In addition, he is the author of *Politics on the Endless Frontier: Postwar Research Policy in the United States* (1995, Duke University Press) and the editor of *Science, Technology, and Democracy* (2000, State University of New York Press). Kleinman's current research centers on public views of biotechnology in different national settings, and on the changing nature of the university in the contemporary world.

Javier Lezaun is a doctoral candidate in the Department of Science and Technology Studies, at Cornell University. His dissertation, "Policing Purity: Testing, Traceability and the Governance of Genetically Modified Organisms" analyzes the constitution of some of the new market infrastructures and bureaucratic instruments used to govern transgenic organisms in the agri-food system. The research for his essay was supported by the National Science Foundation and the Luigi Einaudi Foundation.

Raul Necochea is a doctoral candidate in the School of History and Sociology of Technology and Science at the Georgia Institute of Technology. His research centers on the work of medical practitioners in Latin America. He has published in the *Journal of Management Inquiry* and in *Advances in Qualitative Organizational Research*. Currently, he working on the history of cancer for the US National Cancer Institute, while studying the relations among power, knowledge, and contraceptive technologies in rural areas of Peru.

Gísli Pálsson studied anthropology at the University of Manchester (Ph.D. 1982). He is professor of anthropology at the University of Iceland and the University of Oslo. Among Pálsson's main books are *The Textual Life of Savants* (1995), *Nature and Society: Anthropological Perspectives* (1996, co-editor), *Images of Contemporary Iceland* (1996, co-editor), and *Writing on Ice: The Ethnographic Notebooks of Vilhjalmur Stefansson* 2001, editor and introduction). Currently, Pálsson's research focuses on the social implications of biotechnology and concerns about the collection, storing, and exchange of human bodily material and medical information. Also, he is engaged in research on Inuit genetic history, human-environmental relations, ecological knowledge and the social implications of climatic change. Pálsson has done anthropological fieldwork in Iceland and The Republic of Cape Verde.

Susanna Hornig Priest is associate professor of journalism and director of the master's program in science journalism at Texas A&M University. A social scientist with degrees in anthropology and sociology, as well as communication, she has followed the interaction of media coverage and public opinion in the biotechnology area for the past decade. Her book on this subject, *A Grain of Truth: The Media, The Public and Biotechnology,* was published by Rowman & Littlefield in 2001. Her interest in biotech is part of a broader interest in risk communication and risk management in contemporary democracies, including the study of public discourse about other kinds of risky technologies. She is associate editor of the journal *Public Understanding of Science* and an active member of the editorial board of *Science Communication.* For the past several years she has been collaborating with a group of European and Canadian scholars on a comparative study of North American and European responses to biotech.

Eugene A. Rosa is the Edward R. Meyer Distinguished Professor of Environmental and Natural Resource Policy in the Thomas S. Foley Institute for Public Policy and Public Service, Professor and Past Chair of Sociology, Faculty Associate in the Social and Economic Sciences Research Center, Affiliated Professor in the Program in Environmental Science and Regional Planning, Affiliated Professor of Fine Arts, and Faculty Associate, Center for Integrated Biology all at Washington State University. He currently serves on the National Academy of Sciences/National Research Council Board on Radioactive Waste Management. His research program has focused on environmental topics—particularly energy, technology, and risk issues—with attention to both theoretical and policy concerns. He has investigated the relationship between levels of energy consumption and societal well-being, public opinion about energy problems and policies, factors affecting the adoption of solar technologies and conservation practices, and public attitudes toward and acceptance of nuclear power and nuclear policies. Most recently his research is focused on two complementary topics: technological risk and global environmental change. The principal activities associated with the first topic are recent service on the National Research Council Committee on the Staging of Nuclear Repositories, membership on the National Agricultural Biotechnology Committee, and publications on risk technologies such as nuclear power and biotechnology. The principles activities associated with the second topic are current membership on the National Research Council Committee to Review the U.S. Climate Change Science Program Strategic Plan, research devoted to specifying the anthropogenic (human) causes of greenhouse gases and ecological footprints, to the historical relationships between CO_2 loads and societal well-being, to the history of social thought on climate, and to testing theories of environmental impacts.

Nikolas Rose is Professor of Sociology and Convenor of the Department of Sociology at the London School of Economics. He is managing editor of *Economy and Society*, one of Britain's leading scholarly interdisciplinary journals of social sciences, and Director of the BIOS Centre for the Study of Bioscience, Biomedicine, Biotechnology and Society at the LSE. He has published widely on the social and political history of the human sciences, on the genealogy of subjectivity, on the history of empirical thought in sociology, and on changing rationalities and techniques of political power, and he has also published in law and criminology. He is author of a number of books including *Inventing Ourselves* (Cambridge University Press, 1996), *Governing the Soul* (Second Edition, Free Association Books, 1999), and *Powers of Freedom* (Cambridge University Press, 1999). His current research concerns biological and genetic psychiatry and behavioural neuroscience, and its social, ethical, cultural and legal implications. Together with Paul Rabinow, he is co-editor of the Fourth Volume of Michel Foucault's Essential Works (Free Press, 2003) and edits a Cambridge University Press book series on *Society and the Life Sciences.*

Martin Schulte is Professor of Law and Dean of the Faculty of Law at the Technical University of Dresden, Germany. He is also Director of the Institute for the Law of Technology and Environmental Law and Director of the Center for Interdisciplinary Research of Technology at the Faculty of Philosophy at his university. Martin Schulte has held visiting appointments at the Catholic University of Nijmegen/NL (1989–1991) and the Emory University Atlanta/USA (1998). Among his recent publications are "Zum Umgang mit Wissen, Nichtwissen und Unsicherem Wissen im Recht dargestellt am Beispiel des MSE—und MKS-Konflikts", in: Engel/Halfmann/Schulte (eds..), *Wissen, Nichtwissen, Unsicheres Wissen.* Baden-Baden 2002; "Wissensgenerierung in Recht und Rechtswissenschaft Selbstbeschreibung und Fremdbeschreibung des Rechtssystems," in: Armin Nassehi (ed.), *Szenarien der Wissensgesellschaft,* 2003 (in print); ed. *Handbuch des Technikrechts.* Berlin: Springer Verlag Berlin 2003.

Alexander Somek is a Professor of Law at the University of Iowa College of Law. His current research focuses on anti-discrimination law and its role in the transformation of the European social model. His publications in English include: "German Legal Philosophy and Theory in the nineteenth and twentieth centuries," in: *A Companion to Philosophy of Law and Legal Theory,* ed. D. Patterson (Oxford: Blackwell 1996), pp. 343–354; "'National Solidarity, Global Impartiality," and "The Performance of Philosophical Theory," *Ratio Iuris* 11 (1998), pp. 103–125; 'A Constitution for Antidiscrimination. Exploring the Vanguard Moment of Community Law', *European Law Journal* 5 (1999), pp. 243–271.

Nico Stehr is Senior Research Associate, Institut für Technikfolgen-abschätzung, Forschungszentrum Karlsruhe and Institut für Küstenforschung, GKSS, Germany; he also is a fellow in the Center for Advanced Cultural Studies in Essen, Germany, editor of the *Canadian Journal of Sociology* and a Fellow of the *Royal Society of Canada*. During the academic year 2002/2003 we was Paul-F.-Lazarsfeld Professor at the University of Vienna, Austria. Among his recent book publications are *Knowledge Societies* (Sage, 1994); *Governing Modern Societies* (with Richard Ericson, University of Toronto Press, 2000); *Werner Sombart: Economic Life in the Modern Age* (with Reiner Grundmann, Transaction Books, 2001); *The Fragility of Modern Societies: Knowledge and Risk in the Information Age* (Sage, 2001); *Knowledge and Economic Conduct: The Social Foundations of the Modern Economy* (University of Toronto Press, 2002; *Wissenspolitik: Die Überwachung des Wissens* (Suhrkamp Verlag, 2003) and *The Governance of Knowledge* (2004).

Toby Ten Eyck is an Assistant Professor in the Department of Sociology and the National Food Safety and Toxicology Center at Michigan State University. In addition to holding a Ph.D. in sociology from Louisiana State University, Dr. Ten Eyck spent nearly seven years as a radio broadcaster in Oregon, Florida, Wyoming, and Washington. His interests include media presentations of biotechnology, food irradiation, and general food safety issues, as well as interpretative processes among audience members. He is currently studying attitudes toward regulation among food industry managers and developing theoretical frameworks to understand new information technologies.

Steven P. Vallas is an associate professor of sociology at the Georgia Institute of Technology. His research has focused on the changing nature of managerial regimes in both traditional and science-intensive industries, a topic on which he has written or edited three books. His most recent articles have appeared in the *American Sociological Review*, *Social Problems*, and *Theory and Society*, among others. He is currently writing a book on the restructuring of factory work while also continuing to study the careers of molecular biologists in both industry and academia (with Daniel Lee Kleinman).

Name Index

Subject Index